MEN IN CRISIS

"Men fight and lose the battle, and the thing they fought for comes about in spite of their defeat, and when it comes turns out to be not what they meant, and other men have to fight for what they meant under another name."

WILLIAM MORRIS

MEN IN CRISIS

THE REVOLUTIONS OF
1848

BY

ARNOLD WHITRIDGE

CHARLES SCRIBNER'S SONS, NEW YORK

ACKNOWLEDGMENTS

My first acknowledgments must go to Mr. James T. Babb and the staff of the Yale University Library. My task would have been much more difficult without the generous help they have given me. I am also indebted to the staffs of the New York Public Library and the New York Society Library, and to Mr. Mark Kiley, the librarian of the University Club of New York.

It is a pleasure to express my thanks to the scholars who have read the manuscript of this book in whole or in part and have given me the benefit of their wide knowledge. I am particularly indebted to Professor Henri Peyre of Yale University, Professor Robert H. Fife of Columbia University, Professor G. M. Huisman of the University of Brussels, and to Mr. T. H. Thomas of Cambridge, Massachusetts. My wife collected the information on the Icarian settlements in Texas and has helped me in a variety of other ways. I should also like to thank Mrs. John K. Bodel, Jr., for her care in typing the manuscript.

"All around us the world is convulsed by the agonies of great nations. Governments which lately seemed likely to stand during ages have been on a sudden shaken and overthrown. The proudest capitals of Western Europe have streamed with civil blood. All evil passions, the thirst for gain and the thirst for vengeance, the antipathy of class to class, the antipathy of race to race, have broken loose from the control of divine and human laws. Fear and anxiety have clouded the faces and depressed the hearts of millions. Trade has been suspended, and industry paralyzed. The rich have become poor; and the poor have become poorer. Doctrines hostile to all sciences, to all arts, to all industry, to all domestic charities, doctrines which, if carried into effect, would in thirty years undo all that thirty centuries have done for mankind, and would make the fairest provinces of France and Germany as savage as the Congo or Patagonia, have been avowed from the tribune and defended by the sword. Europe has been threatened with subjugation by barbarians, compared with which the barbarians who marched under Attila and Alboin were enlightened and humane."

MACAULAY

CONTENTS

MEN IN CRISIS

INTRODUCTION

THERE ARE no perfect parallels between the past and the present. History never repeats itself exactly, but the events of our own time may become more comprehensible, or at least more endurable, if we occasionally step back into an age no less chaotic than ours that was struggling, just as we are, to find a working definition of the word "freedom."

The purpose of this book is to examine the various revolutions and counter-revolutions that took place in Europe during the year 1848–49, and to trace the repercussion of those events on the history of America. So many governments were being overthrown simultaneously in different countries that it is difficult to tell the story chronologically. I have adopted a biographical frame, or rather a series of biographical frames, as being the most satisfactory for my particular canvases. The biographical method is open to obvious objections. History is not synonymous with the lives of great men any more than it is synonymous with the tabulation of economic trends, but it has seemed to me that the political, racial, and social issues involved in the revolutions of 1848 can be most conveniently grouped around certain dominant personalities.

In France, Louis Philippe, Lamartine and Louis Napoleon, stand for well-recognized stages in the progress of revolution. First comes the demand for reform, often sponsored by conservatives who foresee the possibility of violence if the reforms are not granted; then, owing to the obstinate stupidity of those in power, the downfall of the dynasty, which is succeeded by a short-lived republic of inexperienced idealists. Unwilling to adopt stern measures, the republic is overthrown and in the resulting confusion the familiar strong man thrusts himself upon the public as the savior of society, the only alter-

I

native to chaos. In Italy, Mazzini, a great moralist as well as a great revolutionary, proclaimed as no revolutionary had ever proclaimed before the duties and responsibilities that freedom imposes on mankind. His words and Garibaldi's deeds convinced the sceptical chancelleries of the Great Powers that Italians had suddenly sprung into being, and that Italy could no longer be considered merely a geographical expression.

In the Habsburg Monarchy, Metternich was forced to flee for his life, and those who believed in reform like Count Széchényi and Francis Deák were swept aside, while Kossuth kindled the flames of a furious and disruptive racialism. In Germany, freely elected representatives of the whole people met together for the first time in the Frankfort Parliament to build a united Germany on a basis of liberalism. Within a year the Frankfort Parliament was dispersed like a mob on a street corner, and the liberalism that was to have flowered in Germany flowered instead in the newly formed states of the Middle West, to which it was transplanted by Carl Schurz and the other forty-eighters who sought and found in America what Germany had failed to give them. Cutting across all these revolutionary movements, Karl Marx, as yet unknown except to a few faithful disciples, was already inciting the proletarians of all countries to unite and overthrow the whole social order. Around these men I have woven the pattern of this year of revolution.

CHAPTER

I

THE REVOLUTION IN FRANCE

1

LOUIS PHILIPPE

"IT WAS a hair-trigger affair altogether," wrote the British consul at Havre to Lord Palmerston, "but thanks be to God everything has gone off admirably." Getting kings out of France has always been a difficult operation, only slightly less difficult than putting them on the throne again. The French people do not like their monarchs to leave the country, even when they have abdicated, and once they have got away they never want them back. Fortunately Louis Philippe was not as stubborn as his cousin Louis XVI. In signing his abdication he surrendered his self-confidence as well as his throne. He left himself and his family in the hands of his friends, and on March 3, 1848, they deposited him and the Queen safe and sound on English soil. Some of the family had already arrived, the others drifted in later.

The appearance of the royal family as they landed at New-haven was not impressive, but being a bourgeois king Louis Philippe was perhaps not as sensitive to appearances as a king by divine right. He wore a rough pea-jacket, borrowed from the captain of the steam packet that brought him over, and gray trousers. He had not shaved for a week, and his eyes were hidden by immense blue goggles. The Queen was muffled in a large plaid coat. Evidently they did not at once realize that disguise was no longer necessary. Immediately upon their arrival they took up their quarters at the Bridge Inn and Louis

Philippe wrote a letter to Queen Victoria. Then the village barber was summoned to remove the week-old beard, an operation he was at first unequal to on account of nervousness but ultimately performed satisfactorily.[1]

By this time the surrounding gentry were arriving to pay their respects. The first to be presented was the local rector whose name happened to be Smith. "Mr. Smith!" exclaimed the King, "that is curious indeed!" The King had escaped from France under the assumed name of William Smith and his meeting with a genuine Smith, as soon as he landed, struck the royal mind as an amazing coincidence. The incident, slight as it was, seems to have broken the ice. Offers of hospitality poured in on them, but the King and Queen, anxious to get in touch with the other members of their family, left Newhaven the next day. They travelled by special train to Croydon where they were joined by two of their children, the Duke de Nemours and the Princess of Saxe-Coburg, and on the same evening they arrived at Claremont, the Surrey villa that was to be their home in exile. It turned out to be a rather unsanitary villa owing to the decomposition of the leaden pipes, and the royal family had to be moved out to the Star and Garter Hotel at Richmond while the drains were being put in order. Meanwhile Guizot, Louis Philippe's prime minister, had arrived in England and found "a little house, close to London, at Brompton, which is almost in the country." There he settled down, imperturbable as ever, to write a constitutional history of England.[2] Greville notes in his diary for March 26 that he dined with Palmerston to meet Guizot and Mme. de Lieven.

> Strange dinner, when I think of the sentiments towards each other of the two Ministers, and of all that Guizot said to me when I was at Paris last year! However, it did all very well. I thought Palmerston and Guizot would have shaken each other's arms off, and nothing

---

[1] The letter of the consul G. W. Featherstonhaugh to Lord Palmerston will be found in 'Queen Victoria's Letters', edited by A. C. Benson, London, 1907. Vol. II, 184–187. For another, slightly different, account of the King's flight from Havre, see the 'Am. Hist. Review,' XXX, 557–560.

[2] Walter Savage Landor commemorated Guizot's escape in a characteristic quatrain:

> Guizot, in haste to cut and run,
> A lackey's livery has put on,
> But whosoever calls disguise
> In him the lackey's livery, lies.

could exceed the cordiality or apparent ease with which they conversed.

Within a few weeks other interesting exiles, a certain Herr and Frau von Meyer, better known as Prince and Princess Metternich, were installed in a Hanover Square hotel. The royal princes and princesses had also fled the storm and found refuge in England. Last to arrive were the Prince de Joinville and the Duc d'Aumale, forced to abandon Algeria in the very hour of victory. History is full of dramatic reversals of fortune but seldom have they been as sudden or as unexpected as those of 1848. The fall of Louis Philippe is all the more remarkable because in many ways he was a shrewd man, not a hero or a coward, but a good bourgeois who had apparently profited by the mistakes of his predecessors. Most of the kings of France had been ruled by a father confessor or by a mistress, often by both at the same time. Louis Philippe was never the tool of a priest or of a woman.

He was born in 1773, the eldest son of the Duc d'Orléans, the future Philippe Egalité, whose one virtue seems to have been that he brought up his children very sensibly. The Duchesse d'Orléans, daughter of the rich Duc de Penthièvre, played as small a part in the education of her children as she did in her husband's affection. She resigned herself to seeing them brought up by her husband's ex-mistress, the intelligent Mme. de Genlis. It may not sound sensible to entrust your children's education to your husband's cast-off mistress, but Mme. de Genlis proved an excellent choice. She brought up the children of Philippe Egalité on a system of her own, adapted from Rousseau but more rigorous than that of Emile. Her pupils—there were four Orléans children, several cousins, and an unexplained and very beautiful child named Pamela, said to be an afterthought of Mme. de Genlis and the Duke—got up at six o'clock every morning, winter and summer. Their diet consisted of bread, milk and meat. No delicacies such as pastry were allowed. Vegetables are not mentioned. All day they worked hard, physically and mentally, and at night they slept on boards with no mattresses. "Thanks to Mme. de Genlis," Louis Philippe told Victor Hugo years afterward, "I know something about most trades. I can bleed my man like Figaro. I am a carpenter, a farrier, a mason and a blacksmith." [3]

[3] Victor Hugo, *Choses Vues* (Paris, 1887), p. 79.

Modern languages were emphasized. In the morning they spoke German, English in the afternoon, and Italian at supper. Mme. de Genlis did not pay much attention to Latin and Greek, or even to the study of French literature. Her system was eminently utilitarian. Buffon's *Natural History* and the *Encyclopedia* of Diderot and D'Alembert were the books of the moment. The children must be taught physics, chemistry, mathematics and geography. Naturally she was not able to teach all these subjects herself, but the German gardener, the English *valet de chambre*, and the other tutors employed, were strictly supervised. Physical exercise played a great part in the day's routine. Fencing and hunting, the athletics usually required of the aristocracy in the eighteenth century, did not appeal to the practical mind of Mme. de Genlis, so the children developed their muscles by jumping and running—the jumps were carefully measured—and by carrying heavy loads of wood and pitchers of water. In an age when water had to be drawn from a well and often carried long distances it was obviously an advantage to be accustomed to great weights. Louis Philippe, or the Duc de Chartres as he was then known,[4] was not as nimble as his brothers but he was the strongest of the family and could carry a weight of 225 pounds up and down stairs.

In many ways Mme. de Genlis did well by her charges. The eighteenth century was an age of educational experiment, and some of her practices, such as taking the children to factories and workshops to learn something of the lives of other people, would not be out of place in a modern progressive school. Metternich, born in the same year as Louis Philippe, was brought up in much the same way. He acquired his knowledge of foreign languages, including Latin, by conversation, and he was also taught carpentry, housework, agriculture and mechanics. The weakness of the system lay in its terrible reasonableness. Mme. de Genlis did not want to waste a moment. Every minute of the fourteen-hour day had to be accounted for. If the children were out of doors they must be doing gymnastics or studying botany. Every meal must show definite progress in a foreign language.

[4] Louis Philippe became the Duc de Chartres upon the death of his grandfather, the father of Philippe Egalité, in 1775. It was only upon his father's death that he became the Duc d'Orléans. While his father and grandfather were both alive he bore the title, Duc de Valence. It was not until he became king that he was ever known as Louis Philippe.

The Duc de Chartres developed exactly as Mme. de Genlis wanted. She noted with satisfaction that his character showed no trace of frivolity. He was a strong, healthy boy, he spoke foreign languages exceptionally well, and his conversation was intelligent, a little pedantic perhaps, but that was a fault which time would cure. If he did not possess the graces of a *grand seigneur* he was free from the immorality that cultivation of the graces seems to involve. Above all, he was never guilty of the luxuriant romanticism which made Napoleon a lover of Ossian and of Rousseau's *Confessions*. By the time Mme. de Genlis had finished with him the main outlines of the future Citizen King were already discernible. Everyone agreed that he was *très sage*.

The outbreak of the Revolution in 1789 found the Orléans family openly critical of the King and delighted to see him floundering from one blunder to another. The feud between Louis XVI and his Orléans cousin was of long standing. With the fatal tactlessness which alienated the very people who should have supported him, Louis XVI had refused the Duc d'Orléans any share in the government. He was debarred from politics and from the army, the only two professions open to a man of his position. He indulged his taste for women and for political intrigue but the Revolution offered something even better. Why should he not put himself at the head of the discontented nobility, pose as champion of the oppressed by advocating a few obvious reforms, and ultimately perhaps take the King's place? It was with such plans in view that the Duke insisted that his older son should join the Jacobin Club as proof of the family's sympathy with the Revolution. The husband of Mme. de Genlis acted as sponsor. Conscientious and intelligent, the eighteen-year-old Duc de Chartres attended the sessions of the club, listened to endless speeches and took notes of everything he heard. Fortunately the threat of invasion cut short his career as a Jacobin. He was appointed colonel of a regiment of dragoons and in that capacity he joined the army of General Dumouriez and fought at the battle of Valmy. It was his baptism of fire and he acquitted himself with distinction. The total casualties at Valmy were less than five hundred—about three hundred Frenchmen and one hundred and fifty Prussians—but it has been classed quite rightly among the fifteen decisive battles of the world. Here for the first time a ragged army of Frenchmen, badly equipped but passionately imbued with a sense of the rights of the common man, defeated what was reputed to be the finest professional army in the world.

The routine of army life suited General Egalité, as the Duc de Chartres had now become, to perfection. Thanks to Mme. de Genlis he was better able to stand hardships than most of his brother officers. Garrison life did not bore him. He was one of those methodical, detail-devouring officers who are just as essential to the well-being of an army as the brilliant strategist. Every morning he was up for stables at six o'clock, earlier, as he notes in his journal, than the other officers. He visited municipal authorities to make a complaint about the number of prostitutes in the vicinity. Once he plunged into a river to rescue a man from drowning. Such things win the respect of troops. Nor did they escape the watchful eye of General Dumouriez, who was particularly impressed by the military qualities of this competent young man.

Dumouriez was one of the best of the many good generals produced by the French Revolution, but he was older than the others and he was a royalist. "I was a republican," he said afterward, "for just three days of my life." Too old to believe that the new-born republic marked the beginning of the millennium, he was convinced that the monarchy was bound to come back. With Louis XVI dead, his son in prison, and his brothers fighting in the ranks of the enemy, the General's eye lighted on the Orléans family as providing the most likely candidates for the throne. The Duke himself was a wretched creature who had put the finishing touch on a useless life of debauchery by yielding to the clamor of the extremists in the Convention and voting for the King's death, but his oldest son, the Duc de Chartres—surely he was the man with the brightest future in France. He had fought at Valmy, thereby proving himself a good patriot. He was young, he was vigorous, he was intelligent, and most important of all he was a great admirer of General Dumouriez. With a victorious army at his back the General felt confident that he could march on Paris, overawe the Convention, and put the young Duke on the throne.

Whether or not some inkling of these plans reached the Convention, it was not long before the Committee of Public Safety despatched three of their dreaded *Commissaires* to his headquarters ordering him to appear before the Convention. Dumouriez arrested the *Commissaires* and handed them over to General Mack, commanding the Austrian army, with whom he was already in contact. From then on there was no going back. France was too small for both the Committee of Public Safety and a general who defied its authority. As long as Dumouriez retained control of his army he was master of the situation, but if the army could be made to feel that their general was a traitor then he would go the way of all enemies of the Republic.

Dumouriez was too much a man of the *ancien régime* to understand the revolutionary fervor of 1793. The art of war he understood and, within certain limits, the art of politics, but this wild enthusiasm for new ideas, this war of propaganda, manifestos and proclamations to soldiers bewildered him. Given enough men he could defeat the Austrians but he could never defeat the terrible cry *Vive la République!* The army melted through his fingers. There was no question that as between the Convention and their general they recognized only the authority of the Convention. By the beginning of January, 1793, it was obvious that the choice lay between arrest, almost certainly followed by the guillotine, and a quick dash for the Austrian lines. Dumouriez jumped on his horse and galloped for Austrian headquarters. With him into exile went the Duc de Chartres and a few squadrons of cavalry, not more than a thousand men altogether.

Orders had already arrived summoning General Egalité, the *ci-devant* Duc de Chartres, to the bar of the Convention. Anyone so closely associated with Dumouriez could hardly escape suspicion, and in 1793 suspicion and conviction were almost synonymous. He can hardly be blamed, therefore, for not walking into the lion's mouth, but it was a sad decision for him to have to make. The immediate result was the imprisonment of all the members of his family living in France. His father was subsequently executed but the brothers and a very devoted sister lived to join him in exile. For himself it meant that he would not see France again for twenty-one years. Dumouriez would have had him continue the fight against the Convention from the *émigré* camp on the Rhine, but the twenty-year-old duke was wiser than his general. Looking far into the future he may have foreseen that no man who had borne arms against his country could ever hope to be king. Foreign bayonets might prop him up on the throne but the people of France would never accept him. Even divine right was not a substitute for the people's respect.

Meanwhile he was an outcast with no standing among royalists or republicans. During the next three years he wandered through Europe learning to accept philosophically the loneliness, the petty insults and the hardships inherent in his peculiar position. The *émigrés* could never forget the infamy of his father, while his own career, honorable as it had been at first at least from the point of view of the republicans, had ended abjectly in desertion along with the traitor Dumouriez. In the eyes of the world the Orléans family had made a bad record. Actually there was no French exile who behaved with more dignity than the Duc de Chartres.

Instead of joining the discontented nobility who had settled in Germany just across the frontier, where they spent their time gazing across the Rhine and praying for the restoration of the monarchy, he made his way to Switzerland and there, in the village of Reichenau, after being hunted from one canton to another, he managed to earn his living teaching mathematics and languages in a boys' school. A hotelkeeper at Zurich noted a characteristic detail that apparently distinguished the Duc de Chartres from other exiles. He never failed to ask the price of everything on the menu and he paid for everything he ordered. Already the same carefulness that made him a reliable officer was standing him in good stead as an impecunious civilian. Whatever sympathy with the Revolution he may once have had evaporated during those hard years in Switzerland. The guillotining of his father, who had begun by flirting with the Liberals because he was jealous of the King, had taught him a terrible lesson, a lesson that had made him swing equally far in the opposite direction. His father had started off gaily on a path of reform not knowing where it would lead him. Henceforth the son would never adopt any policy unless the goal of that policy were clearly in view. He might make mistakes but the mistakes would be made in spite of careful reflection.

One of the questions to which he gave careful thought at this time was a projected trip to the United States. By 1796 Robespierre and his crew had been swept away and their place had been taken by the Directory. The politicians were still nervous of a reaction in favor of the monarchy and, though the Duc d'Orléans, as he had now become, was not a formidable candidate, the mediocre men who made up the Directory felt they would sleep more easily if the Orléans princes disappeared from the scene entirely. Two of the brothers were still in prison in France. The Government hit on the plan of releasing them on the condition that they and the Duc d'Orléans would all emigrate to America.

The Duke had already been planning to visit the New World with Gouverneur Morris, a friend of his earlier days, but at the last minute the plan had fallen through. Morris did not relish the idea of acting as the Duke's host during his stay in America and the Duke was equally unwilling to insure his property in Morris' favor.[5] "It would be quite possible," as he said, "that having left everything to make my fortune in America I should have to devote twenty or thirty years to working for Morris." As they were both excellent business men and both intent on driving a bargain it was perhaps just as well that they decided to go their ways separately. Once again the Duke set off on his travels. Tired of Switzerland and unwilling to join his fellow *émigrés* on the Rhine in a life of aimless intrigue, he set forth on a tour of the Scandinavian countries. His curiosity about strange places and his perfect readiness to undergo hardships made him a good traveller. Long marches through the deserted regions of Sweden and Lapland, camping night after night in the wilderness, would have appealed to very few princes in Europe except Louis Philippe. He even explored the Lofoten Islands that had remained practically unknown except to fishermen until they suddenly flashed into history in the early days of the World War as the scene of one of the most successful commando raids.

At the same time, his curiosity about life was strictly limited. If he visited a mine or an arsenal the fact was duly noted, but the casual meeting with strangers, the unexpected adventures of the road, made no impression upon him. One of his friends describes him at the age of twenty-four as a good son, a good brother and a good friend, but he reproaches him at the same time as being *peu susceptible d'enthousiasme*. This complete absence of enthusiasm at a time when men cared passionately for their ideals and even went to the scaffold for them is one of the most consistent traits of his character. Often it enabled him to size up a situation dispassionately and accurately—no one was more shrewd than Louis Philippe—but at the most critical moment of his life the completely pedestrian

[5] For Louis Philippe's relations with Gouverneur Morris, see Raymond Recouly, *Louis Philippe, Roi des Français* (Paris, 1930), p. 118.

character of the man was to cause his downfall. As a young man, however, it proved an asset rather than a handicap. His relations with the older branch of the family illustrate his level-headedness at its best.

After the death of the Dauphin in 1795 the next in line to the throne was the Comte de Provence, who immediately assumed the title of Louis XVIII. He and his younger brother, the Comte d'Artois, who afterwards became Charles X, were the two members of the family of whom it could most truly be said that they had learned nothing and forgotten nothing. It was important for Louis XVIII if he wanted his title to be recognized by the European Powers that there should be no other claimant to the throne. He decided therefore to become reconciled with his cousin the Duc d'Orléans to whom some of the more liberal-minded royalists were beginning to turn. His method of winning the Duke's support was to summon him to his headquarters at Coblenz and to order him to join the army of the Prince de Condé in which all the *émigrés* were enrolled. The Duc d'Orléans refused. Until the King was prepared to promise the French people a constitutional monarchy (*une monarchie limitée comme en Angleterre*) the Duc d'Orléans would not recognize his authority, and on no account would he join the army of the Prince de Condé, as it was serving under the command of an Austrian general, an acknowledged enemy of France. Nothing could be more firm or more reasonable than his response to the King's demand for submission, but his refusal to rally to the royal standard widened the breach between himself and the royal princes. It was never healed. Years afterward for appearance's sake they pretended to be reconciled, but beneath the surface jealousy and suspicion were always festering.

The Duke's refusal to throw in his lot with the Legitimists left him with no future in Europe. The Scandinavian tour had whetted his appetite for travel. Why not extend his horizon still further by visiting the New World as he had originally planned? Bankers could be found who were more accommodating than Gouverneur Morris. It was either that or a hole-and-corner existence in Germany. The French consul at Hamburg, egged on by the Directory in Paris, offered him every facility, reminding him at the same time that his brothers would be set free when he reached America.

On September 24, 1796, he finally set sail from Hamburg

for Philadelphia. It was a quick voyage, only twenty-seven days, during which time he plied the captain with factual questions about the manners and customs in the New World. Of the many distinguished Frenchmen who sought refuge in America during these troubled years no one was more likely to make a good impression. Chateaubriand, who preceded him by five years, was too much wrapped up in his own thoughts to make friends easily. Talleyrand, whom he missed by only a few weeks, was too caustic. The New World is always ready to welcome the aristocracy of the Old, provided the visitors are willing to be pleased, and provided that they do not volunteer any comments that are not complimentary. Society in the *ancien régime* dreaded boredom. Everything was forgiven to a man who was witty. In the drawing rooms of Philadelphia, still the literary and intellectual capital of America, boredom was not dreaded nearly as much as criticism, even if the criticism was disguised as a dispassionate enquiry into the social problems peculiar to a democracy. It was easier and pleasanter to accept things as they were. Talleyrand's rapier wit made him the best company in Paris, but he was not sought after in Philadelphia as much as the Duc d'Orléans.

This serious-minded young man possessed just the qualities that made for success in a society that was not yet too sure of itself. He was delighted with everything he saw. The simplicity of life and the strict economy practiced in every household suited him perfectly, nor did his own lack of distinction, noted long ago by Mme. de Genlis as a *manque de grandeur* unfitting him for any important office, affect his American friends. On the contrary, it probably contributed to his success. He was democratic without being too casual in his manner. It was a nice distinction which many visitors have missed. Lewis Cass admired him for keeping an accurate record of every dollar he spent while he was in the United States. The qualities, which forty years later, when he was King, made him so easy to caricature, did not seem ridiculous to the hostesses in Philadelphia.

The Duke's two brothers, Montpensier and Beaujolais, released from prison in Marseilles as soon as his arrival in America was made known, joined him early in 1797. The three brothers settled down together in a house on Prune Street belonging to the Spanish consul. Society, including the President of the United States, opened its doors to them. Washington did not receive everybody—Talleyrand tried in vain to meet him—

but his reception of the Orléans brothers seems to have been very friendly. They must have been almost the last Frenchmen to see Washington as President. Shortly afterwards they were invited to Mount Vernon where they spent four days. It was from Washington, certainly the best possible source, that they got advice about their grand tour. Like good travellers they were determined to see something of the West, and the West in 1797 meant the Ohio and the Misssissippi rivers. By the time they sailed home they had seen Niagara Falls and the Great Lakes, they had camped in the Kentucky wilderness, they had poled their way through ice floes down the Ohio River, they had slept in wigwams and they had huddled around tavern stoves with guides and trappers. Once when they arrived at an inn more than usually tired they forgot themselves so far as to ask to be served at a table by themselves. The innkeeper replied that if they did not care to mix with the other guests they could go elsewhere. Mrs. Morris tells of another occasion when they arrived at her house penniless and in rags and were revived by a dinner cooked by a French chef.

In all their travels the force that drove them ahead was not a romantic yearning for strange places. The Orléans princes were not dreamers or sentimental travellers, and they were not looking for noble savages or northwest passages. They travelled to collect facts. The Duke, who was very much the head of the family, had the mind of an enquiring reporter. Wherever he went he made careful notes on the food, which he found bad, the housing, the racial stock of the inhabitants, and the institution of slavery, of which he disapproved. The younger brothers were more carefree, particularly the happy-go-lucky seventeen-year-old Beaujolais, who loved above all things to be amused.

Meanwhile, much had been happening in their own distracted country. Napoleon's star was still rising and the restoration of the Bourbons appeared more remote than ever. All members of the Bourbon family including the Duchess of Orléans, the Duke's mother, had been expelled from France. As soon as he learned of her whereabouts—she had taken refuge in Spain—the Duke, acting impulsively for once, decided to cut short his travels and return to Europe. Family loyalty was one of his most attractive traits, and though in his childhood he had been more attached to Mme. de Genlis than to his mother, the years of separation had brought them together. It was time for the family to be reunited even if France was still barred to them. The decision was easier to make than to carry out. For a year the Orléans princes waited in Havana while a very leisurely Spanish Government considered whether they should be allowed to land in Spain. Eventually they had to go back from Havana to New York and wait for a British ship to take them to England.

The Duke had left Europe when he was twenty-three. By the time he landed in England he was twenty-seven. During those four years he had seen more of America than most Americans. He had lived among people with whom no other royal prince had ever come in contact, and yet though he had acquired a mass of interesting facts he had not changed for the better or for the worse. Experience had not moulded him as it does the really intelligent, it had only confirmed traits that already existed. There is a depressing similarity in the accounts of the impression he made on his contemporaries. Everybody agreed that he was a vigorous, well-informed, pedantic young man. No one denied that he was sensible, but no one suggested he was charming. Society noticed that, unlike most princes, his conduct was irreproachable. Supported by the British Government, he lived simply, but on a better scale than most of his exiled compatriots, in a villa at Twickenham.

There the Duke settled down to wait for the Napoleonic star to set. Always an astute observer of the political scene, he realized that Napoleon, being a dictator, was condemned to a febrile career of conquest. The long string of victories must lead sooner or later to defeat. From his villa in Twickenham he wrote to the King urging him to tell his agents in France not to conspire actively against Napoleon but merely to implant the idea that France could never expect to enjoy peace except under a monarchy. No other *émigré* read the signs of the times so accurately.

The pleasant country-house life at Twickenham, studious as well as social, for the Duke was a great reader, was cut short by the death of his two brothers. Neither of them had followed his regime of plain living. They were typically fashionable young men bent on making the most of London society and probably too convivially inclined for the constitutions they had inherited from their dissolute father. Montpensier, who appears to have been blessed with the charm and the ease that the Duke lacked, died in England in 1807. Beaujolais, already a sick man when his brother died, was ordered south to escape the English winter. Malta was decided on as one of the few health resorts not occupied by Napoleon's armies, but already it was too late. For a few weeks the climate seemed to agree with him and then suddenly on May 29, 1808, he died, leaving the Duke and his sister Adelaide as the sole surviving children.

Before returning to England, the Duke paid a visit to the court of the King and Queen of Naples who had been ousted from Italy by Napoleon and were now reigning in Sicily. The visit was not dictated by idle curiosity. Like everything else the Duke did, it was carefully calculated. He was looking for a wife. So much of Europe was now barred and so many thrones had been toppled over that the selection of desirable princesses was limited. One of them was Marie Emilie, the daughter of Ferdinand IV and Marie Caroline. From their point of view the Duc d'Orléans was not a particularly desirable match. Though he was known to possess great estates in France no one knew what would become of them, and meanwhile he was entirely dependent on the generosity of the British Government. Furthermore, Queen Marie Caroline, being a sister of Marie Antoinette, had no reason to look with favor on any member of the Orléans family, but her daughter Marie Emilie felt differently. Never was there a more perfect case of love at first sight. Compared to her father, a man of no interests, no energy and no talents, the Duc d'Orléans must indeed have seemed a fairy prince. He had travelled in so many strange places and he talked so authoritatively on what he had seen. If not exactly handsome he was in every sense of the word a big man. To Marie Emilie, to whom life had disclosed nothing beyond the trivialities of the court, Louis Philippe represented the great world. It was the old story of Othello and Desdemona. She loved him for the dangers he had passed and he loved her that she did pity them.

Two years were to pass before they were married, during which time he went to Spain to bolster up the Spanish guerrillas against Napoleon. Tired of the intrigues of the Spanish Cabinet, Napoleon had decided that he could wage war against Europe more effectively if he removed the Bourbons from the throne and substituted his brother Joseph in their place. The change necessitated the backing of a French army. The Duke of Wellington, who was to distinguish himself by defeating one marshal after another until he finally drove the Napoleonic armies out of Spain, did not require any help from the Duc d'Orléans. Even if England had not regarded Spain as her own private affair the Comte d'Artois in London and his little cohort of irreconcilable *émigrés* were always working against the Orléans family. The last thing they wanted was for the Duke to make a name for himself in Spain as a successful general. The Duke himself never wanted to fight against his own countrymen, but he dreamed of detaching the French armies from their allegiance to Napoleon and rallying them around his own standard.

The dream faded into nothingness and the Duke went back to his old occupation of waiting and watching, waiting for the last act of the Napoleonic drama and watching to see the effect upon his own fortunes. His marriage had brought him great happiness and he was soon busying himself over the plans for his new home. More practical than most of the *émigrés*, while waiting for the future he never lost sight of the present. Having decided to live in Palermo, at least for the time being, he set to work to reproduce in Sicily the conveniences to which he had grown accustomed in England. His agent was ordered to send out a *batterie de cuisine*, a billiard table, two spaniels for his father-in-law, and a portable water-closet. As soon as the house was furnished to his liking there was the problem of servants. Every mail brought the unfortunate agent new orders. There must be no delay and no extravagance. The Duke knew just what he wanted and he wanted it at the lowest possible price. Usually he got it, thereby proving to his wife that he was not only the best but also the wisest and most discreet husband in the world.

So engrossed was he by his wife and his family—three children were born during the first three years of marriage—that Napoleon's abdication caught him unawares. On May 3, 1814, his cousin, King Louis XVIII, made a triumphant entry into Paris. The Duc d'Orléans left Sicily immediately upon hearing the news, landed at Marseilles and posted across France to present his respects. The King was pleased to greet him most cordially and to appoint him one of the new lieutenant-generals who were to take the place of the Napoleonic marshals. Later on the Duchess arrived, travelling more slowly as she was expecting another baby. The Duc de Nemours was born in the summer of 1814 and christened in the chapel of the Tuileries.

So far so good. The Duke's position seemed to be assured

socially and financially, but the era of good feeling was not destined to last. At eleven o'clock on the night of March 5 the Duke was hurriedly summoned to the palace. There he learned that Napoleon had landed in the south of France. The King was not particularly disturbed by the news. Nothing ever ruffled his placid temperament. He thought that if the princes showed themselves at the head of the troops the usurper's triumphant progress would soon be arrested. The Duc d'Orléans, however, instead of being given an independent command as he would have liked, was ordered to proceed to Lyons at once and report there to the Comte d'Artois.

Events moved quickly in the spring of 1815, more quickly and more disastrously than the gouty old King thought possible. On March 1, Napoleon landed in the south of France; on the 10th he occupied Lyons; and on the 20th his eagles, which had flown from steeple to steeple from Cannes to the capital, fell exhausted among the chimney pots of the Tuileries. Once again the legitimate monarchy lumbered into exile. The Duc d'Orléans retired to his villa in Twickenham, whereas the rest of the royal party took refuge in Ghent. After Waterloo, when everybody in France was busy explaining just why he had acted as he did, the Duke insisted that if the King had followed his advice and gone to Dunkirk instead of Ghent he would have stayed with him, but that as soon as the King crossed the frontier and went into exile the Duke felt himself relieved of the responsibility of his command.

This excuse, coupled with reproaches to the King for not having taken him more into his confidence, marked the reawakening of the old distrust with which the two branches of the family had always eyed each other. It was not until 1817 that the Duke came back to Paris to live, and even then he played only a minor part in state affairs. As he watched the Bourbons make one mistake after another, sacrificing everything for the benefit of the faithful few who had been in exile with them, he may well have preferred to have as little to do with politics as possible. Instead, he directed all his energies to the recovery of the vast Orléans fortune. He engaged the best lawyers and started a whole series of lawsuits. Whoever had laid hands on any of his properties during his absence was forced to disgorge. The Duke was a shrewd man of business and it was not long before he became, as his father had been before him, one of the richest men in France. Anyone who has read the novels of Balzac will know that the deadly sin of avarice was peculiarly prevalent during the Restoration. The Duke was an avaricious man. After the long lean years of exile he meant to feather his nest and live, if not splendidly, at least comfortably. His tastes were the tastes of a *grand bourgeois*, rather than of a *grand seigneur*. He rebuilt the Palais Royal on a lavish scale, but when it came to furnishing he was careful not to compete with the Tuileries or with Versailles. Unlike his royal cousins, he was a man of the nineteenth rather than of the eighteenth century. Convenience was the note rather than beauty, solid comfort rather than elegance. He and his adoring wife with their growing family of eight healthy children were a symbol of new values and new standards.[6] In the eyes of the bourgeoisie the Duc d'Orléans stood for just the things they admired—respectability in private life, cautious liberalism, affable manners, and a talent for making money.

The Revolution of 1830, that cost Charles X his throne and doomed his family to eternal exile, offered the Duke the opportunity for which his critics insisted he had always been scheming. Whether he wanted to be king or not, as long as the crown was rolling on the ground he was quite willing to pick it up. The publication of the Ordinances, whereby King Charles X dissolved the Chamber and suspended the liberty of the press, had kindled a flame of resentment that the Duke knew could only be extinguished by the King's abdication. His own reaction was very characteristic. Whatever happened he would stay in France. If the King chose to follow a course that must lead him inevitably into exile, that was his affair. For the moment there was nothing for him to do but wait, not to thrust himself forward but to remain available if the people wanted him. During the "three glorious days," July 27, 28, and 29, 1830, while men were dying on the barricades, he remained at Neuilly, intent only on watching the drama from the wings. As soon as it became clear, after the capture of the Hotel de Ville by the mob, that the King would not be able to impose his will upon the people, placards began to appear all over Paris proposing the Duc d'Orléans as the only possible candidate for the

[6] The three oldest children, the Duc de Chartres and his two sisters, Louise, the future Queen of Belgium, and Marie, princess of Wurtemberg, were born in Sicily before the Restoration. The five others came after the return from exile: Nemours in 1814; Clementine, princess of Saxe-Coburg and mother of Ferdinand of Bulgaria, in 1817; Joinville in 1818; Aumale in 1822; and Montpensier in 1824.

throne. The alternative was a republic which would lead to civil war and embroil France with the rest of Europe.

The placards were known to be the work of a clever young journalist named Thiers. Writers and journalists had more at stake in the Revolution than men of any other profession, as the Ordinances deprived them of their means of livelihood. Forty years later this same Monsieur Thiers was to become the great champion of the Third Republic, but in 1830, as a young man of thirty-three, he fancied himself in the role of king-maker. On the 30th he visited Neuilly and persuaded the Duke to accept the throne if it were offered to him. He pointed out not only to the Duke but to his sister Mme. Adelaide, who was more ambitious for her brother than he was for himself, that what France needed was a new dynasty headed by a king who owed his throne to the people. Everyone knew that the Duke had not sought the throne but he must not hang back too long. He must put himself at the head of the Revolution. Thrones were not to be won by waiting; they belonged by right to the first occupant.

Never before had the frontier doctrine of squatter sovereignty been applied to the throne of St. Louis and never had it been made to sound so plausible. But Thiers was not only a good psychologist, he had a sense of the theatre as well. After persuading the Duke to come out of his retirement and present himself as a candidate for the throne, he then had to convince the people that what they really wanted was a king, a reasonable king whom they would choose themselves, a king who reigned but did not govern. How could the shrewd but eminently prosaic Duc d'Orléans be "made up" so that Paris would accept him as an authentic fairy prince without any of the objectionable features of the Bourbons? It was a nice problem in publicity and only Thiers could have solved it. He decided to stage a meeting between the Duke and the venerable Lafayette, who was well known for his republican sympathies. The meeting took place at the Hotel de Ville where a provisional government had been established with Lafayette as president. The old gentleman had had his hour of glory in America fifty years before, but whatever powers of decision he possessed then had long since evaporated. In the hands of an accomplished politician like Thiers he was mere potter's clay. Thiers gave him the limelight but he coached him carefully before allowing him on the stage.

In the *Mémoires d'Outre-Tombe* Chateaubriand does full justice to the climax of this charming little comedy:

> Monsieur de la Fayette, seeing the growing uncertainty of the assembly, suddenly decided to relinquish the presidency; he gave the Duc d'Orléans a tricolor flag, went out on the balcony of the Hotel de Ville, and embraced the Prince before the eyes of the astounded crowd, while the Duke waved the national flag. The republican kiss of la Fayette created a king. Strange conclusion to the life of the "hero of Two Worlds"! [7]

On August 9, the Chamber of Deputies confirmed Lafayette's kiss, and the Duc d'Orléans became King Louis Philippe.

Throughout these days the Duke played his part with considerable dignity. The people liked to think that he was their man, not King of France as the Bourbons had been, but King of the French people. They were delighted with him, as any man is by a tool he has fashioned with his own hands, and for some time he had to submit to the terrible familiarity that a sudden burst of popularity brings in its wake. The crowds invaded the Palais Royal and insisted on seeing him and his family at all hours of the day or night. His friendliness and good temper made a generally good impression except upon the two extremes of political opinion, the republicans and the legitimists. The republicans felt they had been swindled into accepting a government that might or might not be democratic but was certainly not republican, while the legitimists always maintained that Louis Philippe had stolen the crown, if not from the King himself at least from his grandson, the Duc de Bordeaux, in whose favor he had abdicated. Until the death of the Duc de Bordeaux in 1883 the royalists in France were divided into camps, the Orléanists who rallied to Louis Philippe, and the legitimists who remained faithful to the elder branch of the family.

To these orthodox royalists Louis Philippe was always a usurper. They might have accepted him as president of a republic but they would never acknowledge him as king. Louis Philippe himself was always troubled by the question of his title to the throne. He was never quite willing to start afresh and base his claim entirely on the people. Anxious to make the

[7] Chateaubriand, 'Mémoires d'Outre-Tombe,' 6 vols. edited by Edmond Biré, Paris, n.d. Vol. V, 345.

best of both worlds he wanted to create a new dynasty and at the same time cling to the prestige of legitimacy. Napoleon III was wise enough to reinforce his claim to the throne by a plebiscite, but the "Citizen King" had no such national support behind him.

Accordingly he took refuge in a quasi-legitimacy that satisfied no one but himself. To a logical people like the French there was a fundamental flaw in a regime that tried to blend the popular appeal of a republic with the historical glamour of the legitimate crown. The English could do it because they have a talent for make-believe that has long been the despair of the rest of Europe. Whether or not French children ever respond to the cry "Let's pretend," their parents certainly don't, and the attempt to graft a typically British compromise upon the relentlessly rational people of France ended, just when the grafting seemed most secure, in a peculiarly inglorious failure.

As for Louis Philippe, the qualities that made him a good father, a good husband and a good man of business were not the qualities that made a *Roi Soleil*. France was in an exacting mood. She demanded an affable, democratic monarch who at the same time was every inch a king. The poet-politician Lamartine summed up the verdict of the people in the deadly phrase *La France s'ennuie*. After the novelty of him had worn off, the bourgeois King with his tiresome domestic virtues was condemned as a bore.

Louis Blanc, the great French socialist who undertook to guarantee work to everybody by creating national workshops, once said that whereas Charles X had fallen because his throne rested on a false principle, Louis Philippe fell because his throne rested on no principle. And yet after the caricaturists have had their say, after the Chateaubriands and the Lamartines and the Louis Blancs have belabored the Orléans monarchy to their hearts' content, the solid achievements of the years 1830–48 cannot be minimized. During Louis Philippe's reign the country was more prosperous than it had ever been before. Compared to the era that preceded it, or to the era that followed, it was indeed a golden age. Guizot was not exaggerating when he said that during these years France enjoyed the most just, mild, free, and sensible government she had ever known. Certainly Guizot was not an impartial witness, but his opinion has never been seriously challenged. A generation that has been brought up to think of the maintenance of a high standard of living as the be-all and the end-all here must think twice before criticizing the policies of Louis Philippe.

Nor can it be said that French prestige abroad suffered during these years. The consolidation of the Algerian conquest begun under Charles X, the creation of a free Belgium for which the diplomacy of Talleyrand was mainly responsible, the establishment of free elementary education, the beginning of railroad development, these were the solid achievements of the bourgeois monarchy. In France the railroads made their way more slowly than in England, and there were consequently fewer railroad panics. The public, even the supposedly enlightened public, was suspicious of the innovation. In 1840, Thiers, at that time president of the Council, stated in the Chamber that he envisaged for the future a maximum construction of thirty miles of railroad track a year. Arago, the great astronomer, was afraid that if the army took to travelling by railroad, the soldiers would lose their stamina. It was only with the passage of the long-delayed railroad law of 1842, in accordance with which the state was to buy the land, build the stations and lay the tracks, while the rolling stock was to be provided by private companies, that the public finally caught the scent. From then on everybody was speculating, and every deputy was determined that the railroad should run through his *arrondissement*. The catastrophe on the Versailles line on May 8, 1842, in which the famous admiral Dumont d'Urville was killed, temporarily convinced the Parisians that the railroad was a wicked and inexorable machine, but gradually opinion veered until finally the railroad came to be regarded as a symbol of progress. In *L'Education Sentimentale* Flaubert described a painting as representing progress or civilization in the guise of Jesus Christ driving a locomotive through a virgin forest.[8]

Louis Philippe's policy, "Peace and Industry," sounded eminently sane. With the peasants and the bourgeoisie united

---

[8] The evil-monster point of view is represented by Alfred de Vigny in *La Maison du Berger*, which was written with the Versailles accident in mind:

> Sur le taureau de fer qui fume, souffle et beugle,
> L'homme a monté trop tôt. Nul ne connaît encor
> Quels orages en lui porte ce rude aveugle,
> Et le gai voyageur lui livre son trésor;
> Son vieux père et ses fils, il les jette en otage
> Dans le ventre brûlant du taureau de Carthage,
> Qui les rejette en cendre aux pieds du Dieu de l'or.

behind him, and the vagaries of the extremists on either flank —the legitimists and the republicans—rigorously repressed, he had every reason to believe that he had founded a government as popular and as firmly established as any in Europe. How was it then that after eighteen years the edifice that he had fabricated so laboriously suddenly toppled over? The collapse was not provoked by any internal or external crisis such as the Ordinances of 1830 or the surrender of Napoleon III in 1870. There was no battle, only a little half-hearted fighting in the streets of Paris in which less than a hundred soldiers were killed. Historians have described the revolution of 1848 as a result without a cause, but like all epigrams this statement is only half true. Louis Philippe fell just as an apple falls from the tree when it is sufficiently ripe, though no one can predict the day or hour it will drop. In the early spring of 1848 the wind of Revolution was rustling through Europe, and one government after another came tumbling to the ground. He had wanted to create a stable government and he succeeded so well that when the storm came no one could persuade him that it might fall. It stood there rigid to the last and then suddenly crashed to the ground.

It was Louis Philippe's misfortune to have been guided during the last eight years of his life by a minister whose political ideas harmonized far too closely with his own. François Pierre Guillaume Guizot was blessed with all sorts of good qualities. He was a man whose personal integrity nobody ever questioned, a splendid orator, a statesman with a wide knowledge of history compared to whom his protagonist Palmerston was a high-spirited amateur,[9] and yet he never caught the imagination of the French people as Palmerston caught the imagination of England. His father, a Protestant lawyer of Nimes, had been guillotined by the Jacobins when his son François was only seven years old. This terrible tragedy influenced Guizot's whole career. He was so horrified by the anarchy the French Revolution left in its wake that he never got away from the idea that the one function of government was to preserve order, to maintain peace at home and abroad.

Guizot never understood the importance of social questions. The people might have tolerated his foreign policy, his subservience first of all to Palmerston and then to Metternich,

[9] E. L. Woodward, *Three Studies in European Conservatism* (London, 1929), p. 183.

though it was never popular at any time, but his indifference to
the thoughts and aspirations of the workingman, his placid
assumption that political intelligence was only to be found
among people of substantial wealth, this they could not forget.[10]
At a time when the average wage of the workman in France
was one franc seventy-eight centimes a day, and when crimes
due to poverty were steadily increasing, Guizot honestly believed that his government had reached the limit of enlightenment. Let the people sit back and enjoy their blessings. The
country was on the right track. The rich were growing richer
and eventually prosperity would seep down to the lowest strata
of society.

But there were many who did not believe that the country
was on the right track. In the industrial centers, particularly
in Lille and in Alsace, workmen were suffering as they had
never suffered before. The industrial workman was not the
representative Frenchman in 1848—he is not even today—but
the slow shifting of the economic center of gravity from the
side of agriculture to that of industry was beginning to make
itself felt. Generally speaking, the French factory employee was
better off than the Englishman of the same kind in Manchester
or Birmingham. The textile workers of Lille were an exception.
Victor Hugo describes in *Les Châtiments* how these unfortunate creatures lived, huddled together on top of each other in
wretched underground cellars, and his passionate indignation
is echoed in the more prosaic complaints of the workers themselves.[11] These conditions, horrible as they were, were confined
to a small minority. In 1848, industry in France had absorbed
only one thirty-fifth of the population, and of this thirty-fifth
many lived in comparatively comfortable surroundings.

The fall of Louis Philippe cannot be attributed then to the
resentment of the working classes. If factory conditions be the
test, England was far more ripe for revolution than France, but
there were other forces making for revolution to be considered.[12] During the last few years of its life the Bourgeois

[10] Louis Blanc's *Histoire de la Révolution de 1848*, 2 vols. (Paris, 1880),
illustrates very clearly the contempt of the intellectual for the studied materialism
of the July Monarchy.

[11] See also A. M. Gossez, *L'ouvrier lillois du textile, 1848*, No. 14, Bibliothèque de la Rév. de 1848.

[12] Karl Marx's friend Friedrich Engels, who knew England well, makes this
abundantly clear in his book *The Condition of the Working Class in England
in 1844.*

Monarchy was confronted with a succession of poor harvests. The years 1845 and 1846 were notoriously bad ones. Crop failures all over France caused a sharp rise in food prices, particulary in the case of bread, and in some districts, more especially Alsace, the dreaded potato disease swept away another fundamental article of French diet.[13]

In Paris, in the winter of 1847, one third of the million inhabitants were said to be in receipt of charity .The 1842 edition of Galignani's *New Paris Guide* notes that there were eighty thousand paupers. Criminal gangs were organized for the more systematic exploitation of society, and the number of foundlings, always a good indication of the sickness of society, was steadily mounting. One hundred thousand in 1820, it had climbed to over 130,000 by 1847. Still more dangerous to the State was the alarming physical deterioration of the people. In 1840, out of every ten thousand called up for military service in *départements* that were predominantly manufacturing, nine thousand were rejected as physically unfit, and even in the agricultural *départements* that were predominantly nonmanufacturing, four thousand out of every ten had to be sent back.[14]

Louis Philippe might point to the enormous increase in national wealth, but by 1848 the combination of bad harvests, unemployment and wild speculation had produced that feeling of uneasiness throughout the country which is so often the precursor of revolution. On the surface France appeared prosperous enough. Only a very intelligent observer would have noted that the vast sums of capital that were being absorbed by railroad construction and other public works were not producing any immediate return. "Works of great importance," says Galignani, "are in progress, and more may be expected every year; the Government leads the way in this march of national improvement, and what is undertaken by public order is now not only begun, but quickly finished." [15]

Such activities impressed the casual visitor; they did not impress the factory worker or the peasant. Least of all did they impress the growing army of communists, Christian socialists, utopian enthusiasts, and hard-headed liberal deputies who, though they disagreed on many things, were unanimous in their

[13] Mme. M. Kahan-Rabecq, *La Crise des subsistances dans le Haut-Rhin à la vieille de la Rév. de 1848*, No. 12, Bibl. de la Rév. de 1848.
[14] E. Lavisse (ed.), *Histoire de France contemporaine*, Paris, 1921, V, 216.
[15] Galignani's *New Paris Guide* (Paris, 1842), p. 146.

conviction that until Guizot was dismissed no genuine social progress was possible.

In 1847, a series of scandals in high social and political circles still further undermined the prestige of the monarchy. The bribery of the President of the Cour de Cassation in which General Cubières, an ex-Minister of War, was implicated, the horrible crimes committed by the Duc de Praslin and the Prince d'Eckmuhl were seized upon by the opposition press as proving the rottenness of the whole social structure. To all this rumbling discontent Guizot, the sixty-year-old President of the Council, turned a deaf ear. He had come to Paris as a young man determined to make his way by his pen, and he had succeeded so well that at the age of twenty-five he had been appointed to the chair of modern history at the Sorbonne. Since then he had devoted his life to history and politics. Under the first restoration he held the post of secretary-general of the interior, and when Louis XVIII went to Ghent during the Hundred Days he represented the moderate royalists at the court of the King in exile. His contemporaries knew him as an austere Protestant who could be relied upon to fight the more reactionary policies of the Bourbons and to support the cause of the bourgeoisie in any controversy. A man of aristocratic manners with something of the Englishman and the puritan about him, was Alfred de Vigny's description of him.

Guizot's great achievement during the early days of the July Monarchy was the passage of a law making primary education compulsory. Between 1830 and 1840 he was in the Cabinet three times, and for eight months, during a crisis in Eastern affairs, he was ambassador in London. No man in France was better qualified by study and experience to direct the policy of a supposedly constitutional monarchy. No man was ever more confident of his rightness or more blindly unaware of the causes of his failure.

The first warning came on December 28, 1847. On that day the King pronounced an address, written for him by Guizot as President of the Council, at the opening of the two Chambers. It was an important speech outlining the policy of the Government, and the deputies and peers had met together for the occasion. Unfortunately Louis Philippe was no longer the canny judge of character, the affable democratic prince that he had been at the time of his accession, but a worn-out old man of seventy-five who had lost all his resiliency and all his flair for politics. The mortal illness of his sister Adelaide, who died three days later, the one person to whose advice he still listened, had still further aged him. The speech opened innocuously enough with a reference to the improved economic condition of the country, and then launched forth into an attack upon the opposition.

> In the midst of the agitation fermented by blind or hostile passions one conviction animates and sustains me, that we possess in the constitutional monarchy, in the union of the great powers of the State, the sure means of surmounting these obstacles and of satisfying all the moral and material interests of our dear country.

The significant words here are "blind or hostile passions," significant because they prove that Guizot in spite of his very real abilities had not yet learned the rules of the game. In a constitutional monarchy His Majesty's loyal opposition must never be accused of blindness or hostility. By aligning the King with the conservative party Guizot served notice on the country that no reforms would be tolerated.

His position was all the more dangerous because his majority in the Chamber did not reflect the sentiment of the country. A strong, serious, unoriginal mind such as Guizot's, once it gets hold of an idea, does not change easily. He prided himself on being a great tranquilizer and he thought he could keep the country tranquil by refusing to extend the franchise. Out of a population of 35,500,000 only 250,000 were entitled to vote, and most of the deputies that those electors sent to Paris were anxious to maintain the status quo at any cost. Tocqueville, a shrewd observer of the French as well as of the American scene, described the government of France at the end of the reign of Louis Philippe as "a business company, all the operations of which were undertaken in view of the profit which would accrue to the stockholders." [16] Guizot knew that he could depend on the votes of his stockholders in any emergency. He had strapped the nation into a strait jacket from which there could be no escape until he was driven out of office.

The moderate wing of the opposition, headed by Thiers, a more supple intelligence than Guizot but without his courage, and Odilon Barrot, a popular orator, had no intention of overthrowing the monarchy, but they were intent on getting rid of

[16] A. de Tocqueville, *Souvenirs*, p. 27. Paris, 1942.

Guizot and on extending the franchise. Their method of appealing to the country at large was to hold public banquets at which inflammatory speeches were made castigating the Government's policies at home and abroad and demanding electoral reform. At one of these banquets, held at Mâcon, Lamartine had lashed an audience of 6000 into a lather of indignation.

Infuriated by the King's speech, the opposition decided to hold a banquet in Paris at the Champs-Elysées. The price was set at six francs, thereby excluding the poorer and more radical element of the population. Though feeling was running high, as yet they were aiming at a dignified protest rather than a popular demonstration. Rather than prohibit the banquet the Government hit on a compromise whereby they would allow the meeting to take place, protest against the proceedings, and afterwards try their legality in court. The question seemed to be settled, at least temporarily, when three of the opposition newspapers published an official program of a public demonstration to be held in connection with the banquet. Furthermore, they called upon members of the National Guard to attend in uniform "for the purpose of defending liberty by protecting order and preventing interference by the police."

This was clearly an illegal step, for it was the attempt of a number of private individuals to usurp the functions of the Government. Guizot, now in a much stronger position and perfectly willing to force the issue, immediately prohibited both the banquet and the demonstration. Early in the morning of February 22, the day set for the demonstration, it looked as if Guizot had won an easy victory. It was a cold, rainy morning, the worst possible weather for a demonstration. Louis Philippe looked out of the windows of the Tuileries and remarked that Parisians were not in the habit of making revolutions in winter. By ten o'clock a few groups of workmen, not very formidable at first, started to converge on the Place de la Concorde and from there streamed across the river to the Chamber of Deputies. There they were joined by a number of students—the Latin quarter could always be relied upon to provide its quota to any demonstration—and together, workmen and students, they began shouting *Vive la Réforme, à bas Guizot!* A squadron of dragoons cleared the area in front of the Chamber and the crowd were driven back to the Place de la Concorde.

Meanwhile, the deputies, still confident that the demonstration had fizzled out, were indulging in an academic discussion on the finances of the Bank of Bordeaux. The opposition benches were empty. At five o'clock Odilon Barrot, tired of the futile little comedy that was being enacted, recalled the Chamber to the actualities of the moment by offering a resolution impeaching the ministers on the grounds that they had falsified the principles of the Constitution, and by a systematic course of corruption attempted to substitute for the free expression of public opinion the calculations of private interest, and of having thus prevented the functioning of representative government. Guizot read the resolution, smiled contemptuously, and announced that the discussion would take place on the following day.

While the Chamber was sitting, the situation in the streets had worsened though there was still no sign of a full-scale revolution. The King went to bed still thinking that his government was perfectly secure. The Queen was more nervous but she knew nothing about politics. The King assured her that the Parisians were sensible people, that it was foolish to suppose they would trade a throne for a mere banquet.

The next morning, February 23, the troops who had been called out the previous afternoon and had then gone back to their barracks were again summoned to keep the peace. The crowds still had no apparent purpose, but they were being hustled by the troops and they had started throwing up barricades. So far the National Guard had not been used. At the beginning of the reign the Guard had been conspicuously loyal, but the fatal habit of electing officers had transformed it into a quasi-political organization, which the Government could no longer trust. Now that it became necessary to occupy the principal points of the city the National Guard was needed, and with some trepidation the Government called them out. Had they supported the regular troops of the line it is possible that Louis Philippe's descendants might still be reigning in the Tuileries, but they were in no mood to stem the current of the crowd. A faithful few kept their ranks, but for the most part they mingled with the mob, shouting for reform and the dismissal of Guizot. From the moment of the defection of the Guard, upon whom he had always counted, the King became a beaten man. He who had been so unreasonably optimistic suddenly gave way to despair, although there was no talk of anything but a change of ministry. During the next twenty-four hours, unable to make any decision or to stick to any one policy, he drifted beyond the help of his most ardent supporters.

It now became obvious that order could not be re-established without fighting, and the King shrank from shedding blood. "I've seen enough blood spilt," he kept reiterating. Perhaps he felt, for he was essentially a kindly man, that since he had received the crown from the people it was not right for him to hold it by force. Reluctantly he decided to yield to the mob to the extent of dismissing Guizot, but would that be enough? In politics, as in private life, concessions should be made before the crisis has arisen or after it is over. To yield in the middle of the struggle is only to encourage the other side to ask for more. The Queen and two of the princes, the Duc de Nemours and the Duc de Montpensier, were eager for a change of ministry. The other two sons, the Prince de Joinville and the Duc d'Aumale, both very popular, were unfortunately in Algeria but they, too, had long been opposed to Guizot's relentless conservatism. Fond as he was of his children the King was very much the head of his family and he was not accustomed to accepting their advice. Now the moment had come to give way. He did it with a bad grace.

Instead of sending for Thiers and Barrot, which would have been hailed as a genuine change of heart, he summoned Count Molé, a relic of the Napoleonic era, an aristocrat unknown to the masses, not by any means a fool but not the man to drive the monarchy through the storm. Molé arrived at the Tuileries at four o'clock in the afternoon of the 23rd. No sooner had he agreed to try to form a cabinet, no easy task at that moment, than the King began to change his mind. Molé would want to make all sorts of changes that might not suit him. Perhaps he should not have dismissed Guizot after all. The King was growing more and more bewildered. Everybody was urging him to appoint Marshal Bugeaud to take command of the Army and restore order in the streets. Bugeaud himself said that though he was a good doctor he would prefer to be called in before the patient was dying. Certainly something had to be done, but Bugeaud's remedy was the old familiar whiff of grapeshot and the King still shied away from it. On the whole he thought he would wait another day and see what happened. Meanwhile, Molé had disappeared and no one knew where he was. Finally he returned to the Tuileries at midnight and reported that the situation had got beyond him. A few hours earlier he might have succeeded; now it was too late. He could not form a cabinet.

During the eight hours that had elapsed since Guizot's dismissal a street clash occurred that turned an ugly, but not yet desperate, situation into a full-grown revolution. Just after sundown the crowd that was pouring down the Boulevard des Capucines headed for the Ministry of Foreign Affairs found itself confronted by the 14th Regiment of the Line. The soldiers refused to give way and as the mob became more threatening a shot was fired. No one knew where it came from but the soldiers, believing themselves attacked, fired a volley into the crowd. Some fifty people were killed or wounded. This was just the incident that the extremists wanted. Sixteen corpses were loaded onto a passing omnibus and paraded through the streets followed by the crowds shouting for vengeance. The question of electoral reform was now an academic issue.

By this time the King was convinced that only Bugeaud and Thiers could save the monarchy, but the choice of these two men illustrates how hopeless the situation had become. Bugeaud stood for repression and Thiers for conciliation. Once again the King could not make up his mind. He did not like Thiers because Thiers had always insisted that the King should reign rather than rule, and though that had been the understanding in 1830 he had never accepted it in his heart. Furthermore, Thiers had in the past advocated a bellicose foreign policy of which he disapproved. Now this obstinate little man was telling him he would have to accept ministers like Barrot, whom he hated even more than he did Thiers, and that he would have to submit to a whole series of thoroughgoing reforms. The appointment of Thiers was equivalent to a confession of past mistakes and a promise to mend his ways.

On the other hand Bugeaud's name was a symbol of brute force. The King seemed to be holding out an olive branch in one hand and a sword in the other. Any conciliatory effect that Thiers might have had upon the mob was paralyzed by his association with Bugeaud. "It is a little late," said Bugeaud upon finally being given the command, "but I have never yet been beaten and I am not going to begin now. There will be some blood spilt but by this evening the mob will have learned their lesson."

He planned to restore order by the use of three columns.

The commanders of these columns were to announce the formation of the Thiers ministry, disperse the mob, clear the barricades, and occupy the principal points in the city. Two of the columns reached their objectives, the Panthéon and the Hotel de Ville, without much difficulty, but the third, commanded by General Bedeau, was held up by a barricade in the rue St. Denis. General Bedeau had distinguished himself in the conquest of Algeria, but it was one thing to lead a charge against the Arabs in the desert and quite another to storm a barricade defended by his own countrymen in the streets of Paris. Instead of carrying out orders he allowed himself to be drawn into negotiations with the leaders of the mob, as a result of which he agreed to wait for further instructions from headquarters. Bugeaud himself, suddenly infected by the virus of indecision, gave Bedeau the order to withdraw. From that moment everything was lost.

As soon as he heard of the Bedeau fiasco Thiers made up his mind that Bugeaud must go, but once again it was too late. During these fatal days the Government was always lagging twenty-four hours behind public opinion. Paris had now passed completely into the hands of the populace. The march of events had swept far beyond the original leaders of the reform party and by now even Thiers was inacceptable. It was no good his sending agents out into the crowd to announce that Bugeaud had been relieved. Bugeaud should never have been appointed in the first place unless the ministry approved of his policy and was willing to back him. The cry had now changed from *Vive la Réforme, à bas Guizot!* to *Plus de Thiers! Plus de Barrot! Le peuple est le maître! A bas Louis Philippe!*

In the Tuileries the King and the royal family were at last aware that they were facing the greatest crisis of the reign. The King debated whether or not they should leave the Tuileries. Thiers was in favor of escaping from Paris to some point outside from which Bugeaud with a force of 60,000 men could reoccupy Paris and crush the Revolution. This was exactly the course that he himself followed when Paris was in the hands of the Commune in 1871. The Queen, suddenly displaying an unexpected courage, urged the King to gather the family around him and wait for whatever fate the future might have in store for him.

Inspired perhaps by the determination of his wife, hitherto considered the timid member of the family, Louis Philippe resolved to stake everything on one last throw. He would review the troops assembled in the Place du Carrousel to defend the Tuileries. If they gave him a rousing welcome that would prove there was still something worth fighting for. The idea was not a bad one and might well have succeeded if the King had been twenty years younger, but the ponderous seventy-five-year-old Louis Philippe, buttoned into the uniform of a lieutenant-general, was not a figure to kindle men's imaginations or to revive their flagging loyalty.

At eleven o'clock that morning, February 24—how much had happened since the afternoon before when he dismissed Guizot—Louis Philippe mounted his horse and rode out of the Tuileries accompanied by his two sons, Thiers, Marshal Bugeaud and a few other officers. The Queen and the princesses watched him from the windows of the palace. The first troops greeted him with *Vive le Roi*. The Queen's spirits rose. The King passed on through the arch of the Carrousel to where some four thousand troops were drawn up, including the first and tenth legions of the National Guard. Again he was greeted with cries of *Vive le Roi*, interspersed with an occasional *Vive la Réforme*. So far the review had gone well, but before coming to the troops of the regular army he had to face another legion of the National Guard who had forced their way into the Place du Carrousel with the express idea of making a demonstration. This time there were no cries of *Vive le Roi* but merely *Vive la Réforme! A bas les ministres! A bas le système!* Several of the men broke ranks and crowded around the King brandishing their weapons.

Now or never was the moment for the magic of personality to assert itself. Napoleon would have won these men over by stepping forward and baring his breast, but Louis Philippe was made of different clay. While everybody waited for the right word and the right gesture he slumped in his saddle, turned around, and rode slowly back to the Tuileries without giving a thought to the other troops who were waiting to be reviewed. The spectacle of the old King, utterly discouraged by the demonstration of a handful of the National Guard, turning tail at the first rebuff, was hardly calculated to raise the prestige of the monarchy in their eyes. If the King was so easily discomfited, why should they fight for him?

In the Tuileries the moral collapse of the King was reflected in the general listlessness of the ministers. The King sat with his head buried in his hands. Thiers kept reiterating, "The flood is mounting, the flood is mounting," but seemed incapable of formulating any policy. All semblance of etiquette had disappeared and people wandered in and out of the palace at will. A lawyer named Crémieux, who professed to be friendly, suggested that the monarchy might still be saved if Thiers resigned and Barrot took his place. In the general confusion only Queen Marie Amélie, who had sensed the catastrophe before anybody else, kept her head. She knew that abdication was in the air but she was a granddaughter of Maria Theresa, a niece of Marie Antoinette, and a brave woman in her own right. If she had had her way there would have been no abdication. The Duc de Nemours was not lacking in courage but he was a quiet, close-lipped young man accustomed to taking orders rather than to giving them. On this last day of the monarchy he said nothing to influence the King one way or another.

The only other member of the family who urged the King not to abdicate was the Duchesse d'Orléans. Hélène of Mecklenburg, Duchesse d'Orléans, was the widow of the oldest and most attractive of the King's sons, who had been tragically killed in a carriage accident at Neuilly. For the sixth time since Louis XIV the heir to the throne had died before his father. At the time of the Duke's death in 1842 there had been some discussion about the regency. Louis Philippe would probably die before his grandson, the Comte de Paris, came of age. The question was whether the Duchess as mother of the heir, or the Duc de Nemours as the King's oldest surviving son, should be appointed regent after the King's death. The Chamber, guided by Guizot, who was disturbed by the Duchess's leanings toward liberalism, voted for the Duc de Nemours.

Now that the word "abdication" was being bandied about in the Tuileries, the question of the succession became very urgent. The first person to force his way into the King's presence and demand his immediate abdication was Emile de Girardin, editor of *La Presse*, a well-known newspaperman of the day, who introduced France to the doubtful blessings of cheap journalism. Girardin announced that the people were clamoring for the abdication of the King, the regency of the Duchesse d'Orléans, the dissolution of the Chamber, and a general amnesty. The King scanned the faces around him to see if he could count on any support. Not a sign of encouragement from anyone, nothing but the persistent demands from the antechamber—"abdication, abdication."

Louis Philippe had already proved that he was not the man to face a threatening crowd. Bewildered by the waves of unpopularity that were lapping around him, he stood up, opened the door of the salon where the Queen was sitting so as to make sure she would hear what he said, and pronounced the words for which everyone was waiting: "I abdicate." The Queen and the Duchess were aghast. "You can't do such a thing," they exclaimed; "how can you leave to your grandson a burden that you cannot bear yourself?" But the King by now was a thoroughly beaten man. "I am a peace-loving king," he said; "since defense is impossible I will not shed French blood uselessly."

The next step was to write out the terms of abdication. There was no time to lose. The crowd would be surging into the Tuileries at any moment, but the King refused to be hurried. Helpless and apathetic he was, but not panic-stricken. He sat down at his desk, selected his pen carefully, and began to write. The shooting outside was growing louder and the Duc de Montpensier urged him to hurry. "I have always been a slow writer," replied the King, "and this is not the moment to change my habits." At last he had finished. He pushed back his chair and read his statement aloud in a clear voice: "I relinquish the crown which the will of the people called me to bear, in favor of my grandson, the Comte de Paris. May he succeed in the great task which falls to him today."

"May he resemble his grandfather," exclaimed the Queen, and then added, raising her eyes to Heaven, *"O mon Dieu, ils le regretteront."*

A few of the bystanders pointed out to the King that he had not appointed the Duchess regent, but on that point he was adamant. Others could do that if they wanted, but it was against the law. He had never broken any law so far and he was not going to begin now.

No one in the royal family seemed to realize that abdication meant the end of the Orléans monarchy, not a regency but a republic. Only a few people in the crowd knew it, but they were the manipulators of public opinion, the men who make up their minds quickly, say nothing in public until the moment is ripe, and then insinuate that the policy upon which they had decided long before represents the considered judgment of the public. The Government had always been aware of a republican opposition, but it was so small that no one took it very seriously. The King and his ministers forgot that revolutions are hatched by one or two men in a back room. There must be a grievance to begin with—a stamp tax or a question of electoral reform—but the men who are set on changing the whole structure of government, a Samuel Adams in 1776 or a Lamartine in 1848, will never be satisfied with the mere elimination of the grievance.

Up to the last moment Louis Philippe supposed that in abdicating he was only substituting his grandson for himself, and exchanging an arduous life in the Tuileries for a carefree existence in one of his numerous country chateaux. That he and the Queen and the whole royal family would be lucky if they escaped from France alive never occurred to him. After signing the abdication he went to his room, took off his uniform, put on a travelling suit, collected a few things he was taking with him and waited for the *berlines*, the big lumbering coaches drawn by four horses easily recognizable on account of the postillions in the royal livery, in which he was planning to drive away.

Meanwhile, the announcement of the King's abdication only whetted the ardor of the mob. Their blood was up and they were determined to force their way into the Tuileries. This was all the easier as the soldiers still had orders not to fire except in self-defense. The army was in no mood to fight for a king who had made such a sorry exhibition of himself at the review. As the royal *berlines* clattered out of the stable they were immediately spotted. The coachman and two of the horses were killed while the mob took possession of the vehicles. At last the King began to take in his danger. The day of the twenty-fourth must have seemed interminable. It was still early in the afternoon, only two hours since he had gone out to review the troops on the Place du Carrousel.

Luckily the Duc de Nemours had had the presence of mind to order three less conspicuous carriages, two coupés and a cabriolet, in which the royal family finally made their escape. A few faithful members of the National Guard acted as escort and the pathetic little party was bundled off in the direction of St. Cloud. It was only just in time. Within a few minutes the crowd was flooding through the Tuileries. What an ill-starred building it was, and how many of its famous occupants—

Louis XVI, Napoleon, Charles X, Louis Philippe, and before long another Napoleon—took up their residence there in splendor, and fled from it with anguish in their hearts!

From St. Cloud the royal fugitives made their way to Dreux where they spent the night. The King had decided to pass the remaining years of his life in comfortable seclusion at the chateau d'Eu, a pleasant country house on the Normandy coast where he had entertained Queen Victoria only a few years before, but as soon as he heard on the morning of the twenty-fifth that the regency had been swept away and a republic established, he knew that he and his whole family must follow his Bourbon predecessor into exile. So great was the danger that the party scattered in different directions. The King and Queen, travelling separately, arrived at Honfleur on the twenty-sixth, and through the good offices of the British consul at Havre slipped over to England a few days later.

The arrival of ex-King Louis Philippe and his family ruffled the waters of journalism for about forty-eight hours, and then the ripples died away. "Sophist Guizot, sham King Louis Philippe and the host of quacks, of obscure spectral nightmares under which France lay writhing, are fled . . . Egalité Fils, after a long painful life-voyage, has ended no better than Egalité Père did. It is a tragedy equal to that of the house of Atreus." [17] So wrote Carlyle, and the world agreed with him. In a less prophetic vein Queen Victoria wrote to her uncle, the King of the Belgians, "What is your opinion as to the late events at Paris . . . there is an impression they fled too quickly. Still the recollection of Louis XVI! . . ." [18]

During the last two years of his life—he died in 1850— Louis Philippe was to spend much of his time explaining why, during those three days of February, he had not acted more heroically. The explanation was really quite simple. He could not bring himself to shed blood. What he did not explain, probably because he did not understand it himself, was that the very circumstances which made him politically merciful made him also politically unprincipled. At the end of his life his shrewdness gave way to obstinacy, but at no time in his seventy-seven years was his conduct ever dictated by passionate convictions. His policy on all occasions, as a republican historian described it, was *"toute provisoire."*

[17] The *Examiner*, London, March 4, 1848.
[18] *The Letters of Queen Victoria*, II, 194.

His last two years were not unhappy. He lived quietly and unostentatiously surrounded by his children and grandchildren. British visitors were impressed by his philosophic indifference to misfortune. As he stood up to carve the roast beef for dinner —he never surrendered that prerogative of the head of the family to anyone else—it must have been hard to realize that this big bourgeois *père de famille*, whom the caricaturists found so irresistibly comic, had been a general before the world had even heard of Napoleon. He had been a member of the Jacobin Club, he had shot rapids on the Ohio River, he had been a Swiss schoolmaster, a Twickenham ratepayer, and a king of the French people—not King of France. On August 26, 1850, this painful life-voyage, as Carlyle called it, was brought to an end by an attack of pleurisy. He died at Claremont, the Surrey villa given to him by his son-in-law the King of the Belgians. If he had set his sights a little higher he might have died in the Tuileries, but the code he lived by—*chacun pour soi, chacun chez soi*—represented everything that liberal Europe hated. Liberal Europe was bent on revolution, and Louis Philippe personified those characteristics of a conservative society—family solidarity, acquisitiveness, and material prosperity—that every revolution is bound to destroy.

2

LAMARTINE

ON FEBRUARY 22, 1848, Richard Rush, the American Minister to the court of the Tuileries, noted in his diary that he had just returned from a pleasant *soirée* at the La Rochefoucaulds'. The party was small but agreeable. The Reform banquets were spoken of but no one seemed under any uneasiness. Why should anyone be uneasy? If the King was known to have a cold there might be some reason for anxiety, but every diplomat in Paris knew that as long as the King was well there could be no serious disturbance. His health was the key to the political stability of Europe.

Forty-eight hours later the King and Queen had fled, the Tuileries had been completely gutted, the whole seemingly solid structure of government had crumbled to pieces, and such families as the La Rochefoucaulds were probably wondering whether once again the mob would be lusting for their blood. Within a week Mr. Rush, acting on his own initiative—there was no transatlantic cable yet—had recognized the provisional government. Lord Normanby, the British Ambassador, thought that Mr. Rush had acted rather hastily.

For one brief moment on the afternoon of February 24 it looked as if Louis Philippe's abdication in favor of his nine-year-old grandson, the Comte de Paris, might yet save the monarchy. The abdication of the King had left the question of the regency unsettled. According to the law of 1842 if anything happened to the King his eldest surviving son, the Duc de Nemours, automatically became regent, but the Duc de Nemours, owing to his anti-liberal tendencies, was the least popular of the King's sons. No one was more aware of this than Nemours himself. He was quite prepared to renounce the power which the law had conferred upon him in favor of his sister-in-law, the Duchesse d'Orléans, mother of the young heir to the throne. The Duke's whole behavior during this crisis was entirely disinterested, but a resolution, however noble, founded upon a consciousness of unpopularity does not excite enthusiasm. It was certain that the French people in their present mood would never tolerate the regency of Nemours. Would they tolerate the regency of the Duchesse d'Orléans? She was a foreigner, a German and a Lutheran, but she was an attractive woman and since the death of her husband, the Prince Charming of the Bourgeois Monarchy, her dignity, her devotion to his name, and her rumored dislike of Guizot, had endeared her to the people of Paris as well as to the Orléanist aristocracy. It was just possible that this striking young widow might succeed in rescuing the crown which the old King had so ignominiously surrendered.

The Duc de Nemours proposed that she should escape from Paris while there was yet time and raise the standard of the Comte de Paris in the provinces. While he was making the necessary arrangements for a nucleus of loyal troops to escort the Duchess to safety, the Duchess suddenly decided that instead of joining the royal family in flight she would stay in Paris, go before the Chamber herself and plead her case. It was still early in the afternoon of February 24 when the Duchess and her two sons, accompanied by M. Dupin, one of the older deputies and a devoted friend of the family, made her way on foot from the Tuileries to the Palais Bourbon. All Paris was in the street. The news of the King's abdication had spread like wildfire, and the crowds that had been shouting "*A bas Guizot! Vive la Réforme!*" were beginning to wonder just what it was they really wanted.

The scene in the Chambre des Députés reflected the bewilderment in the street. Everybody was asking for Thiers, for Barrot, for someone to take hold of the situation. The Duchess walked slowly through the Chamber and sat down in front of the President's chair. The sight of this tall young woman dressed in mourning, very pale but very calm, with her children grouped around her, caught the imagination of the house. Dupin mounted the rostrum, announced the abdication of Louis Philippe, and proposed that the Duchess be proclaimed regent. The immediate response was favorable. *Vive la Duchesse! Vive le Comte de Paris!* But though the deputies applauded there was an ominous rumble of dissent from the crowd that had begun drifting in off the street. Obviously there was no time to be lost. Thiers, who played a sorry part on this critical day, thought it was already too late. Odilon Barrot had not yet arrived at the Chamber. Quite ignorant of what was happening, he was busy telegraphing the provinces that the crisis was over. Finally when he did arrive he made a speech championing the Duchess, which began well enough but tailed off with a threat to resign if he were not supported. During the last three days there had been such a merry-go-round of ministers that no one except M. Barrot himself knew or cared whether he were in office or not.

Meanwhile, more and more of the mob were infiltrating into the Chamber. General Ruhlières, a veteran of the Napoleonic wars, and General Bedeau, a hero of the Algerian campaign, who had been charged with the defense of the Tuileries and the Palais Bourbon and given several thousand troops for that purpose, completely failed to carry out their orders. In a revolution, as De Tocqueville has said, it is always the soldiers who lose their heads first.[1]

This same M. de Tocqueville, one of the few cool-headed deputies, a shrewd observer of this particular scene but too exclusively an observer of life to be capable of dynamic action himself, knew that there was only one man who could save the

---

[1] ". . . j'ai toujours remarqué que les hommes qui perdent le plus aisément la tête et qui se montrent d'ordinaire les plus faibles dans les jours de révolution sont les gens de guerre." *Souvenirs de Alexis de Tocqueville*, p. 54.

monarchy, and even he would have to act instantly. That man was the poet-politician, Lamartine, who had always prided himself on playing a lone hand. He had refused to associate himself with any party but he was known to have been one of those who had originally voted for the appointment of the Duchess as regent rather than the Duc de Nemours. "We are losing the battle," said Tocqueville; "you are the only person who can make himself heard. Go to the rostrum and speak." Tocqueville himself was a liberal but not a republican. Sympathetic though he was with democracy in America,[2] he did not feel that France was yet ripe for a republic. Without knowing Lamartine well he thought he could count on him to support the regency.

For a long time Lamartine had been waiting for just such an occasion. He had longed for a crisis that would make him the arbiter of the destinies of France, and now the crisis had come. He alone could dominate the crowd and with his magnificent voice he could swing the people into a revolution the consequences of which no one could tell, or he could throw his weight on the side of the regency and parliamentary reform. Before him stood the Duchess and her Van Dyke children protected by a few deputies from the rising tide of the mob. In his *History of the Revolution of 1848*, written while the memory of these events was still fresh in his mind, he inserts the brilliant speech he might have made that would have swept her into power. But that speech was never delivered.

Before he arrived in the Chamber that afternoon he had been buttonholed by a little group of republicans. They appealed not to the poet in Lamartine but to the politician. Tentatively they suggested that the time had not yet come for the establishment of a republic. Or perhaps it might be possible to found a republic now with someone like M. de Lamartine at the helm? What did M. de Lamartine think? He tells us that he requested a moment's time for reflection "during which he invoked the inspiration of that Being who alone never deceives." Like Mr. Gladstone, Lamartine never acted in an emergency except under direct orders from the Deity. After five or six minutes spent in almost breathless thought he announced his decision. "As a statesman in God's presence and in yours . . . if the hour in which we are deliberating is big with a revolution, I will not conspire for a half-revolution. I

---

[2] Tocqueville's *De la Démocratie en Amérique* was published in 1835.

conspire for none; but if there must be one, I will accept it entire; I decide for a republic!" [3]

Tocqueville, of course, knew nothing of this conversation but Lamartine's answer to his appeal was not encouraging. He would not speak as long as the Duchess and her children were in the Chamber.

By this time the crowd in front of the President's chair had become so dense that there was a real danger of the young princes being crushed to death. President Sauzet, utterly inadequate to the occasion, ordered all strangers out of the Chamber. No one paid any attention. Then he begged the Duchess to withdraw with her children. She refused to leave, but her friends dragged her away from the semicircle to a less exposed position on one of the rear benches. There she sat down to wait, to wait for a miracle that never happened. A few republican deputies fought their way to the tribune and demanded the establishment of a provisional government. The bulk of the deputies sat glumly silent while the steadily growing crowd of intruders roared their approval. Once again the President tried to assert his authority. As is still the custom in the Chamber of Deputies, he put on his hat as a signal that the session was over, but this last pathetic effort to impose parliamentary law excited nothing but derision. In his hurry he grabbed the hat of his secretary, which came down over his eyes. The crowd cheered, and from that moment on deputies who wanted to speak rushed for the tribune simultaneously and tried to shout each other down.

In the midst of all this tumult Lamartine, who had been standing in the tribune waiting for his noisier colleagues to exhaust themselves, began to speak. He had the presence, the voice, and above all that indefinable quality of leadership which compels the attention of the unruliest audience. He began with a glowing tribute to the courage of the Duchess, and the crowd, never insensible to the appeal of beauty in distress, started to applaud. Quickly he tipped the scales on the other side. If he felt the greatest respect for her gallant gesture in coming before the Chamber of Deputies that afternoon, he was no less moved by the gallantry of the people who had been fighting for three days to oust a corrupt government and to re-

[3] Lamartine, *History of the French Revolution of 1848* (London, 1849), p. 98.

establish the reign of order and of peace. He did not think that the momentary acclamation of an assembly melted to tenderness by natural feeling could establish a stable and undisputed authority over a population of thirty-six millions. On the contrary, he felt there was no way of establishing a national popular government except upon the will of the people.

This speech, containing just the right mixture of flattery and idealism, was interrupted by the mob breaking their way into the upper galleries. Hitherto little groups of workmen and National Guards had infiltrated into the main floor of the Assembly, but now, just as Lamartine was calling for the appointment of a provisional government, an armed mob battered down the doors of the galleries and surged through the entire building. A few devoted friends gathered around the Duchess and her children and managed to get them out by a side door. One of the boys was lost in the confusion but he was restored to his mother that evening. A few days later she crossed the frontier into Germany, never again to set foot on French soil. Her dream of establishing a dynasty was never to be realized.

The Duchess had played for the highest stakes and she had lost. It was a gamble that might well have come off if the deputies had not been so thoroughly demoralized, but the collapse of the monarchy in spite of the comfortable majority so carefully built up by Guizot and Louis Philippe left a Chamber bereft of faith in government itself. It would have been willing to accept the Duchess as regent and the Comte de Paris as king, but it was not willing to fight for them against a rowdy opposition. Men do not fight when they are bewildered. They submit to whatever Fate throws in their way.

A small group of republicans with the rabble of Paris at their back and a matchless orator as their mouthpiece had imposed their will on the rest of the nation. Once again the Chamber failed, as it has failed so often in French history, to assert its right to debate isssues and to decide policy without being intimidated by the mob. If Louis Philippe won the throne by unscrupulous methods, certainly his descendants have paid the price. Ever since the little Comte de Paris was hustled out of the Chamber on that afternoon of February 24, 1848, one generation after another of Orléans princes have been hovering in the wings of French history waiting for the cue that will bring them back onto the stage. Meanwhile the mob had taken possession of the Chamber and there was no longer any pretense of orderly government. The President was heard muttering something about adjournment, and was then seen to scramble down off his platform and melt into the crowd. Tocqueville had never seen such an exhibition of abject terror.[4]

Dupont de l'Eure, an eighty-year-old veteran of liberalism, was called upon to take the President's chair. Lamartine, still at the tribune but now conversing with the mob rather than addressing them, announced that the President would read off the list of names proposed for the provisional government. He was too old to make himself heard, so the names had to be shouted out by those nearest to him. "Arago, Lamartine, Dupont de l'Eure, Ledru-Rollin." The crowd roared its approval. "No more Bourbons! We want a republic!" Three more names are put in nomination. "Crémieux, Marie, Garnier-Pagès." The crowd starts arguing. "We don't want Garnier-Pagès. Yes we do. Crémieux put down his own name. We will take him any way." The seven men were finally elected by sheer lung power.

By now Lamartine was wondering how to bring this wild session to a close. Riots and revolutions are like novels in that they are easy to start but difficult to finish. A provisional government had been formed and approved by popular acclamation. What was to become of it, where was it to install itself? How was it to get its authority recognized by the country at large, by Paris, even by the Chamber, where men were already clamoring for the immediate declaration of a republic? Lamartine clutched at a voice in the crowd. *A l'Hotel de Ville!* Yes, that was it. Make sure of the Hotel de Ville and you had Paris, and whoever held Paris held France.

The Hotel de Ville, a grandiose building with a highly wrought façade that Louis Philippe had just finished renovating at enormous expense, was the one palace of which the people were not jealous. It was their palace, situated in their quarter, the seat of municipal government, the heart of city life. It was from the central window of the Grande Salle that Louis XVI had spoken to the populace with the cap of liberty on his head. Here was the room where Robespierre held his council and where he tried to commit suicide, and here, too, Lafayette had embraced Louis Philippe and recommended him to the people as "the best of Republics." All the revolutions of France had been ratified in the Grande Salle and confirmed by

[4] Tocqueville, *Souvenirs*, p. 63.

the people in the Place de Grève below. This was obviously the place for the new government.

With a cheering crowd at his heels Lamartine hurried away from the Chamber and along the quays, past the Ile St. Louis to the Place de Grève. The bridges were thronged. All Paris was out on the streets. "Place au Gouvernement! Make way for the government!" shouted Lamartine's bodyguard, and not without difficulty the provisional rulers of France forced their way through the dense crowds into the Hotel de Ville. There they barricaded themselves against further interruption by the mob and drew up a proclamation to the French people. Lamartine, the most facile writer among them, wrote the first draft which was approved by his colleagues with a few changes, and despatched to the printer. The proclamation declared that a reactionary government had fled and that the "republican form" had been provisionally adopted until such time as the nation could be consulted.[5] Nothing was said in the proclamation about their program for the future but, considering that the members of the government had had no chance to consult together, this vagueness was inevitable. The next step in organization was the allotment of cabinet positions. Dupont de l'Eure was unanimously elected President. It was understood that Lamartine, as Minister for Foreign Affairs, would exercise the real authority, but Dupont's venerable age and his standing in the community were assets too important to be ignored. As a symbol of republican virtue he was invaluable. Even before the execution of Louis XVI he had been advocate to the Parliament at Rouen. In the time of Robespierre he had been judge in the old city of Louviers. He had been President of the Court of Appeals under the Empire, a Deputy under Louis XVIII, and the senior of Louis Phlippe's ministers as far back as 1831. He was not brilliant, he was not an orator, and he was afflicted by that all too common disease, a passion for popularity, but he was known to be honest and his flowing white locks gave the new government an aura of respectability.

Another distinguished figure in the provisional government was the famous astronomer François Arago. He became Minister of the Navy and shortly afterwards Minister of War as well. Always a scientist at heart, he had dragged himself away from his observatory to examine the growing problems of industrialism. What he saw in the workshops and the factories

[5] Pierre Quentin-Bauchart, *Lamartine, Homme Politique*, Paris, 1903, p. 160.

convinced him of the callousness of the monarchy, but though he was converted to the necessity of republicanism he was irritated by the unpredictability of politics. As a scientist he was more at home in a world of facts that could be verified than in a world of ardent but undefined aspiration. That great forehead and those piercing eyes alienated the rank and file with whom he had to deal, and it was not long before he began to express contempt for the revolution he had hailed with such delight.

Ledru-Rollin, who took over the Ministry of the Interior, was as nearly as possible the exact opposite of Arago. He was the born politician, the author of the classic phrase "I must follow the people, I am their leader." One of the founders of ultraradical *Réforme*, a restlessly ambitious man but always chopping and changing, he conceived of himself as the Danton of his generation, but he was a Danton without the zeal or the courage.

The Ministry of Justice fell to Crémieux, a Jewish lawyer who, in the general confusion in the Chamber of Deputies, was suspected of having put his own name in nomination. His passion for intrigue was notorious. He supported the regency in the morning and, with equal conviction, the republic in the afternoon. The world may not have respected Crémieux but everybody liked him. Lamartine described him as "ever present and ever popular."

Garnier-Pagès, a pompous man with an unjustified respect for his own opinions, was named mayor of Paris but afterwards transferred to the Ministry of Finance, and Marie, a successful lawyer who had the distinction of being the first man to propose the provisional government, was given the Ministry of Public Works.

The guiding spirit of the government was unquestionably Lamartine. In 1848 he was fifty-eight years old, a Catholic, an aristocrat, and a great poet who had convinced himself that poetry was merely the distraction of his youth and that his real vocation was politics. Like Byron, for whom he had the greatest admiration, he encouraged the idea that he wrote his poetry with the careless ease of a man of quality.[6] Elected to the

---

[6] "Sachez que, pour moi, la poésie est une simple distraction à laquelle je n'attache aucune importance. Le matin, avant déjeuner, je fais des vers que j'écris au crayon sur quelques morceaux de papier. Puis sans y songer davantage, je jette tous ces morceaux de papier dans un sac où Mme de Lamartine va les chercher

Chamber in 1833 at a time when pocket boroughs were as common in France as they were in England, he had refused to throw in his lot with any party. He was already a public figure and the role of splendid isolation he assigned to himself, though it lessened his influence in the Chamber, gradually built up for him in the country at large a reputation for independence that was later to prove very useful. His family came from Mâcon in the south of France and no poet was ever more devoted to the scenes of his childhood, but it was as deputy from Bergues in Flanders that he first entered the Chamber. In his own district he would have had to make commitments whereas in the distant corner of Flanders he could be elected through the influence of his brother-in-law as a wholly free agent. Lamartine frankly admitted that it was a family affair engineered by his sister Eugénie and her husband, M. de Coppens. The family of M. de Coppens possessed large interests in the Département du Nord.[7]

After passing through the conventional sorrows of a young romantic—writing poetry that no one would publish, falling desperately in love with a fisherman's daughter, and still more desperately in love with Madame Charles, a married woman older than himself—the skies had finally cleared. He had put away childish things. By the time he took his seat in the Chamber Alphonse de Lamartine could be reckoned a successful man. He had represented his country as *chargé d'affaires* in Florence, he was happily married, and the Academy had opened its doors to him, but his full intellectual energy, his ability to bend an audience to his will, had not yet been revealed. It is not often that romantic poetry, religion and politics are as inextricably intertwined as they were in Lamartine. His political faith sprang from a religion of pure sentiment, a tender pantheism that had nothing to do with the Vatican, combined with a genuine kindliness that was repelled by any form of injustice. He was a man of extreme sensibility, and the growing incoherence of capitalism—pauperism, low wages, child labor—afflicted him as a poet and challenged him as a politician. Unlike most of his contemporaries, certainly those

pour les classer à son gré. Ma véritable vocation, c'est la politique, ce sont les affaires, ce sont les chiffres."

"Notes inédites de Duvergier de Hauranne," quoted by Thureau-Dangin, *Histoire de la Monarchie de Juillet*, V, 139.

[7] H. Remsen Whitehouse, *Life of Lamartine*, 2 vols. (Boston, 1918), I, 342, 357.

who craved as he did a life of activity, he was never bewitched by the Napoleonic legend. The vision of military glory did not blind him. He believed in the Bourbons whom he had been brought up to revere, but he believed in them, not because of some fancied divine right, but because he thought they had been specially commissioned to rid France of the evils of arbitrary government. The obtuseness of the Bourbons and the smug materialism of the Bourgeois Monarchy gradually led him to believe that the reign of God could only be realized in a republic.

His *History of the Girondins*, which appeared in 1847, made converts for republicanism even before Lamartine was aware of the change in himself. It was one of those books, like *Uncle Tom's Cabin*, which scholars may criticize but which drive men to action. The hero of this history is Robespierre, who is portrayed as the incarnation of Revolution. Lamartine follows his career step by step. He likes him and he makes his readers like him. Under the spell of a richly romantic style the reader unconsciously accepts the Revolution as the fulfillment of Christianity. The seed of liberty, he argues, could not have flourished except in the bloodshed of the Reign of Terror.

> This book is in itself a revoluton [wrote Mme. de Girardin], a portent, a decree perhaps, for God cannot carelessly have permitted such a book to be written. . . . M. de Lamartine speaks of revolutionary ideas as a man who has discovered the secret of applying them without crime and without violence. God grant that he may be right, and that his book may be the beginning of such an enterprise.[8]

Lamartine's wide popularity not only in Paris but in the provinces, his freedom from any party allegiance, and his eloquence on the platform, marked him out as the obvious leader in any revolutionary government. He had other qualities as well. His aristocratic good looks, his height, his exquisite distinction, the rare combination in him of the democrat and the *grand seigneur*, counted heavily in his favor. But it was above all by the magic of his voice that he dominated Paris during those critical months of 1848. In the Chamber he was merely one of a number of good parliamentary debaters, but in the

---

[8] Vicomte de Launay, *Lettres Parisiennes*; quoted by Quentin-Bauchart, *Lamartine, Homme Politique*, p. 124.

street in front of a hostile crowd he was one of the great orators of all time. Many speakers have inflamed those who wanted to be inflamed, but Lamartine was one of the very few who have changed men's opinions, who could persuade an audience that was panting for war to go away clamoring for peace, and who, with no weapon but his own voice, could subdue a crowd that was determined to throw him out of office.

We must not expect from him a coherent constitutional program. Actually he was a bad choice for the head of a government, for his ideas were never clearly defined. The only field in which he had had any experience was diplomacy, and here he showed real statesmanship. Confronted by an effervescent Europe that might have boiled over into war at any moment, he managed to keep the peace, and at the same time to conduct a more dignified foreign policy than any of Louis Philippe's ministers.

Almost as soon as Lamartine and his colleagues had arrived at the Hotel de Ville they were forced, much against their will, to take into the government several new members— Marrast and Flocon, two popular journalists, Louis Blanc the well-known socialist, and an unknown workman, a protégé of his, named Albert. These new men, who wanted to set up a socialist republic at once, were the candidates of the Hotel de Ville. If the Chamber could elect men to govern the country by shouting for them, why could not the Hotel de Ville? Louis Blanc and Marrast thrust their way without ceremony into the back room where the members of the provisional government were trying to conduct business, protected from the mob by a few sentries. "Gentlemen, let us begin our discussions," said Louis Blanc. "Certainly," replied Arago, "provided you withdraw first." [9] Louis Blanc threatened to appeal to the crowd outside. Finally a compromise was arrived at, by which the four new members were accepted in the government as secretaries, but the distinction amounted to nothing and after a few days it was ignored.

Louis Blanc, who now became the leader of the radical group within the government, was a small beardless man, a bourgeois by birth and education, who had had a miserable childhood which still haunted him. He became the spokesman of the working classes whose sufferings he had shared. Lamar-

[9] Daniel Stern, *Histoire de la Révolution de 1848*, Third ed., Paris, 1868, 3 vols., I, 251.

tine's passionate but rather vague faith in progress irritated him. The idea of a bourgeois republic instead of a bourgeois monarchy would never satisfy men like Louis Blanc. What he wanted was a pure socialist state including the abolition of capitalism.

These were the men who undertook to launch the republic. None of them had had any experience in government. As in every revolution there were two groups—those who wanted to correct flagrant abuses but were reluctant to alter the structure of society, and those who were determined to tear everything down and to reconstruct the nation on an entirely new model. The differences in temperament between the two groups are obvious, but at the same time they possessed certain traits in common which should not be ignored. They were all idealists, tremendously in earnest, convinced that the future welfare of mankind was in their hands. If they talked endlessly about love, patriotism, and humanity, at least they meant what they said. Their language may strike the twentieth century as pompous, but it was not insincere. It was incredibly naïve. In 1848 men had no doubts about anything. The France of Voltaire, sardonic and fiercely anti-clerical, was temporarily submerged by a wave of romantic idealism. As yet there was no rift between religion and republicanism. That was to come later as a result of Louis Napoleon's first venture into Italy, but for the moment the church and the republic went hand in hand. It is significant that the mob that sacked the Tuileries and tossed Louis Philippe's throne out of the window did not desecrate the royal chapel. They paused at the threshold and, headed by a student of the Ecole Polytechnique, removed the magnificent ivory crucifix from the altar and bore it reverently to the Church of St. Roch. "Citizens," they cried as they marched down the rue St. Honoré, "off with your hats. Salute Christ."

Property, unless it were royal property, was also respected. Even the mob in the Tuileries took more pleasure in destruction than in looting. Anything to do with Louis Philippe seemed to excite the crowd to madness. The royal palace at Neuilly was burnt, also Baron Rothschild's property at Suresnes, under the impression that it, too, belonged to the royal family. On discovering their mistake the rioters sent a deputation to the baron apologizing for their carelessness. With these exceptions the fall of the monarchy was not marked by vandalism.

For several days the life of the Provisional Government hung by a thread. Again and again Lamartine had to harangue the crowds in the square and in the great hall. What was the Provisional Government doing? Why did it not boldly announce the establishment of the republic instead of pretending that it must wait to see what the rest of the country wanted? Perhaps these men elected in the Chamber of Deputies were not really republicans at all. Lamartine was not a man of the people. What did he know of their needs? Why did he not promise to guarantee work for everybody? It rankled with the Paris workingman that the bougeoisie had foisted a monarchy upon him in 1830 out of which he gained nothing. This time it was going to be different. He would not be dismissed and sent home with a pat on the back after fighting for three days on the barricades. He wanted guarantees that he was going to profit by this revolution, and he would follow anybody who proposed to exact those guarantees from the new government. Meanwhile, the eleven men were frantically issuing decrees from the Hotel de Ville and passing them out of the window as quickly as possible, but the crowd was not satisfied. The decrees were not definite enough. Once again Lamartine was called to the window.

"By what right have you taken over the government?" someone shouted.

"By what right?" he cried. "By the right of the blood that has been spilt, the flames that are devouring your buildings, by the right of a Nation without leaders, without order, and perhaps tomorrow without bread. By the right, Citizens, as long as you ask me, of those who were the first to risk their lives, to expose themselves to the vengeance of mobs or of kings in order to save the Nation. . . . You and I want a republic but we would be unworthy of the name of republicans if we assumed an authority that has not yet been given to us. We propose therefore to proclaim a provisional republic and to leave it to the thirty-six million people of France to approve or to modify our decision." [10]

Lamartine's eloquence, impossible to reproduce by the written word, stilled the crowd, but even Lamartine failed to

[10] Paul Bastide, *Doctrines et Institutions de la Seconde République,* 2 vols. (Paris, 1942), I, 116.

arouse interest in the nice juridical problem he was trying to expound. Again and again in French history Paris has led the way and the provinces have followed. The Hotel de Ville was in no mood to tolerate quibbling about properly constituted authority. The weary men who stretched out in the corridors, or who kept watch and ward by the bivouac fires in the Place de Grève, knew their power and meant to exert it. Nothing less than unequivocal statement would satisfy them. If Lamartine and his friends from the Chamber of Deputies would not proclaim the republic, one and indivisible, they would proclaim it themselves. While Lamartine was addressing the crowd inside the Hotel de Ville, the diminutive Louis Blanc standing on a table on the steps outside had captured the imagination of a still larger audience with the promise of an immediate declaration of the Republic. At the same time two workmen hoisted a large strip of canvas on the front of the building upon which was written, "The Republic is proclaimed in France." Lit up by the flare of the torches this sign excited even greater enthusiasm than the speeches. It was still only the night of the 24th. In less than twenty-four hours the people of Paris, the laboring class as opposed to the bourgeoisie, had won a great victory. At their orders Guizot had been dismissed, the King compelled to abdicate, the attempt to establish a regency defeated, a provisional government elected and forced to do their bidding. No one had dared oppose them. They had carried every point in their program.

The political revolution was now finished. The social revolution was about to begin. Old Dupont de l'Eure, worn out by the bewildering events of the day, stole away from the crowd just after midnight and clambered over the barricades to his distant home in the rue de Madame. For Lamartine and the others there was no rest. They worked on through the night, drafting decrees, arguing among themselves what should be done now and what should be left to the National Assembly, wondering always how long their fragile little ship of state would withstand the buffeting of the waves.

From the very first day the Provisional Government ran into stormy weather. On the morning of February 25 a delegation of workers with an ugly crowd on its heels forced the doors of the Hotel de Ville, thronged every hall and passage until they reached the room where the Government was sitting, and demanded, gun in hand, that the Government should immediately issue a proclamation guaranteeing the *Droit au Travail*. The Right to Employment—from those magic words flowed the future happiness of all mankind. Lamartine tried to reason with the angry spokesman of the delegation. Once again he turned on the ever-ready flow of eloquence, but this time he was rudely interrupted. "*Assez de phrases comme ça.*" "No more glowing oratory, M. de Lamartine." The people were willing to grant the Government three months, but at the end of that time work must be guaranteed to all applicants.

Under this menace Louis Blanc, standing in the embrasure of a window, surrounded by the more articulate members of the delegation, drafted the following decree:

> The Provisional Government engage themselves to guarantee the existence of the workmen by means of labor.
> They engage themselves to guarantee labor to every citizen.
> They take it to be necessary for the workmen to associate with one another, in order to reap the legitimate reward of their toil.
> The Provisional Government restore to the workmen, who are its real owners, the million francs which will shortly be due on the Civil List.

The decree was published in the *Moniteur*, February 26, probably without the knowledge of Lamartine and the more moderate members of the Government, Dupont de l'Eure, Arago, and Marie. Louis Blanc had put the moderates in the position of repudiating the decree, which would have meant their downfall, or of accepting it and thereby accepting the Socialist Revolution.[11] Once men have tasted the joys of office they do not resign easily. Lamartine, who had a boundless faith in the ability of his eloquence to manage everybody, chose to accept the decree. The others followed suit. Under the guidance of Louis Blanc socialism was to emerge from Utopia into the arena of daily life. He conceived of the State as filling the role in modern society of a benignant banker of rare imagina-

[11] Louis Blanc made no bones about it. In his history of the Revolution he congratulates himself upon his finesse: "Je n'ignorais pas jusqu'à quel point il (le décret) engageait le gouvernement; je savais à merveille qu'il n'était applicable qu'au moyen d'une réforme sociale ayant l'association pour base, et, pour but ultérieur, l'abolition du prolétariat. Mais, ce que je voulais, c'est que le pouvoir se trouvat lié par une promesse solennelle, et amené de la sorte à mettre activement la main à l'oeuvre." Louis Blanc, *Histoire de la Révolution de 1848*, I, 129.

tion and infinite kindliness. In his *Organisation du Travail*, a brilliant pamphlet written in 1839, Louis Blanc looked out upon the chaotic world created by the Industrial Revolution, and found it wholly evil. He knew that Louis Philippe and his ministers had cared nothing for the principles of equality and fraternity, and now that a new era had dawned nothing could stop him from putting his principles to the test. At Lyons the silk weavers had adopted the gloomy device, *Vivre en travaillant, ou mourir en combattant*. Live working or die fighting. "No," said Louis Blanc, "you shall not die fighting. The State shall see to it that you live by labor." [12]

It was all very well for the Government to guarantee work to all applicants, but the fulfillment of the promise proved as difficult in 1848 as it has shown itself to be ever since. Louis Blanc proposed that a Ministry of Progress should be appointed, with himself at the head of it, to organize co-operative associations along the lines he had already laid down, but the Government, chafing at his dictation, produced an alternative solution which had the advantage of manoeuvring the restless young socialist into a position where he could do no harm. On February 28 Louis Blanc was installed at the Palace of the Luxembourg as president of a Commission "charged to examine the claims of labor and to insure the well-being of the working class." In those days such a Commission constituted a startling innovation. Louis Blanc saw it as a forum from which he could address the working classes of Europe. What he did not see was that his Commission had no power to carry into effect any of its recommendations. Nevertheless, the Luxembourg Commission plunged into its problems full of confidence. In the spring of 1848 anyone who had doubts about the certainty of progress was not a good republican. Employers participated in the conferences with the workmen, for during these days of crisis everyone expected help from the State.

Letters poured in offering factories and workshops to the Government as a gift, provided the Government would agree to employ the "patron" at a reasonable salary as director of the new establishment. No one was discouraged over the dislocation in commerce and industry since no one thought it would last. Naturally there was a certain confusion after the fall of the monarchy but in some miraculous way the new government, being dedicated to the interests of the people, would set

[12] Louis Blanc, *Organisation du Travail*, p. 4.

all that to rights. Only gradually did it dawn on the public that Louis Blanc had been given an impossible task. The Luxembourg Commission had no budget and no authority. All it could do was to recommend. Among other things it recommended that the working day should be reduced to ten hours in Paris and eleven hours in the country, and this particular recommendation was approved by the Government, but there was no provision for its enforcement, and within three months it was being generally ignored.

Meanwhile the Provisional Government, though it had shaken off Louis Blanc, could not shake off the consequences of Louis Blanc's decree guaranteeing labor to every citizen. It may be that the decree was practically extorted from them by force but the fact remained that the Government had promised much more than it could possibly extemporize into performance. Marie, the Minister of Public Works, a man who had no sympathy with Louis Blanc's socialistic theories, hoped to skirt the difficulty or at least to postpone the evil days that lay ahead by the establishment of National Workshops. The Provisional Government had proclaimed its acceptance of the *droit au travail* on February 25. On the twenty-seventh it had decreed the immediate establishment of National Workshops, and on the twenty-eighth Marie announced that "on Wednesday, March 1, important operations would be organized in various quarters, and that any workmen who wished to take part in them must apply to one of the mayors of Paris, who would receive their application and direct them promptly to the workyards." [13]

As director of these National Workshops Marie chose a young republican named Emile Thomas, a man with a real talent for organization who, it was hoped, would build them up as a counter attraction to the Luxembourg Commission. It was particularly important for Lamartine, as the leader of the more moderate element in the Government, not to allow himself or his colleagues to be outdone by Louis Blanc in zeal for the people's welfare. Emile Thomas himself had no illusions about the National Workshops. He undertook to provide a semi-military organization of the unemployed, founded on the principles of Saint-Simon, but he did not undertake to provide work. Lamartine, who was always enamored of grandiose ideas, dreamed of a great campaign in the interior of France with

[13] Emile Thomas, *Histoire des Ateliers Nationaux* (Paris, 1848), p. 28.

agricultural implements for arms, like the campaigns undertaken by the Romans or the Egyptians for digging canals or
draining the Pontine marshes. The proposals that Emile
Thomas outlined at the Hotel de Ville were more sober:

> In a word, the scheme I propose is the opening of a
> Labor Exchange, gratuitous and open to all, which during
> this crisis shall perform the additional duty of centralizing
> the distribution of doles at present in the hands of the
> mayors. This office will first register the workmen accord-
> ing to their trades, and will then arrange them according
> to their *arrondissements*, with a view to avoiding contact
> and consequently union between men of the same trade,
> such as might—at any rate in certain trades—lead to
> grave inconvenience, if not danger.[14]

Thomas knew perfectly well that the success of his plan
depended upon the regular employment of a majority of the
men who registered, but the idea of guaranteeing work to everybody seemed to him preposterous. How was it that Lamartine,
who had spoken so eloquently against the *Organisation du Travail* as recently as 1844—Thomas quotes the speech in full—
had suddenly reversed himself? [15] The fact was, according to
Thomas, that since February 25 the Government had been
operating under the influence of fear. Lamartine, at times brilliant and courageous, never quite dared cut himself off from
the things he knew were wrong. The Government made a mistake in surrendering to Louis Blanc in the first place, they had
been wrong in assuming that public works should provide for
the growing army of unemployed, and they had blundered still
more seriously when they started paying money, instead of
supplying food, to those for whom they could not find work.
The criticism to which the National Workshops were subjected
has a strangely familiar ring. In the France of 1848 as in the
United States of 1936–40 the Government was accused of
making it too easy to get on relief, and of conjuring up unemployed where there had never been any before.

By March 5, less than a week after the Workshops had
been founded, seventeen thousand men were registered as
unemployed. The "important operations" promised by Marie
—our generation would have used the word "boondoggling"—

[14] Emile Thomas, *Histoire des Ateliers Nationaux*, p. 52.
[15] Emile Thomas, *Histoire des Ateliers Nationaux*, pp. 22–26.

consisted in levelling the Place de l'Europe, terracing the Quai de la Gare, and repairing some of the State roads in the suburbs. These jobs accounted for about 3000. A further 6000 were employed by the Ministry of War in the Champ de Mars. That left 8000 men for whom no work could be provided, a figure which rose steadily until it reached a peak of 49,000. By June 20 there were approximately 120,000 men employed by the National Workshops, in addition to the 49,000 to whom admission in the workshops had been refused.[16]

Each workman who was employed received two francs a day, regardless of how much or how little he accomplished. To those who were not employed the Government paid 1.50 francs a day on the production of a ticket showing there was no vacancy for them in the Workshops. Consequently, as Emile Thomas points out, "the workmen made the following simple calculation, and made it aloud: 'The State gives me 30 sous for doing nothing, it pays me 40 sous when I work, so I need only work to the extent of 10 sous.' This was logical." [17] The characteristically French common sense of this calculation explains the alarming rise in the numbers of the unemployed. This was the situation with which Emile Thomas had to cope. Unable to find any further work beyond road-mending and grubbing up the stumps of trees on the boulevards, which had been cut down to make barricades, and planting new trees in their places, he undertook to convert the floating masses of unemployed into a well-disciplined army to be held at the disposition of the Government. Thirty sous is not high pay, but it was to be had for nothing, and hopes of advancement were held out. Every group of eleven persons formed an *escouade*, and the chief *escouadier*, elected by his companions, got half a franc a day extra. Five *escouades* formed a brigade, and the brigadier also elected by his subordinates received three francs a day. Above these were the lieutenants, the *chefs de compagnie*, the *chefs de service*, and the *chefs d'arrondissements*, appointed by the Government and receiving progressively higher salaries. Besides this, bread was distributed to their families in proportion to the number of children.

Quite naturally Louis Blanc resented what he called the "rabble of paupers" created by the Government to offset the

[16] P. Quentin-Bauchart, *La Crise Sociale de 1848*, Paris, 1920, p. 241.
[17] Emile Thomas, *Histoire des Ateliers Nationaux*, p. 30.

genuinely socialist reforms he had in mind.[18] The paupers may not have been created by the Government but they were certainly organized with a view to doing the Government's bidding. Thomas's account of his interview with Marie goes a long way towards substantiating Louis Blanc's charge.

> Marie took me aside and asked me in a whisper if I could count upon the working men.—"I think so," I replied, "but their number increases so rapidly that I find it difficult to keep as direct an influence over them as I could wish."—"Don't be uneasy about the number," the Minister replied, "if you keep them under your control the number can never be too great, but find some means of attaching them to you. Don't economize. If necessary, you may be supplied with secret service funds."—"I don't think I shall need that, indeed it might be the source of pretty serious difficulties. But for what purpose other than public tranquillity do you make these recommendations?" —"For public safety. Do you think you can command the loyalty of these men? The day may not be far off when we shall really need them." [19]

Thus once again the split in the Provisional Government yawned wide open. From the very beginning the moderates in the Hotel de Ville and the radicals in the Luxembourg distrusted each other. The National Workshops were the tool of the moderates, whose good fortune it was to constitute a majority. They were created by Marie and approved by Garnier-Pagès, Arago and Lamartine, though Lamartine insisted that they were only a temporary expedient, terrible but necessary.[20]

The minority, headed by Louis Blanc, felt that socialism was being undermined by a device that was economically unsound as well as morally indefensible. Ledru-Rollin wavered between Lamartine and the socialists. Beyond being ambitious for his own advancement he does not seem to have had any definite policy. He was generally regarded as a red republican rather than a socialist, one who looked back with longing eyes to the days when France was ruled by the Committee of Public

---

[18] Louis Blanc, *Pages d'Histoire de la Révolution de février*, Paris, 1850, pp. 63, 64.

[19] Emile Thomas, *Histoire des Ateliers Nationaux*, p. 147.

[20] Lamartine, *History of the French Revolution*, p. 543.

Safety. During three critical months the "army" created by Emile Thomas served its purpose, but a pretorian guard is notoriously difficult to disband, and the stupidity of the Assembly eventually transformed the Government-supported "army" into bitter rebels against the State. On June 21, the Government issued a decree ordering all workmen in the National Workshops, between the ages of 17 and 25, to enroll in the Army. The men over 25 were to be ready to leave Paris at a moment's notice. They would be employed in public works in the provinces.

This was the decree that precipitated the terrible struggle in the streets of Paris, June 23–26, in which the republic finally triumphed over socialism but in so doing destroyed itself. The workmen refused to be disbanded and once again, as so often in French history during the nineteenth century, the issue had to be fought out on the barricades. The experiment of the National Workshops had failed, but not as completely or as irrevocably as the men of 1848 believed. The "preposterous" idea that a State could guarantee work did not seem so preposterous when it was translated to Russia seventy years later.[21]

At the same time that the Provisional Government was fighting for life by apparently granting the mob everything that was demanded—the right to employment, the appointment of the Luxembourg Commission, and the establishment of the National Workshops—it did manage to hold its own on the issue of the red flag. The Revolution of 1789 had substituted the tricolor for the white standard of the Bourbons. Would the Revolution of 1848 adopt the red flag and thereby stamp itself as unequivocally socialist? It was only a question of symbols, but in France even more than in other nations symbols assume tremendous importance. In 1871 the man who might have been Henri V gave up the throne rather than give up the white cockade of his family.

The red flag has had a curious history in France. During the first revolution it was the symbol of martial law, only to be flown in case the police or the army had to be called out to

---

[21] One of the most vigorous critics of the National Workshops was Victor Hugo. In a speech in the Assembly, June 21, he spoke of it as a disastrous experiment. Self-respecting men had been debauched by the "hand-out" (*la honteuse puissance de la main tendue*). The wealthy idler was bad enough but the Government had now created the "pauper idler," a hundred times more dangerous to himself and to society. Victor Hugo, *Avant l'Exil*, 2 vols. (Paris, no date), I, 155.

break up a demonstration. It remained the symbol of law and order until 1832. On June 5 of that year the funeral ceremonies of General Lamarque, a Napoleonic hero popular with the masses, were made the excuse for a demonstration against the regime of Louis Philippe. As usual, the red flag was flown before the troops went into action. In the early days of the Bourgeois Monarchy these street disorders were a common occurrence, and on every occasion the red flag was displayed. Theoretically it was the emblem of authority, but gradually the population of Paris came to associate it with scenes of disorder. In 1830 the workmen and the bourgeoisie had hoisted the tricolor, and fighting under that banner they had overthrown the Bourbon dynasty, but by 1848 the tricolor had lost its prestige. The workmen, in particular, craved some emblem that would represent their social and economic aspirations. They found it in the red flag, the flag that the Government had formerly used to suppress the rumblings of their discontent.[22]

On the afternoon of February 25 the Paris workman was beginning to feel that this was his revolution. There were no limits to his power. The Government was putty in his hands. Far from being difficult to learn, as he had been led to understand, the art of politics was delightfully simple. It consisted in getting up a demonstration for whatever was wanted, and, provided the demonstration was noisy and threatening enough, Lamartine and his friends would always give way. By that system the workmen had swept away Government opposition to the declaration of the republic and the right to employment. Now they would clinch the victory they had won by hoisting the red flag, storming into the Hotel de Ville, and insisting that the Government accept their banner as the symbol of a new order. For once Lamartine stood firm. To him and to most Frenchmen the red flag had recently become the emblem of anarchy. Possibly he overestimated the danger, but on that afternoon he and Marie and Garnier-Pagès—the other members of the Government had gone home—went out to face the crowd expecting to die and ready to die rather than accept the red flag. Lamartine's speech on this occasion was one of the greatest of his triumphs. The story of how he quelled the mob loses nothing in his telling:

[22] For a full discussion of this question see Gabriel Perreux, *Les Origines du Drapeau rouge en France* (Paris, 1930).

"Citizens, you have the power to lay hands on the Government, you have the power to command it to change the banner of the nation and the name of France. If you are so ill advised and so obstinate in error as to impose upon it the republic of a party and the standard of terror, the Government, I am well assured, is as determined as myself to perish rather than to dishonor itself by obeying you. As for myself, never shall my hand sign such a decree! I will reject, even to death, this banner of blood, and you should repudiate it still more than myself, for this red flag you offer us has only made the circuit of the Champ de Mars, dragged through the people's blood in 1791 and 1793, while the tricolor has made the circuit of the world, with the name, with the glory and liberty of your country!"

At these last words, Lamartine, interrupted by almost unanimous cries of enthusiasm, fell from the chair which served him as a platform into the arms stretched out to him from every side. . . . A general commotion, seconded by the gestures of Lamartine, and the exertions of the good citizens, made the rioters fall back as far as the base of the great staircase with cries of "Vive Lamartine! Vive le drapeau tricolore."[23]

Lord Normanby, the British Ambassador, who liked Lamartine but was by no means blind to his faults, "did not suppose that in the history of the world there was ever such an instance of the triumph of a courageous man inspired by noble sentiments over the brute force of the masses."[24]

Lamartine made the most of his victory by announcing from the steps of the Hotel de Ville that the Revolution was now over. The Monarchy was abolished, the Republic proclaimed, and the Provisional Government was taking this opportunity of announcing the most recent of its decrees—the abolition of the death penalty for political offenses. This, he maintained, was the noblest decree ever promulgated by a free

[23] Lamartine, *op. cit.*, p. 229. Lamartine's allusion to the use of the red flag on the Champ du Mars was oratorically effective but historically quite inaccurate. On the particular day to which he referred, July 17, 1791, Bailly was accused of negligence for not having flown the red flag sooner, or of not flying it in such a way that the populace could see it. There was no question at that time of its being the symbol of revolution.

[24] Phipps, Constantine Henry, First Marquis of Normanby. *A Year of Revolution, from a Journal kept in Paris in 1848*, London, 1857. 2 vols. I, 135.

people in their hour of victory.[25] Guizot, Louis Philippe and the Duchesse d'Orléans could rest assured that the Government harbored no designs against them. The Republic had no time for vengeance.

This constant flattery of the people, this emphasis on their idealism and their magnanimity, goes far toward explaining Lamartine's success as an orator. Whatever course of action was expedient, he presented as nobly unselfish. Such practices are the common tactics of politicians, but Lamartine was exceptional in that he really believed what he said. No man was more completely devoid of cynicism or more naïvely vain. To cajole a hostile audience, to manipulate the prejudices of a mob of angry workmen, and finally to swing them over to enthusiastic support of his policies, was what he understood as the business of the statesman, and it was only by his desperate feats of oratory that the Provisional Government survived its first week.

By the beginning of March, after successfully negotiating a series of crises, it looked as if the Provisional Government had at last arrived at the point where it could function without looking over its shoulder every minute to see whether it were going to be stampeded by the mob. But, first of all, it had to decide what were its functions. On that question among the members themselves there was no unanimity. Lamartine assumed that the Government's role was that of a temporary chairman. He and the other moderates conceived of themselves as bridging the gap between the King's abdication and the convening of the Assembly. The Government had no right to use the power which fate had thrust into its hands except to maintain order and to assure complete freedom of election. Universal suffrage, which was decreed on March 2, automatically guaranteed a body of deputies that would reflect the will of the nation. Under these circumstances it was important to hold the elections as soon as possible, and thus bring the interregnum of the Provisional Government to an end. It took a long time to dispel the myth that democracy was something that the voting booth could guarantee.

These ideas were not peculiar to Lamartine. To a great extent they represented the political philosophy of the *National* which became the official organ of the Republic. During the July Monarchy the *National* was a cautiously republican paper

[25] *Moniteur,* February 27, 1848.

committed to a rather timid program of step-by-step reform. It deprecated the growth of industrial feudalism fostered by Louis Philippe, but it was more concerned with political than with social reforms. Louis Blanc considered its program woefully inadequate. The Paris workman spoke of it with contempt as *le journal des messieurs*. The *National* was edited by Marrast, an elegant rather than a vigorous writer who disliked the materialism of the Guizot regime and dreamed of a republic as an ideal state in which arts and letters flourished at the expense of business and commerce. The welfare of the working classes was an obvious by-product of the revolution, but it was not an end in itself.

The organ of the more radical republicans was the *Réforme*, edited by Flocon and supported financially by Ledru-Rollin. The first number appeared in 1843. In its early days it was not an inflammatory paper, but before long it developed marked socialist tendencies. Louis Blanc drafted the editorial credo.[26] "All men are brothers. Where there is no equality, liberty is a lie. In a well-constituted democracy the rulers are nothing more than the agents of the people. If they do not carry out the wishes of the people they should be summarily deposed." Alfred de Vigny expressed the same idea when he described the men who govern the nation as glorified coachmen, to be employed only so long as they demonstrated their capacity to drive. The press should be untrammelled and all education should be free. To the young and vigorous the State owes employment, and to the old and feeble it owes security. Foreign policy consisted in championing oppressed nations, particularly Poland, and presumably, in order to carry out this policy effectively, every citizen should be trained as a soldier. In 1848, these two papers, the *National* and the *Réforme*, filled the part afterwards taken by the organized political parties. It was in their offices that the list of names for the Provisional Government was originally drawn up. Though they were both opposed to the Monarchy, as soon as the Monarchy disappeared they became bitter rivals for power. On broad questions of national policy they might agree but on the much more difficult questions of procedure it was impossible for them to work together. The real barriers to understanding, among individuals as well as nations, are built out of differences of temperament rather than differences of opinion.

[26] Louis Blanc, *Histoire de la Révolution de 1848*, I, 59.

The program of Ledru-Rollin, Louis Blanc and Flocon differed very sharply from that of the conservatives, but it was the temperament and the background of Lamartine and Louis Blanc that made the differences insuperable. Being out-and-out radicals, the men of the *Réforme* were impatient of constitutional processes. Louis Blanc made no bones of his determination to stay in power until the country was committed to socialism. It was the duty of the Government to put through necessary reforms, not to abdicate as soon as they were in office and leave everything to a possibly reactionary Assembly. The radicals wanted to draft the Constitution themselves and submit it to the Assembly for approval. Whatever we may think of Louis Blanc, he was at least more of a realist than Lamartine. He knew perfectly well that in political maturity the provinces lagged a long way behind Paris, that the Socialist party in France represented only a tiny minority of the population, and that the easy collapse of the Orléans Monarchy did not mean that republicanism, far less socialism, was widely popular.

Emile Thomas, himself a republican, estimated the number of convinced republicans in Paris on February 24 at ten thousand. In the provinces the number was negligible. The press may not be an entirely fair test, as newspapers under the Monarchy were so highly taxed that they were beyond the reach of the workingman, but it is at least significant that before the Revolution the circulation of republican papers outside Paris never exceeded six thousand.[27]

From the point of view of the radicals, therefore, it was essential to delay the convening of the Assembly as long as possible, and in the meantime to launch an intensive propaganda campaign that would insure the election of liberal-minded deputies. The wheel of fortune had whirled Louis Blanc into power. Not for a moment was he prepared to renounce that power in deference to the principle of popular sovereignty. The people had to be guided before they could vote intelligently, and the radicals would see to it that the people were guided in the right direction.

The Government decision to hold elections on April 9, which was much earlier than Louis Blanc or Ledru-Rollin would have liked, required swift action on their part to forestall the election of a conservative Assembly. Ledru-Rollin

[27] P. Bastid, *Doctrines et Institutions Politiques de la Seconde République*, I, 91.

wasted no time. As Minister of the Interior it was his duty to replace the great army of civil servants appointed under the Monarchy with men who were sympathetic to the new regime. One hundred and ten delegates were selected for this purpose and despatched into the four corners of France. It goes without saying that they were carefully coached before they left Paris, but on March 11 the Minister followed up their instructions with a circular still further explaining their duties and their powers. This circular received wide publicity. It appeared that their powers were unlimited. They were responsible only to their own conscience. The elections were to be their work. Republican sentiments must be strongly excited and the Assembly animated by a revolutionary spirit.[28]

This circular, which Lamartine never saw until it was published, scandalized not only the conservatives but also the great middle class who had watched the fall of Louis Philippe with perfect equanimity and hailed the Republic as the beginning of a better world. An atmosphere of gloom now settled down over Paris. The rising tide of unemployment, the well-known split within the Government, culminating in Ledru-Rollin's openly avowed purpose of tyrannizing over the provinces, a policy which Lamartine did not dare to repudiate, all pointed toward another and far more serious political convulsion. Men began to wonder whether the Provisional Government could possibly hold out until the National Assembly met. The innumerable political clubs which a crisis in France always spawns were bent on forcing the Government into more revolutionary channels. Several of these clubs voted petitions demanding postponement of the elections. At the same time they planned a *journée*, a day given over to a demonstration which would overawe the Government and compel them to accept the dictation of the mob. These skilfully organized demonstrations have always been characteristic of French political life. Without the clubs they could hardly have been organized. Among other things the Revolution had established the right to hold public banquets, the right to foregather in political or any other form of assocation, and Paris reveled in the new-found freedom. Two hundred and fifty clubs opened within a month, and before long the number reached 450. There were clubs for Frenchmen, and clubs for strangers, clubs for dra-

[28] The circular is quoted in full in Lord Normanby's *A Year of Revolution,* I, 219–22.

matic artists, for grocers, for students, for workingmen, clubs for every profession and for every walk of life. There was even a women's political club with the arresting title, *Le club légion des Vésuviennes*. Not all of the clubs were political but almost all of them could be enlisted in a political cause if necessary.

The two guiding spirits in the organization of discontent were the arch conspirators Louis Auguste Blanqui and Armand Barbès. Dreaded equally by the radicals and the conservatives, Blanqui was one of those men for whom revolution is an end rather than a means. A thin-lipped, small, haggard man, who looked as if he had spent his life in a sewer, he inspired fear and disgust in all who knew him. And yet this apparently repulsive revolutionary dominated the masses. They were fascinated by his hatred of all authority and by the lustre which a life-time of imprisonment had conferred upon him. He had been imprisoned for life in Mont St. Michel for conspiring against the Monarchy, and released after the fall of Louis Philippe. He was imprisoned again in May, 1848, released and imprisoned under the Empire, and again under the Third Republic. He rebelled against any and every form of authority. Around him grew up a legend of terror. Wherever he passed secret societies sprang up behind him dedicated to the overthrow of the Government. It made no difference what Government was in office. Statesmen of every complexion, Louis Blanc as well as Guizot or Napoleon III, dreaded him. The only man in power who ever took Blanqui into his confidence was Lamartine, probably because Lamartine could never believe that there was anybody whom his personal charm could not win.

In contrast to Blanqui, Armand Barbès was a generous and romantic figure, the Don Quixote of the Revolution. Barbès gathered around him in the *Club de la Révolution* a group of republican enthusiasts, men who admired him for his devotion to the cause of freedom. He, too, had been imprisoned in Mont St. Michel for conspiring against the Monarchy. Intellectually he had little to offer beyond a fervent belief in the sacredness of republicanism, and the conviction that republicanism meant something more than political reform. The text adopted by his club indicates his aspirations: "So far we are only a Republic in name, now we must realize the thing itself. The Republic must satisfy the workers and the proletariat." In the beginning of March he supported the Provisional Government, but he had no faith in the moderates whom he suspected of wanting to divert the Revolution from its glorious course. Lamartine regretted that so honest a man as Barbès should have drifted into the ranks of the desperadoes of democracy.

Although Blanqui and Barbès were the most prominent of the club leaders, there were many others—Raspail, a veteran republican politician, but also a doctor whose services to the poor were never forgotten, and Etienne Cabet, an earnest high-minded communist, who afterwards emigrated to America and founded a very unsuccessful "ideal" community on the banks of the Red River in Texas.

These few men had so organized the clubs that they could always threaten the Government with a demonstration. By the middle of March Lamartine knew that his few days of respite were over, and that once again the Government must fight for its life. This time the threat was even more serious as it came from two quarers at once. The conservative element, which had been heartened by Lamartine's stand on the red flag, was very much disturbed by Ledru-Rollin's circular. On March 13, he alarmed the conservatives still further by decreeing the dissolution of certain aristocratic companies of the National Guard. Ledru-Rollin claimed to be acting in a spirit of republican equality which demanded the fusion of the famous *bonnets à poil* with the rest of the Guard, but the conservatives saw it as an attempt to remove the one last bulwark against anarchy. From their point of view the tactics of the radicals were all too obvious. Weaken the National Guard, keep the regular army out of Paris and postpone the elections indefinitely. In that way mob dictatorship was assured. The *bonnets à poil* marched to the Hotel de Ville and demanded a recall of the obnoxious decree. The Government stood firm, and the National Guard retired, threatening to return the next day with arms in their hands.

The clubs, irritated by this demonstration in favor of privilege, seized the moment to press their demands for postponement of the elections. After successfully withstanding the National Guard, the Government was now called upon to face the more formidable opposition of the clubs. Fortunately Louis Blanc and Ledru-Rollin, the two members of the Government most sympathetic with their demands, could not stomach the prospect of being under obligations to Blanqui. Instead of throwing in their lot with the clubs they decided to bide their time. Lamartine rose to the occasion as usual with a glowing speech in which he reiterated the Government's intention of convening the Assembly immediately, and once again the crisis was averted.

The Government had won a victory, but it was Ledru-Rollin and Louis Blanc who carried off the honors rather than Lamartine. It was their decision to withhold support from the clubs, rather than Lamartine's eloquence, that kept the Government in power. Lamartine took stock of the situation and decided that if he were to achieve his two great objects—the preservation of peace abroad and the meeting of the Assembly —he must align himself more closely with the ultra-republican party. Any party that was as firmly entrenched as they were would not allow the election of an Assembly to tear it from power. Gradually he drew away from the moderates, Arago, Marrast, Marie and Garnier-Pagès, and was seen more and more with Ledru-Rollin, whose star was steadily rising. The moderates might have a majority in the Council chamber but they did not have a majorty in the streets, and Lamartine was beginning to realize that that was what counted. His association with the demagogue Ledru-Rollin cost him the respect of the conservatives but the drop in his popularity was only temporary. He was still haunted by the vision of himself as the great conciliator, the one man who could rally all France around him by the sheer magic of his personality.

With this end in view he consulted with the leaders of the principal clubs, and at the same time entered into negotiations with General Négrier, commanding the army of the north, to make sure of his support in case the Provisional Government should be driven out of Paris. Lamartine believed that in the event of another demonstration the moderates would be forced to resign, but he himself was determined not to go down to defeat with them. On the night of April 15 he was warned by some of his friends in the clubs that the Government would be attacked the next day by more than 100,000 men. The only hope of defense lay in the National Guard, which had just elected its officers and received its arms. It had not yet been called out, and no one could foresee whether, since the dissolution of the *bonnets à poil*, it would side with the clubs or with the Government. The *journée* of April 16 was to prove that the National Guard could still be relied on to support the friends of order.

The success of the Government, however, seems to have

depended on the accidental presence of General Changarnier at the Hotel de Ville. By the merest chance General Changarnier, who had just been appointed Minister to Berlin, called at Lamartine's office that morning for his instructions. What happened can best be described in his own words:

> On the morning of the 16th I was an ambassador. At a quarter after twelve I went to M. de Lamartine's to take his final instructions, and to request that I might be sent off to Berlin immediately. I found there a secretary, and asked some questions about Holstein. "Don't talk of Holstein," he said; "at this instant M. de Lamartine may be killed." Madame de Lamartine entreated me to go to the Hotel de Ville. I found there Marrast. Lamartine soon arrived. He seemed disturbed, talked of the divisions of the Government, and complained of Louis Blanc and Ledru-Rollin, whom he believed to be engaged in the insurrection. As he took no steps, I acted of my own accord. General Courtais had summoned only a *piquet* from each legion. I though the *rappel général* ought to be beaten. Marrast wrote the order at my dictation; and this was the summons which called out the National Guards.[29]

Before two o'clock, the hour at which the popular demonstration was to start from the Champ de Mars, 130,000 men of the National Guard were under arms, of which 50,000 were massed around the Hotel de Ville. The army of insurgents marching along the left bank crossed the Seine by Pont Royale. As they neared the Hotel de Ville their procession was checked, and they were allowed to advance only by single file through columns of bayonets. Under these circumstances the club leaders, who had started out in a truculent mood intent on the resignation of the Government and the appointment of a Committee of Public Safety, suddenly changed their minds. They decided instead to take up a collection and present it to the Government as a token of their loyalty.[30] Lamartine graciously consented to receive the deputation, and the day ended as usual with his haranguing the crowds from the steps and from the windows.

The *journée* of April 16 was a decided victory for the

---

[29] Quoted by Nassau William Senior in *Journals Kept in France and Italy from 1848 to 1852*, 2 vols. (London, 1871), I, 82.

[30] *Memoires de Caussidière*, 2 vols. (Paris, 1849), II, 19.

bourgeois republicans as opposed to the socialists.[31] It raised the prestige of the Government and restored to the National Guard a consciousness of their own power, but it would be difficult to prove that any one of the principal actors emerged from the crisis with any credit. Only General Changarnier distinguished himself, and he was not a member of the Government. Ledru-Rollin showed himself as vacillating as ever, always ready to betray his colleagues but never quite willing to throw in his lot with Blanqui. Louis Blanc, who organized the demonstration and hoped to jockey himself into dictatorship as a result of it, was completely surprised by the spirit of the National Guard. Lamartine, who called the day the happiest of his political life, was as completely nonplussed by the turn of events as anybody. On the next day the Government published a proclamation making it appear that everything was for the best in this best of all possible worlds.[32]

Never did any government whistle more vigorously to keep up its courage. Every escape from disaster was translated into a great victory for the Republic. Nevertheless, it must be admitted that Lamartine and his ill-assorted team did succeed in holding the Government together until the Assembly could be elected. The conservative element, at least, never lost sight of that as their first duty. The Assembly met on May 4, and on May 6 Lamartine rendered a glowing account of his stewardship. If he had not founded the United States of Europe to which the *Moniteur* had confidently looked forward in the first flush of excitement after the fall of the Monarchy, under the Provisional Government France for the first time had enjoyed complete political liberty. They had been in office forty-five days backed only by moral force. Now they could surrender their dictatorship and mingle in the market place again without having anyone demand of them, "What have you done with so-and-so?" That was a unique achievement. The abolition of slavery in the colonies, universal suffrage, freedom of the press and freedom of assembly—all these things had become a reality, while at the same time he, Lamartine, had staved off all efforts of the extremists to get control of the Government. Seen from a different angle the picture was not so smiling. The nation was on the verge of bankruptcy, and the

[31] Le 16 avril fut la première journée publique où la bourgeoisie réactionnaire reprit le dessus." Caussidière, II, 18.

[32] Caussidière, II, 25.

army of unemployed was steadily rising, but after Guizot's long reign of materialism there were worse things in the world than a financial crisis. The generation of 1848 craved above all things generous sentiments, and Lamartine did not disappoint them.

The elections proved him to be the most popular man in France. Ten *départements* proclaimed him as their representative, and in Paris he headed the list of succesful candidates with 259,800 votes. When Marrast announced this unprecedented triumph, he is said to have remarked, "Now I am greater than either Alexander or Caesar!" and then added reflectively, "at least, so they tell me." [33] As Lord Normanby noted in his journal, there was "a simple candour in Lamartine's self-esteem which is peculiar and not without its charm."

*   *

*

All through the difficult months of March and April, while Lamartine was struggling to keep the Provisional Government in power, he was also carrying on his duties as Secretary of Foreign Affairs. It was no easy task to maintain peaceful relations between the new-born Republic and the European Powers. Revolutions were germinating all over Europe. Palermo had struck the first note even before the fall of Louis Philippe. In February, Pius IX had published an allocution beginning with the strange words "God bless Italy," to which Metternich took sharp exception. What did the Pope mean by blessing "Italy"? Italy was not a nation; it was only a geographical expression. During the next month Vienna had risen in successful insurrection, there had been fighting in the streets of Berlin, Manin had driven the Austrians out of Venice, and the kings of the various German states had tumbled over themselves in their hurry to grant liberal reforms. In April the *Vorparlament*, meeting in Frankfurt, had acknowledged it to be their sacred duty to co-operate in the restoration of Poland. What should be the attitude of the French Republic to these revolutionary rumblings? If Lamartine gave too much encouragement to the reform movements in other countries, which might well prove only a flash in the pan, those countries would combine against him. On the other hand, the people of Paris were eager to show their sympathy with any nation that was

[33] E. Regnault, *Histoire du Gouvernement Provisoire* (Paris, 1850), p. 358.

stretching out toward freedom. The foreign refugees in Paris, of which there were a great number—Irish, Belgians, Germans, Italians and Poles—were all clamoring for the Republic to champion the cause of oppressed nationalities. As usual, certain members of the Government—among them Ledru-Rollin —were only too eager to champion anybody or anything that might add to their popularity.[34]

Lamartine's first step was to inform the Corps Diplomatique privately that France had no intention of attacking anyone. At the same time he published a manifesto to Europe in which he catered to domestic opinion by skilfully mingling defiance with conciliation. He repudiated the treaties of 1815, which were obnoxious to French opinion because they confined the nation within fixed limits, and in the next breath he assured Europe that the proclamation of the French Republic was not an act of aggression against any form of government in the world. Without veiling her democratic principles abroad and her hope of seeing the other nations of Europe tread the same path, Lamartine reminded the world that it was the dynastic ambitions of Louis Philippe that had nearly plunged Europe into war. The Republic had no such aspirations.

Palmerston ignored what he called the "gaseous parts" of the Manifesto, and decided that Lamartine wanted to keep the peace. Meanwhile the ambassadors in Paris had to submit to the threatening demonstrations of different bodies of foreigners. Lord Normanby was troubled by the Club of United Irishmen residing in Paris, "persons of no social respectability." He impressed upon Lamartine the necessity of abstaining from giving the slightest encouragement to such deputations. Since good relations with Great Britain was the cornerstone of Lamartine's foreign policy, he found no difficulty in dismissing the Irish delegation with words that cannot have sounded very encouraging. After assuring the Irish of his sympathy he added that it was not right for any nation to mingle in the private affairs of another. Shortly afterward the Irish began quarrelling among themselves, and thus simplified Lamartine's problem.

The Government had a more serious problem on its hands in the refugees of other nations. In the first few days of the Republic a German democratic society raised a legion of 15,000

[34] Between February 27 and April 28 the Government received twenty-one deputations from foreign countries. D. Stern, *Histoire de la Révolution de 1848*, II, 370.

volunteers for a march on Berlin. Pressed by the *Club des droits de l'homme* Ledru-Rollin lent them a few thousand francs. Lamartine had to reassure the German states by a note in the *Moniteur* that this legion of refugees did not have the backing of the Republic. The Belgian democrats, also intent on organizing a Republican foray into their native land, won the support of Caussidière, the prefect of the Paris police, as well as that of Ledru-Rollin. Again Lamartine hastened to assure a foreign government that France wanted only to live at peace with her neighbors. His colleagues were constantly putting him in position from which he had to extricate himself as best he could. They were always ready to embarrass him by proclaiming that it was the business of a republic to make war on kings and organize crusades on behalf of martyred nations. Such statements were the stock in trade of the red republicans.

On May 13, when the news of a Polish revolt, brutally suppressed by Prussian troops, became known in Paris, workmen and students thronged into the Place de la Concorde shouting *Vive la Pologne!* Poland had long been the favorite victim. Even during the reign of Louis Philippe the French chambers had gone on record at the opening of every session as favoring the restoration of a free Poland. The Republic could hardly do less, but, as Lamartine said, the wishes of a great people are but a mockery when they are merely words unaccompanied by acts, and to translate the words into acts by declaring war against Prussia, Austria and Russia on behalf of the Poles would have been like "entering on a crusade to win a sepulchre." [35]

For the great army of restless, discontented republicans sympathy with Poland was the excuse for another *journée*. The elections had gone against the radicals. They saw themselves suddenly deprived of their authority in Paris by an omnipotent National Assembly. Out of the 900 deputies elected the clubs could only claim 200 sure votes. The remaining 700 seats were divided between legitimists, Orléanists, and moderate republicans. Odilon Barrot, who had championed the Duchess of Orléans, came back into public life; Count Molé, the former minister of Louis Philippe; Lacordaire, the famous Dominican preacher; Tocqueville, the critical and dispassionate student of democracy; and Béranger, the poet who was busy fabricating the Napoleonic legend. These were not the men to rebuild

[35] Lamartine, *History of the French Revolution*, p. 421.

society. According to the poet Clough, who had come over from England to hail the birth of a better world, the Assembly "was extremely shopkeeperish and merchantish in its feelings, and would not set to work at the organization of labor at all." [36] That was not the kind of Assembly to suit Blanqui and Barbès.

The first task that confonted the Chamber was the appointment of an executive, either a president or an executive committee. The great majority of the deputies were ready to throw themselves at the feet of Lamartine and appoint him temporary President of the Republic, but Lamartine unexpectedly declined the honor. Apparently he did not believe that he could maintain himself in the Chamber if he admitted among his ministers members of the ultrarepublican party. Nor could he maintain any influence in the clubs if he excluded them. On these grounds he supported the motion that the Assembly should vest the executive power in a committee, and he refused to serve on such a committee unless Ledru-Rollin were included.

Lamartine's loyalty to his former associates, whether it was inspired by weakness or a genuine passion for national solidarity, marked the beginning of his downfall. He carried his point about the committee and he forced the Assembly to accept Ledru-Rollin, but when the votes were counted it was evident that he was no longer the most popular man in France. Arago, the old astronomer, now disillusioned with republicanism, headed the poll with 725 votes; Garnier-Pagès and Marie, safe conservatives both, followed with 715 and 702. He himself received 643 votes, and Ledru-Rollin 458.

These political manoeuvres within the Assembly excited nothing but contempt outside. Louis Blanc was chafing at his exclusion from power, and still agitating for the appointment of a "Minister of Progress." The leaders of the clubs, though not eager to risk another demonstration after their failure in April, were willing to go along with the hotheads if they insisted. Actually the *journée* of May 15 was organized by Polish sympathizers, but as soon as the crowds stormed into the Chamber the fate of Poland became a secondary issue. More than anything else the clubs wanted to demonstrate their power, not necessarily to overthrow the Government but to make it feel that it was their creature, dependent for its very existence on their good will.

[36] A. H. Clough, *Prose Remains* (London, 1861), p. 120.

Tocqueville, ineffective in debate but with a pen in his hand always trenchant, describes the eruption of the mob into the Chamber with his usual vividness:

> Wolowski was at the tribune mouthing some commonplace about Poland when the mob signalized its approach with a great roar that dropped on us through the open windows in the roof as if out of the sky. . . . Several representatives yielding to curiosity or fear stood up; others shouted "Sit down." Everyone sat down again, and Wolowski continued his speech. I think it was the first time in his life that he was ever listened to in silence; and yet we were not listening to him but to the hubbub outside that was steadily growing nearer and more distinct.[37]

Once again the troops detailed to guard the Chamber, bewildered by supine leadership, had allowed themselves to be thrust aside. The crowds swept past them, broke down the doors, forced their way into the low-hanging galleries, and from there dropped down to the floor of the Chamber. A few were armed but most of the men who invaded the Chamber were mere idlers with no particular object in view except the intimidation of the deputies. In France there is always a good deal of satisfaction to be had out of shaking one's fist in a deputy's face. Occasionally someone would force his way to the tribune, but even the most popular orators could not make themselves heard. Even Barbès, the Bayard of the republicans, was not able to get a vote on his motion that an army should be sent to Poland immediately, and a tax of a milliard francs levied on the rich.

This extraordinary session lasted for two hours, at the end of which time the *rappel général* was heard, a signal that the National Guards were at last coming to the rescue of the Assembly. At this moment Huber, one of the club leaders, a man who had only recently been discharged from an insane asylum, climbed up on the President's dais and declared the Chamber dissolved.[38] Satisfied with this exhibition of its power the mob melted away from the Chamber and once more made for the

---

[37] A. de Tocqueville, *Souvenirs*, p. 118.

[38] Tocqueville insists that many of the revolutionary leaders, including Blanqui and Barbès, were touched with insanity. "J'ai toujours pensé que dans les révolutions et surtout dans les révolutions démocratiques, les fous, non pas ceux auxquels on donne ce nom par courtoisie, mais les véritables, ont joué un rôle politique très considérable." *Souvenirs*, p. 124.

Hotel de Ville, just as they had done on February 24. A revolutionary government must always get control of Paris, and the strategic center of Paris was in the Hotel de Ville. Lamartine and Ledru-Rollin, at the head of a detachment of National Guards, followed in the wake of the mob, entered the Hotel de Ville with them, and arrested the ringleaders.

These two men invariably gravitated toward each other in moments of crisis. Presumably they thought that together they could prop up the tottering Republic, but actually they only compromised each other and they ended by losing the confidence of their supporters. Neither one of them ever regained his influence. Men who are willing to solve every issue by compromise must first of all convince the public that their compromises are not dictated by cowardice or self-interest. Lamartine was not a coward, but he was too ready to be guided by the inspiration of the moment, and in time the men who would naturally have supported him came to realize that his inspiration did not always spring from pure selflessness. He could never get away from the idea that he was the great amalgam, that it was his hypnotizing eloquence that held the Republic together.

As soon as the storm was over the deputies drifted back into the Chamber and resumed business. Lamartine, bursting with pride over his success at the Hotel de Ville, announced that the insurrection had been put down and the leaders arrested. The people, he said, had risen as one man to give back to the Assembly the sovereignty that for one moment had slipped from its hands. From now on, the people and the Assembly were bound together in life and in death.[39] The deputies cheered him to the echo. "It was the last time," said Tocqueville, "that I ever heard him applauded."

The events of the next month hardly confirmed Lamartine's radiant optimism. Within less than six weeks over a hundred thousand men were to be engaged in a life-and-death struggle on the barricades. The Assembly began to gird itself for the battle between represetnative government and anarchy that all thoughtful men knew was inevitable. Gradually the conservative elements, the monarchists and the moderate republicans, coagulated. Men realized that since the fall of the Monarchy the country had not been governed. It was obvious

[39] P. Bastid, *Doctrines et Institutions Politiques de la Seconde République,* I, 208.

that no Government could function without the sure support of the Army. The first step therefore was to summon to the Ministry of War a general who could be trusted. Eugène Cavaignac was the man. He had been offered the post before but he had refused it because the Government would not allow him to bring into Paris the troops that he thought necessary. Now they turned to him again. The people of France had grown tired of a collective executive. They had been willing to see Lamartine lead them out of the wilderness, but he had shied away from the responsibility and insisted on sharing it with men they did did not trust. Cavaignac was forty-six years old, a good general, an honest man and an out-and-out republican. Lamartine "scanned his character at a glance, and doubted not that he was the man to whom the preservation of the Republic could be trusted." That was true, but it was also true—and this Lamartine did not realize—that Cavaignac's rise to power would thrust Lamartine into a limbo of political insignificance from which he was never again to emerge.

3

LOUIS NAPOLEON

PARIS HAD hardly recovered from the irruption of the mob into the Assembly when the inhabitants were summoned by the Government to a great national Feast of Concord. On Sunday, March 21, the National Guard in whose honor the feast was given assembled in the Place de la Concorde and marched to the Champs de Mars. At the head of the procession came the five members of the Executive Commission, then the representatives in the National Assembly followed by the delegates of the different *départements* from Calais to the Pyrenees, each with its appropriate banner, and the inevitable contingents of oppressed peoples. Anxious to emphasize the peaceful character of the occasion, the Government arranged that Agriculture, Art and Industry should be represented in the review by allegorical figures carried on floats. One of the floats, which was drawn by sixteen horses, carried three trees, an oak, a laurel and an olive, symbols of strength, honor and abundance. In the middle of the Champ de Mars towered a colossal statue of the Republic crowned with a Phrygian cap and guarded by four plaster cast lions.

Had not the Republic promised the people to abolish

tyranny and to guarantee full employment? The Feast of May 21 was the consecration of that promise. No expense was spared. The weather was favorable, the Champ de Mars was ideally suited for pageants of this kind, the decorations were as beautiful as they always are in Paris. The only thing lacking was the right spirit on the part of the people. The incorrigible Parisian insisted on regarding the Feast of Concord as a joke. The chariot of Agriculture, displaying a lonely plough surrounded by flowers and ears of corn, was greeted with hoots of derision. Five hundred maidens, dressed in white muslin, chanting patriotic songs, fared no better. One of the five hundred stopped in front of the reviewing stand and recited an ode to Lamartine. Little by little, as the ode developed, she lashed herself into a frenzy of enthusiasm. The crowd roared its approval. Tocqueville, who was sitting near by, observed that Lamartine embraced the perspiring poetess with the most embarrassing reluctance.

It was only too obvious that in undertaking to stage this Feast of Concord the Executive Commission had misjudged the temper of the people. The refusal of the Archbishop of Paris to play any part in the proceedings should have warned them that something was wrong. Archbishop Affre was not a reactionary priest. He had given the Republic a more vigorous support than he ever gave to Louis Philippe, but like all intelligent Frenchmen he had a certain sense of the fitness of things. He was willing enough that the clergy should bless innumerable trees of liberty, as they had been doing for the last two months, but he was not willing to allow them to be used to bolster up the waning popularity of the Executive Commission. Nor did he smile upon the place in the program assigned to him, between the chariot of Agriculture and the chorus of the Opera. On this occasion at least Paris and the Church saw eye to eye. Everyone was disgusted by the Government's assumption that the people could be distracted by anything so palpably false as a Feast of Concord. There was no sign of concord in the Assembly or in the street. The bourgeoisie felt that the Government was playing the fool instead of protecting it against the possibility of another uprising. The conservatives in the Assembly were uneasy because they did not feel themselves masters of the situation. Lamartine and Ledru-Rollin knew that their popularity was oozing away from them. Worst of all, the people were restless. Barbès was in prison, Blanqui had been arrested. The National Workshops, deliberately omitted from the program of the Feast of Concord and threatened by the hostility of the Chamber, were girding for the inevitable conflict.

The relations of the Government with the 100,000 workmen employed in the National Workshops had steadily deteriorated since that fatal February afternoon when the State had guaranteed work to all its citizens. Originally Marie had viewed the workshops "as a reservoir into which could be drained the unemployed and troublesome members of the Parisian populace." [1] The Government had acted reluctantly, but after all something had to be done to pacify the unemployed, and the idea of transforming them into a pretorian guard had distinct possibilities. Unfortunately the provision of adequate public works had not kept abreast of the steadily increasing enrollment. In April the Director of the Workshops had been able to deliver the workmen's vote for the list of candidates prepared by the conservative *National*, but by May 15 the workmen were demonstrating against the Government and shouting *Vive Louis Blanc!* The Workshops had now become an incubus. The Assembly, the Executive Commission and the Ministers were all eager to get rid of them, but no one could decide how or when they should be suppressed.

The new Minister of Public Works, Trélat, was a kind-hearted man with no administrative experience, a doctor who knew the Paris workmen only from having treated them when they were ill. [2] The workman clamoring for his rights was a very different creature from the grateful patient, and Trélat did not understand him. He accused Louis Blanc of having perverted the simple hard-working laboring man, as he had always known him, by inspiring him with a strange Spanish hatred. [3]

Trélat's first step was to summon Emile Thomas, the Director of the Workshops, and inform him that the presence of 100,000 idle workers in Paris constituted a menace that no

[1] Donald Hope MacKay, *The National Workshops*, Harvard Univ. Press, 1933, p. 12.
[2] Marie had had to resign from the Ministry of Public Works on being elected to the Executive Commission.
[3] Louis Blanc was born in Spain. The myth that the Spaniard is the most cruel of Europeans dates from the Inquisition, and was probably given a new lease on life by the activities of the Spanish "underground" during the Napoleonic occupation of Spain.

government could stand. At the same time Trélat appointed a commission which met on May 18, and brought in a report on May 19, recommending a complete transformation of the Workshops.[4] The speed with which the report was prepared indicates that the Government had already laid down the lines it was to follow. Emile Thomas made certain counter-proposals but Trélat would tolerate no delay. He issued peremptory instructions prescribing drastic measures for the dissolution of the Workshops. Among other things a census of workers was to be taken at once. Those resident in Paris less than six months prior to May 24 were to be dismissed. Unmarried workers, eighteen to twenty-five years of age, were to be given the option of enlistment in the army or dismissal from the Workshops.

Thomas, an independent character who would neither go along with the Government nor resign, was bundled off to Bordeaux in charge of two policemen without even being allowed to communicate with his family. Under the *ancien régime* a *lettre de cachet* would have been necessary, but the Executive Commission dispensed with even that formality. The forcible abduction of the popular Director of the Workshops was one of their worst mistakes. The workers, realizing that their means of existence was threatened, now began to make common cause with the delegates of the Luxembourg Commission. Thus the antagonism between the National Workshops and Louis Blanc, carefully fostered by the Provisional Government, began to disappear. Up till now the workers had not been organized as a labor party. On the contrary, they had voted with the Government, but the time was fast coming when in the place of the bogus loyalty to law and order they would follow anyone who promised them a rosier future than the choice between starvation and conscription offered by the Executive Commission. Meanwhile, Lamartine and his associates hesistated to take a step that must lead to civil war. For a few weeks longer they stared helplessly at the monster that sooner or later would devour them.

Although the Workshops were an ever-present problem, the Assembly could always thrust them aside temporarily in view of other pressing decisions that had to be made. After all, the principal business of a Constituent Assembly is to make a

[4] This report was printed on May 20, and 1200 copies were delivered to the Minister. Subsequently it mysteriously disappeared. A single copy found its way into the Bibliothèque Nationale where it was recently unearthed by Mr. Donald Hope McKay.

Constitution, and the function of the Executive Commission was merely to preserve order until the Constitution could be written and put into effect. Under the best conditions government is an organism of slow growth. In France, where the people are quick to destroy an institution as soon as they discover its faults, no Constitution has lasted very long. The Constitution of 1848 was no exception to the rule. The eighteen representatives who drafted it included every shade of political opinion except the Legitimist party. Though they can hardly be compared with the framers of the American Constitution, they were by no means nonentities. Cormenin, the chairman, was a recognized authority on international law. Tocqueville had written what is still the standard book on American democracy. Lamennais, an ex-priest, was one of the greatest humanitarians France had ever known. His quarrel with the Church had alienated the Catholics, but no one questioned his ability. Odilon Barrot was a successful lawyer and a seasoned parliamentarian. Considérant was the most reasonable of socialists. These men and their colleagues worked, as one of them said, "like Archimedes during the siege of Syracuse," and yet the Constitution they produced lasted less than three years, and left no trace on the political life of France. Tocqueville declared that the work was too hurried, and that the members the Constitution they produced lasted less than three years on outside. He was perfectly aware that they were not measuring up to the American example.

The first draft of the Constitution was produced in exactly one month. Subsequently a good many alterations were introduced, and it was not finally approved until October 30.[5] Even so, judged by American standards of constitution-making, it was a hasty piece of work. In France the Constitution was adopted by the Assembly four months after the Committee sat down to write it. In America the Convention of 1787 devoted four months to drafting the Constitution and it took the thirteen states another two years to ratify it. Judging by the experience of France it would seem that impatience were fatal to a good Constitution.

Contrary to Tocqueville's recommendation, the Commis-

[5] Though it was passed by a big majority, most of the representatives voted for it on the grounds that there was no alternative. A vote against the Constitution would have been interpreted as a vote against the Republic. The Duc de Broglie called it "un oeuvre qui a reculé les limites de la stupidité humaine." Lord Normanby, *Journal*, II, 281.

sion decided that there should be one chamber rather than two, and that the President should be elected directly by the people instead of by the Chamber. In this way they hoped to make the President immediately responsible to the whole electorate. Under Louis Philippe the basis of government had been absurdly narrow. The Second Republic would broaden that basis to coincide with the nation. Actually what the Commission did was to pave the way for dictatorship. It was obvious that in a country where there were no clearly defined political parties anyone who could capture the popular imagination would be elected. Once he was elected he could always appeal to the people over the heads of the Assembly. The people were in that state of mind so dangerous to freedom when the craving for order, the dread of reaction or revolution, crowds out every other instinct. The Commission was all the more to blame because already, by the time they submitted their first draft, the shadow of Louis Napoleon had begun to darken the horizon.

In February, 1848, there was no such thing as a Bonapartist party. The heir to the dynasty, Louis Napoleon Bonaparte, son of Napoleon's brother Louis, the ex-king of Holland, and Hortense Beauharnais, was living in London as an exiled pretender. He had only recently escaped from the castle of Ham, where he had been imprisoned for six years, and he was making the most of his liberty. He was enjoying the society of the beautiful Miss Howard and at the same time casting about for a more permanent connection. Like many other political refugees, before and since, he managed to live comfortably enough on borrowed money. It was a pleasant existence but not one that could last indefinitely. Nor was it a way of life that suited a man who, whatever his faults, was never content like the rest of the family to doze through his three score years in the shadow of a great name. Louis Napoleon has often been called a visionary, but he was at least a visionary who strove to make his dreams come true.

Personally he was not well known in France. His mother, exiled after Waterloo, had finally settled down in Switzerland, and it was there in the chateau of Arenenberg that the young prince grew up. He enrolled as a volunteer in the artillery school at Thun, and was later elected a citizen of the canton of Thurgovie and member of the Grand Council. In 1834 he was appointed a captain of artillery, an honor that he cherished even more. Switzerland always treated him kindly.

My own country [he wrote to a friend in Berne] or rather the government of my country, rejects me because I am the nephew of a great man; you have been more just. I am proud to count myself among the defenders of a State where the sovereignty of the people is the basis of the Constitution and where every citizen is ready to sacrifice his life for the liberty and independence of his country.[6]

With the death of the Duc de Reichstadt in 1833 Louis Napoleon became the virtual head of the Bonaparte family. According to the Emperor's will, in default of direct issue of his own, the succession was limited to his brothers, Joseph and Louis and their male descendants. Joseph was not one of the doers of the world. He was essentially a peace-loving man who did not want to disturb anyone or to be disturbed. His unhappy experiences as king of Naples and king of Spain had only intensified his longing for a quiet life. At the time of the death of the Duc de Reichstadt, Joseph was living at Bordentown, New Jersey. He had two daughters but no son. Obviously the professional Bonapartists would have to look elsewhere. Louis, the former kind of Holland, was as lacking in ambition as his brother Joseph. The mantle of Napoleon, if it was to fall on anybody, would have to fall on his son Louis Napoleon. This young man was now the heir to the glories of the Empire, and he was immensely proud of it.

Even as a child he had always talked about his star. Now at the age of twenty-five he was more than ever convinced that one day he would rule France. The word "Empire" was never used, but he spoke of himself quite openly as the future leader of French democracy. It was difficult for strangers to understand his extraordinary self-confidence. Certainly he did not suggest the champion of a lost cause. The first impression was distinctly disappointing. His body was too long and his legs were too short. He spoke French, like all Bonapartes, with a foreign accent. His tutor complained that he was lazy and only moderately intelligent. An indolent manner and a somewhat expressionless face seemed to corroborate the tutor's opinion. Years later his cousin, the witty Princess Mathilde, wanted to bore into his head with a chisel to find out if there was any-

---

[6] D. Stern, *Histoire de la Révolution de 1848*, III, 74.

thing behind the mask. And yet anyone observing Louis Napoleon more closely would not have dismissed him as a nonentity.
On horseback, if not on foot, he became a commanding figure.
His tutor may have thought he was lazy but his friends noticed
that if he took up a subject at all he mastered it. Nor was he
always the shy, taciturn recluse. Lord Malmesbury, who met
him in Rome in 1829, describes him in his memoirs as

> a wild harum-scarum youth, what the French call *un
> crâne*, riding at full gallop through the streets to the peril
> of the public; fencing and pistol-shooting, apparently
> without serious thought of any kind, although even then
> he was possessed with the conviction that he would one
> day rule France.[7]

While he was in Rome, Louis Napoleon is supposed to
have become a member of the Carbonari, the most powerful of
the secret societies that kept alive the cause of Italian independence. Whether he did or not, he certainly acted generously
and recklessly in joining one of the many hopeless insurrections
against the papal government. The Romagna insurrection of
1831 was easily suppressed, but it proved that Louis was something more than an indolent dreamer. At least he did not indulge in the kind of dreaming that precludes action. Incidentally this willingness to adopt other people's quarrels as his
own cost the life of his older brother Charles, who developed a
malignant fever during the campaign and died after three days
of illness. Louis was now more than ever certain that fate had
chosen him as the standard-bearer of the family. Queen Hortense encouraged him at every turn. She was always reminding
him of his heritage and predicting a glorious future, but it was
the chance visit of a M. de Persigny that systematized and
translated into fact what was already becoming known at
Arenenberg as the *idée napoléonienne*.

Fialin de Persigny was one of those apparently insignificant men who attach themselves to characters stronger than
themselves and never cease pushing them forward along the
road they must travel. What Herndon was to Lincoln, Persigny
was to Louis Napoleon. He was also, and this is something
which the twentieth century should admire, one of the first ex-

[7] Lord Malmesbury, *Memoirs of an ex-Minister*, 2 vols. (London, 1884),
I, 33.

ponents of the art of propaganda. No modern publicity agent was ever more successful in dangling the name of his client before the eyes of the public.

Persigny began by telling his host and hostess at Arenenberg the very things they wanted to hear, that in the course of his journey from Paris he had found the portrait of Napoleon hanging in every barracks, every inn and every café. Everywhere the memory of Napoleon was alive. Everywhere people associated the name of Bonaparte with glorious achievements, while the subsequent rulers of France, the Bourbons and now Louis Philippe, called to mind the humiliating treaties of 1815, the domination of priests and nobles or the reign of lawyers and business men and a parliament imitated from England that the people neither admired nor understood.

On the strength of these revelations and some judicious army contacts established by Persigny, Louis embarked on the first of two enterprises that were to make him the laughing stock of Europe. On the evening of October 31, 1836, a telegraphic despatch from Strasbourg transmitted by semaphore threw the cabinet of Louis Philippe into a panic. It read as follows:

> Strasbourg, October 30, 1836. This morning about six o'clock, Louis Napoleon, son of the Duchess of St. Leu, who had in his confidence the colonel of artillery, Vaudrey, traversed the streets of Strasbourg with part of . . .

Here the despatch broke off abruptly. A fog along the line of signals prevented the transmission of the concluding portion.

It had taken thirty hours to get the message from Strasbourg, and even then it was incomplete. For all Louis Philippe knew, the young Bonaparte was already marching on the capital. Memories of Napoleon's return from Elba must have flitted through his mind. Were the royal armies going to melt away before the usurper as they did in 1815? The concluding instalment of the despatch, which arrived the next morning, made them ashamed of their forebodings. The conspiracy, such as it was, had collapsed in three hours. No blood had been shed, and the pretender was already under lock and key.

The Government wisely decided to minimize the whole affair. Instead of giving him a trial, which he very much wanted, the foolish young man was shipped off unceremoniously to the United States. It was given out that he had promised to remain in America for a term of years, but this the Prince indignantly denied. He had originally intended to make a grand tour of the United States, but the illness of his mother cut short what promised to be an agreeable visit. Before leaving America he was careful to write a polite note to President Van Buren expressing his regret at his inability to visit the President in Washington. It was characteristic of him to assume that as head of the Bonaparte family his comings and goings would be of interest to the President of the United States.

By the beginning of July, 1837, he was back in Europe. He arrived at Arenenberg in time to spend a few weeks with his mother before her death. The relationship between mother and son had always been very close. His consideration for her comfort and for her feelings was something he gave to no other woman. Later on in life he humiliated the Empress Eugénie with his promiscuous amours, but he never did anything to humiliate his mother. In her eyes he was the perfect son.

The French Government was very much annoyed by his return, and still more annoyed at the prospect of his settling down in Switzerland. Even though they considered him personally insignificant, they knew that he would always be a center of intrigue. Republicans and revolutionaries, all the worst elements in the State, would automatically gravitate toward him. Count Molé, the President of the Council, demanded that he be expelled from Swiss territory at once. For a few weeks it looked as if Prince Louis might be the spark that would set fire to the whole inflammable European structure. The Swiss refused to be intimidated, and the French, having once asked for his expulsion, could not back down. Finally the Prince cut the Gordian knot by offering to leave Switzerland of his own accord. He had embarrassed the ministers of Louis Philippe, he had earned the gratitude of the Swiss Government by not insisting on his rights as a Swiss citizen, and, most important of all, he had kept his name before the public.

The next few years were spent in London, ostensibly amusing himself, but always watching and waiting for another chance. A house in Carlton Terrace, where he gave dinners twice a week, notable, according to Disraeli, for "the finished appointments and the refined cuisine," [8] a good stable, a host of friends and acquaintances including perhaps more riffraff than

---

[8] The character of Prince Florestan in Disraeli's novel *Endymion* is a thinly disguised portrait of Louis Napoleon.

he would have liked—but an exiled prince cannot always choose his society—all this gay worldly life was suddenly sacrificed to another desperate venture.

The failure at Strasbourg, far from shaking his self-confidence, had only strengthened it. The Prince was a born conspirator to whom success or failure were almost equally irrelevant. What difference did the world's opinion make to him? The same people who called him insane because he had failed would have tumbled over themselves to acclaim him if he had succeeded.

Early in the morning of August 6, 1840, a small British pleasure steamer anchored off the port of Wimereux, a few miles north of Boulogne. The passengers were landed by boat. They included Prince Louis in imperial disguise complete with a tame eagle and fifty-three more or less ardent followers who had only the vaguest idea of what was expected of them. The Prince made them a brief speech from which they gathered that they would be in Paris in a few days. According to a version circulated by his enemies, "the eagle was to hover about Napoleon's head, attracted by a piece of bacon concealed in the historic hat." [9]

A crowd of curious civilians were easily induced to raise the cry *Vive l'Empereur!* Largess was scattered, and the party marched off to Boulogne in high spirits. There the little opera bouffe invasion petered out to an ignominious finale. Unable to rally the soldiers of the garrison to his cause, or the civilians, the Prince hurried his little company to the monument of the Grand Army half a mile outside the town. The imperial flag was duly hoisted, but it proved a futile gesture. By now it was too late to escape. The party made their way to the shore, pursued by the National Guard who fired at them as they were struggling into an empty lifeboat. Louis Napoleon himself was fished out of the water slightly wounded.

Louis Philippe and his ministers revelled in the completeness of the fiasco. They had dealt kindly with the young man after the Strasbourg affair. This time he must be taught a lesson. On October 7 he was condemned to perpetual imprisonment in the fortress of Ham. By a curious coincidence the frigate that was to bear Napoleon's body back to France anchored in St. Helena on the same day. The Prince was soon forgotten in

[9] Albert Guérard, *Reflections on the Napoleonic Legend* (New York, 1924), p. 148.

the excitement over the return of the ashes. The great Emperor was being laid to rest in the Invalides. No one was thinking about the crack-brained nephew in Ham.

No one, not even Persigny, could have foreseen the effect of the sentence of perpetual imprisonment on the public mind. The Prince had failed at Strasbourg and he had failed even more abjectly at Boulogne, but his faith in himself and in his destiny remained as strong as ever. In the long run the world takes a man at his own valuation. Contemporary opinion, if not posterity, is bowled over by self-confidence. Reasonable men dismissed Louis Napoleon after his failure at Boulogne as a mountebank, just as reasonable men dismissed Hitler after the Munich beer "putsch," but all the time he was in prison this "mountebank" was steadily drawing to himself a real following from the rank and file of the people.

The Prince made the most of his lonely years of imprisonment by plunging into the study of social questions. He wrote a pamphlet on the extinction of pauperism that attracted some attention from the socialist press, another on the problem of national defense in which he advanced the extraordinary theory that the Prussian military machine was more efficient than the French. Occasional articles from his pen began appearing in the leading reviews. He interested himself in a fantastic project for the junction of the Atlantic and Pacific Oceans by means of a canal. The Prince recommended the Nicaraguan rather than the Panama route. These pamphlets, together with a solid two-volume history of artillery, could not be described as the work of a mere trifler.[10] Gradually the details of his life in prison leaked out. The public began to take an interest in the prisoner of Ham. His correspondence with Louis Blanc and other leaders of liberal opinion indicated that he was thinking very seriously about the welfare of his country. Those who went to see him were charmed by their reception. No one could help admiring his courage under adversity. "Louis Napoleon is no longer a pretender," wrote the republican *Journal du Loiret*. "He is a citizen, a member of our party, a soldier fighting under our flag."

The government of Louis Philippe was annoyed by the

[10] *Etudes sur le passé et l'avenir de l'artillerie*, 2 vols. (Paris, 1846). The Prince had already written a *Manuel d'Artillerie*, 1835, described by an English biographer as "a closely reasoned volume of over 500 pages, succinct in form, precise in detail, clear and lucid in expression—almost a model of what such a book should be." F. A. Simpson, *The Rise of Louis Napoleon*, London, 1925, p. 90.

steadily growing interest in his favor. The request that he might
be allowed to visit his dying father was curtly refused. By that
time, the beginning of 1846, his fellow prisoners had been set
free and the Prince himself felt justified in trying to escape.
As long as his followers were still undergoing punishment in
his cause he had felt bound to remain in prison too. Now he
was once more at liberty to pursue his own ends. At seven
o'clock on the morning of May 25, 1846, Louis Napoleon, disguised as a workman in blue trousers and a blue blouse, carrying a plank on his shoulder to hide his face from the sentinel,
walked across the drawbridge of the Fortress of Ham, through
the castle gate and out on to the main St. Quentin road. He
reached Brussels that afternoon and on the following day he
was safe in London. After nearly six years of prison once more
he was a free man, free to take the waters at Bath, much
needed after the years of confinement, free to enjoy the pleasant
round of English country-house hospitality, free to marry some
attractive English heiress, but not free to set foot on French soil.

Never had Louis Philippe seemed more secure on his
throne, never had the chance of a successful *coup d'état* seemed
more remote. Guizot held the Chamber in the hollow of his
hand, and then suddenly the whole corrupt system he had
evolved collapsed. Rather than fight for his throne the old King
threw up his hands, leaving the road open for Louis Napoleon
—the road to Paris, to the Assembly, to the Presidency and to
the Empire.

Before Louis Philippe had smuggled himself out of France,
Louis Napoleon was already on his way to Paris. He was not
going to repeat the mistake made in 1830 when the Bonapartes
let slip a golden opportunity by not presenting themselves
boldly at the capital. This time a Bonaparte would be on the
spot. He arrived at the Hotel de Castille in the rue Richelieu,
where he met a group of friends including the faithful Persigny,
at a time when the Provisional Government was fighting for its
life in the Hotel de Ville. The meeting marked the beginning
of a propaganda campaign that has served as a model for all
the dictatorships of the twentieth century. Every trick of the
trade was used—persuasion and intimidation, the simultaneous
appeal to the noblest sentiments and the basest instincts, and a
blaring publicity that kept the people whipped up to such a
frenzy of excitement that the shrewdest peasant and the most
cautious bourgeois were finally convinced that Napoleon was

the only guarantee of security for the family or of safety for the State.

Starting with no other assets than his name, no money and no influential friends, and not even possessed of that eloquence which counts for so much in French political life, he built up a machine that crushed every attempt at opposition. The first step was to announce his arrival to the Provisional Government. He had hastened from exile to place himself under the flag of the newly proclaimed republic. His letter met with a very discouraging reply. The Provisional Government requested him to leave France at once. The Prince made no difficulties. He had hoped that after thirty years of exile and persecution he had earned the right to find a home in his native land, but if the Government thought that his presence in Paris might cause them any embarrassment he would obey their wishes and retire from the scene for the time being.[11] The phrasing of the letter, like all Louis Napoleon's letters during this period, was masterly. It was extremely polite. At the same time it indicated that the Government was perhaps not very sure of itself, and that he, Louis Napoleon, would feel at liberty to return whenever he wanted.

It was one of the Prince's virtues that he knew when to yield to circumstances. He was just as convinced that he was the instrument of destiny as the Bourbons were of the divine right of kings, but he was willing to bide his time. Once he had manoeuvred his way into power he became blocked psychologically by his very genuine respect for popular opinion and his inherited dislike of representative government. Caesarian democracy can never tolerate any third party between the ruler and his people. As a conspirator or a candidate for office he did not have to consider this particular problem. There was no obstacle ahead of him that he could not circumvent. After a week in Paris he withdrew to London with a good grace, knowing that both his friends and his enemies were paving the way for his return.

While France was drifting helplessly between anarchy and reaction, Louis Napoleon was patrolling the streets of London as a special constable. On April 10 the Chartists were to present a monster petition to the House of Commons demanding annual parliaments, universal suffrage, equal electoral districts,

[11] André Lebey, *Louis Napoleon Bonaparte et la Révolution de 1848*, 2 vols. (Paris, 1907), I, 173.

no property qualifications, and payment of members. The British Government, warned by events in France, had made extensive preparations. "Every gentleman in London," wrote Greville in his diary, "is become a constable . . . it is either very sublime or very ridiculous." The demonstration, from which the Paris radicals expected great things, turned out to be a complete failure, but the fact that Louis Napoleon had ranged himself unequivocally on the side of law and order was not without significance. A *coup d'état* resulting in a change of government in accordance with the wishes of the people was never to be confused in his mind, or in the mind of his supporters, with mob rule. His brand of Napoleonism may have meant democracy with a socialist tinge; but Bonapartism stood also for order and security. "If it came to a choice, the preservation of order would be his first consideration." [12]

Paris was too much absorbed in its own affairs to pay much attention to the Chartists. The representatives of the National Assembly, which met on May 4, after proclaiming their unswerving devotion to the Republic, soon fell to squabbling among themselves. If only the business of government could have been confined to planting trees of liberty, and to listening to splendid orations by Victor Hugo about the importance of spreading French ideas of liberty throughout the world! Unfortunately even Victor Hugo's eloquence could not drown out the ominous rumble of discontent. The widespread feeling of uneasiness, partly due to the growing scandal of the National Workshops but also to the lack of any executive ability in the Government, provided the perfect seed-bed for Bonapartist intrigue. Louis Napoleon had wisely refused to allow his name to be presented at the April elections. While Persigny and his friends were planting their agents in the National Workshops, covering the walls of Paris with his name in enormous letters, and distributing thousands of medals and lithographs labeled simply "Lui," he himself was living quietly in London apparently quite indifferent to the course of events in France. This time there would be no tame eagles and no Boulogne. He would wait until the people clamored for "the man."

Meanwhile Colonel Vaudrey, another disciple who was more of a Bonapartist than the Prince, was hiring organ grinders and street singers to predict the return of another Na-

[12] Albert Guérard, *Napoleon III* (Cambridge, Mass., 1943), p. 80.

poleon.[13] And in the evening along the boulevards could be heard the tramp of workers chanting: *Poléon, Poléon, nous l'aurons, nous l'aurons.* The Napoleonic legend built up in the songs of Béranger and the histories of Thiers was an invaluable asset, but it needed a slight twist to the left. As long as the prevailing mood was so definitely republican the regret for the past glories of the Empire had to be played down. Louis Napoleon was a man of his time. He would emphasize the duties inherent in his name rather than the rights. Around him, and only around him, could be built a democracy free from anarchy. At the same time, his agents did not forget to woo the less vocal but not less active parties that scoffed at the very idea of a republic.

The success of the campaign amazed everyone. In the supplementary elections held in June to fill the vacancies which resignation or double election had already created, four of the twenty-three *départements* vacant elected Louis Napoleon.[14] Without lifting a finger to help himself, and without the support of any responsible paper, the Prince was elected in Paris, in the Yonne, in the Charente-Inférieure, and in Corsica. Two hundred thousand voted for him. They had neither seen him nor heard him, but he was a symbol of what they thought they wanted. In the Yonne whole villages with the mayor at their head marched to the voting booth to the sound of the drum, shouting *Vive l'Empereur!* and *A bas la République!* [15] Would he be allowed to take his seat, or would the National Assembly invoke the law of 1832 under which all Bonapartes were banished from France? Lamartine's political instinct warned him that a Bonaparte was a greater danger to the Republic than any member of the royal family, but Lamartine's hold on the Assembly was waning. Even his eloquence could not withstand the wave of sympathy that was flooding through France for all those who had suffered for their political beliefs. *Vive Barbès! Vive Napoléon! Vive* anybody who had been imprisoned by Louis Philippe.

Meanwhile, couriers were plying to and fro between the Prince in London and his friends in the Assembly. Every letter

[13] D. Stern, *Histoire de la Révolution de 1848*, III, 88.

[14] Under the electoral system of that time a candidate could stand for any number of constituencies. If he happened to be elected in more than one, new elections were necessary. In the original election Lamartine had been chosen by ten *départements*.

[15] A. Lebey, *op. cit.*, I, 201.

that he wrote—and he wrote a great many—was carefully calculated from the point of its effect on the voter. What had he done, he asked the Assembly, in a letter written on May 24, to deserve exile? Was it because he had always publicly declared that France was not the property of any one man, of any family, or of any party? Was it because in championing the principle of national sovereignty he had twice become the victim of a government that had since been overthrown? As this letter produced no reply he followed it up with another, written after his election to the Assembly, in which he stated that he "would know how to discharge any duties that the people might impose upon him." His name was a symbol of order, nationalism, and glory. He would rather remain in exile than see it used to increase the dissensions that were rending the country.[16] The tone of this letter infuriated the Assembly, particularly the ominously Caesarian phrase, "if the people should impose duties upon me." Cavaignac pointed out that the word "republic" was not even mentioned. This time the Prince had gone too far, but it was not too late to retrieve the situation. Back went one of the faithful friends to London. Another letter was written, and within twenty-four hours the President of the Assembly was able to announce that the Prince had submitted his resignation. "I was proud of my election," wrote the Prince. "In my eyes it was an ample reparation for thirty years of exile and six years of captivity; but the suspicions to which it has given rise, the disorders for which it is a pretext, the hostility of the executive power, impose upon me the duty of refusing an honor which I am suspected of having obtained by intrigue. I desire order, and the maintenance of a wise, great, and intelligent republic; and since involuntarily I am the excuse for disorder, I place my resignation with deep regret in your hands." [17]

Once again the Prince had scored over the Assembly. His willingness to withdraw his name rather than force the issue made a most favorable impression. He had been legally elected in four *départements*. The Assembly apparently resented his election. All right, he would remain in exile until he could return to France as an ordinary private citizen devoted to the welfare of his country. Even an ardent republican like Mme. d'Agoult had to admit that Louis Napoleon had somehow

---

[16] D. Stern, *op. cit.*, III, 106.
[17] D. Stern, *op. cit.*, III, 109.

come to represent that ideal of revolutionary dictatorship which an ignorant, tumultuous, irrational democracy will always prefer to liberal government. The more intelligent section of the middle class gravitated toward Cavaignac in the hope that he would find some halfway house between anarchy and reaction, but society as a whole, the comfortable and the well-to-do who instinctively dreaded republicanism, flung themselves into the arms of the man who would preserve them from the threat of chaos. In the last hundred years many other nations besides France have cheerfully surrendered their birthright to those who promised to maintain order. There are moments in the lives of most of us when a hot steaming mess of pottage is almost impossible to resist.

*   *
*

With the gradual fading out of Lamartine the Assembly looked hopefully to General Cavaignac to stem the torrent of Bonapartism. The battle between liberty and license had been won. The never-ending struggle between representative government and dictatorship was about to begin. In the eyes of the Assembly Cavaignac had much to recommend him. He had the right background. He came of good republican stock. No one had ever questioned his honesty. He was a capable if not an inspired public servant, one of those wheel horses so dear to democracy who possess every virtue except the uncomfortable one of initiative. Unfortunately his very virtues militated against him. The soldier's single-minded devotion to duty often hampers him in the council chamber. In one of the crises of the First World War General Lyautey, a great organizer and a brilliant general, was summoned from Africa to become Minister of War. He proved utterly incapable of getting on with the Chamber of Deputies. After a few weeks he begged to be sent back to Africa. Cavaignac was not as able a man as Lyautey but he was blessed or cursed, depending on the point of view, with the same soldierlike rigidity. As a citizen and a soldier he wanted to serve the Republic, but he could never make up his mind just what a republic should be. The revolutionary tradition of his family, which he held dear, was always at odds with his own respect for authority. His father had been a member of the Convention, one of those who condemned Louis XVI to death. His brother had been an equally uncompromising republican. It was difficult for him to square the family hatred of authority with his own almost superstitious respect for it.

In the struggle with Louis Napoleon, Cavaignac was under a perpetual disadvantage. He was always waging a private war with himself that had to be fought out on every issue before he could turn his attention to outsiders. The Prince labored under no such handicap. His moral or political convictions could always be adjusted to meet the emergency of the moment. If he found it difficult to make decisions it was not because the family tradition was pulling him in a different direction from his own conscience, but because every decision restricted his liberty of action in the future. Once in power he found himself attracted simultaneously by the most contradictory ideals, each of which required a different decision, but for the moment his path was clear. His opponents prevented him from taking his seat in the Assembly and thus saved him from any responsibility in the fatal June days. It was not his fault if he was riding in Hyde Park with Miss Howard while his countrymen were killing each other on the barricades. Had he been in Paris there was nothing he could have done to avert the crisis, but in a curious way the simple fact that he was not there contributed to his reputation for political sagacity.

While the Assembly was wrangling over the laws of banishment, trying to decide whether a Bonaparte was eligible or not, it became increasingly obvious to everybody except the Executive Commission that a matter of much greater importance was clamoring for a decision. The future of the National Workshops had to be settled one way or the other. The Executive Commission had changed its mind half a dozen times and was now in favor of postponing the dissolution indefinitely, but the Assembly had taken a directly opposite view. *Il faut en finir,* was the refrain that ran through every speech. "We must get rid of them."

On June 15 Goudchaux, the Jewish Minister of Finance in the Provisional Government, atacked the fumbling policy adopted by Trélat and approved by Lamartine. He expressed the sentiments of capitalism and the business world: "The National Workshops must go, they must be dissolved. It is not a question of reducing the numbers. Let there be no mistake about this. We must get rid of them." [18] In vain the delegates

[18] P. Bastid, *op. cit.,* I, 284.

of the Workshops protested that it was not their will to
work that was lacking. The fault lay with the Government
for not providing the kind of work for which they were
trained.

Once again the fundamental discrepancy between the two
conceptions of the National Workshops was revealed. The
workers believed that the Workshops were intended to guarantee now and forevermore to each and every worker regular
employment in his own chosen trade or profession. Everyone
else conceived of the Workshops as a temporary expedient, a
device for tiding the unemployed over the inevitable slump resulting from the Revolution. With the best will in the world no
nation could discard a monarchy and create a republic without
causing some slight dislocation of industry. That was the bourgeois position and it was impossible to harmonize it with Louis
Blanc's dream of an entirely new and more equitable society.
There was no room for compromise. Either the Government,
representing the great bulk of national opinion, or the workers,
must give way.

The delegates demanded to know what was to happen to
the 110,000 workers employed in the National Workshops.
Were they to be abandoned to the evil counsels of famine and
despair? The parliamentary commission appointed to find a
solution recommended dissolving the Workshops and granting
a subsidy to private employers. On June 19 and 20 the Assembly listened to a number of speeches including a characteristically vapid oration by Victor Hugo, in which he offered as
his solution the extension of a more abundant life to everybody.[19] Finally the Assembly pushed the Executive Commission
over the brink by refusing to grant any further appropriation.
That settled the question. On June 21 the decree already
drafted was published, requiring the workers to enroll immediately in the Army or to hold themselves in readiness for ship-
ment to such destination in the provinces as might be assigned
to them. The first convoy left for the marshes of Sologne on the

---

[19] "Quant à moi, j'en comprenais ainsi la solution: n'effrayer personne,
rassurer tout le monde, appeler les classes jusqu'ici désheritées, comme on les
nomme, aux jouissances sociales, à l'éducation, au bien-être, à la consommation
abondante, à la vie à bon marché, à la propriété rendue facile."
Plusieurs Membres—"Très bien!"
De toutes Parts—"Nous sommes d'accord, mais par quels moyens?"
To that tiresome question Victor Hugo deigned no answer. It was enough
to have noble ideas. Let the Government devise means of putting them into effect.
V. Hugo, *Avant l'Exile*, I, 159.

next morning. They were to be employed on a drainage project under the direction of Government engineers.

To Goudchaux, the Jewish banker, it seemed that common sense had triumphed at last. The whole scheme of the National Workshops was financially unsound. He was a republican, not a socialist, and he did not approve of socialist experiments. To Tocqueville, the dispassionate student of society who foresaw the cataclysm but could do nothing to avert it, the dissolution of the Workshops and the insurrection it provoked was the culmination of a long series of political blunders going back to Guizot's obstinate refusal to extend the franchise. To the warm-hearted Mme. d'Agoult, who loved Liszt and Freedom and all humanity except her husband, the Government's action was nothing less than a betrayal of principle. She realized even more clearly than Tocqueville that it was not only the workers who would go down to defeat on the barricades. It was the Republic itself. Some new order would emerge out of the flames of civil war but it would not bear the imprint of liberty.

The Government was not unprepared for the struggle. Cavaignac had at his disposal about 50,000 men, most of them concentrated on the west side of Paris, between the Champs-Elysées and the Ecole Militaire, so as to protect the Assembly. In the last two revolutions, in 1830 and again in February, 1848, the Army had been humiliated. Split up into small units, badly supplied and badly led, it had allowed itself to be surrounded and disarmed by the mob. Officers with splendid records in Africa had proved utterly incompetent. The very different tactics of street fighting had bewildered them. Then, too, their heart had not been in the business. A desert charge against Arabs was a glorious adventure, but there was nothing glorious about shooting down your own countrymen in a quarrel which nobody seemed to understand. To a man with the schoolboy virtues of Cavaignac the real issue at stake was the prestige of the Army. The workers had challenged the Government, and it was his duty as Minister of War to accept the challenge and stamp out the insurrection. If so much as one company were disarmed he would feel disgraced. He had drawn up his plan of operations, and no political pressure would induce him to swerve from it. Instead of scattering his forces all over the city he massed them around the Assembly, which had to be defended at all costs, and from there sent out powerful columns in the directions threatened. General Bedeau was to clear the way to the Hotel de Ville, General Lamoricière was responsible for circulation along the boulevards.

Cavaignac was subsequently criticized for standing by passively while the insurgents were throwing up the barricades. It was even suggested that he deliberately allowed the insurrection to develop so that he might be given dictatorial powers in dealing with it.[20] Actually Cavaignac was probably thinking more of the morale of the Army than of his own powers. He would not be stampeded into committing his forces piecemeal, and he would not give the order to fire until the troops could see for themselves that the workers were bent on another revolution. Nothing was done to prevent a solemn demonstration in front of the column of the Bastille, where the crowd invoked the heroes of July, 1830. *"Du pain ou du plomb! Du plomb ou du travail!"* "Bread or bullets, bullets or work!" This was no common midsummer madness. The mob was desperately serious. By the morning of June 23 half of Paris appeared to be in their hands. Barricades had sprung up as if by magic in the faubourg St. Antoine, in the faubourg of the Temple, in the Cité, and on the left bank of the Seine as far as the Panthéon. The discipline of the insurgents was excellent. Each barricade was commanded by an officer of experience who utilized the defensive possibilities of the narrow winding streets to the best advantage, but whether there was any commander-in-chief of the workers who dictated an overall plan of campaign has never been known.[21] Cavaignac, a lonely self-contained man with no understanding of the instincts that swayed the masses, was mystified by the fanaticism of the defense.

The members of the Executive Commission dreaded giving

[20] This opinion was openly stated in *La Presse*, June 22. The editor of *La Presse*, Emile de Girardin, was one of Cavaignac's bitterest enemies. He afterwards supported Louis Napoleon.

[21] All historians of the period are mystified by the organization of the insurgents. Tocqueville was particularly struck by the anonymity of the defense. To him the insurrection was "la plus singulière dans notre histoire . . . car les insurgés y combattirent sans cri de guerre, sans chefs, sans drapeaux et pourtant avec un ensemble merveilleux et une expérience militaire qui étonna les plus vieux officiers." Tocqueville, *Souvenirs*, p. 135.

Mme. d'Agoult was of the same opinion. "A chaque barricade, on entend, dans le silence qui garde les combattants, la voix d'un chef qui paraît commander militairement; mais on ne sait si ces chefs eux-mêmes obéissent à un order supérieur. Pas un nom, pas un cri, pas un emblème qui révèle le caractère ou le but de l'insurrection. On n'a vu jusqu'ici que des drapeaux tricolores. En inquiétant l'imagination du soldat, le mystère de cette guerre des rues en double la force." D. Stern, *op. cit.*, III, 166.

the orders for a general attack. As a last resort Arago, an old republican who had always been sympathetic with the masses, marched up to one of the barricades and demanded of the defenders why they had revolted against the Government. "Monsieur Arago," came a voice from the barricades, "you are an honest man but you have never starved. You don't know the meaning of misery." Further discussion was useless. Arago withdrew in despair. The issue could only be settled by force. For three days the battle ebbed to and fro. Barricades were captured and recaptured. At one moment it looked as if the Government forces would be beaten. Everyone was asking for reinforcements. On the night of June 24 Cavaignac made a gloomy report to the Assembly. The *garde mobile*, a force of seventeen-year-old boys originally organized by Lamartine, had shown the greatest heroism, but the Assembly must be prepared for further losses. The workers were unfortunately fighting with the most extraordinary tenacity. After the endless rhapsodies over the Republic and the dawn of a new freedom, to which they had been subjected, the Assembly listened with relief to the General's frank appraisal of his difficulties. Here at last was a man who did not sidestep uncomfortable facts. They responded by voting a decree whereby all the executive powers were placed in his hands. Once again the usual destiny of popular revolutions was accomplished. France was in the hands of a dictator.

The Executive Commission had failed, not because the members individually were lacking in courage or ability but because they were dogged by disunity. The typically French individualism, so fatal in politics and so charming in every other walk of life, bound them to inaction. They never made up their minds what they wanted to do or what they could do. Only a sincere belief in the superior virtues of republicanism held them together, and that was not enough.

No sooner was Cavaignac invested with supreme powers than he had to face the usual criticism of the amateur strategists in the Assembly. Monsieur Thiers in particular was not satisfied. As the official historian of the First Empire he had studied Napoleon's campaigns to such good effect that he felt he understood military affairs far better than Cavaignac. It was impossible to storm every barricade. The Government should abandon Paris to the insurrection and withdraw to the provinces. It was the same advice he had offered Louis Philippe and that he himself adopted in 1871 when the Commune was in control of Paris. Cavaignac was exasperated. He had been ordered to crush the insurrection. Now that he had been appointed dictator, nothing would induce him to order a retreat. For the first time in modern history Cavaignac took the Army into his confidence. Instead of the usual grandiose appeal to patriotism and glory he spoke to them of the cruel war they were fighting. In the past the Army had too often been used as the tool of despotism. That was no longer true. This time they were not the aggressors. This time they were fighting for the sovereignty of the people, for a government strong enough to guarantee liberty and justice to all.[22]

With this new appeal for democracy ringing in their ears the Army set about the grim task of reducing the barricades one by one. Two generals had already been killed, and the pile of corpses was still mounting around the barricades when another general, appalled by the senseless slaughter, determined to make one last appeal to common sense and humanity. The Assembly had just voted three million francs to be distributed among the families of the needy regardless of whether they were fighting for or against the Government. Armed with this offer General Bréa, a kindly man who thought that a few simple words from an old soldier would set everything right, advanced to the *barrière d'Italie* [23] and pleaded with the insurgents to lay down their arms. He and his chief of staff were lured inside the barricade and assassinated.

On the same day the Archbishop of Paris, Monsignor Affre, was also murdered. He had been urged by some young Catholics to intervene in the struggle. As long as the politicians had failed to avert the senseless bloodshed the Church must exert her authority. Cavaignac warned him that he was going to his death, but the Archbishop, hitherto considered a timid man, was suddenly transfigured into a hero. "My death is of so little account," he replied. Dressed in his most gorgeous vestments, crucifix in hand, he penetrated into the rabbit warren of barricades in the faubourg St. Antoine. He had asked for an hour's truce, but before he could make himself heard someone fired a shot and in the general fusillade that followed, the Archbishop fell mortally wounded. The news of these two murders spread through Paris all too quickly. From now on even

[22] D. Stern, *op. cit.*, III, 339.
[23] Today the Place d'Italie.

the most tolerant bourgeois shuddered at the very mention of socialism. Every hour brought fresh accounts of the barbarities committed by socialists upon all who fell into their hands. They were poisoning their victims, pouring vitriol into their wounds, violating nuns—all the familiar stories that spring up in the wake of war were freely circulated and freely believed. On the barricades the *garde mobile* were being similarly accused of the most hideous cruelties. The precise number of casualties has never been known, but not less than 1500 soldiers and 3000 insurgents are said to have been killed. Lord Normanby estimated the cost of the destruction of property at thirty million francs. "From this it would appear," says the British Ambassador, "as if the erection of barricades were a more costly luxury than the building of palaces." [24]

By the time the last barricade was carried, on the evening of June 26, Cavaignac was more than ever the hero of the hour. Two days later he remitted his powers into the hands of the Assembly, who immediately reappointed him Chief Executive for an indefinite period. General Cavaignac had deserved well of the country. He had crushed the insurrection but the victory had left him lonelier and more disillusioned than ever. No sooner was the fighting over than he was beset by innumerable demands, reproaches and warnings. The newly arrived National Guards from the provinces marched through the city shouting, *Vive la République des honnêtes gens!* But who were the *"honnêtes gens"?* Who were the decent, honest people to whom the maintenance of order should be entrusted? Cavaignac was determined to stay in the middle of the road, but his conception of the middle of the road was so literal that it left room for nobody except the conservative republican representatives in the Assembly. The man who pursues the golden mean too relentlessly will sooner or later find himself alone. The great bulk of public opinion was aghast at the measures of repression. Every individual captured with arms in his or her hands was to be immediately deported. Subsequently the order was amended and two thirds of the prisoners were released, but even so the long convoys of destitute men and women on their way to Algeria confirmed the popular belief that Cavaignac was an enemy of the people.

After having struck at the insurgents, the Assembly was determined to reach the instigators of the rebellion. Louis

[24] Normanby, *op. cit.*, II, 95.

Blanc and Ledru-Rollin escaped to England before their sentences were pronounced. Proudhon, the most extreme socialist of them all, who believed, or thought he believed, that property was theft and Christianity a humbug, could not be convicted of having any share in the insurrection—he was not a conspirator like Blanqui—but his theories were condemned by the Assembly as an odious attack on the principles of public morality.

All the political clubs were closed and only those newspapers could be published which paid a *cautionnement*, or good-conduct pledge, of 24,000 francs. Lammenais flayed the Government's policy in the last number of his *Peuple Constituant:* "One must be rich, very rich, to have the right to speak. We are not rich enough. Silence to the poor."

If he antagonized the republicans by these measure Cavaignac was equally careful to rebuff the leaders of the non-archical party, many of whom had done good service in the June fighting. This rigid man insisted in clinging to an ideal of duty which was shared by nobody else. No one could quarrel with the principles to which he anchored himself, but he was so unyielding that he alienated those who should have been his friends. From the first day he came into power Cavaignac believed that the editors of the *National* were the only genuine republicans. Everybody else was a socialist or a disguised monarchist. "Whoever does not want the Assembly," he said in a speech to the Assembly on Septmber 2, "is our enemy, our everlasting enemy. Against any attack on the idea of a Republic we will use all the weapons that the Republic has given us." He was determined to wage war upon anyone who attacked the republican principle, anyone who hinted that the Republic was inadequate, anyone who yearned to bring back the Monarchy. To such persons there was no answer but irreconcilable war.[25] This was the speech of a fanatic rather than of a statesman. The French people were less than ever willing to fight for forms of government. They were only willing to fight for men who could restore credit and maintain order. The passion for independence was giving way to a fear of free institutions amounting almost to terror. As usual after a revolution, the pendulum was swinging back to the necessity of a strong government.

More and more during that summer of 1848 it became

[25] A. Lebey, *op. cit.*, II, 6.

obvious that France was interested in personalities rather than political systems. The election of the President by universal suffrage had weakened the Assembly's hold on the nation. The candidate elected, if he secured a big enough majority, would shape the future of the country as he wished. By the end of the summer all France knew that the choice for the Presidency had been narrowed down to two men—Cavaignac and Louis Napoleon. At first glance it appeared that the General had the advantage. His character was well known. His political honesty, his courage, his immense services to the cause of order, assured him the votes of the Paris bourgeoisie, the clergy, the provincial nobility, the officers of the Army and the Navy, and the whole civil service. They might not be enthusiastic about him but at least they liked him better than a Bonaparte they did not know.

Prince Louis had nothing to count on but his name. The prestige of that name was something beyond the reckoning of Cavaignac's supporters. Even in an unsympathetic Assembly it exercised an influence that the political wiseacres found it hard to explain. The Prince had refused another election in July. He wanted to wait until the commission appointed to investigate the causes of the insurrection had conclusively proved his innocence, but when that was done and when in September he was again elected, this time by no less than five *départements*, he felt that the time had at last come for him to take his seat.

On September 24 he arrived in Paris and drove to the Hotel de Hollande, in the rue de la Paix, where he had rented a three-room apartment. On the 26th he took his seat in the Assembly. A big crowd was waiting for him outside the doors but he avoided the noisy ovation that had been prepared for him and slipped in by a side entrance. The meeting had hardly begun when a ripple of excitement spread through the Assembly. Citizen Louis Napoleon Bonaparte, no longer a Pretender, was being formally admitted to the Assembly as Representative of the Yonne. All eyes turned instinctively to examine the newcomer. Those who looked for a resemblance between the nephew and his uncle were disappointed. He was more of a Beauharnais than a Bonaparte. What they saw was a short, awkwardly built man with a large impassive face and a head that was too big for his body. Only the more curious would have noticed the rather attractive combination of diffidence and self-possession in his manner. He accepted the interest of the Assembly as his due without either demanding it or chafing under it. He was completely unaffected by the general atmosphere of hostility. Cavaignac, Thiers, Lamartine, none of the great leaders in the Assembly welcomed him. He might be popular in the provinces but he was not popular in the Assembly, nor would he ever be. And yet this unobtrusive enigma of a man who spoke French haltingly with a strong foreign accent could hardly be considered a threat to the Government. He very rarely spoke in the Assembly. It was almost as if he ignored it. At the same time his mere presence in Paris caused uneasiness. Before long he moved into the more fashionable Hotel du Rhin where he and his ever-growing entourage occupied three floors. In these more spacious quarters and in a villa he rented at Auteuil there seemed to be a great deal of activity. The new Representative was always interviewing people. Newspaper editors were seen going in and out of his house, also prominent socialists and army officers. It was all very mysterious, so mysterious that some of the more suspicious in the Assembly grew restive. A proposal was brought forward to exclude from the Presidency all members of houses that had reigned in France. Even Cavaignac opposed this amendment to the Constitution, urging with justice but without much foresight that since the Chamber had decided to trust the people it must do so without any reserve.

The proposal was so obviously aimed at Louis Napoleon that for once he decided to break his silence. He was not prepared, he was never a good impromptu speaker, and the result was a complete failure. In the few stammering sentences he managed to utter before he trailed off into silence, he convinced the audience that they had grossly exaggerated the danger his candidacy might present. It was impossible for the Assembly to take anybody seriously who was so little of an orator. The mover of the amendment announced that he would not press his proposal. After what they had just heard it was obviously quite unnecessary.[26] The sarcasm was not lost on the victim but Lord Normanby, an eyewitness of the scene, noted that he behaved with amazing *sang-froid*. He appeared neither irritated nor disconcerted. Once again the Prince proved that a setback would not deflect him from his course.

Never has any failure proved more fortunate. By his timely ineffectiveness in debate Louis Napoleon had surmounted the

[26] Lord Normanby, *op. cit.*, II, 242.

last obstacle in the race. Everything had played into his hands. If he had spoken brilliantly the Assembly would probably have sustained the amendment against him. A clever orator would have been too dangerous to ignore. If Lamartine had not insisted on direct election of the President by the people instead of by the Assembly, Louis Napoleon would have been beaten by Cavaignac. Lamartine realized the dangers of Bonapartism but he was intoxicated by the idea of universal suffrage. To him it was the panacea for every ailment. The Assembly should never venture to set aside the verdict of the people. If the Prince had been allowed to take his seat in the Assembly when he was first elected he would have had to take sides in the struggle between the bourgeoisie and the socialists. As it was, he escaped all responsibility for the mismanagement of the National Workshops, for the slaughter on the barricades, and for the repressive measures that every unsuccessful insurrection brings in its wake. There was nothing to be said against him, and from the point of view of the masses there was much to be said for him. His name represented the victory of equality over privilege, the victory of democracy over kings and nobles, the victory of the French Revolution over European dynasties. The more prominent men in the Assembly, who at first had been bitterly opposed to him, soon felt that it was hopeless to stem the great wave of Bonapartism that was flooding the provinces. The opinion they had formed of his very mediocre abilities made them prefer him to Cavaignac. This awkward, timid Louis Napoleon, this burlesque hero of Strasbourg and Boulogne who made such a fuss about being admitted to the Assembly and had then broken down in his maiden speech, was hardly the kind of man that need be taken seriously. The Legitimists and Orléanists ended by voting for him on the theory that the surest way to restore the monarchy was to elect a second-rate man as President, who could be counted upon to demonstrate the weakness of the republican form of government.

As the summer wore on the Napoleonic machine gathered momentum. He had made his way without the help of the big newspapers. Then gradually the seed sown by Persigny began to bear fruit. *La Presse*, edited by Emile de Girardin, the respectable *Constitutionnel* for which Sainte-Beuve was soon to be writing his *Causeries du Lundi*, suddenly discovered that it was their duty to support the new champion of order and liberalism. Victor Hugo, later a relentless enemy but for the moment a friend, claimed that the candidacy of Louis Napoleon dated from Austerlitz. While the army was reminded that he was the inheritor of the glories of the Empire, the middle class were made to feel that this new Napoleon was essentially a man of peace.

Today we all know that in a national election party organization counts for more than the personal qualifications of the candidate, but that great truism was only discovered in 1848. Louis Napoleon built up the first great political machine. It manipulated public opinion, divided the opposition and crushed it with all the terrifying efficiency of a twentieth century dictator. He was not the standard-bearer of any one party. All political parties stood for the privileges of some special group. He stood for a principle, the principle of unity. He was the champion of all those who were dissatisfied with the present state of confusion. Bonapartism brushed aside special interests in order to establish direct contact between the Chief Executive and the people. Our generation knows the results of these theories all too well, but to a people unversed in the ways of demagogy their force is incalculable.

Like all dictators in their early stages the Prince was always short of money. He borrowed wherever he could, from friends in Italy, from the faithful Miss Howard, who was as generous as she was beautiful, and from the financier Achille Fould. A gamble on his political future had become "a good thing." [27] With the help of these funds the country was saturated with Bonapartist propaganda. Throughout the campaign he displayed the astuteness of a seasoned politician. As a private individual he possessed certain attractive qualities. He was friendly, easily approachable, unassuming about himself though immensely proud of his origin. Certainly he was no great orator or even a good conversationalist, but he was a good listener, and the candidate who can listen intelligently and sympathetically will often pick up votes that his more articulate rival disdains. The world forgives a man more readily for speaking badly than for speaking too much. Louis Napoleon wrote a great deal, but after his first failure in the Assembly he rarely spoke at all unless he was carefully prepared.

The flexibility of his character made the downright Cavaignac appear stiff and arrogant in comparison. In 1848 a candidate's written declarations and manifestos were more im-

[27] A. Guérard, *Napoleon III*, p. 92.

portant than his speeches, which were not widely reprinted. Louis Napoleon's proclamations were models of political adroitness. He spoke of guaranteeing freedom of education, of reducing taxes, of protecting the workers, of decentralizing the Government, and above all of the reign of the worldwide peace which was to be ushered in by enlightened administration. He even had a word of comfort for those who had been temporarily banished. After undergoing the rigors of exile himself he would know how to spare them the sufferings that he had experienced. There was no limit to his humanity or to his far-seeing patriotism. He had a solution ready for every problem.

The election was held on December 10. Long before that day it was obvious that France had succumbed once more to the magic of the Napoleonic name. Out of the seven and a half million votes cast Louis Napoleon received 5,534,520 to the 1,442,302 for Cavaignac. There were several other candidates. Ledru-Rollin received 371,431 votes, Raspail 36,920, and Lamartine, who did not expect to be elected but did expect to poll at least 500,000 votes, 17,910! No Shakespearean hero ever fell more quickly or more irretrievably from public esteem. At the May elections Paris alone had given him 259,800 votes. It was significant that the more "red" *départements* gave Louis Napoleon the biggest majority. The socialists never forgave Cavaignac for the slaughter of the June days. On December 20 Louis Napoleon took the oath of acceptance and made a short speech, this time without breaking down. He concluded his remarks with a promise to found a government that would be firm and just without being reactionary or Utopian. "I shall consider as enemies of the country all those who attempt to change by illegal means what the people of France have established." No doubt he spoke with complete sincerity. Unfortunately, human nature is capable of successive and contradictory sincerities.

At the end of the speech he turned to shake hands with Cavaignac, but the General was apparently thinking of something else. The hand outstretched toward him found nothing to grasp. It was an embarrassing moment but no slight could ruffle the Prince's imperturbable good humor. At last he had come into his own. Five and a half million votes outweighed the bad temper of a disgruntled general. That evening he gave a dinner at the Elysée Palace. A few rooms had been hastily prepared for him, and the dinner was sent in from a restaurant on the

Place de la Madeleine. The indefatigable Persigny had arranged for it to be served by footmen dressed in the imperial livery. The guests were his uncle King Jerome, Odilon Barrot, the newly appointed prime minister, and his companions in the mad adventures of Strasbourg and Boulogne. It was thirty-three years since Napoleon had abdicated in this same palace in favor of the Duc de Reichstadt. Mme. de Pompadour, Murat, Napoleon after his return from Elba, the Duke of Wellington, and the Czar Alexander had all lived there. Now it was to be his home, the official residence of the President of the Republic. As his eye wandered over those rooms so full of Napoleonic memories he must have contemplated his own achievement with no little satisfaction. The campaign that had swept him into the Presidency had been no less skilfully planned, no less brilliantly executed, than the campaigns of Jena or Austerlitz.

What was to be the effect on France of the election of another Bonaparte? It was the first time that the people had chosen their ruler. How far would his election satisfy their dreams? George Sand confessed that the prospect of universal suffrage bewildered her. She spoke of it in a letter to Mazzini much as we today speak of the atom bomb. It was a new force let loose in the world. Man had created something that he was powerless to control. For one thing the election of Louis Napoleon represented the victory of equality over liberty. The instinct of liberty which had been the driving force behind the Paris bourgeoisie as long as the vision of a Republic beckoned to them was suddenly thwarted. The instinct of equality with its implication of social revolution, which would affect not only the well-to-do but the mass of the people as well, swept everything before it. The people had voted for a name without realizing that they were choosing a master. Cavaignac would have given them an honest Republic without summoning help from the extreme left or the right, but that was not enough. What the peasants and workingmen of France sought above all was the abolition of privilege. As Albert Guérard points out, "they never attached any other meaning to 'democracy.' " [28] From now on, France was Louis Napoleon's, and his not only to serve but to govern.

The English conception of a king obedient to the wishes of Parliament had never suited the French temperament. To

[28] A. Guérard, *Napoleon III*, p. 120.

preserve the respect of the people the sovereign, whether he were called president or king, had to act. If he acted contrary to their wishes he might be deposed, but if he announced his intention of governing through the Assembly he would never be elected. With that infinite optimism so characteristic of the men of 1848 France was once more willing to start all over again. The Bourbon and the Orléans monarchies had failed; so had the bourgeois republic. It remained to be seen whether authoritarian democracy would success. The fact that the universal suffrage had inadvertently designated a candidate for the Empire instead of merely electing a President was not realized until 1851.

For the first few weeks there were no difficulties. The moderate conservatives in the Assembly, including such men as Thiers and Odilon Barrot, had plumped for Louis Napoleon instead of Cavaignac, and it was hardly possible for the President to break with them overnight. His first ministry, in deference to their wishes, contained only one republican. This honeymoon period could not last long. Between the airy dreams of Louis Napoleon and the earthbound policies of a timidly bourgeois cabinet, steeped in parliamentary tradition, there was no common meeting ground. The Ministers were not interested in the vaguely humanitarian faith of their President, in the possibilities of a Nicaraguan canal, in the fostering of some sort of European patriotism, or in any of the other fantastic schemes around which his imagination liked to play. Nor did they look with much favor upon his demand to see the dossiers of the Boulogne and Strasbourg affairs. The private papers of a judge were not to be delivered up to the citizen he had convicted, even if that citizen had since become President of the Republic.

There were other and more pressing questions that divided the President and his cabinet ministers. What was to be the attitude of France toward the revolutionary movements in Italy? In his youth Louis Napoleon had been mixed up in a Carbonari uprising. As a Bonaparte he could not help being sympathetic to the struggles of the Italian states to drive out the Austrian invader, but as a good Catholic, or rather as a Frenchman who recognized the tremendous weight of Catholic opinion in France, he could not tolerate the spectacle of the Pope at bay, his prime minister murdered, and the republican rabble master of Rome. Pius IX had discovered early in 1848 that his duties as Pope and his sentiments as an Italian necessarily diverged. After a dangerous flirtation with liberalism he had suddenly realized that he must choose between being a Pope and an Italian patriot. The assassination of his minister Count Rossi convinced him that a liberal Pope was an impossibility. Cavaignac had offered to rescue his Holiness and bring him to France, but at the last moment the negotiations broke down and instead of seeking an asylum in republican France the Pope took refuge in the reactionary court of Naples.

The problem of re-establishing Pius IX in the Vatican without crushing the liberal movement in Rome was the most unpleasant legacy Cavaignac could possibly have bequeathed to the new President. His tactics as a conspirator had been comparatively simple, but now that he had reached his goal he found himself incapable of adopting one line and pursuing it to the exclusion of everything else. More than any other ruler of his time Louis Napoleon was tortured by dreams that could never come true. It was all very well for him to have faith in himself, the faith that makes men endure all things with resignation, but that faith could not alter the fact that he was at heart a sentimentalist attracted simultaneously by the most contradictory ideals. He believed in peace and he thought he could establish peace by making war. He wanted to be more powerful than his uncle, and at the same time more idealistic than Mazzini. A liberal and a nationalist by temperament, he drew his chief support not from the liberals—least of all after the *coup d'état* of 1851 that made him Emperor—but from the deeply conservative rural masses. He revealed to the French people glorious visions of European peace congresses and national prosperity.

> Great schemes they were, grandiose, magnificent; sometimes even noble in their failure, magnanimous in their partial success. But while the dreamer gazed on far horizons he stumbled ever more often over the obstacles at his feet, and at last fell headlong, tripped by an antagonist who never lifted his eyes from the ground.[29]

The history of France during the ten months that elapsed between the fall of Louis Philippe and the election of Louis Napoleon can be interpreted in many ways. To the cynic it will appear that France had made a political somersault. By

[29] F. A. Simpson, *The Rise of Louis Napoleon*, p. 330.

December 31, 1848, the situation was apparently not so very different from what it had been on January 1. Louis Napoleon's first set of ministers were surprisingly like the ministers of Louis Philippe. No one of them had played any part in the setting up of the Provisional Government or in the founding of the Republic. The budget was no smaller, the Army certainly no less powerful. There were more Representatives in the Chamber and they were more noisy, but they exercised no more influence in the country than the Chamber of 1847. Louis Philippe, his children and grandchildren, had been bundled out of the Tuileries. Louis Napoleon, a gay bachelor, had begun his reign where Napoleon had ended his, in the Elysée Palace. After shouting *Vive la République!* vociferously for ten months France was beginning to wonder whether she really wanted a Republic at all. It still remained to be seen whether Frenchmen could take up any intermediate position between political torpor and revolutionary violence. In February Baudelaire had welcomed the Revolution as offering him a chance to shoot his stepfather.[30] That may have been bravado, but after witnessing the horrors of the June Days the cynic might well wonder whether the mood represented by Baudelaire could ever be affected by a change in the political regime.

And yet there is another, less cynical and perhaps more plausible, interpretation of these crowded months. The Revolution of 1848 cannot be dismissed as a mere flash in the pan. It produced solid results, though these results were not immediately apparent. After 1848, in spite of the defeat on the barricades, the worker was a political factor that had to be reckoned with. He had acquired a new status in the community. Never again could a politician suggest that a worker should accept his lot with humble resignation. Heaven knows that the Revolution of 1848 did not put an end to political corruption, but at least it did put an end to the idea that any administration could perpetuate itself by working exclusively through the meaner and more selfish impulses of mankind.

Guizot had thought it absurd to maintain that all men should be allowed to exercise political rights. He believed that two or three hundred thousand landowners and prosperous business men adequately represented the whole of France. That belief, honestly and tenaciously held, coupled with an indifference to social reform, precipitated a revolution that marked

[30] E. Seillière, *Baudelaire* (Paris, 1931), p. 49.

the end of an era. The new industrial economy with which the newborn republic had to grapple propounded problems to men who were incapable of solving them. These men of 1848, and particularly Lamartine, never sensed the danger to a republic of the ignorant voter. They believed that liberty and social justice could be conjured into being by winged words, and when the magic did not work they persuaded themselves that dictatorships, because they sometimes abolish specific evils, can therefore create a lasting good in their place. In the very act of failure they stumbled on the road leading to the twentieth century. Incredibly naïve though they were, they belong to the present, just as the worldly-wise Guizot and Louis Philippe belong to the past.

CHAPTER

II

THE REVOLUTION IN ITALY

1

ITALY AFTER THE CONGRESS OF VIENNA

OF ALL the nations overrun by Napoleon, Italy was the one that suffered the least and profited the most. From the Alps to the Strait of Messina the administrative system of France was introduced in all its centralized efficiency. That in itself was an incalculable benefit. Napoleon had swept away the cobwebs of the eighteenth century. Not very tenderly, but most effectually, he had roused Italy from her long slumbers. At the same time he had redrawn the map to suit his own convenience. He annexed directly to the Empire a large slice of the richest territory including Piedmont, Tuscany, and the Papal States up to the Apennines. The rest of the peninsula was divided into the Kingdom of Italy, consisting of Lombardy, Venetia, Modena, Romagna, and the Marches, and the Kingdom of Naples, which coincided roughly with the Bourbon Kingdom of the Two Sicilys except that Sicily itself had been lopped off by British sea power.

The Kingdom of Italy was ruled by Eugène Beauharnais, Napoleon's stepson and one of his best lieutenants, a keen professional soldier rather than a statesman, but even as a statesman above the average of Italian rulers. Naples was given to Napoleon's brother Joseph, and, when Joseph was appointed King of Spain, to Murat. They were both genuinely interested, almost too interested from Napoleon's point of view, in the welfare of their subjects. Thanks to the skill of Roederer, Joseph Bonaparte's Minister of Finance, the revenue of the Kingdom of Naples was soon doubled. In education, as in civil administration, the Napoleonic regime effected many reforms. Modern education on scientific and military lines was substituted for the prevailing clerical obscurantism. Every university was endowed with a free school for both sexes, and every province with a college. General Pepe, a Napoleonic veteran and afterwards commander-in-chief in Manin's defense of Venice, declared: "We made more progress on this side of the Strait within the space of ten years, than our ancestors had done in three centuries." [1]

In French Italy Napoleon made the mistake of arresting the Pope and transporting him to France, but otherwise the Napoleonic rule was generally popular. The careers open to the talented, equality in the eyes of the law, honest judges, the Code Napoleon—these things more than compensated for the insult to the Pope, the burden of conscription, and the lack of political independence. It is true that the government was a despotism, but the despotism was made palatable by the rapid increase in national prosperity, the tremendous momentum given to life, the outburst of fraternization and the general atmosphere of excitement.

The Congress of Vienna was so bent on preserving Europe from the domination of another Napoleon that in Italy at least it tried to push back the hands of the clock and to recreate the conditions that had existed in 1789. Fearful that France might once again surge over the Alps, Austria was appointed to mount guard in Italy just as Prussia mounted guard on the Rhine. Maria Theresa had ruled Lombardy. What was more natural than that this province should be given back to her grandson, the Emperor Francis? Meanwhile the Venetian Republic having died of old age, Venice was added to Lombardy to form the Lombardo-Venetian Kingdom. Of the ten states set up in Italy by the Congress of Vienna no less than five were to be ruled by Habsburgs: the Kingdom of Lombardo-Venetia directly under the Emperor, the Grand Duchy of Tuscany under his brother Ferdinand III, and the Duchy of Parma under his daughter Marie Louise, the wife of Napoleon. Modena was given to Francis IV, an Austrian Este grandson of Maria Theresa, and the duchies of Massa and Carrara to

[1] *Memoirs of General Pepe*, 3 vols. (London, 1896), II, 115.

another Habsburg, Marie Beatrice d'Este. The arrangement insured the predominance of Austrian influence throughout the Italian peninsula.

Two states were restored to their Italian rulers. The Kingdom of Sardinia, consisting of Sardinia, Savoy, Nice, Piedmont and Genoa, reverted to the aged Victor Emmanuel I, who celebrated his return by closing the Botanical Gardens on the ground that they had been founded by the French, and the Papal States, which lay across the center of Italy stretching from the frontiers of Venetia to the outskirts of Naples, were given back to the Pope. The little republic of San Marino was left intact, as it had been by Napoleon.

Two other states were ruled by Bourbons: The Duchy of Lucca under Maria Louisa de Bourbon, which was to revert to Tuscany after her death, and the Kingdom of the Two Sicilys (Naples and Sicily) under Ferdinand I. On the basis of population this state was the most important in Italy, but it was so split up by the mutual jealousy of Neapolitans and Sicilians that it never challenged the leadership of Piedmont. Strangely enough, in recent years the Savoy monarchy proved to be more popular in southern Italy than in the provinces where it originated.[2]

The Italy conjured into being by the Congress of Vienna bore no relation to the wishes of the inhabitants or to the changing spirit of the times. Even in the Papal State, where Pius VII, released from his prison in Fontainebleau, was acclaimed by wildly enthusiastic crowds, it was not long before the pontifical government had squandered all its reserves of good will. Leo XII, who succeeded Pius, reintroduced many of the obnoxious laws that had been swept away under the French occupation. He took away from the Jews the right to hold property and confined them once more to a ghetto. He surrendered the entire system of education into the hands of the clergy and he flouted public opinion still more outrageously by establishing a ramified system of espionage for watching over the morals of his subjects. This was not the way to make the old order popular.

At the same time, though there was an ever-growing demand throughout Italy for liberal institutions, the people were

[2] For further details on Italy and the Congress of Vienna see G. F. H. Berkeley, *Italy in the Making, 1815–46*, (Cambridge, 1932), and R. M. Johnston, *The Napoleonic Empire in Southern Italy*, 2 vols. (New York, 1904).

not yet clamoring for independence. It was only gradually that
the idea of liberalism in Italy became divorced from French
culture and efficient government, and associated with the idea
of national unity. In Germany and Spain national sentiment
was the inevitable result of the Napoleonic wars, but Italy had
always been governed by foreigners. It was not a conquered
nation, for it had never been a nation at all. The intellectuals
fixed their gaze on Paris, and the rank and file of the population were imbued with a fierce local patriotism that left no
room for romantic ideas about nationalism. Byron and Shelley
would have us believe that all Italy was chafing for freedom
and independence, but the greatest Italian historians of the
Risorgimento make it very clear that there was no tradition
of unity. Liberty in Italy meant neither unity nor federation.
On the contrary, it meant the self-determination of each separate community.[3]

The man who did more to regenerate his countrymen, to
convince them that they had emerged from the small autono-
mies of the past into a new world where the old narrow loyal-
ties could no longer satisfy their needs, was Mazzini. His principal aim was to unite all Italy into one indivisible republic.
Mazzini was the born conspirator, his hand against every government in Italy. Against him were ranged not only Metternich, who could never believe that the unity of Italy was more
than a dream, but also Pius IX, the "liberal" Pope elected in
1846, and Charles Albert, King of Sardinia, the nation that
was destined in due time to absorb the whole of Italy. The influence of Pius IX was of incalculable value. He alone could
reach the great rural population that always lags behind in
every national movement. Even though at the last moment he
balked at sending troops to fight against fellow Catholics he
made the national cause popular with great masses of the
people whom no radical or intellectual propaganda would have
touched. "His adhesion to the cause sanctified it to the peasant
and made it respectable to the bourgeois." [4]

In spite of the zeal of Mazzini, the gallantry of Garibaldi,
and the official blessing of Pius IX, the national movement of
1848 ended in failure. The Italians themselves were not ready
for it. Not until 1859 when Cavour persuaded his countrymen

[3] E. Masi, *Il Risorgimento Italiano*, 2 vols., I, 38.
[4] G. M. Trevelyan, *Manin and the Venetian Revolution* (London, 1923),
p. 166.

to follow Piedmont could Italian unity be achieved, and even then it was not the unity dreamed of by Mazzini.

The great causes of history are never clear-cut, certainly not as clear-cut as Mazzini and Garibaldi believed them to be, but though Mazzini played no part in the actual unification of Italy, these two men in the year 1848–49 arrested the attention and commanded the respect of the civilized world. The exploits of Garibaldi gave the Italians that pride and confidence in themselves without which a people can never be quickened into a nation. Without the *garibaldini* the Roman Republic would have crumbled at the first blow. He proved to the sceptical foreign offices of Europe that Italians were just as capable of heroic action as any other people. As his biographer, G. M. Trevelyan, puts it, "Garibaldi gave to the warfare of the extreme republicans something of the spirit of Thermopylae, so often mouthed by orators whose stock in trade was classical history, but at last brought by the red-shirts into the region of fact."

Mazzini's faith was no less essential to the justification of Italy than Garibaldi's works. His doctrine was a dangerous one and the Fascists were quick to "interpret" it to suit their ends, but Mazzini's nationalism, unlike theirs, was not exclusive. He believe that nations were the citizens of humanity, as individuals are the citizens of the nation, that the free development of the national spirit was the instrument by means of which a richer life for the individual would be achieved. So far as it served that end, the national spirit was a benefit to humanity. As soon as it throws itself athwart that end, it becomes an enormous evil.

Revolutions invariably produce a crop of disillusioned idealists, men like the Girondins in the first French Revolution or Lamartine in the second, who after watching the current of opinion flow as it seems to them in the wrong direction, shrug their shoulders, give up the fight and either creep back into obscurity or are led to the scaffold. Mazzini was not one of those. He was continually being disappointed by the backslidings of his friends and the failure of his plans, but he never grew disillusioned or embittered. To the end of his life he fought for the principles of Young Italy as he had first conceived them in his prison cell in Savona. He quarrelled with Garibaldi, with Manin and with Cavour, but he never lost faith in the ability of humanity to build a better world. He was a great patirot, but his patriotism was a silent thing that recoiled from the display of emotion. He tested it by its fruit in the individual life. No shady character could be a patriot in his eyes. "You must keep your country pure of selfishness," was his maxim of patriotism for Italian workingmen. Today when the world is struggling to raise a superstructure of internationalism on a foundation of individual sovereign states there is no better guide for the bewildered statesman than Giuseppe Mazzini. The world still clings to nationalism. Let us accept that fact, but at the same time let us conceive of nationalism as Mazzini conceived of it—an instrument for ennobling the life of the individual. He wanted, first of all, to emancipate his country from the tyranny of unjust laws and unjust governments. But that was not enough. All his labors for his country had the supreme end in view, that Italian men and women should lead more perfect lives. Only on such a foundation, thought Mazzini, could a durable superstructure ever be raised.

2

MAZZINI AND GARIBALDI

IN THE YEAR 1830, when the King of France was driven into exile and when in every country in Europe the liberals were thrilled with the news of the first successful revolution since 1815, a young Genoese lawyer was arrested on the charge of conspiracy and confined in the fortress of Savona. It turned out that he was the son of Dr. Mazzini, professor of anatomy at the university. The Governor of Genoa complained to Dr. Mazzini that his son Joseph was altogether too fond of solitary walks at night, and that when questioned by the police he was obstinately silent as to the subject of his meditations. "What on earth," wondered the governor, "has he at his age to think about?" Evidently Joseph Mazzini was not one of those fat, sleek-headed men such as sleep o' nights. Like Cassius he had the lean and hungry look that autocratic governments have always distrusted. After three months' solitary confinement in the rock fortress of Savona, where from his window he could see nothing but a patch of sea and a patch of sky and where his only welcome visitor was a greenfinch "full of pretty ways," his case came up for trial before the Senate of Turin and he was acquitted.

Years later Giovanni Ruffini, one of his childhood friends,

wrote a novel about those early days in Genoa containing a strikingly sympathetic portrait of Mazzini in the first phase of his career:

> Fantasio [Mazzini] was my elder by one year. He had a finely shaped head, the forehead spacious and prominent, and eyes black as jet, at times darting lightning. His complexion was pale olive, and his features, remarkably striking altogether, were set, so to speak, in a profusion of flowing black hair, which he wore rather long. The expression of his countenance, grave and almost severe, was softened by a smile of great sweetness, mingled with a certain shrewdness, betraying a rich comic vein. . . . His life was one of retirement and study; the amusements common with young men of his age had no attraction for him. His library, his cigar, his coffee; some occasional walks, rarely in the daytime, and always in solitary places, more frequently in the evening and by moonlight —such were his only pleasures. His morals were irreproachable, his conversation was always chaste. If any of the young companions he gathered around him occasionally indulged in some wanton jest, or expression of double meaning, Fantasio—God bless him!—would put an immediate stop to it by some one word, which never failed of its effect. Such was the influence that the purity of his life, and his incontestable superiority, gave to him.[1]

Mazzini flattered himself that at the time of his arrest he was carrying on his person matter enough for three condemnations: "rifle bullets, a letter in cipher, and the formula of the oath for the second rank of Carbonari." In this delicate situation he showed that coolness and adroitness that characterized him all his life. "I succeeded," he says, "in getting rid of everything." The connection with the Carbonari was in itself more than sufficient to damn him in the eyes of the Genoa police. The Carbonari were an offshoot of Italian Freemansonry with similar ceremonies and a similar elaborate symbolism. God was the Grand Master of the Universe, Christ "our good cousin" the Honorary Grand Master.[2] The Society hatched

---

[1] This novel, *Lorenzo Benoni: Passages in the Life of an Italian: Edited by a Friend*, was published anonymously in Edinburgh in 1853. It ran through several English editions.

[2] The Carbonari oath mentions Christ as "il nostro buon cugino."

plots against all the governments of Italy and initiated ineffective insurrections aiming at the expulsion of the Austrians from
Italy. At one time Byron was chief of the Carbonari in Ravenna
but the revolt which he longed for did not break out during his
lifetime. Mazzini admired the courage and persistence of the
Carbonari but he soon wearied of the elaborate hocus-pocus
that was choking the growth of any genuine patriotism. During his months of solitary confinement he conceived of a society
equally revolutionary but more in harmony with the spirit of
the coming age, a society that would look beyond the liberation of Italy to the intellectual and social uplifting of the
masses of her people.

Upon his release from Savona, although he had been acquitted, Mazzini was not allowed to return to Genoa. The Government offered him a choice of exile or internment in a small
inland town, where presumably his anti-social habits could be
more effectively supervised. He chose exile and set out cheerfully enough for the haven of a free Switzerland, confident that
the Revolution would soon repatriate him. At Geneva he made
the acquaintance of Sismondi and his nice English wife, who
welcomed him cordially but were not as enthusiastic about
Italian unity as he would have liked. They advised him to join
the colony of Italian exiles in Lyons.

No sooner had he arrived in Lyons than he got wind of a
conspiracy for the invasion of Savoy. The republican flag had
already been raised in Romagna, and it was hoped by a few
very optimistic refugees that a simultaneous rising in Savoy
and Piedmont would set the whole peninsula ablaze. French
volunteers had promised their support and the prefect of Lyons
was said to be well disposed. Before the expedition could get
under way the French authorities changed their minds. Louis
Philippe's title to the throne was so questionable that he could
not afford to support insurrections in other lands. The conspiracy petered out ignominiously. Some of the exiles including
Mazzini escaped to Corsica, still bent on aiding the revolutionaries in Romagna, but before they could reach the mainland
the rising had collapsed. It was the first of many disappointments.[3]

Mazzini returned to Marseilles, his ardor only whetted by

---

[3] It was in this insurrection that Louis Napoleon first came into public
notice. He and his older brother Charles both joined the revolutionaries. Charles
died of a fever contracted during the campaign.

failure, and promptly set to work forging a new and more effective instrument for the regeneration of Italy. The Carbonari movement had failed. It had no machinery for simultaneous and concerted action. Worse than that, it had no program, no lofty ideal. During the months of imprisonment at Savona Mazzini had thought out his religion and the manner in which it was to find expression, for to him the independence of Italy was fundamentally a religious or ethical problem. In April, 1831, he founded the republican society of "Young Italy" (*Giovine Italia*). The aim of the society was very definitely set forth in the statutes drawn up by Mazzini himself:

> Young Italy is a brotherhood of Italians who believe in a law of Progress and Duty, and are convinced that Italy is destined to become one nation—convinced also that she possesses sufficient strength within herself to become one, and that the ill success of her former efforts is to be attributed not to weakness, but to the misdirection of the revolutionary elements within her—that the secret of force lies in constancy and unity of effort. They join this association in the firm intent of consecrating both thought and action to the great aim of reconstituting Italy as one independent sovereign nation of free men and equals.[4]

Young Italy was republican and unitarian, that is to say, unity was to be achieved through fusion of the different provinces into one nation rather than through any system of federation. But Mazzini went further than that. He thought of himself as a prophet of righteousness. He and his associates were to be not only the precursors of Italian regeneration but the founders of a new religion.

This was indeed a strange doctrine to most Italian liberals. They were all agreed that the expulsion of the Austrians was the first prerequisite, but they looked for leadership to the Pope or to the House of Savoy. Mazzini's inseparable bases of unity, liberty and independence, seemed to them as impractical as they were undesirable, and the ethical wrapping of his doctrine with its implication that the Pope as a temporal sovereign must go, frankly un-Christian. Farini, a contemporary of Maz-

---

[4] The Italian text will be found in vol. I of the National Edition of Mazzini's writings—*Scritti editi ed inediti*—Imola. 1906 *et seq*. This edition has been in process of publication since 1905, the centenary of Mazzini's birth.

zini, a moderate but a genuine patriot, criticized Mazzini for excluding from his association anyone over forty, thus showing that he "based his calculations on the buoyant enthusiasm of youth and not on judgment and experience." [5] He also resented Mazzini's being a refugee and stirring up factions at home from a safe distance outside the country. "I do not find," says Farini, "that the enterprises of refugees have often been successful. I see, rather, how commonly they failed, and worsened their own condition, as well as that of their friends, and of their native place."

Nevertheless Young Italy grew and prospered. Mazzini and his little band of disciples worked with tireless energy. There were no illustrious names among them, they had no influential friends and no financial resources beyond the voluntary contributions of friends, but they had the faith that moves mountains. Every ship that sailed out of Marseilles bound for Itally carried its quota of Mazzinian tracts. The bundles were put aboard in barrels of pitch or pumice stone. These barrels, secretly marked, were sent by means of commercial agents ignorant of their contents to equally ignorant commission agents in Milan or Genoa, where one of the faithful had been previously warned to pick up his pitch or pumice stone on a certain date. It was not long before the missionaries of Young Italy were pushing their prohibited writings throughout the length and breadth of the peninsula. The Carbonari had preached nothing more definite than a passion for liberty. Young Italy made war against the existing idolatry of material interests. It taught men to think of democracy and social reform, words which in Italy a hundred years ago were charged with tremendous significance. Among those who joined the society was a good-looking young sailor from Nice named Garibaldi, just promoted captain in the Genoese mercantile marine. Garibaldi did not always see eye to eye with Mazzini, but years later when he was the chosen hero of all Europe he bore witness to the galvanizing patriotism of one he was proud to call his friend and teacher.[6]

The success of Young Italy was phenomenal. In less than a year it had become the dominant association of its kind. The scattered remnants of Carbonarism willingly took orders from

[5] Farini, Luigi Carlo. *The Roman State from 1815 to 1850.* London, 1851, 4 vols. I, 81–82.

[6] J. W. Mario, *Supplement to English Translation of Garibaldi's Autobiography,* London, 1889, p. 372.

it. Even Metternich saw the importance of Young Italy and demanded as many copies of the dangerous little newspaper as could be found. By the beginning of 1833 the organization, not yet two years old, was strong enough to think seriously of action. The accession of Charles Albert to the throne of Savoy had already given Mazzini just the publicity he needed. Like many other revolutionary leaders before and since, Mazzini was not unaware of the importance of getting his name before the world. He had accordingly addressed an open letter to "Charles Albert of Savoy, an Italian," exhorting him to become the Napoleon of Italian liberty, and concluding with a threat—"If you do not act, others will, without you and against you." (*Se voi non fate, altri faranno, e senza voi e contro voi.*) [7] As a young man Charles Albert was known to have had nationalist sympathies. He had even been involved in a liberal conspiracy with other army officers from which he had extricated himself with some difficulty. Now that he was crowned King the moment had surely come to act on the generous instincts of his youth, put himself at the head of a national movement and drive the Austrians out of Italy. Young Italy would help him.

If Mazzini really expected the King to head a movement for independence he could not have devised a worse method of approach. Kings do not take kindly to open letters from their subjects, particularly when those letters under a guise of patriotism demand the impossible. It was absurd to think that a revolution could be engineered overnight. The only answer he received was a further sentence of indefinite banishment. But from Mazzini's point of view the letter had served its purpose. It had brought his name before the public and it had proved, at least to his own satisfaction, the hopelessness of looking for leadership to the King of Sardinia. Mazzini never lost an opportunity of putting the ruling princes of Italy in a bad light. He was fond of writing flamboyant letters, and when the letters were ignored, as they always were, he pointed out that the people of Italy must learn to rely on themselves alone. There was no such thing as a really liberal pope or a patriotic king. The temporal power of the Pope, dependent as it was on Austria, and the narrow interests of Piedmont, must always block the way to Italian independence.

The appeal to King Charles Albert did not interrupt the

[7] Mazzini, *Scritti*, II, 75–82.

steady stream of propaganda flowing out from Marseilles. It was not long before all Piedmont was honeycombed with republican societies. By the end of 1832 the French Government, prodded by the Piedmontese police, ordered Mazzini to leave the country. Mazzini read the order and decided to stay where he was. Marseilles was a convenient headquarters and there were plenty of French sympathizers, among them a certain Demosthenes Ollivier whose son grew up to be the last premier under Napoleon III, ready to give him shelter. Even so, to live with the police perpetually on your heels was a dangerous business. For a year he never went out of doors except at night and in disguise. And all the time he was organizing for revolution, building up depots of ammunition and muskets, interviewing likely refugees, signing up volunteers, and writing those pamphlets that breathed into his countrymen a new purpose and a new hope.

War was to be waged upon the Austrians, upon all the governments of Italy, upon the very idea of a prince or a king. Having failed to win over Charles Albert, "Young Italy" undertook to launch a strictly popular revolution. The plan was simple enough. First, republican converts in the Piedmontese army with the help of Mazzini's civilian agents would gain control of a few strategic centres. This success would be followed up by a spontaneous national uprising in the course of which the hated "white coats" would be driven headlong out of Italy over the Brenner Pass. Mazzini never outgrew the idea that the whole country was on the eve of revolution.

By the beginning of 1834 Mazzini felt that the hour of liberation had struck. There had already been too many delays, disappointments, and even tragedies. The unfortunate discovery by the custom-house authorities in Genoa of a double-bottomed trunk containing copies of the *Giovine Italia* together with secret instructions signed "Filippo Strozzi," Mazzini's name as chief of the association, had led to the arrest of Jacopo Ruffini, his closest friend as well as his ablest lieutenant. Ruffini committed suicide in prison rather than run the risk of being tortured into betraying the plans of the Society. The drunken quarrel of two Genoese artillerymen revealed to the police the names of other conspirators. Mazzini never got over the death of Jacopo Ruffini, but nothing could swerve him from his plans. With infinite difficulty he had collected some small store of arms in the cantons of Vaud and Geneva, and had gathered together about a thousand refugees, Italian, German, Swiss and Polish. Under command of General Ramorino, a veteran of the Grand Army—the Piedmont Committee insisted on an experienced soldier leading the expedition—Mazzini's little column was to march through Savoy and join forces with the insurgents of Piedmont. Partly owing to the incompetence if not treachery of Ramorino, who proved to be a very poor specimen of the Grand Army, and partly owing to the inadequacy of the whole plan, the expedition ended in ignominious failure. It was founded on the belief that the Savoyard peasants would rise at the first opportunity and fight for a free Italy. Actually, the Savoyards were not much interested in the rest of Italy, and not at all interested in dying for an unborn republic. A few of the volunteers were rounded up by Piedmontese troops, taken to Chambéry and shot. The main body was disbanded by General Ramorino without ever having come in contact with the enemy.

Young Italy's first enterprise had ended in defeat, and not even in glorious defeat. Everyone was discouraged. The equipment necessary for the expedition had been seized; the slender financial resources of the association were exhausted. Nevertheless Mazzini kept on extending his program. Not content with Young Italy, he laid the foundations for a Young Switzerland, a Young Germany, and a Young Europe. The Savoy fiasco only whetted his ardor. The man was indefatigable. After the first inevitable reaction of despair he recovered himself and set to work to persuade others as well as himself that the defeat was practically equivalent to victory. Why, he inquires, if we are so cowardly, so impotent, and so inept, should we be pursued so ruthlessly? Why, because each one of us represents an idea which must sooner or later cause the downfall of tyrants, because these tyrants know their victories are Pyrrhic victories that must lead ultimately to their defeat.[8]

Mazzini felt he was fighting for all humanity, not just for Italians. He believed that nations, no less than individuals, were created free and equal, but this equality involved duties as well as rights. Nations must learn to share each other's burdens. "Young Europe" was founded at Berne in April, 1834, three days after the failure of the insurrection of Savoy. There was no mistaking the object of the Association. It was designed to help any people rising against their rulers to overthrow the

[8] Mazzini, *Scritti*, III, 383.

government. "I did not deceive myself," says Mazzini, "with any hope of immediate results." In the meantime he turned his attention to Switzerland, where the prospects were more promising. Many of the cantons were ruled by an oligarchy, and the federal executive was powerless to assert its authority. Mazzini got in touch with the leading Swiss liberals, somehow or other funds were provided, and in July, 1835, another Mazzini journal was launched—*La Jeune Suisse*. The Swiss authorities had so far ignored foreign protests about the Ramorino expedition, but a small and none-too-secure republic that harbored conspirators against neighboring Powers was in a very delicate situation. When the conspirators started to agitate for specific reforms in Switzerland the Government decided to act. Writers, printers, all concerned in the publication of *La Jeune Suisse* were arrested. A decree of the Diet condemned Mazzini to expulsion, and forbade his return.

Mazzini had now been expelled from his own country, from France, and from Switzerland. He might have continued his life in hiding, but there were others to be considered besides himself. Giovanni and Agostino Ruffini, brothers of Jacopo who had committed suicide for his sake, had thrown in their lot with him. What right had he to subject them to unnecessary dangers? There was still one country in Europe left that was said to be hospitable to exiles, a country where the police did not hound you and where you could live a free man. Swiss and French officialdom was only too ready to supply passports and safe-conducts for Monsieur Mazzini and his friends. On January 13, 1837, they landed in England. They sailed directly from Calais to Tilbury Docks. It was a cold rough trip, and they were all seasick.

3

Mazzini's first impressions of London were not unpleasant. The customs authorities were polite, and it was a relief to know after seven years of police surveillance that he need have no fear of midnight visits from inquisitive officials. The London fog was mysterious and exciting. It transformed the whole city into something ghostly that reminded him of Ossian's poems. Others might not like it, but he did.

There was only one trouble. London was terribly expensive. A single room cost 40 francs a month, and cigars—Maz-

zini's one extravagance—were threepence each. The little party
that had travelled together—Mazzini, the two Ruffini brothers,
and Angelo Usiglio, a poet and a devoted henchman, who had
joined them in France—insisted on remaining together. It was
not easy to find suitable accommodations within their means.
They moved from the Hotel Sablonnière, where the food was
execrable (*si spesa maledettamente*), to modest lodgings at
24 Goodge Street, Tottenham Court Road, but their landlord
was not able to give them single rooms. An unfurnished cottage
seemed to be the best solution, particularly if the families in
Italy could send them some of the necessities. They needed
everything: sheets, towels, curtains, knives and forks (not necessarily silver), and of course provisions of all kinds, oil, vin-
egar, macaroni, cheese, and sausages. The Mazzini and Ruffini
households must have been staggered by these demands. Probably Signora Mazzini did not confide the full extent of the list
to her husband. The doctor was always harping on the importance of "establishing oneself in an honorable independence."
Surely it was time for Giuseppe to give up this moonshine
about Italian unity, and start earning his living. The doctor
had friends in England, Panizzi who afterwards became Librarian of the British Museum, and the Rossettis, who would
be only too willing to help him. If only Giuseppe were not so
obstinate! Even his mother, who understood him better than
anyone else, began to wonder whether her beloved Giuseppe
were not mistaken in trying to fight things that the rest of the
world seemed willing enough to accept. In one letter she suggested that he might apply for a position in the consul's office
in London. As if he, the founder of Young Italy, the exile with
a price on his head, could think of such a thing! "Do you not
realize," he writes in answer to this strange suggestion, "that all
embassies, consular offices, etc., are and always will be for me
forbidden territory?" It was like urging a soldier to go over
to the enemy's camp.[1]

These were hard days for Mazzini. It was all very well to
write gay letters to his mother about the beautiful unfurnished
cottage, but there was no gaiety in his heart. All through the
year 1836 he had battled his way through what he called a
tempest of doubts. Had he after all been right in urging others

---

[1] "Direste a un soldato d'andare nel campo nemica? Niente, niente, e non
pensiamo a siffate cose." Mazzini, *Scritti*, XII, 313.

to follow him on the path of exile, poverty, and apparently useless sacrifice? Everything he had put his hand to failed. People
were losing faith in him. The Ruffinis themselves were growing
restive. At the moment when he thought he had plumbed the
lowest depths of despair he overheard a friend say: "Let him
alone. He is in his element, conspiring and happy." If this was
what those who professed to love him believed, what chance
was there of being understood by strangers?

London might remind him of Ossian's poems but the interesting atmospheric effects of a London fog hardly compensated for the loneliness of a great city. Yet he had no desire to
make new friends. He would live on his memories. It was impossible for anybody who had been through what he had to
form new ties.[2] The decision to ignore his surroundings and to
wrap himself in the past was all the more remarkable in that
Mazzini was a naturally companionable man whose nature demanded sympathy and affection. He made friends easily, both
men and women; sometimes too easily. There was a Mlle.
Mandrot in Lausanne who had fallen in love with him without
his even being aware of it. The father and mother had shown
him great kindness when he was in Switzerland, but he did
not remember exchanging more than a few words with their
daughter. Now that he was in London she had begun writing
him heartbroken letters. Sometimes he felt there was a curse
on him. He even warned his friends to keep away from him.
He brought unhappiness wherever he went.

Then there was always Giuditta Sidoli, an ardent patriot,
described by the police as "beautiful" and "extremely dangerous." She had nursed Mazzini through a long illness. They
were desperately in love with each other but marriage was out
of the question. The mother of four children—her husband
had died in exile and her father-in-law, a strict conservative
who shared none of her republican sympathies, had wrested the
children from her—how could she dream of settling down to
any domestic life? Mazzini himself knew that marriage was
impossible, but he never felt free to marry anybody else. It was
one of those hopeless situations about which there was nothing
to be done. Time would relieve the suffering but it would never
extinguish the memories. He was always in love with her. He

---

[2] "Affezioni nuove nè so, nè posso, nè voglio averne. Mi bastano le an-
tiche. . . ." Mazzini, *Scritti*, XII, 287.

would never see her again. For a long time they had not even been able to write. Letters from him would involve her with the police and prejudice her chances of getting possession of the children. He would die alone. He had no more happiness to offer, and he did not wish to share his sorrows.[3]

This was the mood in which he arrived in London. Fortunately it did not last. The love for Giuditta Sidoli, deep and lasting though it was, could not preempt his whole life. He was too resilient to live permanently in the past. Gradually the clouds lifted, his writings slowly made their way among English liberals, and he began to feel at home in England. "There," he says, "friendships develop slowly and with difficulty, but nowhere are they so sincere and lasting."

The first of his great English friendships was with the Carlyles. Mazzini made the acquaintance of Carlyle in 1837 but it was not until several years later that the acquaintance ripened into anything like a friendship. Mazzini's review of *The French Revolution*, cordial but not entirely eulogistic, resulted in an invitation to dinner, and before long he was dining with the Carlyles regularly every week. At first glance it would seem that the two men could have had little in common. Carlyle, as Mazzini said, comprehended only the individual; the unity of the human race escaped him. To Mazzini, history was not the biography of great men; it was something greater, more divinely mysterious, than all the great men. It was "the earth that bears them, the human race that includes them, the thought of God which stirs within them . . ."[4] Yet the dyspeptic Scotsman thundering against "irrational flabby monsters" like universal suffrage, and the gentle Mazzini—but not so gentle that he could be swept aside by Carlyle's torrent of talk—recognized in each other the essential element of sincerity. There were obvious blind spots in Carlyle, but he knew a genuine man when he saw him. Mazzini made an impression that was unforgettable:

> A small square-headed, bright-eyed, swift yet still, Ligurian figure; beautiful and merciful and fierce; . . . True as steel, the word, the thought of him pure and limpid as water: by nature a little lyrical poet; plenty of fun in him too, and wild emotion, rising to a swift key, with

[3] Mazzini, *Scritti*, XII, 367.
[4] Mazzini, *Scritti*, XXIX, 94.

all that lies between these two extremes. His trade, however, was not to write verses.[5]

Such was Carlyle's impression. Others were struck by the clear olive complexion, the delicately fine features, the wide brow, and the expression grave and almost severe, softened by a smile of extraordinary kindliness. Jane Welsh Carlyle was even more completely won over than her husband. Between Mazzini and Mrs. Carlyle sprang up the kind of friendship that Mazzini needed. He would never love anybody again as he had loved Giuditta, but he always responded to affection, and Jane Carlyle scolded him and teased him, looked after him when he was sick, and generally did her best to prevent him from making himself, as she said, into "minced meat for the universe." Her letters are full of Mazzini. He is at Cheyne Row every week, "dining, gossiping and smoking." They are caught regaling themselves with wine figs and gingerbread, and again, much to her annoyance, they are interrupted "just when they have put their two pairs of feet on the fender." Not the least of his virtues in her eyes was that unlike her husband, he seemed to be able to resist the fascinations of Lady Harriet Baring.[6]

If she did not always see eye to eye with Mazzini in his schemes for the regeneration of Italy, that was because her Scotch canniness was outraged by the impracticality of his conspiracies. One day in October, 1842, he came in to see her in high spirits:

> Mazzini was here yesterday—radiant over an *aviso interessante* (sic) which he produced from his pocket, setting forth that one Mussi, or some such name, had discovered a power for regulating balloons as perfectly as a steamboat or railway carriage, in confirmation whereof behold certificates from the Grand Duke of Tuscany and the heads of the Academy of Science at Florence, etc., etc., before whom his model had been displayed! The practical application you cannot for a moment be at a loss about! The man, having not a shilling in the world, no means of subsistence but simply this small model-balloon,

---

[5] J. A. Froude, *T. Carlyle, A History of His Life in London*, 2 vols. (London, 1884), I, 454.
[6] Jane Welsh Carlyle, *Letters to Her Family*, edited by Leonard Huxley (London, 1924), p. 179.

is willing to sell his secret for the trifling sum of two thousand pounds. If Mazzini can find him work in the interim, the man may be induced not to part with it!—till some member of the Association in Italy may be found to make the purchase. "Then," says Mazzini, "the power of directing balloons ours: all is ours!" "You mean you would invade Italy in balloons?—that the Association would descend on the Austrians out of the skies!" "Exactly! . . ." All this with eyes flashing hope, faith and generous self-devotion! Surely between the highest virtue and the beginning of madness the line of separation is infinitesimally small! But is it not almost a desecration, a crime ever to jest with that man? He lives, moves and has his being in truth, and take him out of that, he is as credulous and ignorant as a two-year-old child . . .[7]

Men who set out to make a revolution cannot perhaps afford to calculate too nicely the results of every step they take, but Mazzini was far from being the credulous child Mrs. Carlyle's letter suggests. If he was sometimes childlike in his enthusiasms he was a man in his dogged pertinacity. The man who dreamed of parachuting into Italy—not so fantastic an idea to us as it was to Jane Carlyle—could be severely practical when the occasion demanded. Carlyle's friend, David Masson, found him the most tenacious man he had ever met. Early in 1841 his attention was drawn to the pathetic little organ grinder boys and terra cotta vendors who thronged the streets of London. He discovered that these children, sent over from Italy to make their fortunes in England, were being exploited by a vicious ring of London Italians who herded them in squalid dens, kept them half-starved, and appropriated their earnings. It was not in Mazzini's character to preach the redemption of Italy and neglect the unredeemed little Italy at his door. As soon as he had assured himself of the facts, he raided the Whitechapel haunts of the ring and brought some of the culprits to justice. The thought of building up better citizens for Italy induced him to open up a free school for the boys, where from nine o'clock every evening they might learn reading and writing, as well as something of the civic duties which must eventually be theirs. Along with the night school he

[7] Jane Welsh Carlyle, *Letters to Her Family*, p. 34.

founded an Italian Workingmen's Association, where once again he could spread the tidings of Young Italy. He himself undertook a large share of the teaching and all the responsibility of raising funds for the maintenance of the school. Some of his fashionable subscribers may not have been aware of the tinge of propaganda in his philanthropy, but Mazzini's conception of education could never be divorced from the sacred doctrines of Italian unity. Carlyle growled about "Mazzini's nest of conspirators," but supported the enterprise.

Through his friendship with the Carlyles, the founding of the Italian Free School, and his articles in *Tait's Magazine*, the *Monthly Chronicle*, and various other reviews to which he was now a regular contributor, Mazzini was gradually making a name for himself in literary and political circles. John Stuart Mill and Harriet Martineau, William Lloyd Garrison and Margaret Fuller, these and many others, English and American, were among his friends and acquaintances. With such people he was sure of sympathy and understanding, but something more was needed to force the Italian question upon the mind of the whole country.

The necessary something was provided most unexpectedly by Sir James Graham, the Home Secretary. Acting under instructions from Lord Aberdeen at the Foreign Office, who wished to prevent the hatching of foreign revolutions on English soil, the Home Office had formed the habit of breaking the seals of Mazzini's letters, forwarding any pertinent information to the Austrian Government, and then resealing the letters and sending them on to their destination. Mazzini suspected the tampering with his correspondence. A few ingenious experiments with hairs and sand in the envelopes confirmed the suspicion. He placed the whole matter in the hands of Thomas Duncombe, a radical M. P., who brought it up in the House.

The indignation that swept the country when it became known that the Government was in the habit of opening private letters was still further fanned by the report that two young Italan patriots, the brothers Bandiera, had been seized and shot on the strength of information contained in Mazzini's letters. Later researches have proved that the British Government was not guilty of betraying the Bandieras, but the hue and cry served Mazzini's purpose.[8] Macaulay denounced the

---

[8] See documents published in *The Times,* August 12, 22, and 24, 1907.

Government in Parliament, *Punch* published a caricature of Sir James Graham as Paul Pry at the Post Office,[9] and Carlyle wrote a generous letter to *The Times* declaring that though he knew nothing of Italian democracies and Young Italy's sorrows, he did know that Mazzini was a man of striking veracity and nobleness of mind. Furthermore, he considered it vital that sealed letters in an English post office should be respected as things sacred. Mazzini himself wrote a masterly letter to Sir James Graham. Hitherto his words had reached only a small circle; now he had the attention of all England. Englishmen were naturally concerned with the gross interference with their rights, but he, Mazzini, would have them know that there were other, even more momentous, questions at stake.

Englishmen were being assured that all was quiet in Italy. Yes, that was true. In Italy nothing speaks. Silence is the common law. The people are silent by reason of terror; the masters are silent from policy. One might fancy the very steps of the scaffold were spread with velvet, so little noise do heads make when they fall.

The words struck home. Carlyle was not far wrong in asserting that the best thing that had ever befallen Mazzini was the opening of his letters. It marked, as one of his biographers has said, "the beginning in England of that pro-Italian interest and growing sentiment which Garibaldi's later exploits were to excite to passionate sincerity."[10] Unwittingly Sir James Graham had swung British opinion in the direction Mazzini wanted.

Of all the expressions of sympathetic indignation that poured in on him the tribute that bore the greatest personal consequences was that of the Ashurst family. William Ashurst was one of those vigorous-minded Englishmen of the nineteenth century whose radicalism does not fit into the conventional picture of Victorian complacency. As a solicitor, his reputation for befriending the oppressed was such that he once received a letter from a persecuted Russian, addressed simply to "The Old Jews' Advocate, London."[11] His four daughters were "emancipated" women, who smoked, studied art, discussed util-

[9] *Punch*, VII, 7.
[10] G. O. Griffith, *Mazzini*, London, 1932, p. 167.
[11] *Mazzini's Letters to an English Family*. Edited by E. F. Richards, 3 vols. London, 1920. I, 23.

itarianism, and read the novels of George Sand. In a letter to his mother Mazzini described the Ashursts as "a strange and excellent family": three sisters smoked; the fourth brought him flowers and took tea in his house—"all capital crimes against English mores!" [12] According to Mrs. Carlyle, the Ashursts made themselves ridiculous by pursuing Mazzini, but he managed to become a part of their family circle without sacrificing weekly visits to Cheyne Row. One of the daughters, Emilie, subsequently married an Italian and wrote the first and most eulogistic of the many Mazzini biographies.[13] When asked what her religion was, she used habitually to answer: "I am a Mazzinian." The devotion of Jane Welsh Carlyle and the Ashursts compensated, as far as anything could compensate, for the spiritual loneliness from which Mazzini could never escape. Even in his own beloved Italy, to which events were now drawing him, he was never to know the joy of complete "oneness" with the people around him. Wherever he went, he dragged the chain of exile behind him.[14]

4

On the night of April 8, 1848, Mazzini wrote to his mother from Milan that the crowds were shouting *Viva Mazzini!* under his window. It was a moment that might well have given him, as he knew it would give his mother, a thrill of pride. The fall of Louis Philippe had opened the Continent to him, and here he was—back in Italy—after seventeen years of exile. At the frontier the customs-house officers greeted him with his own watchwords. For once, the prophet was not without honor in his own country. Everywhere he was recognized and acclaimed. Was not his free Italy almost an accomplished fact? The Austrians had been driven out of Milan, a republic had been proclaimed in Venice, Metternich was in flight from Vienna, and Italian soldiers in the service of Austria were deserting by hundreds. The very day after he arrived in Milan the entire Ceccopieri brigade, 2000 strong, had passed under his windows shouting *Viva l'Italia!* And yet after a few weeks in Milan he writes to Emilie Ashurst: "I cannot deny my feel-

---

[12] Cited by Harry W. Rudman, *Italian Nationalism and English Letters* (New York, 1940), p. 73.

[13] E. A. Venturi, *Joseph Mazzini: A Memoir* (London, 1875).

[14] Mazzini, *Scritti*, XXXV, 97.

ing entirely an exile in my country; feeding my soul with its own substance, like the Pelican with its little ones." Always there were antagonistic forces at work in Italy, even in this glorious springtime of revolution, so-called "moderates" who put aside as a dream the goal of Italian unity, which was to Mazzini the most important thing of all, and would substitute for it a kingdom of northern Italy or a federation of states under the presidency of the Pope. Always men swerved away from his conception of an Italian nation as if it were something impractical, the idle fancy of a few refugees who had lived out of Italy so long that they had lost whatever understanding they may once have had of things as they actually were.

The guiding spirits among the moderates were the Abbé Gioberti, Count Cesare Balbo, and the Marquis Massimo d'Azeglio, all three accomplished men of letters who preached the necessity of liberal reforms but steered away from the stony road of revolution. Vincenzo Gioberti, a Turin priest who had been exiled in the early days of Charles Albert for suspected sympathy with Mazzini's Young Italy, had grown wiser or at least more cautious with the years. In 1843 he published a book on the civil and moral primacy of the Italians (*Il Primato civile e morale degli Italiani*) which was well calculated to flatter the sensibilities of his countrymen. By appeals to history and geography he claimed to show that Italy alone had the qualities to become the leader of nations, and that though for the moment she had almost completely lost that leadership it was still within her power to recover it. At the beginning of his career Gioberti was a Mazzinian, but while Mazzini expected the new Italy to be born out of popular revolution Gioberti relied on the regenerating power of Catholicism. Everything that could be construed as progress had to be grafted on to the trunk of Catholic tradition. The right man in the Vatican would promote an Italian confederation of which he would be President. A confederation of Italian rulers, presided over by the Pope and fortified by the consent of Christian peoples—that was the surest guarantee of liberty and Italian *grandezza*.

What would be the attitude of this confederation toward Austria? Gioberti was significantly silent on this issue. He did not believe in Italian unity, and consequently he did not find it necessary to mention the Austrian occupation. Cesare Balbo's treatise on the hopes of Italy (*Delle Speranze d'Italia*) published a few months after Gioberti's *Primato*, found an agreeably painless solution of the Austrian problem. Balbo was an old Napoleonic officer who had served the Empire in Florence, Rome and Paris. As the president of Charles Albert's first constitutional cabinet he was one of those champions of moderation to whom sovereigns who have renounced absolutism instinctively turn. "A safe tiller-man for a quiet voyage" is William Roscoe Thayer's description of him, but at least he had wit enough to see that neither internal reform nor political federation was feasible until the Austrians had been expelled. Independence must be sought before all else, but Balbo thought independence might be attained without war. The approaching break-up of the Turkish Empire might entice Austria eastward, and thus allow her to make Italy a present of her independence. Unlike Gioberti, Balbo planted his hopes in Turin rather than in Rome. Around him rallied the so-called Piedmontese school, who insisted that if there were to be a league or confederation of princes it should be headed by the King of Sardinia.

Balbo's plea for faith in Italy's future was echoed by his friend the Piedmontese aristocrat, Massimo d'Azeglio. Already in 1846 a popular man of the world, a novelist and an artist, Massimi d'Azeglio suddenly found himself swept into fame by the publication of a pamphlet on the incompetence of the papal government. D'Azeglio had undertaken an unofficial mission to the province of Romagna to investigate the brutalities that were said to have followed on the suppression of the insurrection of Rimini in September, 1845. The results of this investigation were contained in the short but scathing *Recent Events in Romagna (Gli ultimi casi di Romagna)*, in which he pointed out the terrible disparity between the sordid practices of the papal government and the divine principles which it professed. The indictment was all the more effective in that Massimo d'Azeglio was no revolutionary fanatic. He deplored the petty local revolts which always ended in bloodshed and failure. Let the people bide their time, let them put their trust in Piedmont and in Charles Albert, the king with an Italian soul. When the time came for the Italians to fight, everyone must fight, but first they must school themselves by organizing public opinion. The alternative to revolt was a spirited and unremitting public protest. The time was not ripe for war.

Such was the doctrine of the moderates, and it was a doctrine that Mazzini found wholly unpalatable. Of course the time was not ripe for war. It never would be for men like Gioberti, Balbo and Massimo d'Azeglio, who could never bring themselves to contemplate an Italy free from the domination of Pope or King. They prattled about railways and banks, agricultural societies and scientific congresses, as if these things, admirable as they were, could ever make a nation. As for d'Azeglio, he was

> narrow in his political conceptions; narrow in his love for his country, which amounts to a little feeling of pride and nothing else; despising the people; sensuous in his life; a sceptic in everything, from woman to religion; a true emanation of the eighteenth century.[1]

These men were the servants, rather than the masters, of events. They possessed little of that faith that creates new forces and rejects the experience of history. Yes, it was true that Italy had never been united since the Roman Empire, but under the aegis of "God and the people" (Mazzini's watchword) a new Italy was being born. This was what the "Albertists" and the Papalists, all the "moderate" men who were so anxious to avoid the risks of revolution, could not or would not understand. So it was that when, after the "Five Glorious Days" of street fighting in Milan culminating in the defeat of the Austrian garrison, Charles Albert declared war against Austria, and when first Lombardy and then Venice voted for fusion with Piedmont, Mazzini was disgusted rather than elated. A swollen Savoy monarchy was no substitute in his eyes for the Federal Republic, the "thing of the people," to which he had dedicated his life. Metternich, the reactionary chancellor, he had always recognized as an enemy, but there were other enemies as well— practical men who would have nothing to do with his utopias. Between him and his splendid vision of an Italian republic that was to be the center of a new moral unity for Europe and mankind, loomed the ever more powerful house of Savoy and the massive bulk of the papacy. With them there might be an occasional truce, but any lasting peace founded on mutual respect was out of the question.

Gregory XVI, the Pope who quarreled with Lamennais and alienated liberal Catholicism in France, had only been dead two weeks when the Sacred College, acting in a great hurry so as to elect their candidate before the foreign cardinals

[1] Mazzini, *English Letters*, I, 266.

arrived, chose Cardinal Mastai Ferretti, Bishop of Imola, to take his place. The new Pope was elected on June 16, 1846; he announced that he would take the name Pius IX. He was a likable, good-looking man, fifty-four years old, with kind eyes and a winning smile. If he was a little too anxious to make friends, that was not a fault that the Roman populace would hold against him. The death of Gregory XVI opened the hearts of all good Catholics to the hope of something new. His government had been a byword of corruption and incompetence all over Europe. The cardinals did not want a great reformer or a fanatic "Italian," but they did want someone who could administer his domains with reasonable honesty and efficiency, someone, too, who was sufficiently of his time to approve of railways, gas lighting, savings banks, and the telegraph—innovations which Gregory XVI had invariably condemned. Two of the cardinals are said to have discussed the election among themselves: "Who will be the next Pope?" "If the Holy Spirit has anything to do with the elections it will be Mastai; if the Devil meddles in it, it will be you or I." [2]

The election made no immediate impression on the Italian people. Cardinal Mastai was an unknown quantity. As Bishop of Imola, a small town in the Romagna, a district that was always in revolt against papal rule, he had won golden opinions by his moderation and kindliness, but Imola was a long way from Rome. Few people outside his diocese knew anything about the new Pope, except that as a young man he had visited South America on a diplomatic mission—he was the first Pope to have seen the New World—and that he was reported to be generally sympathetic to reform movements. Metternich would have preferred someone whose opinions on important subjects were more definitely known. Could it be, as Metternich had heard, that Pius IX was a liberal? Surely a liberal in the Vatican would be the strangest of all the strange things he had witnessed in his lifetime.

The first act of the new Pope, the proclamation of a general amnesty for all political prisoners throughout the Papal State, seemed to confirm Metternich's worst fears. The amnesty freed 394 prisoners and restored to Italy 477 political exiles. More important than that, it started a wave of enthusiastic liberalism throughout Italy. The news was received in Rome with the wildest excitement. "It seemed," said Farini, a his-

[2] E. Masi, *Il Risorgimento Italiano*, Firenze, 1917. 2 vols. II, 76.

torian who is not by any means a wholehearted admirer of Pius IX, "as though a ray from the love of God had unexpectedly descended on the Eternal City." [3] Day after day crowds surged into the square in front of the Quirinal Palace, shouting *Viva Pio Nono!* and clamoring for the papal blessing. Whenever he went out young men would lie in wait for his carriage, unharness the horses, and insist on dragging the vehicle themselves. Almost overnight the Pope had become the most popular man in Europe. The excitement was understandable. For the first time within the memory of living men the Vatican, instead of thundering imprecations upon an already troubled world, had spoken a word of Christian charity. To the populace of Rome the amnesty meant a great deal more than it said. It meant that the Pope was an "Italian" at heart, that the Vatican had declared its independence of Austria, that the new head of the Christian church was an enlightened ruler who had sounded the death knell of human misery. Rossi, the French ambassador in Rome, wrote to Guizot: "Peace is now signed . . . between the Holy See and the populations of its states. Yesterday I said to a cardinal with perfect sincerity, 'Today I know of only one person who could make the whole of this country rise like one man: it is Pius IX.' " [4]

Actually the Pope was nothing like the Carlyle hero the people supposed him to be. He was a kindly man blessed with a gift of inspiring affection wherever he went, but he was not a man of any great executive ability or intellectual distinction. He himself regretted that people wanted to make a Napoleon out of him whereas he was nothing more than a poor country priest. The amnesty was followed up by various other administrative reforms which encouraged men to believe that Pius IX, as Gioberti said, had reconciled men to religion by proving himself a friend of civilization. The air was thick with schemes of charity and education, with projects of railways, projects for grappling with the terrible problem of unemployment and for reforming the outworn criminal code. Meanwhile he set an example of plain living by selling most of his horses, reducing the number of courses at his dinners from seven to four, and limiting the quantities of ice cream that Gregory XVI had been in the habit of serving to his friends in the papal gardens. [5]

[3] Farini, *op. cit.*, I, 181.
[4] Berkeley, *Italy in the Making*, p. 50.
[5] Vimercati, César, *Histoire de la Guerre en Italie* (Paris, 1857), p. 31.

One small incident seems to have won more popular sympathy than all the others. On July 2, the Feast of the Visitation, the Pope actually walked to church. The Roman people had been accustomed to rulers who drove about the city surrounded by a great train of armed guards. The sight of the Holy Father strolling along the street without any retinue of servants hedging him off from his flock, gave immense pleasure. It was a long time since any Pope had set such an example of apostolic simplicity.

By the beginning of 1847 Pius IX had reached the high-water mark of his popularity. Not only in Italy but in France and even in Protestant England "the world saw," says Carlyle, "with thoughtless joy, which might very well have been thoughtful joy, a real miracle not hitherto considered possible in the world—a reforming Pope." [6] Guizot and Lord Palmerston were genuinely delighted. They were not interested in the unification of Italy, but administrative reforms within the papal dominions would keep the Austrians in check and prevent their further expansion through the peninsula. The British Government had no ambassador in Rome, but, in order to show his sympathy with the cause of liberalism, Palmerston sent out Lord Minto to Italy as a Whig propagandist with a roving commission to proceed from state to state advising and encouraging Italian sovereigns to continue their liberal reforms. Besides these rather indefinite duties he had a secret mission to perform with Pius IX: he was to ask His Holiness to "interpose his authority" to forbid priestly agitation in Ireland. [7]

During this honeymoon period, before the Pope realized that reforms must lead to political concessions that he was not prepared to grant, no stranger of any importance set foot in Italy without paying his respects to this extraordinary man (*questo miracolo di papa*) who had suddenly become the idol of his people. Rome was kept in a fever of excitement by the visits of celebrities—Prince Maximilian of Bavaria; the Prince de Joinville, son of Louis Philippe; Daniel O'Connell, the Irish patriot, who hoped to invigorate himself by the benediction of the Holy Father but died before he could reach Rome; Richard Cobden, the great apostle of free trade; and perhaps most remarkable of all as an acknowledgment of papal prestige, Chekib Effendi, the Turkish ambassador at Vienna.

[6] Carlyle, *Latter Day Pamphlets*, No. 1.
[7] Berkeley, *op. cit.*, p. 345.

Chekib Effendi expressed himself in the most complimentary terms:

> As at a former time the Queen of Sheba came to salute King Solomon, so the Envoy of the Sublime Porte is come today to render homage, in the name of his Lord, to Pope Pius IX. As the wonderful and lofty acts of his Holiness not only have filled Europe with the sound of his praises, but have spread throughout the whole world, my potent Master has honored me with a commission to tender to the sovereign Person of the Pope the most cordial congratulations on his elevation to the throne of the Prince of the Apostles.[8]

All through 1847 messages of congratulation continued to pour in on him from every nation in the world. Rossini wrote a cantata in his honor that was performed in the great senatorial hall of the Capitol. Torchlight processions would march to the Quirinal in the warm summer nights, and the Pope from his balcony would bless the kneeling multitude. It was roses, roses, all the way.

While Pius IX was basking in the sunshine of this unheard-of popularity did he ever wonder how it would all end? Professor Masi, the great historian of the Risorgimento, thinks that neither the Pope nor the people knew where they were going, but there was one Italian at least, an exile living in London, who knew that the Pope's popularity could never last. Mazzini was disgusted by the enthusiasm of his English friends for the reforming Pope.

> I am furious against your countrymen! [he writes to the Ashursts] I cannot meet with any one of my English acquaintances by the street, without being complimented, congratulated with—guess—the Pope! The Pope has forgiven! The Pope has lowered the duties on cotton and raw silk! Therefore go and feel happy! The bright days of Italian regeneration have begun—and so forth in newspaper style. As if we could clothe our soul with cotton and forgiveness of other people's sins![9]

The reason for this outburst is understandable. Mazzini knew that the Pope was being jockeyed by well-meaning mod-

[8] Farini, *op. cit.*, I, 211.
[9] Mazzzini, *English Letters,* I, 38.

erates into an impossible position. They wanted him to become a national leader, a role for which he had no qualifications and no desire. How could the Pope discharge his duties as the president of a league of Italian states, which were all straining at the leash against Austria, and at the same time maintain his position as head of the Catholic Church, of which Austria was the chief mainstay?

Mazzini had never believed that the salvation of Italy could be achieved "now or at any future time by Prince, Pope or King," but he wrote an open letter to Pius IX, just as he had written to King Charles Albert, urging him to put himself at the head of the national movement. "Italian unity was a thing of God . . . It would be achieved with him or without him." (*L'unità italiana è cosa di Dio . . . Si compierà con voi o senza di voi.*) [10] Either he must break with tradition and go forward, regardless of Austria and the Jesuits, or he must settle back in the old papal rut and let the future of Italy be decided by others. With Mazzini it was always "either . . . or." His method with popes and kings never varied. He would present the case to them, shorn of all its complications, as one would to a slow-witted child, knowing perfectly well that they would balk at the terrible simplicity of his conclusions. That was precisely what Mazzini wanted. He must show the moderates that they were living in a fool's paradise. A few years ago they had pinned their hopes on the King of Sardinia, today it was the Pope, tomorrow it might be the king of Naples. When would they learn that Italy could only become a nation when the people learned to rely upon themselves? Enlightened rulers in the various Italian states, such as the Pope and the King of Sardinia appeared to be, were more of a menace from his point of view than Metternich himself. If the Papal States, Piedmont, and Tuscany, were well administered, the fires of Italian patriotism that he had been stoking for nearly twenty years would inevitably die down. So it was that when he heard that seventy-six arrests had taken place in Tuscany, "the mildest government we have in Italy," he looked upon it as "a rather fortunate event." [11]

In Rome there were many good Italians who believed that Mazzini was a visionary, and that since God had granted his people a liberal Pope they must work through him rather than

[10] Mazzzini, *Scritti*, XXXVI, 225-33.
[11] Mazzini, *English Letters*, I, 49.

against him. One of the dominant forces in the city was the burly Angelo Brunetti, better known as Ciceruacchio, the man who first won the populace of Rome to a sense of their place in the national movement. Unlike Mazzini, Ciceruacchio had to feel his way from sentimental loyalty to revolutionary liberalism. He was a man of the people, a wine-carter of the Trastevere—one of the famous slums of Rome that is crushed in between the Tiber and the Janiculum. No one in Rome, unless perhaps Pope Pius himself, was more popular than the genial Ciceruacchio, the man with the quick wit and the loud voice who spoke to the people in the natural eloquence of the Italian market place. As a young man he had been a Carbonaro and a member of Mazzini's Young Italy; now, in 1847, he was the leader, if not the creator, of a boisterous democratic party in Rome, always ready to stage a demonstration for the Pope as a a means of obtaining further concessions. How far his enthusiasm for the Pope was genuine, and how far it was based on the Pope's willingness to yield to his demands is hard to tell. During one of these carefully engineered demonstrations of enthusiasm Ciceruacchio is said to have clambered up on the back of the papal carriage, and unfurled a banner bearing the strange device, "Justice, Holy Father, the people are with you." [12] No wonder the Pope was seized with an attack of faintness. The people seemed to have forgotten that he was the Vicar of Christ, that it was for them to recognize his generosity, not to dictate to him about justice.

Another of his more embarrassing supporters was the noisy, restless Prince of Canino, son of Napoleon's brother Lucien. The Prince of Canino was an ornithologist and a revolutionary politician. As a young man he had emigrated to America, married his cousin Zénaïde, the daughter of Joseph Bonaparte, and published an *American Ornithology* which established his scientific reputation. On his return to Italy he managed to combine his strangely assorted interests by founding scientific congresses which were held annually in different parts of Italy. These congresses were among the forces that made the new nationalism. It was impossible for cultivated Italians from Piedmont, from Rome, from Naples, to meet together year after year without giving something of a national complexion to their meetings. Economic questions suggested a customs league, social problems led up to politics, geography to

[12] G. Spada, *Storia della revoluzione di Roma*, Roma, 1868. 3 vols. II, 10.

free-spoken talk of Italy. At these sittings the Prince of Canino made a regular practice of turning the conversation to politics, praising Pius IX to the skies, and abusing Austria, Metternich and the Jesuits. The discussions of the Congress at the meeting in Genoa, December, 1846, were more than usually inflammatory. At Genoa "this strange individual (the Prince of Canino) began his career as a notable busybody in theatrical politics." [13]

Surrounded by supporters like Ciceruacchio and the Prince of Canino on the one hand, and reactionary ecclesiastics who disapproved of any change on the other, Pius IX can hardly be blamed for not living up to the extravagant hopes founded on the amnesty and the early reforms. After all, he was only a reformer, and not a very radical reformer at that. Once he had recalled the exiles, authorized the Civil Guard, and granted a partial freedom of the press and a consultative assembly, his stock of mild benevolence was exhausted. By that time the people had begun to think of a pope who would rule as a constitutional monarch obedient to their wishes. In other words they were thinking of a pope who would surrender to their clamor for a war against Austria. At last the logic of events had driven the Pope into the dilemma Mazzini had foreseen. A secret letter from Delessert, the Paris prefect of police, to Guizot, dated January 1848, indicates how persistently Mazzini was working for a republic:

> I am told that Mazzini has arrived in Paris to consult with such members of "Young Italy" as happen to be here about the means of raising money for sending agents into Tuscany, Piedmont, Rome and Naples, with instructions to support the existing movement and to ingratiate themselves with the patriots. They have been advised to study the character of Ciceruacchio, the popular leader in Rome, and to draw him into their party by inducing him to believe that everything will be done for the greater glory of Pius IX. In other words, the plan of Mazzini is to avail himself of the present excitement to further the plans of "Young Italy," which repudiates monarchy under any form. [14]

By the spring of 1848 the Pope had about reached the end of his tether. He was now begging the people not to make

[13] Farini, *op. cit.*, I, 195.
[14] Mazzini, *Scritti*, XXXIII, 41.

demands upon him (*i.e.*, a declaration of war against Austria) that he could not possibly grant. As the head of a church that prided itself above all things on being Catholic, he could not identify himself with the aspirations of one nation. When he used the phrase *Benedite, Gran Dio, l'Italia* (O Lord God, bless Italy), he made it clear that he was not blessing the war. Mazzini was satisfied that he was witnessing "the last great agony of Popedom-Authority."

5

The opening gun of the revolutions of 1848 was fired by the Sicilians in Palermo, six weeks before Louis Philippe was driven out of Paris. The Sicilians were not interested in federation or fusion, in a league of free states or a united Italian republic. What they wanted above all things was to free themselves from the hated Neapolitans. Once free they intended to re-establish the Constitution of 1812, enjoyed during the Napoleonic era when Sicily, detached from Naples, was living under the protection of the British navy. Inspired, perhaps, by all the excitement in Rome, the Sicilians issued a proclamation on January 10, announcing a rising for January 12, the birthday of Ferdinand, King of Naples. Revolutionaries do not usually announce their plans beforehand, but this was an unusual revolution. For once, priests, nobles and peasants were fighting side by side. Insurrections are more apt to succeed because of the weakness of the party in power than because of the skill of the conspirators. Certainly that was true in this case. The Neapolitan army proved extraordinarily incompetent, and within two weeks the island was free. Unfortunately the Sicilians ignored the wise advice of Mazzini, not to be satisfied with their successful revolt aganst Naples, but to think of themselves as having struck the first blow for a united Italy.[1] That was demanding too much of a people who only gradually learned to think of themselves as having anything in common with Italians in Piedmont or Tuscany. A few months later, when Piedmont declared war against Austria and summoned the other states of Italy to join in the struggle for independence, the Sicilian fear of the Neapolitans prevented their responding to the appeal of Charles Albert in any numbers,

---

[1] Mazzini's pamphlet, *Ai Siciliani,* was published in Paris in 1848 shortly **after** the insurrection.

but they sent a detachment of a hundred men to show their good will.

The triumph of the Sicilians, short-lived though it was, seemed to justify the Mazzinian belief that any popular uprising was bound to succeed. One concerted push and the rickety fabric of despotism would collapse. Within a year the lava of revolution boiled over from Palermo to Paris, and from Venice to Vienna, Prague, Budapest and Berlin. In Italy the chapter of reforms was closed, and the chapter of constitutions began. Ferdinand II, known as King Bomba on account of the bombardment of Messina, badgered by the Pope and King Charles Albert to make a few concessions to the liberal spirit of the times, decided to go them all one better. On January 29 he forestalled a revolution and at the same time he put himself in the forefront of liberal rulers of Italy by promising his people a constitution. The so-called "reforming" states had wanted to coerce him into doing something he did not want; now he would coerce them.[2] Representative government, liberty of the press, a civic guard, the expulsion of the Jesuits, whatever was wanted he would grant with the mental reservation that what had been freely granted could be freely taken away.

The example set by King Ferdinand, hitherto known as the most reactionary ruler in Italy, was one that had to be copied by the other states. The moderates regretted that first by an excess of obstinacy, and then by a new excess of weakness and of haste, he had shifted the Italian movement off the line of measured progress. Everywhere men were standing on tiptoe expecting more and more extensive changes in the government. Whenever a courier arrived in the market place, men would crowd around him to find out if a constitution had been granted, or was about to be granted, in the neighboring state. Mazzini was disgusted that "that most infamous king should be hailed as a reformer"[3] but, infamous or not, King Bomba forced the other rulers of Italy into granting free assemblies, and without free assemblies the sentiment against Austria would never have found an outlet.

Between the end of January and the middle of March the Kingdom of Naples, Kingdom of Piedmont, the Duchy of Tuscany and the Papal States, all passed from absolute to

[2] "Ils ont voulu me pousser, je les pousserai à mon tour." Vimercati, *op. cit.*, 61. Cf. also Spada, *op. cit.*, II, 29.
[3] Mazzini, *Scritti*, XXXV, 15.

constitutional government. Strange that these constitutions should all have been built on the French model of 1830, and that, before the finishing touches could be added, the model that the liberals had been so anxious to copy was toppled over by the Paris mob! Karl Marx complained that "the Revolution of February upset, in France, the very same sort of government which the Prussian bourgeoisie were going to set up in their own country." [4] If that was true of the Prussian bourgeoisie it was equally true of the Italian, who was no less convinced that the Orleans Monarchy represented the summit of political enlightenment. The notion that a constitution, any constitution, would make men happy as well as rich, died hard. Faith in political machinery, in a brand-new constitution or in the extension of the franchise, was the great fallacy from which nineteenth century liberalism never freed itself. Mazzini may have been an impractical idealist, as his enemies charged, but he was one of the few liberals of his generation who realized that liberty was a means and not an end, and that democracy implied duties as well as rights.

While constitutional government was finding its feet in Piedmont, revolutionary fires were breaking out all over Europe. On February 24 Louis Philippe abdicated. When the news of the Provisional Government reached St. Petersburg the Emperor Nicholas, so it is said, strode into the ballroom of the palace and silenced the music with the words, "Saddle your horses, gentlemen. France has proclaimed a republic." Those ominous words recalled the evil days of 1791 when the establishment of a French republic had heralded a war that ended by engulfing all Europe. Little as he cared for the bastard monarchy of Louis Philippe, the Russian emperor would fight to defend it. Not for a moment would he hesitate to accept the challenge to civilization thrown down by the wild men in Paris. On March 1 the French catastrophe was known throughout Austria. On March 4 Kossuth, one of the great revolutionary orators of all time, made a ringing speech against "the preposterous policy of the Austrian ministers." In Bavaria the Lola Montez scandal compelled King Ludwig to abdicate in favor of his son Maximilian. In Paris, the forcing-house of revolution, where bar-room republicans of every nation were congregating, refugee Poles, Germans, Italians, Irish, were clamoring for arms and demanding that France should once again declare

[4] Karl Marx, *Revolution and Counter-Revolution*, Chicago, p. 68.

war against reactionary governments all over the world. The Chartists were marching on London, Metternich and Guizot had fallen, Louis Philippe was living like any other bourgeois in a Surrey villa—how was it all to end?

For Austria it was a sad time. The governing power had fallen into the hands of insignificant men, honest and respectable but without authority or discernment, and already more or less won over to the ideas which it was their duty to resist. Metternich, who seemed all-powerful, complained that though he had governed Europe sometimes he had never governed Austria. The Emperor Ferdinand, supremely obstinate as only the very stupid can be, refused to accept even the very limited reforms Metternich recommended. The old chancellor, who had watched the Napoleonic hurricane spend itself nearly forty years earlier, knew that another storm was now gathering. In spite of his extraordinary powers as a manipulator, balancing one interest against another, the order that he had so long sustained was nearing its end. Imperial obstinacy, which took the form of never trusting capable subordinates, lack of energy in the internal administration and the restlessness of subject peoples within the Empire seemed to justify Mazzini in his belief that the whole fabric of Europe was crumbling to pieces.

The Tobacco Riots in Milan, during which the police chief wrote to Vienna for instructions, revealed the growing helplessness of the authorities. In imitation of the Boston Tea Party the inhabitants of Austrian provinces in Italy decided to celebrate the New Year by launching an anti-smoking campaign, partly to strike at a source of the Government revenue, and partly to prove to the world that they were capable of united action. For three days no Italian smoked; whenever a cigar was seen the cry was *Fuori!* "Put it out!" Those who refused to obey were mobbed. Before long the police were contributing to the confusion by arresting innocent bystanders. Then the Austrian soldiers began marching through the streets of Milan puffing cigar smoke in the faces of the inhabitants. Every day the situation grew more tense, and on January 3 there was an outbreak of rioting in which five people were killed and sixty wounded. The shedding of blood was just what was needed to stiffen the determination of the easygoing Milanese and prevent any possibility of reconciliation. Before 1848 there had been plenty of complaints that the Austrian rule was clumsy and bureaucratic, but it was not until the To-bacco Riots that the ridicule changed to hatred.

Massimo d'Azeglio, who had been perfectly content to live in Milan under the Austrian occupation before 1848, wrote a bitter condemnation of Austrian brutality in these riots indicating how completely the sentiments of the aristocracy had changed.[5] Milan was a gay city, much more attractive to a man of the world like D'Azeglio than Turin. The opera house was the magnet and epitome of Italian social life, and though the two front rows were reserved for the army of occupation no anti-Austrian feeling was perceptible. As long as Fanny Ellsler was dancing, what difference did it make who occupied Milan? In his *Recollections*, D'Azeglio admits with shame that in spite of the occupation it was only in Milan he felt he could breathe.[6] Now everything was changed. The river of blood that flowed between Austrians and Italians made it impossible for Massimo d'Azeglio and his pleasure-loving friends to ignore the growth of national sentiment. But was it national sentiment or merely a feeling of intense local patriotism? The Austrians had made themselves generally hated, but when they had been driven out of Italy, what then? Count Hübner, the wisest of Metternich's diplomats, felt that Austria was combating a variety of enemies —enthusiasts for a free and united Italy, liberals from every country in Europe who sympathized with their aspirations, secret societies bent on the destruction of all government, and the traditional ambition of the House of Savoy.[7]

Against these imponderable forces stood the Austrian civil administration, bewildered and incompetent, and a polyglot Austrian army commanded by the eighty-one-year-old Marshal Radetzky. This astonishing old man, Father Radetzky as he was known to his troops, had hammered the seventy thousand Austrians, Hungarians, Poles, Croats and Italians that made up his army into a superb fighting machine. The various races were bound together not by any feeling of patriotism— that was obviously impossible—but by professional loyalty and by devotion to Radetzky himself. On the base of the Radetzky statue in Vienna are inscribed the words of the poet Grillparzer: *In deinem Lager liegt Österreich*, "In your camp lies

[5] M. d'Azeglio, *I Lutti di Lombardia* (Florence, 1848).

[6] "Ed io, un odiatore di professione dello straniero, lo dico colla confusione piu profonda, se voleve tirar un fiato, bisognava tornassi a Milano." *I Miei Ricordi*, new edition, Florence, 1934, p. 292.

[7] Hübner, *Une Année de Ma Vie, 1848–49*, Paris, 1891, p. 47.

Austria." It was literally true. When everything else in Austria was crumbling, Metternich in flight, and Vienna in insurrection, Radetzky stood firm. If he had listened to the counsel of despair from Vienna, the Austrian Empire might have disintegrated in 1848 instead of 1918.

Radetzky had learned his trade in the wars against Napoleon. Whether he was a military genius or not, he was an inspiration to the men he commanded. A hard-bitten old soldier with seventeen campaigns and seven wounds to his credit, an indefatigable worker, genial and fearless, they recognized in him their own virtues and their own vices. The youngest of his illegitimate children was born when he was seventy-nine years old. Whenever he appeared on parade he was greeted with shouts of *Vivat, Evviva, Eljen, Zivio,* the cheers of the German, Italian, Hungarian, and Croatian soldiers. That such a man should have endeared himself to his army is not surprising, but there must have been an unusual quality about him to attract young John Ruskin, who met him in Venice in 1851 and describes him as "one of the kindest of men—his habitual expression was one of overflowing bonhomie, or of fatherly regard for the welfare of all around him." It was not an opinion that would have been shared by the citizens of Milan.[8]

On March 17, when the news of the revolution in Vienna reached Milan, Radetzky must have known that the fires that had been smouldering since the Tobacco Riots would soon break out again. It was an ominous sign when the words "Too late" were pasted over the edict promising to all peoples within the Empire liberty of the press and a national guard. The real question at issue was whether Milan would fight alone or whether the other Italian states would come to her rescue. From Venice the news was most discouraging. Count Palffy and Count Zichy, the civil and military governors, unable to get instructions from Vienna and fearful of precipitating bloodshed, allowed themselves to be talked into evacuating the city. The revolutionary leader in Venice was Daniele Manin, a quiet-spoken scholarly Jewish lawyer, who had endeared himself to the people in Venice by his continual agitation against the illegalities of Austrian government. Unlike Mazzini, Manin believed in open agitation by constitutional methods instead of conspiracies and secret societies. He adopted wholeheartedly Massimo d'Azeglio's advice to patriots to conspire in the

[8] Ruskin, *Works*, ed. Cook and Wedderburn (London, 1903), XVIII, 539.

market-place by the light of day. Nothing delighted him more than to produce proof after proof that Austria did not even abide by her own laws when the expression of political opinion was concerned. Once, when he was getting the better of an argument, an Austrian police officer ordered him to be silent. "Is this a piece of advice or an order?" demanded Manin. "If it is advice I reject it. If it is an order it is unjust, and I shall yield only to force." Such a man was in many ways more of a thorn in the side of the authorities than Mazzini.

He had been arrested in January together with his friend Niccolò Tommaseo, a Dalmatian man of letters and an ardent republican though not of the Mazzinian brand, on a vague charge of inflaming the public mind against the authorities. A few weeks later, when rumors of Metternich's fall began circulating in Venice, the crowd staged a demonstration and demanded the release of the two patriots. Count Palffy temporized and finally decided on a policy of appeasement. Perhaps if Manin and Tommaseo were released they would prevent the spread of disorder, and rally decent people to the support of the Government. Up till his imprisonment Manin had never demanded more for Venice than self-government within the Austrian Empire, but as soon as he was liberated his tactics changed. He announced that the only way to avoid bloodshed was for Count Palffy to authorize the formation of a Civic Guard. Again Palffy yielded, and for a moment it looked as if there might be a reconciliation.

Manin's next step was to secure the Arsenal, which would deliver into the hands of the patriots the arms and ammunition they so badly needed. The task seemed hopeless. The Austrians had 7000 troops within call, besides the ships in the harbor, but this appearance of strength was deceptive. Most of the troops were Italians or Dalmatians. Fortunately for Manin, at a critical moment Captain Marinovich, the acting commander of the fort, an Austrian officer of the Radetzky type opposed to any concessions, was murdered by workmen in the Arsenal. Manin deplored the murder—a peaceful revolution was what he wanted—but the death of Marinovich removed the last serious obstacle in his path. Prompt action was needed to save Venice from Austrian revenge.

Acting against the advice of Tommaseo, who had not yet reached the point of believing that the fall of the Austrian Government was possible, Manin set out for the Arsenal with a handful of followers. He knew that he had the sympathy of the workmen there and of the bulk of the marines on guard. Their attitude and Manin's self-confidence frightened the officer in charge into surrendering the keys. From that moment Manin was master of the situation; with the Arsenal in his hands nothing remained for the Austrian authorities but capitulation. They had been driven from one concession to another until finally, without firing a shot, they were forced to abandon the city, surrender the fleet, and evacuate the army.

On March 23, after a solemn service in St. Marks, the Civic Guard and the sovereign people gathered in the piazza outside and elected Daniele Manin by acclamation President of the Venetian Republic. It was an amazing triumph of character. There was nothing of the demagogue about Manin. He never flattered people or told them what he did not believe himself. More flexible than Mazzini and less of an opportunist than Cavour, he was closer to the people than either. No one approached the question of fusion *vs.* federation with more common sense. On July 4, when the newly elected Assembly was hesitating whether to vote for the union of the Republic of Venice with the Kingdom of Charles Albert, Manin's statesmanlike words carried the day.

> "I am going to ask a great sacrifice," he said, "and I ask it of my own party, the generous Republican party. The enemy is at our gates, counting on our divisions. Let us give them the lie. Let us forget all parties today. Let us show that we are neither Royalists nor Republicans but that we are all Citizens. To the Republicans I say—The future is for us. All that has been done or is being done is provisional. The decision belongs to the Italian Diet at Rome." [9]

A few weeks later when the Piedmontese Army was defeated, and it appeared that Venice had given away her independence for nothing, the Assembly once again turned to Manin for leadership. The fusion had proved a fiasco "but it had also been a great fact. It remained in the minds of men as another milestone on the road of Italian unity, and the day was coming when Manin in exile would pronounce in favour of the union of Venice with the rest of Italy under the Monarchy of Charles Albert's son." [10]

[9] Cited by G. M. Trevelyan, *Manin*, p. 203.
[10] G. M. Trevelyan, *op. cit.*, p. 208.

That decision was a great blow to Mazzinian republicanism but a great victory for the cause of unity. In the spring of 1848 the principle of unity was still a long way from realization. The street fighting in Milan, the "Five Glorious Days" from March 18 to March 23, when the people of the city, old and young, men, women and children, armed with whatever they could lay their hands on, drove Radetzky's garrison out of the city, was a miracle of improvisation. With butchers' knives and cooking spits, old fowling pieces and spears snatched from museums and the property rooms of the Scala, the Milanese fought their way into a barracks, where they managed to equip themselves with more up-to-date weapons. In all quarters of the city barricades sprang up like mushrooms. Just as in the Paris revolution, paving stones were torn up, and pianos, beds and sofas were trundled out of the houses to block off the various centers of resistance. No sooner had the Austrians stormed one barricade than the mob surged in behind them to cut off their retreat. Harassed on all sides, with Milanese sharpshooters picking off his men from the room tops, Radetzky wisely decided to retire into the Quadrilateral, the region defended by the four fortresses of Peschiera, Verona, Legnano, and Mantua, there to lick his wounds and wait for reinforcements.

For the people of Milan it was a great achievement. To Mazzini the victory over Radetzky was proof conclusive of the people's ability to manage their own affairs. Simultaneously, but without any previous agreement, the population of Venice and Milan, upon hearing the news from Vienna, had risen as one man and expelled the invader. The two great cities of the north were free; Radetzky had been driven into the Quadrilateral. It remained only for the other states to combine, surround the old lion, cut off his means of communication, and starve him into submission. "The Milanese," wrote Mazzini, "had been sublime, beyond all conception . . . far superior to the Parisians," [11] but unfortunately the Milanese were hopelessly divided among themselves.

The two chief factions were headed by Count Casati, the mayor, an aristocrat and a monarchist, and Carlo Cattaneo, a well-known professor at the university, a federalist-republican and an honest man but not an inspired leader. Casati advised waiting for the Piedmontese Army before risking everything

[11] Mazzini, *English Letters*, I, 84.

in an insurrection. He was the kind of official that exists in all countries who hate to do anything that is not authorized by some properly constituted authority. Cattaneo would have preferred to narrow down the conflict to a struggle between Milanese democracy and the Austrian Army, but when King Charles Albert promised assistance if he were formally asked for it, Cattaneo would not take the responsibility of refusing the help of an army which everyone believed would complete the rout of Austria. As a moderate he believed that education, agricultural improvements, and the introduction of railways must take precedence over any political movement. Though not a rebel by temperament, as soon as the fighting broke out he threw himself into it and formed a War Council, separate from Casati's municipal government, to direct the fighting.

In addition to these two groups there were the out-and-out republicans who had no respect for the timorousness of Casati or the anti-Piedmontese attitude of Cattaneo. They were willing to accept support from Charles Albert, or anybody else who was willing to fight the Austrians, provided they gave their help freely without demanding any *quid pro quo*. The circumstances of Piedmont's entry into the war were not reassuring. Radetzky had already been driven out of Milan when King Charles Albert, vacillating between the call of his country and the warnings of France and England against plunging all Europe into war, made his great decision. On March 25 he crossed the Ticino and invaded Lombardy. The case for declaring war was presented in a brilliant article in the *Risorgimento*, a newspaper founded in 1847 by a young liberal, Count Camillo Benso di Cavour. It was this newspaper that gave the name by which the whole struggle for Italian unity was afterwards known. Cavour's famous articles headed "The Supreme Hour of the Sub-Alpine Monarchy" opened like a trumpet call:

> The supreme hour of the monarchy of Savoy has sounded, the hour of decisive resolutions, the hour upon which hangs the fate of the monarchy and the people. In the face of the events in Lombardy and Vienna, hesitation, doubt or delay are no longer possible: they would be a policy utterly deplorable.
>
> We are men of a cold temperament, used rather to

listen to the dictates of reason than to the impulse of emotion, and after having carefully weighed our every word we must in conscience declare it: there is only one path open for the nation, the government, and the King— War! War, immediate and without delay! [12]

Cavour went on to argue that France and England, though they had protested against the war, were not likely to intervene on Austria's behalf. The young French republic was much too busy with its own affairs to embark on a war that did not concern her. As for England, Cavour put his trust in the common sense of the English people. It would not surprise him to see Lord Palmerston and Lord John Russell "grasping the hand of Metternich, still dripping with Polish and Italian blood, but they would never be able to persuade England to co-operate in the barbarous undertaking of keeping Italy in slavery."

Nothing illustrates the difference between Cavour and Mazzini more clearly than their response to Piedmont's declaration of war. Cavour was convinced that, whatever the outcome might be, Charles Albert must not miss the opportunity of proving to the world that Piedmont was the only possible champion of Italy. King Wobble (*Il Re Tentenna*), as his subjects called him, might not be the ideal ruler, but in this very imperfect world men must learn to use the tools that come to hand. With the King's passionate Catholicism—it was said that he flogged himself and wore a hair shirt—a man of Cavour's easygoing morality can have had no sympathy. On the other hand there was nothing to be gained by girding at him. Cavour was always aiming at the "possible" rather than at the "desirable." It had been found possible to induce Charles Albert to set up a constitutional regime and to launch the necessary administrative reforms, which in turn made possible a definite break with Austria. Why should it not be possible to transform this poor bewildered monarch who, despite his broodings and hesitations, was honestly longing to serve his country, into a great patriot king?

Mazzini, who instinctively veered away from what was possible and aimed only at what was morally desirable, was willing to serve under Charles Albert if he would "sign a proclamation to Italy for absolute unity, with Rome as a

[12] Cited by A. J. Whyte, *Early Life and Letters of Cavour* (London, 1925), p. 348.

metropolis, and for an overthrow of all other Italian princes." [13]
Obviously it was impossible for the King to accept any such
terms. The only possible hope of success in the war against
Austria lay in the unity of all the Italian states. Any such proclamation as Mazzini had in mind would have played squarely
into the Austrian hands. Charles Albert's great pronouncement,
"Italy will rely on herself alone" (*Italia farà da sè*), implied
that the various states would rally around Piedmont and Lombardy. This was difficult enough under any conditions; it
would have been quite impossible if the other states had been
made to feel that if victorious they were to be liquidated.
Mazzini could never be convinced that the Italian people, the
bulk of whom were peasants, were not chafing to overthrow
their rulers and establish a national republic. Because of the
success of the "Young Italy" movement among the professional
classes he concluded, quite erroneously, that the rank and file
of the nation would forget their local differences and rise *en
masse* as soon as he gave the signal. This was his great illusion.
It was all very well for him to inveigh against Charles Albert
as "a political Hamlet, condemned to a permanent want of
equilibrium between his conceptions and the faculties which
should realize them," [14] but Charles Albert was far more aware
of the issues involved than Mazzini, and far more realistic in
grappling with them. He was wrong in thinking that Italy
could free herself by her own efforts without the help of allies,
but he was right in not attempting to appeal to the people
over the heads of their rulers. It was not by such tactics
that the Austrians would be driven back over the Brenner
Pass.

General della Rocca, who commanded a brigade in 1848
and afterwards became Victor Emmanuel's chief of staff, could
have enlightened Mazzini on the attitude of the peasants. He
found the townspeople unanimous in wanting to drive the Austrians out of Italy. "Not so the villagers and peasants, generally
conservatives, and afraid lest the passage of troops and a
change of government would only bring requisitions and fresh
taxes. We had proof of this at Borghetto, our first halting place.
Resenting our camping in their fields, the peasants prepared
to open the sluices of the canals to flood the country. I sent for
the syndic, and finding my appeal to the sentiment of Italian

[13] Mazzini, *English Letters*, I, 85.
[14] *Spectator*, December 2, 1848.

brotherhood, proclaimed by Lombardy, useless, threatened to burn the village if my men were not allowed to sleep in peace on dry land." [15]

Whatever Mazzini may have thought about it, Charles Albert's declaration of war was an occasion for general rejoicing in Milan. Radetzky had gone, and the Milanese, ignorant of the recuperative powers of a well-trained army, believed him to be incapable of much further resistance. With the entry into the field of the Piedmontese Army—25,000 troops on the day of mobilization and a further 20,000 in reserve—and with the support of the whole Lombard population, and the promise of troops from Tuscany, from Rome and from Naples, nothing could have looked more promising. Della Rocca was not alone in thinking that an army of 100,000 men would soon be dictating peace at the gates of Vienna. For the first two months of the campaign Charles Albert rivalled Pius IX as the most popular man in Italy. A victory at Goito, in which the Piedmontese troops behaved like seasoned veterans, forced Radetzky to withdraw from Mantua and Peschiera, leaving these two key fortresses to fend for themselves. Could it be that the old Marshal was unable to maintain himself even within the Quadrilateral? All through April volunteers were pouring into Piedmontese headquarters to join in the fight for liberation. The little duchies of Parma and Modena were the first to drive out their princes, declare in favor of a kingdom of northern Italy, and despatch troops to the front. The Grand Duke of Tuscany, ready to do anything to please his subjects as long as the Austrians were not standing at his elbow, issued a stirring war proclamation in which he reminded his faithful people that the cause of Italian independence would be decided on the plain of Lombardy. By the end of the month 7000 Tuscan troops had crossed the river Po and had taken up the positions allotted to them under command of Charles Albert.

Naples contributed 3000 men—a small contingent out of a population of six million, but the Neapolitans were more concerned over their affairs in Sicily than with what was happening in the north. In Rome, where for nearly two years Pius IX had been regarded as the most progressive ruler in Italy, Charles Albert's declaration of war and his appeal for troops was greeted with the wildest enthusiasm. Farini, the his-

[15] Della Rocca, *Autobiography*, English trans., London, 1899, p. 55.

torian of the moderates, was swept along by the tide of patriotic fervor:

> Those days were the brightest that the seasons can bring around: the last blaze of her sun was shining upon Italy. The stranger poet could no longer have called her the land of the dead [a reference to Lamartine, who had described Italy as *"la terre des morts"*]; nor could the overbearing inhabitants of the northward countries, and speakers of the guttural tongues, any longer have confined their eulogies to blue skies, soft melodies, and miracles of art. Those who were then coming into Italy from beyond Alps and beyond seas did not alone admire those paintings and statues, which are her wealth and too much her pride. They saw freemen in arms flinging themselves upon the track of the stranger, to drive him back within the confines which God appointed for him, and from which, in despite of God and nature, he had come down to contaminate for ages the loveliest portion of the earth.[16]

Altogether the Papal State sent about 17,000 men to the war, half of them regular troops, and the other half volunteers.

In spite of the enthusiasm described by Farini, the response to Charles Albert's proud policy, *Italia farà da sè*, was not encouraging. The other Italian states, exclusive of Piedmont and Lombardy, contributed to the common cause only 27,000 men. All through these momentous days, Italy, far from relying on herself alone, was relying on the Piedmontese Army, which even if it had been brilliantly led was no match for the might of Austria. Whether or not Charles Albert missed his opportunity by not following up Radetzky more vigorously, once the old Marshal had caught his breath and established his lines of communication, it would have needed the resources of the whole Italian peninsula to dislodge him. These resources were not forthcoming; the Italian people had not yet learned to fight together in a common cause. Mazzini's explanation of the failure, that "a nation cannot be regenerated by a policy which it does not comprehend, guided by men in whom it has no faith," [17] was only partially true. The people believed in Pius IX and in Charles Albert as much as they believed in anybody, but the ardor of a few volunteers and the bravery of the

[16] Farini, *op. cit.*, II, 24.
[17] *Spectator*, February 17, 1849.

regular troops did not compensate for the apathy of the people at large. Italians were not yet malleable enough to be hammered into a nation.

If the Pope had been able to throw himself heart and soul into the Revolution, that apathy upon which the claims of nationalism made so little impression might have been transformed, but in 1848 the papacy still lay morally as well as geographically in the way of amalgamation. Even some of the liberals could not bring themselves to face the elimination of the Papal State from the map of Italy. The Pope himself, though he never quite realized it, was in an impossible position. His ministers and the Roman populace, egged on by Ciceruacchio, were clamoring for war with Austria, while the majority of cardinals and the diplomatic corps were bitterly opposed to it. By a cruel stroke of fate this well-intentioned but mediocre man, who thought himself a good liberal because he had read Gioberti's *Primato* and Balbo's *Speranze d'Italia*, found himself involved in a dilemma he had never foreseen. He had blessed the papal troops as they marched out of Rome. Obviously he had to define his position further.

On April 28 he addressed an allocution to the cardinals in consistory which may be regarded as the turning point of the Revolution. The gist of this harmless-sounding document was contained in one sentence:

> We have declined to allow the imposition of any other obligation on our soldiers, despatched to the confines of the Pontifical State, except that of maintaining its integrity and security.[18]

In other words, his army was to engage in a defensive war only. Papal soldiers could repel an attack on papal territory, but they were not to join other Italians in driving the Austrians out of Italy. The Pope's refusal to declare war was a disastrous blow to the Italian cause. Even though his generals ignored the order, the fact that the Pope had deserted his people at the moment when his support was most essential could not be forgotten. But had he deserted them? Not in his own eyes. As the vice-regent of Christ on earth, he could not possible declare war against the Austrians on grounds of nationalism, but if his troops should cross the border and serve under the orders of Charles Albert, he would not feel it necessary to disapprove of

[18] The allocution is quoted in full in Farini, *op. cit.*, II, 106–12.

their action.[19] Was he not facing on a very much larger scale the problem that confronts every minister of the gospel when his country goes to war?

Anyone might have foreseen, as both Metternich and Mazzini did foresee, that ever since his elevation to the papacy the Pope had been travelling down a road that ended in a blind alley. Administrative reforms, yes—but sooner or later administrative reforms must lead to popular government, which could only result in a war of independence. Up till the very last moment Pius had deluded himself with Gioberti's idea that a league of Italian states would solve the Italian problem. The failure of his attempt to form such a league, which would have relieved him of the responsibility for war, and his terror of provoking Germany and Austria into schism, were the two motives that drove him unwittingly into the arms of reaction. The Austrian ambassador left Rome, rubbing his hands with delight: "I have placed the Pope in such a predicament that he will never be able to extricate himself." [20]

The results of the allocution were immediately felt in other parts of Italy. On May 18, less than three weeks after the Pope had announced that he could play no part in the war of independence, King Ferdinand of Naples sent out an order recalling his army from the frontier. The meeting of the Chambers on May 15, that was to have formally inaugurated constitutional government in Naples, resulted in a massacre for which the King, the people and the deputies were apparently all equally to blame. The King seized upon the chaotic condition of the country to call the army home. General Pepe, the most unselfish of the Neapolitan patriots, together with about 1200 officers and men, refused to obey the order. The remaining 1500 were probably glad to escape from a war which could produce no tangible benefit to Naples. Ferdinand had already inquired about territorial advantages to Naples, supposing Piedmont were victorious, and the answer had been most discouraging. By recalling his troops just as they were going into action Ferdinand served Austria as effectively as any ally. "Let this be thoroughly understood," says Farini, "that the greatest, and perhaps the only effective cause of our misfortunes, and of the Austrian victory, in so far as the human mind can judge, was the desertion of the troops of Naples." [21] These two inci-

[19] "Se esse le varcheranno, non sarà colpa mia." Masi, *op. cit.*, II, 252.
[20] Masi, *op. cit.*, II, 281.   [21] Farini, *op. cit.*, II, 179.

dents, the allocution and the defection of the King of Naples, provided excellent material for republican propaganda. Not through such rulers as Pius IX and King Bomba could Italy hope to achieve her independence. It remained to be seen whether King Charles Albert would cut a better figure.

6

The King of Sardinia was far from being the miserable creature that Mazzini had depicted, but he was not a military genius, and only a military genius could have defeated Radetzky once he had recovered himself and established his lines of communication. As the summer wore on, Charles Albert's chances of success grew steadily slimmer. By the end of May, Radetzky had received important reinforcements, the papal volunteers had been defeated at Cornuda, and the Neapolitans had been recalled. The Piedmontese Army scored its last victories at Peschiera and at the second battle of Goito, and these successes, coming as they did just at the moment when the national war had been abandoned by the Pope, by the King of Naples, and—inevitably—by Tuscany, singled out Piedmont as the only champion of Italy. Whatever hesitation and lack of initiative the Piedmontese generals had shown, the Piedmontese Army had proved itself the most serviceable weapon Italy possessed. The creation of this army was Charles Albert's contribution to the cause of unity.[1]

Meanwhile, behind the lines in Milan, the unity of the Five Glorious Days had given way to apathy and confusion. After toiling so strenuously to create a new world, the Milanese followed the example of the Creator and rested. Albertists were drifting away from republicans, and the republicans were quarrelling among themselves. The Provisional Government, headed by Casati, was from the first in favor of fusing Lombardy with Piedmont and creating a northern kingdom of Italy. One group of republicans, headed by Cattaneo, dreamed of a free autonomous Lombardy; another, inspired by Mazzini, would never be satisfied with anything less than an indivisible Italian republic. At first, both Charles Albert and Mazzini would have preferred to postpone the political wrangling until the war was over, but, as our generation has discovered, politi-

[1] Berkeley, *Italy in the Making*, III, 309.

cal issues cannot be kept waiting. However united allies may be in the face of the enemy, they can never forget that their political interests are not identical. It was this inextricability of war and politics that made Clemenceau exclaim that war was much too important a matter to be left to generals.

Mazzini suspected Charles Albert of being more interested in crushing the republican movement than in fighting the Austrians. While Radetzky was collecting bayonets, Charles Albert was said to be collecting votes, but in view of the chaotic conditions in Lombardy the King's concern over politics was perfectly natural. One reason why the Milanese left everything to Piedmontese initiative, and failed to find either men, money, or supplies for the army, as they had agreed to do, was that the relationship between the two states was so indefinite. Nobody knew whether Charles Albert was to be their king or merely their general, whether Lombardy was to be incorporated into Piedmont, and if so under what terms. Realizing that no people could wage war under such conditions, the King approached Mazzini through a third party, and offered him an important position in the projected kingdom of northern Italy.[2] When we consider that Mazzini had refused to accept the royal amnesty, and that he was therefore technically still an outlaw, this was no small step for the King to have taken. A few weeks later Mazzini "refused to be an M. P. for Genoa, and for I do not know what place in Piedmont." [3]

It was characteristic of Mazzini that he regarded all these overtures as temptations. In a letter to his mother, who had apparently urged him to sacrifice his convictions for the good of Italy, he begged her not to demand the impossible of him. His mother and father must trust his judgment. Why should they think that other people knew better than he what was for the good of Italy? He was not looking merely at Lombardy and Piedmont as the Albertists were, but at Italy as a whole. Come what may, he would never live under a monarchy, nor would he desist for a moment from his republican propaganda. "Meanwhile," he writes, "I am here [in Milan] disliked, dreaded, suspected, calumniated, threatened more than ever: and my writings are burnt in my native town, Genoa, almost

[2] In her biography of Mazzini, Emilie Ashurst states that he was actually offered the prime ministership and invited to write the constitution. For a discussion of this point see G. E. Curatulo, *Il Dissidio tra Mazzini e Garibaldi* (Milan, 1928), pp. 75–7.

[3] Mazzini, *English Letters*, I, 85.

under the eyes of my mother." [4] No wonder that he began to look back to the days of exile—the family gatherings at the Ashursts', the weekly dinners at the Carlyles'—with fond regret. The English Government was hopelessly selfish and obtuse —like all governments—but he could never forget the steady friendship of his English friends.

Rebuffed in his attempt to come to terms with Mazzini and the republicans, Charles Albert can hardly be blamed for pushing forward a plebiscite in Lombardy to decide whether to have fusion at once or postpone the whole question till the end of the war. With the backing of the Provisional Government the result was a foregone conclusion. The people of Lombardy voted for fusion by 561,002 against 681. The duchies of Parma and Modena followed suit, and on July 4, as we have already seen, Venice too voted to join the Kingdom of Northern Italy.

Such was the state of affairs when "General" Garibaldi, fresh from his exploits in South America, presented himself at the royal headquarters, and offered his sword to the King. It was fourteen years since Garibaldi had sat at a café in Marseilles, reading an old copy of the *Peuple Souverain,* the organ of the democrats, and caught sight of his own name listed among bandits of the first category (*di primo catalogo*) to be sought for diligently by all loyal subjects of His Majesty Charles Albert. Considering that Garibaldi had joined the Sardinian Navy, at Mazzini's suggestion, with the express purpose of organizing a mutiny, the sentence of execution that had been passed upon him *in absentia* was not entirely unjust. It was the first time that he or anybody else had seen the name of Giuseppe Garibaldi in print. Other men might have been frightened, but Garibaldi was pleased—very pleased. It always delighted him to see his name in print.

Since then he had found his way to South America, taken service under the infant republic Rio Grande do Sul, and distinguished himself as a buccaneer in the struggle against the giant empire of Brazil. It was significant that the first vessel that he commanded was called the *Mazzini.* He had formed the Italian Legion of Montevideo, consisting largely of political exiles like himself who had enlisted to fight for the liberties of Uruguay. The Italian Legion saved Montevideo, and played a leading part in the victory of Sant' Antonio, the fame of which spread to Europe and established his reputation

[4] Mazzini, *English Letters*, I, 86.

as a great captain, equally successful on land or sea. Above all, he had fallen in love, and his love story—the whirlwind courtship, the honeymoon spent fighting the Brazilian Navy in the lagoons along the coast of Uruguay, the ten thrilling years of married life that were to end so tragically in the marshes of Ravenna—had already made him a popular romantic figure.

The story of Garibaldi and Anita, and the fabulous exploits of the red-shirted legionaries, was carefully followed by many Italians, and by none more carefully than Mazzini. Letters had been passing to and fro between Montevideo and London, the center of Mazzini's spider web of conspiracy. It was important that the world should know that Garibaldi himself was a member of "Young Italy," that Anzani, his chief lieutenant, had won his spurs in the Greek War of Independence, and that every man in the Legion was a republican as well as an Italian.

No man understood better than Mazzini the value of propaganda. He knew that the thousands he had inspired with a hatred of Austria demanded the leadership of a spectacular personality. He could supply the brains, the organizing capacity, and the abiding faith in revolution without which men's spirits would flag, but he needed, to capture the imagination of the world, a man of action. Obviously Garibaldi was the man. Nor was Garibaldi at all reluctant. He had never considered settling down in South America, and now that he was married and that his children were growing up, he wanted to take the whole family back to Nice, to be near his mother, where he felt no harm could come to them. There was another reason, too. As the 'forties rolled by, the Montevidean exiles began to watch more and more eagerly for the letters from his friends in Italy and London. Mazzini saw to it that they were kept informed of the activities of "Young Italy," and of the rising temper of the Italian people. There were better things in store for them both, wrote Mazzini, than to die in London or Montevideo.[5]

The accession of the new liberal Pope, Pius IX, followed immediately by the amnesty to political prisoners, seemed to Garibaldi the signal for a great national uprising. In his mind's eye he pictured an alliance between this new Messiah and the Italian Legion of Montevideo. Without waiting for Mazzini's advice he dashed off a letter to the Pope, to be transmitted

[5] Letter from Mazzini to Garibaldi, June 22, 1845.

through the papal nuncio at Rio de Janeiro, offering the services of himself and of his companions in exile to "the Holy Father who has already done so much for his country and for the Church." He realized that there was probably no lack of loyal defenders nearer home, but he would like the honor of being included among those most eager to fight against the Pope's enemies. Mazzini had also written a letter to the Pope, but it was very different from Garibaldi's. The hero of Montevideo was a simple-minded soul—D'Azeglio said that he had the brains as well as the strength of an ox—who never dreamed that the Pope might hesitate to make war against Austria. Mazzini, equally guileless as far as the great mass of humanity was concerned, was more sceptical than Garibaldi of those in authority.

Whether or not Garibaldi received any answer from the Pope, his mind was now made up. In spite of heartbreaking delays, owing to the unwillingness of the Montevidean Government to see him leave, and the difficulty of hiring a ship, Garibaldi put Anita and the children on a sailing ship bound for Genoa in December, 1847. He himself with eighty-five men embarked on the *Speranza* a few months later. On June 21, 1848, the *Speranza* came in sight of Nice. Garibaldi was afraid they were too late. They had called at Alicante to buy oranges and a goat to provide milk for Anzani, who was at his last gasp with tuberculosis of the lungs, and there they had heard that Charles Albert had granted a constitution and was at war with Austria, that Radetzky had been chased out of Milan, and that all Italy was sending contingents to the holy war.

> The effect produced on us all by this news may be better imagined than described. There was a rushing on deck, embracing one another, raving, weeping for very joy. Anzani sprang to his feet, excitement overpowering his terrible state of weakness. Sacchi absolutely insisted on being taken from his berth and carried on deck. "Make all sail!" was the general cry . . . In a flash the anchor was weighed and the brigantine under sail.[6]

The landing at Nice Garibaldi described afterwards as the happiest moment of his life. Never again was the future to seem so utterly unclouded. The whole town was at the quayside, swarming about Anita and the children, and his mother,

[6] Garibaldi, *Autobiography*, London, 1889. 3 vols. I, 261.

Signora Rosa, who had always hoped that he might become a priest and was now so proud that he had become the "Hero of Montevideo" instead. As soon as the tumultuous welcome was over, and Garibaldi had assured himself that he was not too late for the fighting, it began to dawn on him that the liberation of Italy was a good deal more complicated than it had seemed in the mountains of Rio Grande. With whom should he join up—with the Provisional Government of Milan or with the Piedmontese Army? Where was Mazzini, and what had become of young Giacomo Medici, whom he had sent ahead to enlist volunteers in Tuscany? Pressed to declare himself a republican or a monarchist Garibaldi lost no time in announcing his allegiance to Charles Albert. He had always been a republican, but since the King of Sardinia had become the defender of the people's cause he and his friends were willing to shed their blood for him. "Woe to us if instead of banding together we dissipate our strength in separate insurrections. Even worse will befall us if we sow among ourselves the seeds of discord." [7]

To one man at least the report of this speech in the Genoese papers must have been bitter reading. Mazzini had always considered Garibaldi his protégé. It was he, Mazzini, who had nursed the Garibaldi legend by publishing his American exploits far and wide in the revolutionary press, and now, without a word to his old counsellor and friend, Garibaldi was offering his services to the King. He might at least have reported his actions first to the Mazzinian Committee. "Garibaldi," wrote Mazzini to his mother, "is another disappointment, but I am getting accustomed to them." [8] It was the old story of the pupil growing up and feeling no obligations to his master. Mazzini, after all, was a man of ideas rather than a man of action, and Garibaldi was never at home in the world of ideas. It mattered little to him who the savior of Italy should be—Pope, King or popular demagogue. All that mattered was that men should stop scribbling and chattering. Liberty was never going to be achieved by scattering pamphlets about liberty, and arguing the virtues of a republic versus a constitutional monarchy, but by subjecting oneself to discipline and learning to shoot straight.

So it was that Garibaldi, eager to hurl himself into the

[7] Curatulo, *op. cit.*, p. 86.
[8] Mazzini, *Scritti*, XXXV, 246.

battle for freedom as soon as possible, swallowed his republican
pride and reported on July 4 at King Charles Albert's headquarters. For the moment only the mortal sickness of his old
comrade-in-arms, Anzani, clouded his horizon. Anzani had returned to Italy after twenty-seven years of exile, not to fight,
as he had hoped, but to die. The day before he expired he
spoke his famous words to Medici, who, like Mazzini, had been
irritated by the Chief's sudden conversion to monarchy: "Do
not," said the dying patriot to Medici, "do not be too hard on
Garibaldi; you must follow him. The future of Italy depends
on Garibaldi." [9] The counsel from dying lips sank deep into
Medici's heart. He often disagreed with Garibaldi, but he
never quarrelled with him again.

The details of Garibaldi's interview with the King have
never been reported, but the result must have given Mazzini a
certain savage satisfaction. The "General" by his own appointment was neither accepted nor refused. Obviously the King
was ill at ease in the company of this impulsive, independent
man, who, though he had abjured the republican follies of his
youth, did not seem to realize that his extraordinary experiences in South America did not necessarily qualify him for a
command in the Piedmontese Army. War in northern Italy
was very different from war on the pampas—less picturesque,
perhaps, but more specialized. It required the qualities of a
chess player rather than those of a *beau sabreur*. Garibaldi's
lack of military training, as opposed to military experience,
might prove a serious handicap. Under the circumstances the
King thought it wiser to refer the "General" to the Minister of
War in Turin, who would doubtless be able to find some suitable employment for a man of his unusual talents. Back went
Garibaldi to Turin, two hundred miles from the fighting line,
where he was advised to find his way to Venice. There he might
be given command of a few naval vessels and render important services to the besieged city as a corsair.[10]

Disillusioned by the cold courtesy of the King, and disgusted by the hopeless bureaucracy of the War Department,
Garibaldi betook himself to Milan. The Provisional Government would surely give him a command of volunteers. The
Provisional Government was no more free from red tape than

[9] Trevelyan, *Garibaldi's Defence of the Roman Republic*, London, 1908,
p. 44.
[10] Curatulo, *op. cit.*, p. 69.

the Piedmontese Army, but thanks to Mazzini, who welcomed him as a prodigal son, the hero of Montevideo was finally appointed a major-general in the Lombard Army. As to the equipment of his volunteers, Garibaldi was told that the Government could supply neither arms nor uniforms. Apparently the supposedly democratic committee that ruled Lombardy were no more anxious to accept him than the professional soldiers in Turin. The only uniforms available were those that had been left behind by the Austrian garrison, which the people of Milan refused to touch. Garibaldi took the spotless white tunics and dyed them red. The Minister of War did not like red uniforms; they suggested blood (*troppo apparente alle fucilate nemiche*) but Garibaldi had learned by now to ignore officials. He equipped his little band of volunteers as best he could, and marched it out of Milan to meet the enemy.

Meanwhile Radetzky had received his reinforcements and was pressing the Piedmontese Army back toward Milan. The royal forces were defeated at Custozza at the end of July, and on August 3 Charles Albert arrived at the gates of Milan. He might have retreated into Piedmont via Piacenza and Pavia and abandoned Milan to its fate.

> To defend the Milanese [says della Rocca], Charles Albert had placed the Army in jeopardy, and staked his kingdom and throne. Believing in the fine promises of the Lombard representatives, he had come to Milan expecting to find the city fortified and well provisioned. On his arrival, Generals Chiodo and Rossi, who had preceded us, met him with the news that no preparations had been made for the troops. The city was silent and deserted; the few inhabitants who remained were cold, disappointed, and reproachful.[11]

Unfortunately the Milanese were still divided among themselves. When news of the defeat had first arrived, they had formed a Committee of Public Safety, composed entirely of republicans, which decreed a *levée en masse* and began constructing fortifications. According to Mazzini, the Committee of Public Safety did more in three days than the wishy-washy Provisional Government had done in three months, but whatever it did was not enough. The spirit of the Five Days had evaporated, and to continue the struggle without men, without

[11] Della Rocca, *op. cit.*, p. 86.

ammunition, and without a leader in whom they felt any confidence, was obviously impossible. An armistice was signed on August 5, and the army, beaten but not routed, evacuated the city during the night. It all came, thought Mazzini, from having thrown their sacred flag at the feet, not of a principle, but of a wretched man.

No one felt the humiliation of the surrender more keenly than Charles Albert, all the more so since the Milanese, infuriated at having their city handed back to the Austrians, laid every mistake at his door. As soon as the news of the armistice was known, a howling mob gathered outside his headquarters, and for a few hours his life was in grave danger. Finally Della Rocca came to his aid with a battalion of grenadiers. "The King was on foot, deadly pale, and aged in face and figure. He held his sword tight under his arm, and, when he saw me, said, 'Ah, mon cher La Rocca, quelle journée, quelle journée.' I shall never forget the tone of his voice." [12]

Garibaldi, utterly disgusted by the armistice, decided to continue the war on his own account. He regarded the order to disband his volunteers without fighting as an insult. For the moment he was completely in accord with Mazzini. The royal war was finished, the war of the people would now begin. No prince could deprive him of the right of driving the stranger from the soil of Italy.

The campaign of the next few weeks in the Italian Alps, if it did nothing else, confirmed Garibaldi's reputation as one of the great guerrilla fighters of all time. As Mr. Trevelyan says, "it was a personal and political protest rather than a real war." Garibaldi was encamped at Bergamo when he heard that the victorious Austrians were racing toward Milan. He started in pursuit, intending to harass the Austrian flank and rear, but by the time he reached Monza, fifteen miles north of Milan, he heard that the city had fallen. His men were exhausted after their long forced march, and the spectacle of half the population of Milan drifting out of the city like frightened sheep was not an auspicious beginning for what was at best a desperate adventure. In spite of the armistice he hoped that the dogged resistance of his volunteers would so rouse the spirits of the people of Lombardy that the order to cease firing would be ignored, and that with more and more patriots rallying to his standard he might still be able to drive Radetzky out

[12] Della Rocca, op. cit., p. 88.

of Italy. All that was needed was courage and confidence, but it was precisely courage and confidence that was lacking. By the time he had reached Como—Garibaldi withdrew his troops to the north so as to have his back to the mountains—all but 800 of his original 3000 volunteers had melted away. The nearness of the Swiss frontier was a powerful incentive to desertion. "The majority found it pleasanter," says Garibaldi, "to relate their glorious deeds in the inns and cafes of Lugano, than to stay and endure the hardships and dangers of the camp." [13]

Garibaldi was learning to his sorrow that it was much easier to wage guerrilla warfare in South America, where anyone could make war on his own account and be sure of finding plenty of followers, and where the instinct of independence was almost a religion, than it was in Italy where fighting was considered the business of professional armies. The general apathy of the peasants, their unwillingness to risk anything in the common cause, baffled him as the tactics of the enemy never did. Nevertheless with the 800 men that were left to him Garibaldi staged a campaign in the mountain villages around Lake Maggiore and Lake Como that proved him to be no less resourceful in the unfamiliar conditions of Alpine warfare than he had shown himself to be in the lagoons or on the vast undulating plains of Uruguay.

His first move was the capture of two small steamers on Lake Maggiore. On these he embarked with his 800 Red Shirts, and sailed across the lake from Arona to Luino, followed by an excited flotilla of smaller craft. It was an unorthodox way of starting a campaign, but as his opponents soon discovered, Garibaldi was never one to follow the book of the rules. On the following day, August 15, an Austrian column billeted in the neighborhood launched what they doubtless hoped would be a surprise attack. Garibaldi, a sick man at the time, had gone to bed for two hours while Medici posted the guard, and kept an eye on the roads leading into the village. Before the two hours were up, Medici's scouts came rushing back: "The Austrians!" Garibaldi, forgetting his fever, sprang out of bed, posted half of his men in the fields alongside the road and kept the other half in reserve to protect the flank. A few shots were exchanged while the Austrians occupied the village, and then the 400 men that had been kept in reserve closed in with the bayonet. Bewildered by the impetuousness

[13] Garibaldi, *op. cit.,* I, 274.

of the attack, the Austrians turned and fled, leaving thirty-seven prisoners behind them.[14] Though hardly more than a skirmish, the affair at Luino is important in the history of the Risorgimento as marking Garibaldi's first victory over the enemies of Italy.

> The result of this victory [says Garibaldi] was to leave us masters of the Varese district, which we traversed in every direction without opposition. The inhabitants roused themselves somewhat from their dejection, and we entered Varese amid the enthusiastic acclamations of those good people. On this occasion I was conscious of the revival of a hope I had cherished for many years—that of inducing our countrymen to enter upon a kind of unsystematic guerrilla warfare, which, in the absence of a regular army, might be the prelude of our country's emancipation, by promoting the general arming of the nation, in case the latter was firmly and honestly resolved to free itself. I therefore detached Captain Medici's company (composed of picked young men), and several others, with directions to act independently of each other.[15]

The inhabitants of the Varese district may have been enthusiastic, but their enthusiasm was limited to cheering Garibaldi and entertaining the Red Shirts in the local taverns. The dwindling numbers of these picturesque volunteers, and the meagreness of their resources, did not encourage the wary peasant to risk his life in a struggle that might be magnificent but was certainly hopeless. Evidently Radetzky had decided to make an end of the matter. He had despatched General d'Aspre with a force of not less than six brigades to stamp out the last smouldering fires of rebellion. The Piedmontese Government, fearful that Radetzky might use Garibaldi's continued resistance as an excuse for occupying their territory, was equally anxious for this South American swashbuckler to lay down his arms. Under the circumstances there was nothing for Garibaldi to do but extricate his army from the net in which D'Aspre hoped to catch him, by slipping across the frontier into Switzerland. There was one final brush at Morrazzone, where

---

[14] Guerzoni, author of the standard life of Garibaldi, Florence, 1882, 2 vols., states that the Austrians suffered 180 casualties. Garibaldi himself, in his *Autobiography*, says that "some Austrians were killed, and thirty-seven remained prisoners."

[15] Garibaldi, *op. cit.*, I, 279.

a squadron of Uhlans rushed through the tired Garibaldian outposts and entered the village just as Garibaldi and his officers were sitting down to a meal. They rose, sword in hand, rallied their men and drove out the assailants. The fighting lasted until nightfall, after which, under cover of darkness, Garibaldi infiltrated his men through the Austrian lines, disbanded them, ordered them to cross the frontier by twos and threes, and to meet him again in Switzerland. With Garibaldi's withdrawal into Switzerland the last flicker of resistance in King Charles Albert's dominions was snuffed out. Venice was again flying the flag of independence, but Radetzky had decided to deal first with the insurrection in Lombardy, and the siege of Venice had not yet begun. The best comment on Garibaldi's miniature campaign was made years afterward by General D'Aspre, who recognized the flash of genius in his great adversary long before the Italians themselves were aware of it: "The one man who could have been useful to you in your war of independence in 1848 you never appreciated; it was Garibaldi." [16]

In the retreat from Milan Garibaldi had been joined by Mazzini, a recruit who was not entirely welcome. The misunderstanding between the two men was not easily cleared up. Garibaldi complained that Mazzini joined him for only a few days, and then made his way into Switzerland taking many of his followers with him. It was for the General, not for the private soldier, to decide when the moment had come to give up the struggle. Medici, who admired both Garibaldi and Mazzini, was apparently unconscious of the feud and wrote most enthusiastically about Mazzini's joining the battalion:

A general *evviva* saluted the great Italian, and the legion unanimously confided its banner, "God and the people," to his charge. . . .

The march was very fatiguing; rain fell in torrents; we were drenched to the skin. Although accustomed to a life of study, and unfit for the violent exertion of forced marches, Mazzini's constancy and serenity never forsook him, and, despite our entreaties—we feared for his physical strength—he would never stay behind, nor leave the column. Seeing one of our youngest volunteers dressed in a linen jacket, and with no other protection against the

[16] Guerzoni, *op. cit.*, I, 245.

rain and sudden cold, he forced him to accept and wear his own cloak. Arrived at Monza, we heard the fatal news of the capitulation of Milan, and learned that a numerous body of Austrian cavalry had been sent against us. . . . Garibaldi, not wishing to expose his small band to useless destruction, gave orders to fall back, and placed me with my column as rear-guard to cover the retreat. . . . My column, always pursued by the Austrians, never wavered, but remained compact and united, . . . and kept the enemy in check to the last. In this march, full of danger and difficulty, the strength of soul, intrepidity, and decision, which Mazzini possesses in such a high degree, never flagged, and were the admiration of the bravest amongst us. His presence, his words, the example of his courage, animated our young soldiers, who were, besides, proud of partaking such dangers with him. . . . His conduct is a proof that to the greatest qualities of the civilian he joins the courage and intrepidity of the soldier.[17]

While Garibaldi was criticizing Mazzini for deserting him before the fighting was over, Mazzini was back at his old trade of conspiracy. From Lugano, just across the frontier in Switzerland, he began collecting funds, arms and ammunition, for what was to prove another abortive Savoy expedition. With a few faithful followers he was still confident that he could repair the errors of the "royal war." Once again he became the idol of all the Italian émigrés in Switzerland.

> One talked only of him, one listened only to him; his theories, his words were indisputable and venerated dogmas. His more intimate friends, and the many who wanted to seem intimate, called him simply "Pippo"; and whoever spoke in Pippo's name needed neither to argue nor to adduce proof. The Word was absolute and infallible.[18]

In spite of the usual difficulties—the Swiss were such "degenerated" republicans that they put every difficulty in his way—Mazzini finally launched two "invasions" of Italy, confident as usual that the people would rise as one man. Both invasions proved complete fiascos. In the Val d'Intelvi a re-

[17] J. W. Mario, *Supplement to Garibaldi's Autobiography*, p. 80.
[18] Visconti-Venosta, *Memories of Youth* (Boston, 1914), p. 112.

public was proclaimed, which lasted three days. At Chiavenna, in the Valtelina, the insurgents, disappointed that the population showed no interest, fired a few shots and then dispersed. There were two casualties. However effective his constant campaign for unity, Mazzini's ventures into the field of action were invariably failures. Carlyle made fun of his revolutions "à la Donnybrook fair," but Mazzini's sincerity was so contagious that he could always induce men to embark on the most hopeless undertakings, nor did they seem to lose faith in him when those undertakings failed.

Garibaldi played no part in these pathetic little uprisings. Convinced that he and Mazzini could do nothing together, he made his way to Nice, hoping to recover there in his own home from the continued attacks of fever. Apparently domestic peace did not suit him, for he hurried on to Genoa, which was still a center of revolutionary activity. Sick in mind as well as body, Garibaldi knew that the only cure for him was action. He must always be doing something—not conspiring like Mazzini—but seeking out one of the many centers of revolution, and leading his Red Shirts into the thick of the fighting. Conditions in Italy at the end of September offered him a wide choice of activity. For the moment Austria seemed triumphant. Her position, so desperate earlier in the year, had been restored by a series of unbroken victories. Windischgrätz had crushed the Bohemian revolt, the Hungarians and the Croats were conveniently quarrelling among themselves, and Radetzky had compelled Charles Albert to sue for an armistice, thereby disclosing to the world the hopeless divisions between monarchists, moderates, and republicans. Only Venice still remained undaunted by the catastrophes in Lombardy. But frustrated though they were, the Italians were not crushed. It was perhaps unfortunate that every man did as seemed good in his own eyes, instead of uniting for a common purpose, but throughout Europe, and not merely in Italy, that was the tragedy of 1848.

In Tuscany, Father Gavazzi, a rebellious monk of the Barnabite order, who had been profoundly impressed by the wrongs of Italy and the sins of the Church, had proclaimed a republic. In Rome, Pellegrino Rossi, an honest statesman of the Guizot school, who still thought that the people could be satisfied by merely administrative reforms, was wasting his energy bolstering up the waning popularity of Pius IX. In spite of his efforts, papal authority was everywhere breaking down. Gioberti's dream of a federation of Italian states under the presidency of the Pope had not materialized, and the Pope himself had alienated the liberals and the moderates by refusing to sanction the war with Austria. Further south, in the Kingdom of Naples, Ferdinand II was bent on reconquering Sicily. While Garibaldi was in Genoa looking about him for some new scene to which he and his companions could carry the People's War, a deputation of Sicilians offered him a command in Sicily. A ship was waiting in the harbor ready to carry him and such companions as he could muster to a corner of his country where the people were still fighting tyranny. Garibaldi agreed, but on the way to Sicily the ship touched at Leghorn where he was given an enthusiastic reception. The democrats of the city urged him to stay with them, reorganize their army, take command of it, and march southward through the Papal States toward Sicily, taking Naples on the way. The prospect of fighting his way through Italy, overthrowing the Bourbons as he went, was too alluring to be refused. The ship sailed without him, and Garibaldi and his seventy-two Red Shirts suddenly found themselves plunged into the politics of central Italy.

By the time Garibaldi arrived in Florence he must have begun to doubt the wisdom of his projected march through the Papal States. For one thing, the recruits he had been promised never materialized. There was no flocking to the standard as he had been led to expect by the democrats of Leghorn. The Tuscan peasants were charming people, but they were not crusaders nor were they chafing to overthrow their Grand Duke and establish a republic. Garibaldi was willing to attach his column to the Tuscan Army, if the ministry wished, but no such request was made. Guerrazzi, the chief minister, was anxious only to pass the adventurer and his rabble out of Tuscany. "They are," he wrote, "a swarm of grasshoppers. Let us consider them at once as one of the plagues of Egypt, and let us do our utmost to induce them to get away quickly and contaminate as few places as possible." [19]

The difficulty of reaching Naples and Sicily seemed so insuperable that Garibaldi finally decided to march his Legion to Ravenna, and from there set sail for Venice, which seemed to be the one place in Italy where people were fighting instead

[19] Cited by David Larg, *Garibaldi*, London, 1934, p. 90.

of talking. There at least he would not find himself cold-shouldered by timid ministers, who claimed they were liberals but were unwilling to take any step that might antagonize the Pope or encourage democratic "agitators." While Garibaldi was waiting on the shores of Ravenna for a ship to take him to Venice, the assassination of Rossi, the papal prime minister, once again induced him to change his plans. For two years Rossi had been the Pope's ablest friend and adviser, "the only real statesman Italy had produced before Cavour." [20] An Italian by birth, Rossi had been exiled for supporting Murat in 1815. After living some years in Switzerland, where he made a reputation for himself as an authority on criminal law, he moved to Paris and there became one of Guizot's most staunch admirers. The two men had much in common—a deep and not unjustified confidence in their own abilities, moral as well as physical courage, devotion to the cause of political liberty, combined with a curious lack of imagination manifesting itself in a contempt for human nature.

Guizot thought so well of his Italian friend that he appointed him Ambassador to the Holy See. [21] Rossi, the ex-revolutionary, appears to have made himself so agreeable to the Pope that after the fall of the Bourgeois Monarchy he was urged to remain on in Rome as an unofficial adviser to the papacy. As the situation in Rome grew steadily worse, with the democrats demanding a greater share in the Government than the Pope felt he could allow, he finally turned to Rossi in September, 1848, as the one man who might possibly stave off revolution without sacrificing the temporal power. Rossi promptly introduced a series of administrative reforms in the civil service, in the army, and in the treasury, that definitely alienated the clericals. At the same time he made it perfectly clear to Ciceruacchio, Sterbini, and Prince Canino, that he would maintain the liberal Papal State, that he would not tolerate anarchy, and that he would not embark on a war with Austria, for which, apart from other considerations, he felt the army was totally unprepared. Rossi's relentlessly reasonable policy satisfied nobody. He stood almost alone. Whether he would

[20] E. Masi, *Il Risorgimento italiano*, II, 333.

[21] There was nothing unusual about Rossi, an Italian, being appointed French Ambassador. In 1848 the principle of nationality was not as rigorously applied in diplomacy as it is today. Baron von Meyendorff, the Russian Ambassador to Prussia, was a German nobleman and at the same time a loyal and devoted servant of the Russian Government.

have been able to persuade the Chamber of Deputies to support him will never be known. On the morning of November 15, on his way to the opening of Parliament, he was struck down by a band of assassins on the steps of the Capitol.

Garibaldi hailed the murder as an act of deliverance: "The ancient metropolis of the world, worthy once more of her former glory, freed herself on that day from the most formidable satellite of tyranny, and bathed the marble steps of the Capitol with his blood. A young Roman had recovered the steel of Marcus Brutus." [22] Perhaps the kindest comment on this fustian was made by Henry Adams, when he said that Garibaldi and President Grant were the two most completely unintellectual men he had ever met. "The type was pre-intellectual, archaic, and would have seemed so even to the cave-dwellers. Adam, according to legend, was such a man." [23] And yet, in the long run, the non-intellectuals are not always wrong. Men like Garibaldi, though they may be incapable of thinking, are sometimes astonishingly right in their estimates of a situation. If Rossi had lived, Gioberti's dream of an Italian federation of free states might have been translated into reality, but there would have been no "Italy," and for those who believe in the sanctity of nationality, as all idealists did in the nineteenth century, that would have been a great tragedy. In all revolutions the moderate man—men like Guizot and Rossi who believe in the *juste milieu*—are bound to be destroyed.

7

Even before Pellegrino Rossi had bled to death on the steps of the Cancellaria Palace it was already evident that without him the moderate party was helpless. Rome was now in the hands of Ciceruacchio, the Circolo Populare and the secret societies. No one thought of arresting the assassins. On the night of the murder a mob gathered outside the windows of Madame Rossi's house, singing the couplet, *Benedetta quella mano, che il Rossi pugnalò* (Blessed be the hand that stabbed Rossi). Under these circumstances Pius must have realized that the assassination of Rossi snuffed out the last flickering hope of a liberal Papal State. Henceforward the kindly Bishop of Imola, the beloved "Papa" of the amnesty who had uttered

[22] Garibaldi, *op. cit.*, I, 298.
[23] *The Education of Henry Adams*, Boston, 1918, p. 265.

those prophetic words, *Benedite, Gran Dio, l'Italia,* without being aware of their significance, disappears from history. Pius IX lived on for another thirty years, but the cruelly repressive policy of the papacy was dictated by the sinister figure at his elbow, the grim-faced Cardinal Antonelli.[1]

Obviously the situation was not one that could last long. The new ministry was determined to carry out a "patriotic program," which sooner or later would involve the Pope in a war with Austria. After a fitful flirtation with liberalism Pius found himself back at the old impasse. No, he would bless Italy, but that was as far as he could go. He would not renounce the international character of the Holy See by declaring war on the most faithful daughter of the Church. On the evening of November 24 he fled from Rome, unrecognized by his guards, in the dress of an ordinary priest. The flight was arranged by the Duc d'Harcourt, the French ambassador, and Count Spaur, the Bavarian minister. An inconspicuous carriage waiting outside the gates of the Quirinal—not like the lumbering *berline* in which Louis XVI made the ill-fated flight to Varennes—whisked him along the Appian Way and over the Alban Hills to Gaeta in Neapolitan territory.

The city that two years before had greeted his every appearance with such intoxicating applause had become a prison house. He would come back to Rome again, the armies of the faithful would see to that, but it would never be the same thing. With the murder of Rossi Rome had become for him the land of lost content. A quarter of a century later a little English girl, in her white frock and veil, knelt with her companions before the now aged Pontiff. "The Pope did not seem to be interested in anything but our names. When it came to my turn I answered 'Roma.' The Pope hesitated, and a slight chill seemed to fall. *Brutto nome!* murmured the Holy Father. Ugly name! Has she no other?"[2]

With the Pope's flight from Rome, and the appointment of a Provisional Committee to govern the city in his absence, Garibaldi's fortunes began to mend. At last his services were in demand. His Legion, which Piedmont and Tuscany had found so embarrassing, was finally regularized. Garibaldi wrote

[1] Masi speaks of the *tristo ceffo* (the villainous mug) of Cardinal Antonelli. An equally unflattering description will be found in the *Dublin University Magazine* LXXVII (March, 1871), 308.

[2] Roma Lister, *Reminiscences Social and Political*, London, 1926, p. 29, cited by Griffith, *Mazzini*, p. 203.

to the Provisional Committee and received a not overly enthusiastic reply offering him a lieutenant colonelcy in the Roman Army (hardly a flattering rank to one who had been a general) and ordering him and his four hundred legionnaires to Macerata, a hundred miles northeast of Rome, where the priests were said to be doing their best to provoke a peasant uprising in favor of the Pope. No one wanted the *garibaldini* in Rome. It was rumored that the heroes of Montevideo were wild men who lived off the peasants and stole their cattle, but if they were dangerous as allies they might be still more dangerous as enemies.

The horrible impression, spread abroad, says Garibaldi, "by the calumnies of the clerical party . . . was always changed by the sight of the manly, well-conducted young fellows who accompanied me, nearly all belonging to the cultivated classes of the towns." The bulk of the Legion was made up of shopkeepers, workers and students, a ragged regiment badly equipped—Garibaldi had no war chest—but utterly devoted to their chief and to the ideal of freedom he represented. They were officered for the most part by veterans of Montevideo, who, if they cared nothing for the parade-ground discipline of European armies, knew how to command alertness and absolute obedience. One and all, officers and men, trusted Garibaldi implicitly. He was the paladin of justice, the reincarnation of the *condottiere* of the Middle Ages in a new uniform. No Sforza ever had so complete a control over his men as Garibaldi had over the men of the Italian Legion. There was something about this massive, four-square man, unintellectual perhaps, but kindly, generous and humane, that neither men nor women could resist. Johan Koelman, a Dutch artist, resident in Rome who later fought in the defense of the city, was struck by his peculiarly leonine expression. The nose was broad at the root, the eyes shot forth flames of fire, and the long chestnut hair waved as a mane above his temples.

The picture of Garibaldi and his staff galloping across the *Campagna* in their red shirts and ponchos was easily distorted in the peasant imagination. These men in their strange assortment of uniforms, who sat around campfires roasting whole sides of oxen, and let their horses wander untethered, to be lassoed when necessary, were not the kind of soldiers to which they were accustomed. Strange though they were, the citizens of Macerata soon discovered that the *garibaldini* were not scoundrels. Offenses were rigorously punished, and the few convicts whom Garibaldi had admitted to the Legion "under the characteristic delusion that to fight for Italy would cure all moral diseases" [3] were either discharged or executed.

Meanwhile in Rome events were moving rapidly toward a republic. In the absence of the Pope, who refused to receive any delegations from the Provisional Committee, the democratic ministry appointed after Rossi's death announced the convocation of a Roman Constituent Assembly to be elected by manhood suffrage. On January 21, 1849, the elections were held, and one hundred and fifty deputies elected, including Mazzini and Garibaldi. Mazzini stayed on in Florence trying to persuade Guerrazzi and the republican element in Tuscany to consent to union with Rome, but Garibaldi hurried to the capital at once to take part in the opening meeting. As soon as the Minister of the Interior had finished reading a long inaugural speech, Garibaldi astonished his fellow deputies by jumping to his feet and shouting: "Let us drop the formalities and proclaim the Republic!" [4] Prince Canino seconded the motion, but the other deputies refused to be stampeded. They were looking forward to a philosophic discussion on the nature of democratic government, and they were not going to be deprived of it by this unseemly interruption. Garibaldi left the Assembly in disgust, persuaded, as many soldiers have been before and since, of the ineffable stupidity of politicians. The discussion was resumed in accordance with the usages and forms common with parliaments, and it was finally voted that the papacy had ceased to exercise temporal sovereignty over the Roman State, that the form of the new government was to be "pure democracy," and the name "the Republic of Rome." [5] The yellow and white flag of the papacy was hauled down and the tricolor banner of Italy hoisted. The Revolution, begun in murder, was becoming respectable.

Mazzini received the news in a laconic telegram—"Rome, Republic, Come." On the evening of March 5 a slender figure might have been seen trudging along the Via Flaminia. Anxious to avoid the sort of ovation that had greeted him in Milan, in Leghorn, and in Florence, the inevitable speech from the balcony, and the noisy welcome of the cafés, Mazzini

---

[3] G. M. Trevelyan, *Garibaldi's Defence of the Roman Republic*, p. 89.

[4] Guerzoni, *op. cit.*, p. 257.

[5] Farini, *op. cit.*, III, 221.

slipped into Rome alone and unannounced. As he passed through the Porto del Popolo, he felt an electric thrill run through him—"a spring of new life." Could it be that the new-born Roman Republic would spread from state to state, as he had dreamed it would, until it embraced the whole peninsula? He had always prophesied that a new Rome would arise, greater than the Rome of the Caesars or of the Popes—the Rome of the Italian people. Yet he writes to his English friends in no mood of gay optimism:

> Nothing, till the day of my arrival, has been done for the war: we have no arms: almost all the European Governments are at work against us; and we are going to be involved, sooner than I expected, in a war initiated by Charles Albert for the purpose of preventing us from spreading our republican principles through Piedmont. We shall do what we can.[6]

On the day after his arrival in Rome, Deputy Mazzini, member for Ferrara, took his seat in the Chamber. The other deputies rose to their feet as he entered the hall and gave him a tremendous welcome. Galletti, President of the Assembly, insisted that Mazzini sit by his side. Here was the living symbol of their cause, the man who worshipped the people as the visible embodiment of God invisible. But he was more than the symbol of a cause. He was an agent, and a highly competent one, through whose energy the cause might possibly triumph. Margaret Fuller, an old friend whom he had first met in England at the Carlyles', was not exaggerating when she declared, "if anyone can save Italy from her foes, inward and outward, it will be he." [7] Mazzini had the ability, which Garibaldi so conspicuously lacked, of dominating an assembly without ever antagonizing it. There was no hint of the demagogue about him. "Mazzini's was a spiritual ascendancy ruling by influence and weaving around the souls of men an otherworldly spell." [8] No one contested his superiority. Within a month of his arrival the Assembly balloted for a Triumvirate, with sweeping dictatorial powers, to cope with what had already become a desperate situation. The other two triumvirs,

---

[6] Mazzini, *English Letters,* I, 113.
[7] Margaret Fuller, *Memoirs,* 2 vols. (Boston, 1852), II, 262.
[8] G. Griffith, *Mazzini,* 214.

Armellini and Aurelio Saffi, honest political wheel horses, yielded him the real authority.

Mazzini was now forty-four years old, and eighteen of those forty-four years had been spent in exile, conspiring against every state in Italy. How would this modest, retiring man, whose manner suggested an almost English reserve, acquit himself now that he was faced with the terrific problems of government? William Wetmore Story, the American sculptor, who was sceptical about the whole republican experiment, called on Mazzini and found him

> haggard and worn in appearance, with rather an agreeable face, dim black eyes, full forehead, straight black hair and grizzled beard. He speaks English and wished that America would give the Republic its sympathy and adhesion. His practicality has been veneered over his mind by his English life. Essentially, like almost all Italians, he is a visionary. But he sees and understands the virtue of simple direct action. There was a little the affectation of a busy man with him, and he was of course oppressed with labour and distracted by details. But he had an air beyond this.[9]

The poet Clough found him "a less fanatical, fixed idea sort of person" [10] than he had expected, while Lord Palmerston, whose jaunty, aristocratic whiggism was about as far removed as anything could be from Mazzini's mystical democracy, told the House of Commons that "Mazzini's government of Rome was far better than any the Romans had had for centuries." [11]

To everybody's surprise Mazzini seemed to be able to govern without trials, without prisons and without violence. The charges of communism and socialism that were hurled at him could never be supported.

> All property was safe, except the enormous estates of the Church, which the mildest reform could not have left untouched. In other countries, Catholic and Protestant alike, the wealth accumulated by the mediaeval Church had undergone large curtailment by a process of which

[9] Henry James, *William Wetmore Story and His Friends*, 2 vols. (London, 1903), I, 157.

[10] A. H. Clough, *Prose Remains* (London, 1861), p. 142.

[11] Mazzini, *English Letters*, I, 114.

the propertied classes had been the chief beneficiaries. But it was not for squires, courtiers or capitalists that Mazzini laid his hand on ecclesiastical property. It was for the benefit of the poorer peasants that he decreed the employment of confiscated Church land, as small holdings leased to cultivators at nominal rents; it was for the benefit of the poorer parish priests that he joined in the movement to equalise the emoluments of ecclesiastics.[12]

The Triumvirs were determined that the Church should be subordinate to the State, but there was no persecution of religion as there had been in France under the first French Republic. They themselves heard Mass at St. Peter's, and the Sacred Bambino was borne through the streets in solemn procession as usual. Once when the crowd brought out confessional boxes from the churches to make barricades, Mazzini reminded them that from those confessionals had come words of comfort to their mothers. "It was perhaps the most convincing proof of his grip on the people's hearts that the confessionals were taken back."[13]

The papal court at Gaeta saw nothing to approve of in Mazzini's methodical housecleaning. There could be no peace with the evil men who repudiated the Church's claim to temporal power. Cardinal Antonelli bombarded the Catholic Powers with demands for rescue. Nor would he tolerate the mediation of Piedmont, a dangerously ambitious state under suspicion of seeking to dominate the rest of Italy. The Holy See had spoken. It was for the faithful daughters of the Church—Spain, Austria, Naples and France—to bestir themselves and cleanse the sanctuary of "that band of wretches, which is exercising there, with every kind of enormity, the most atrocious despotism."[14]

The first of the faithful daughters to heed the appeal was France. On April 24 General Oudinot and an expeditionary force of ten thousand men landed at Civita Vecchia, forty miles northwest of Rome. The orders given to General Oudinot by his government were deliberately vague. Odilon Barrot, Louis Napoleon's prime minister, had requested an appropriation for sending an expedition to Rome on the plea of safeguarding liberal institutions, but this did not mean saving the

[12] G. M. Trevelyan, *Garibaldi's Defence of the Roman Republic*, p. 102.
[13] Bolton King, *Mazzini*, London, 1902, p. 131.
[14] Farini, *op. cit.*, III, 280.

Roman Republic. It meant that as long as the Pope was to be restored to power, France was determined to do the restoring.

A succession of Austrian victories had convinced the diplomatic world that, for the moment at least, there was no hope of making alterations in the map of Italy. Early in March, Charles Albert had denounced the armistice and gathered his forces together for one last rush on Milan. The result had been another disaster for the Piedmontese Army. The battle of Novara closed the efforts of the constitutionalists to liberate and unite Italy. Charles Albert abdicated and died shortly afterwards in a Portuguese cloister, leaving it to his son Victor Emmanuel to cope with an implacable Radetzky. On March 27 Venice sent out its last defiance to General Haynau ("General Hyena," his victims christened him), and though the agony of the siege dragged on for some months the end was certain. King Bomba's army crushed the Sicilian insurrection on April 6, and on April 12 the Grand Duke of Tuscany was recalled to his throne by his own people in time to prevent a forcible restoration by the Austrians. By the time the French expedition set sail from Marseilles it was certain that the Pope would be restored to power. The Roman Republic had no friends in any foreign government. Even the United States, usually so quick to welcome republics into the family of nations, withheld recognition on the ground that it could not last. Rather than let the papacy be indebted to Austria or the Neapolitans, Louis Napoleon, anxious to assert his position in the eyes of the world and to curry favor with the conservatives in his own country, elbowed his way into the limelight as the champion of Christendom. At the same time the French Republic must not appear to be supporting a reactionary policy. The French troops, with the Italian and French tricolors intertwined, landed, shouting "Long live the Republic! Long live Italy!" The populace, slightly bewildered but anxious to appear hospitable, cheered them in return. Unfortunately the pleasant fiction that the French were allies rather than enemies was somewhat spoilt when Oudinot refused to allow a battalion of Lombard volunteers to disembark. "What business have you Lombards to meddle in Roman affairs?" asked the French invader angrily. The young Bersagliere captain thought that a citizen of Milan had a better right to be in Rome than any Frenchman.

On the morning of April 30 a lookout stationed in the

dome of St. Peter's reported a French advance guard approaching from the west. The men were marching in undeployed columns, and as they drew nearer the officers were seen to be wearing white gloves. Evidently Oudinot, believing that he had sufficiently paved the way with proclamations, anticipated no difficulty. He had explained to the Triumvirs that without a French garrison Rome could not hope to withstand the imminent invasion of the Austrians and Neapolitans. Mazzini's reply was not as friendly as he could have wished, but the General assured his staff that he knew all about the Italians. *Les Italiens ne se battent pas.* (Italians don't fight.)

By the end of the day the French army was headed back to Civita Vecchia with a loss of five hundred men killed and wounded, and 365 prisoners. At two o'clock the following morning General Oudinot wrote an account of the disaster to the French Government, and demanded effective reinforcements. He would need siege artillery and a corps of engineers. There had been some mistake. The Italians did fight after all, and the capture of Rome was going to prove a serious business.

That night the city was illuminated as it had never been before. The hero of the hour was Garibaldi. If he had not been brought into Rome at the last minute, Oudinot might well have eaten his dinner in the capital as he had confidently expected. The personal magic of Garibaldi inspired the heterogeneous mass of veteran Red Shirts and half-trained volunteers to fight for their city as no one else, not even Mazzini, could have done. As it was, Garibaldi complained that Mazzini deliberately robbed him of the crushing victory he might have won. Given reinforcements, he felt he could have driven the French back to their ships or into the sea, but Mazzini with one eye on republican sentiment in France had no wish to humiliate the French Army. The only hope for the survival of the Roman Republic was that it should rally to its support liberal opinion throughout Europe. So it was that he persuaded the Assembly to send back the three hundred-odd prisoners, after showing them the sights of Rome and loading them down with cigars and snuff, wrapped up in tricolored tracts. Rome was not at war with France but simply in a state of defense. It could afford to be generous.

Garibaldi cared nothing for these subtleties. He was thinking only of victories in the field, whereas Mazzini was always looking beyond the immediate crisis to the regeneration of

Italy. This regeneration could only be brought about if Rome set Italy an example of the perfect republic, unstained by crime or persecution, with peace, good will, and Christianity operating within its walls. Mazzini admitted, years later, that he knew the Roman Republic would fall, but he was determined that in falling it should attract the respect and admiration of Italians all over the world.

It was unfortunate that the two men who galvanized the easygoing Roman populace into such extraordinary feats of heroism should have been perpetually at loggerheads. Mazzini in his tightly buttoned frock coat, listening quietly to his opponents and replying without petulance but never changing his opinion, and Garibaldi on his white horse, his poncho streaming in the wind, were both in their own way great leaders, but they found each other utterly exasperating. Mazzini thought Garibaldi too much concerned with his own importance, and Garibaldi grumbled that Mazzini had a mania for dictating strategy, of which he knew nothing.[15]

After Oudinot's repulse Rome was immediately threatened from another quarter. The Neapolitans, eager to forestall the French in Rome, had crossed the frontier and taken up positions at Albano and Frascati. Garibaldi's Legion, reinforced by the Lombard brigade, was ordered to oust them, but in the moment of victory they were summoned back to Rome to meet another attack. By the time he reached Rome after a night march of twenty-eight miles, he found no attack was impending, but that, on the contrary, a French envoy had arrived from Paris and that an armistice had already been signed.

Back went Garibaldi to the Neapolitan front, this time under the command of General Rosselli, the least incapable of the Roman generals. The Triumvirs hesitated to make Garibaldi commander-in-chief, not because they did not recognize his ability but because they feared the effect of his appointment on an already critical and suspicious Europe. How easy it would be for the papal propagandists to make out that the so-called Roman Republic, governed by apostates and heretics, was defended by a Legion of outlaws commanded by an American filibuster. Garibaldi was disgusted. The Neapolitan Army was defeated—never a very difficult task—but King Bomba himself escaped, and Garibaldi was again prevented

[15] "Quel Mazzini che ha sempre avuto la smania di fare il Generale, e non ne capiva . . ." Guerzoni, *Garibaldi*, p. 272.

from exploiting his success. Disgruntled by the criticisms of Rosselli, Garibaldi wrote to Mazzini that he could serve the Republic in only two ways: as dictator with unlimited powers, or as a simple soldier.[16]

Poor Mazzini! He must have read the letter with a wry smile. He had so often written in that same truculent vein himself. How difficult it was to get men to work together, even in the face of the enemy and in the noblest of causes! Meanwhile the Austrians were overrunning Romagna and the Marches, Oudinot had repudiated the armistice, and now Garibaldi was threatening to sulk in his tent. Fortunately he realized the Triumvirs could not accept either of his propositions. He retained his rank as general of division and continued to devote his entire energies to the defense of the Republic.

In abruptly denouncing the armistice and attacking the city actually two days before the armistice was over, Oudinot showed that the whole business of negotiation had been merely a device to gain time. The French envoy, Ferdinand de Lesseps, who was destined to achieve greater fame as the builder of the Suez Canal than as a diplomat, had been sent out by the French Government to talk the Triumvirs into letting the French army occupy Rome. Himself an honest man, De Lesseps was the victim of a tortuous policy. Louis Napoleon always wanted the best of both worlds, Catholic and liberal. He believed that with the exercise of a little diplomatic finesse it would be possible to bring back the Pope, restore the temporal power (with a few constitutional trimmings), if necessary prop the Pope up with French bayonets, while at the same time posing as the champion of free institutions. De Lesseps, who was really being called upon to reconcile the irreconcilable, began by quarrelling with Mazzini but ended by falling under his spell. At one moment he wrote a letter to his Government describing Mazzini as a "modern Nero," and the Roman soldiers as "the scum of socialism and of secret conspiracies." [17] A few days later he changed his tune and worked out a compromise, according to which the French were to be welcomed as allies and lodged in the outskirts of the city, provided they agreed not to interfere in internal affairs.

---

[16] "Qui io non posso esistere, per il bene della Republica, che in due modi: o dittatore illimitatissimo o milite semplice. Scegliete. Vostro invariabilmente, G. Garibaldi." Garibaldi, *op. cit.*, III, 101.

[17] Farini, *op. cit.*, IV, 121.

This was the settlement that Oudinot, backed up by his Government, refused to accept. The honor of the French Army was at stake. De Lesseps went home to be reprimanded, and on June 2 Oudinot surprised the Romans by occupying the Villas Pamfili and Orsini, key positions to the defense of the city. He justified the violation of his promise not to attack until the morning of June 4 by a subtle interpretation of the word *città*. French and Italian historians have been arguing ever since whether *città* meant the fortress of Rome bounded by its walls, or whether it included points of vantage outside the city itself. It is a nice point for historians, but the wise general does not rely too implicitly on his opponent's acceptance of a debatable definition of a crucial word. Had Garibaldi been in command of the defense instead of Rosselli, Oudinot would never have acquired his foothold so easily.

For the next month 17,000 Italians, some of them, like the Garibaldi Legion and Manara's Lombards, among the best troops in the world, but others only partly trained and badly equipped, defended Rome against a French army of 30,000 men, supported by a powerful train of siege artillery and an expert corps of engineers. Day after day the French trenches crept nearer the city, and the batteries erected under their protection crumbled breaches in the walls that the defenders found it impossible to man. It was obvious that, failing a counter-revolution in Paris, surrender was only a question of time. Ledru-Rollin attempted a demonstration on the boulevards in favor of the Roman Republic, but it petered out ignominiously and Ledru-Rollin himself fled to England. There was now no reasonable excuse for prolonging the struggle but Mazzini refused to give up. He was still looking far ahead to the effect that this supremely gallant defense would have on the opinion of the world.

The night of June 29–30, the Feast of St. Peter and St. Paul, was selected by Oudinot for the final assault. During the earlier part of the night the *festa* was celebrated in the town in right Roman fashion, with lighting of candles in the windows, and sending up of rockets in the streets—functions which that mercurial people would not forgo even under the shadow of impending doom. The Triumvirate gave official countenance to these mild *circenses*, and the dome of St. Peter's blazed with every extravagance of colour. The French officers, as they stood in front of their dark columns, waiting for the signal to mount the breach, saw below them the holy city glowing "like a great furnace, half-extinct, but still surrounded by an atmosphere of fire." Suddenly the heavens were opened in wrath, and a deluge of rain fell on the disobedient children of the Pope, extinguishing their last poor little fires of joy. When the torrential storm had passed away, one light alone, from the top of the great dome of St. Peter's, still shone through the thick blackness, beckoning the crusaders to the assault.[18]

The last struggle was fought around the ruins of the Villa Spada. Garibaldi headed a desperate charge of his own legionaries, but the French could not be dislodged. Summoned before the Assembly, Garibaldi, blood-bespattered as he was, told the deputies that the defense of the city could not be carried on any longer. The Assembly had three choices before them—to capitulate, to defend the city street by street and house by house, or to leave Rome with the Army and continue the war against France and Austria elsewhere. This was the plan that Garibaldi himself had been advocating for a long time. He was tired of the walls of Rome, tired of this relentless war of trenches and bastions which was unlike anything he had met with in all his experience of fighting, and which Oudinot's engineers understood better than he. It had long been his dream to take to the Apennines, to carry the Government and Army into the wilderness. *Dovunque saremo, colà sarà Roma.* (Wherever we go, there will be Rome.) Whatever decision was made by the Assembly, he would go forth with such men as would follow him.

On the night of July 2 Garibaldi at the head of 4000 men marched out from the gate of St. John Lateran. Among the volunteers was Anita, who gladly accepted the conditions her husband offered to her as to the others: "Let those who wish to continue the war against the stranger, come with me. I offer neither pay, nor quarters, nor provisions; I offer hunger, thirst, forced marches, battles and death. Let him who loves his country in his heart and not with his lips only, follow me." [19] It was a desperate project. Chased by French, Austrian,

[18] Trevelyan, *Garibaldi's Defence of the Roman Republic*, pp. 217–18.
[19] The text of this famous speech is first recorded by Guerzoni, *Garibaldi*, I, 331.

Spanish and Neapolitan armies, all of which he eluded, Garibaldi and his constantly dwindling army finally reached the neutral territory of San Marino. The fathers of the little republic gave them shelter and negotiated with the Austrians for the safety of the *garibaldini* as best they could. Disdaining safety for themselves, Garibaldi and his wife and a remnant of 200 men pushed on to the port of Cesenatico in a last heroic attempt to reach the dying republic of Venice. The flotilla of fishing boats which they had launched was over-hauled and captured by the Austrian patrol, but Garibaldi, Anita, and a few others, reached the shore and fled inland. Worn out by the hardships of the fight, Anita, in the last stages of pregnancy, died in her husband's arms. Garibaldi himself, concealed by faithful partisans, escaped into Tuscany, and eventually made his way to America. There we must leave him making candles in Staten Island. It was five years before he returned to Italy, and another five years before he was to astonish the world again with a still more spectacular march.

While Garibaldi's little army was plodding through the silent Campagna on the night of July 2, the Assembly, having decided against the proposal of an official exodus as being impractical, remained calmly at its post. The deputies showed a certain stately gravity worthy of the Eternal City.

> They celebrated the obsequies, and voted aid to the families, of the dead; they accorded the right of citizenship to everyone who had defended the city; then, on July 3, having proclaimed on the Capitol the new constitution—as a man on his deathbed makes his will—they remained calmly at their posts until the French army, which took possession of Rome on that morning, came and dispersed them.[20]

Mazzini, who had never imagined such a finale, refused to be "the executioner of Rome's honour." [21] He and his two colleagues resigned on the ground that they had been chosen to defend, not to destroy, the Republic. Like Garibaldi, he had been eager for the Government with its armed forces to withdraw together into the hills, but Mazzini would not go forth without the Government. An army of a few thousand men

[20] W. R. Thayer, *The Dawn of Italian Independence*, 2 vols. (Boston, 1893), II, 382.
[21] Garibaldi, *op. cit.*, III, 109.

collected at random, without the prestige of a government behind it, meant nothing to him. Nor was he attracted by the
sheer gallantry of Garibaldi's gesture. Each in his own way
loved Italy, but they did not love each other.

For some days Mazzini walked about the streets of Rome
still hoping to rake together the embers of resistance. The
French, fearing perhaps to make a martyr of him, left him
alone although they were hunting for the other leaders.

> One morning in July [the thirteenth] an aged man,
> unheeded by the French patrols, walks aboard the steamer
> *Corriere Corso* [Captain de Cristoferi] bound for Mar-
> seilles. He addressed the Captain: "I am Mazzini. I have
> no passport. Do you dare to take me?" Yes; Captain De
> Cristoferi would dare; but he must point out that he must
> call at Leghorn, where the Austrians are now in occupa-
> tion and have a habit of searching vessels; and if— But
> the aged man waves the objection aside; he will take the
> risk and all responsibility. And at Leghorn the officials
> pass unnoticed the grey-bearded old steward sleepily
> washing the glasses and now and then staring idly at the
> white-coat sentries on the quay-side. And who indeed
> would have recognised him? In five months he had grown
> old. His hair was streaked with grey, his beard almost
> white; his eyes were bloodshot and famished of sleep; a
> slow fever had consumed the flesh from his bones and
> parched his skin; the clear olive of his complexion had
> become a jaundiced yellow. The Triumvir was well dis-
> guised.[22]

So ended the Roman Republic. Within a few months
Mazzini was back in his dingy lodginghouse in London. Jane
Welsh Carlyle found him "the same affectionate, simple-
hearted, high-souled creature—but immensely more agreeable
—talks now as one who had the habit of being listened to—" [23]
He had certainly not returned a broken or humiliated man.
For one splendid hour at least he had brought his dream to
pass. If he had not made Italy in the sense that Cavour and
Victor Emmanuel were to make it ten years later, he had given
Italians a glimpse of unity and independence that was greater
than anything dreamed of in Cavour's philosophy. For Mazzini,

[22] Griffith, *Mazzini*, p. 128.
[23] J. W. Carlyle, *Letters to Her Family*, p. 345.

nationality was the connecting link between the individual and humanity, the appointed means by which the individual was lifted out of himself to a sense of brotherhood with mankind.

He never exalted the nation at the expense of the individual, as the twentieth century dictators did, nor did he ever conceive of nationality as a fixed and absolute principle, but he did believe it was the best channel through which a sense of brotherhood could be brought home to the great majority of mankind. For good or evil the principle of nationality has played a greater part in the affairs of Europe during the nineteenth century than at any other period of recorded history. Mazzini expressed it at its best. The very fact that he could not accept the Italy built by Cavour proves that to him the nation was not, as it was to so many, an end in itself. He was never reconciled to the Savoy monarchy, but for the Italy of his dreams, foreshadowed by the Roman Republic, he dedicated his life. Everything that men hold dear—fame, love, domestic happiness—he sacrificed to this ideal.

On March 10, 1872, a Mr. George Brown, of London, died at Pisa. The doctor who attended him was amazed that this mysterious foreigner should speak such excellent Italian. "But I am an Italian," exclaimed the patient excitedly, "I love my country passionately." Then calming himself, he added, "I was born in Liguria, but I have lived in London for forty years." It was Mazzini, the unpardoned exile, who had come back to Italy to die. He was buried in the Staglieno cemetery, overlooking Genoa. Carducci's noble epitaph would have pleased him more than his belated recognition by the Italian Government:

L'uomo
che tutto sacrificò
che amò tanto
e molto compatì e non odiò mai.

The man who sacrificed everything, who loved much, who pitied much, and who hated never.

THE REVOLUTION IN GERMANY

KARL MARX

ONE AFTERNOON in November, 1843, a young German couple might have been seen unloading their worldly goods at 38 rue Vaneau in the faubourg St. Germain. The man was obviously Jewish. The broad sensitive nose and the mobile mouth were unmistakable. Their name was Marx—Karl Marx, doctor of philosophy, formerly resident of Cologne, and his wife, Johanna Bertha Julia Jenny von Westphalen. Dr. Marx was presumably known to the French police as the editor of the *Rheinische Zeitung*, a radical paper that had been suppressed by the Prussian authorities for its unseemly criticism of Czar Nicholas. That had been in March. Since then he had married Jenny von Westphalen, daughter of an official in the Prussian administration at Trier, and they had spent the honeymoon at Kreuznach with her family, reading constitutional history. It was not an ideal arrangement. Jenny did not mind the constitutional history, but Marx did not get on very well with his wife's *pietistisch-aristokratischen* relations. Still he was head over heels in love, and after waiting for his wife seven long years he could put up with the idiosyncrasies of her family for a few weeks. As for Jenny, she never failed him. Years later his mother is said to have complained that it would be better if Karl were to make some capital instead of always writing about it, but Jenny von Westphalen never questioned her husband's genius, and was always

194

ready to endure discomfort and even grinding poverty if that was what fate ordained.

The decision to leave Kreuznach and settle in Paris was natural enough. In the 1840's everyone interested in the theory or practice of revolution was bound to find his way to Paris, just as in the 1930's all good radicals gravitated to Moscow. By 1843 there were not less than 80,000 *émigrés* from Germany alone living in Paris. It was the mecca for the artists, the idlers and the discontented of every nation. Heine, the most famous of the exiles, was writing letters to the *Augsbürger Zeitung* on the political, social and artistic life of France.[1] George Herwegh, a popular poet whose zeal for revolution was in some danger of melting in the warm sunshine of Paris society, Bakunin, the Russian aristocrat, not yet famous but already full of windy enthusiasm that could not be harnessed to any definite project—these and many other exiles Marx met and appraised with critical eye. Most important of all for his purposes was Arnold Ruge, a writer of some reputation in the radical camp who had paid for his radicalism as a young man with six years in a Prussian prison. Marx had already written to Ruge asking whether he knew of any position abroad. There was no future in Germany for any independent-minded man. Ruge welcomed him eagerly. He needed an assistant editor for a new publication he was hoping to bring out, the *Deutsch-Französische Jahrbücher,* which was to be the rallying point for the real intellectuals of western Europe. Its international character was to be the essential feature of the review.

Ruge hoped to gather together all the important democrats of his acquaintance—Marx, Heine, Bakunin, Herwegh, and along with them Lamartine, Louis Blanc, Proudhon, and other French intellectuals of the same quality. To his great disappointment the French refused to co-operate. Lamartine proclaimed his sympathy with the projected intellectual alliance between France and Germany, and then decided he could have nothing to do with any such revolutionary enterprise as Ruge seemed to be contemplating. Louis Blanc could not bring himself to write for an admittedly atheistic journal. Proudhon was out of town. Considérant, a well-known socialist and a disciple of Fourier, suspected Ruge of advocating the use of violence for the advancement of his ideas, something that

---

[1] These letters were republished later under the title *Lutèce.*

Fourier had always deplored. These unexpected rebuffs meant that the review would have to be exclusively German. Ruge and Marx could only conclude that French socialists were lagging far behind them. If not practicing Catholics, they were all, with the exception of Proudhon, warped by a belief in God. German socialists had reached their conclusions about government via Hegel's philosophy and were therefore convinced atheists, whereas the French, however anti-clerical they might be, were still deists. It was unfortunate that the French knew nothing about Hegel, "the intellectual world navigator," as Heine called him, "who has fearlessly penetrated to the north pole of thought, where one's brain freezes amid abstract ice." [2] Marx could not understand how a nation as celebrated for its intelligence as the French should be unable to grapple with philosophy and should still believe that communism was merely an extension of Christianity.

The fact was that the French liberals to whom Ruge was appealing were not communists at all. They were socialists. During the forties socialism and communism became more and more differentiated. Socialism, a word that made its first appearance in the French language in 1832, had come to stand for a utopianism born of ethics and a desire to improve the world.[3] Communism implied class hatred and the destruction of one's opponent. It was founded on an essential antagonism to absolute property, whereas socialism was antagonistic only to human discord and rivalry. One started from the *thing* and the other from the *person*.

The only Frenchman for whom Marx felt any intellectual sympathy was Proudhon. Pierre Joseph Proudhon was a self-educated workingman who had started life herding cattle in the fields around Besançon, where he was born. Later on he worked in a printer's shop where he acquired, as a by-product of his daily activity, a vast store of undigested erudition. The award of a scholarship by the Academy of Besançon enabled him to read and study more systematically. The first important step in his career was the publication in 1840 of a pamphlet entitled *What is Property?*—the answer being the famous dic-

[2] Quoted by J. G. Legge, *Rhyme and Revolution in Germany*, London, 1919, p. 89.

[3] "The first use of *socialisme* appears to have been in the *Globe* of 13 Feb., 1832, where it was employed in contrast to *personnalité*."—OXFORD ENGLISH DICTIONARY. See Arthur E. Bestor, Jr., "The Evolution of the Socialist Vocabulary," in *Journal of the History of Ideas*, June, 1948.

tum, "Property is theft." Actually Proudhon did not believe that property was theft, but merely that "under certain circumstances property might enable its owner to acquire an income in ways of which he, Proudhon, disapproved." [4] The denial of property was followed by an equally emphatic rejection of God. This assertion of atheism, or rather of anti-theism, was merely part of a revolt against all authority. God and the State were the two great dictators that had to be overthrown before man could feel that he was free.

For a moment Marx had been drawn to Proudhon as a fellow worker in the field of revolutionary agitation, but he was soon disillusioned by Proudhon's unwillingness to co-operate with anybody and by what must have seemed to him the maddening disorder of Proudhon's ideas. Proudhon the moralist, the man who invoked Justice and Conscience, he could never understand. The strong vein of idealism in Proudhon seemed to him merely a mark of weakness. Still less could he understand Proudhon's indifference to the importance of organization. When Marx invited him to take part in a regular correspondence designed to link together militant socialists all over Europe, Proudhon accepted with many reservations. Marx's dogmatism alienated him. "Let us," he answers, "give to the world an example of wise and far-sighted tolerance. Let us welcome disagreement and avoid all exclusiveness." If Marx were prepared to pursue truth in a completely disinterested spirit, then Proudhon would join his association with pleasure, but he could not promise to write many letters. He was a poor correspondent and he had many other irons in the fire.[5] He went on to say that he did not believe in revolutionary action as a method of social reform, and that the working classes of France were thirsting for knowledge rather than for blood. This and many other things he had explained in his new book, *The Philosophy of Poverty,* upon which he invited criticism.[6]

Marx must have read the letter with disgust. It was not with such allies that he could hope to overthrow the bourgeoisie. Proudhon, after all, was nothing but a *petit bourgeois* himself, a man who understood nothing of dialectics. As for *The Philosophy of Poverty,* he explained in a counter treatise

[4] Alexander Gray, *The Socialist Tradition* (London: Longmans, Green, 1947), p. 233.
[5] *Lettres de P.-J. Proudhon* (Paris: Grasset, 1929), pp. 72, 73.
[6] *La Philosophie de la Misère* (Paris, 1846).

entitled *The Poverty of Philosophy,* in which he gave full rein to his talent for invective, that it was the pretentious work of a self-taught "parvenu of science." [7] So ended the projected intellectual alliance between France and Germany.

The *Deutsch-Französische Jahrbücher,* which turned out to be an exclusively German production owing to the lack of interest among French intellectuals, died young. Only one number was published, which appeared in February, 1844. Not only did the French fail to co-operate but the German editors fell to quarrelling among themselves. Herwegh, recently married to the daughter of a rich Berlin silk merchant, had set up a smart establishment in Paris, which Ruge thought occupied more of his attention than it should. Ruge himself might have made a good editor of a learned magazine, but he was not a fighter by nature and gradually he came to think that the German people were not ready for revolution. Marx was more than ever convinced that revolution was the only way. The question of money was another source of friction. The confiscation by the Prussian police of 300 copies of the review that had been shipped into Germany proved a serious blow. Marx had been promised 500 thaler a year from the profits the editors confidently expected to make, but there were no profits, and Ruge refused to put up any more capital. The relationship grew steadily worse. Ruge finally decided that Marx had a destructive, unoriginal mind, whose capacities he had much overestimated. In the end, they would have nothing more to do with each other. Both took refuge in England after 1848, but during their long exile they never met. Ruge became completely reconciled to things as they were, and in the last years of his life, after the war of 1870, which he strongly supported, he received a pension from the German Government.

The collapse of the *Jahrbücher* left Marx penniless, but the venture had been worth while, if for no other reason than that it brought him into contact with the man who was to prove his greatest friend, the man who made the writing of *Das Kapital* possible. Two of the best articles in the ill-fated journal, one entitled "Outlines of a Critique on Political Economy," and the other an enthusiastic review of Carlyle's *Past and Present,* were written by a man Marx hardly knew, Fried-

---

[7] Karl Marx, *Misère de la Philosophie* (Paris and Brussels, 1847). Marx had the book printed at his own expense. A new edition was published in Paris in 1947, Editions Sociales. See p. 141 for the full flavor of Marxian bitterness.

rich Engels, a Rhinelander, son of a well-to-do manufacturer of Barmen. Caspar Engels and Sons had connections in England, and for the last two years Friedrich Engels, the eldest of the sons, had been living in Manchester learning the textile business. He was one of those versatile, popular young men upon whom the gods bestow the questionable gift of facility. Everything came easily to him. He did not care for business, but even his strait-laced father, who disapproved of so much in his character, could not deny that Friedrich was a competent business man. He was popular with the local squires and enjoyed a day in the hunting field, while at the same time he made friends in radical circles and wrote articles on continental socialism for the Chartist papers.

The most fruitful result of his stay in England was a savage book, *The Condition of the Working Class in England in 1844,* in which he showed that even in England, the model country of the liberals, the paradise of parliamentary government and free trade, the great mass of working people lived in "an ever spreading pool of misery and desolation." [8] Engels got much of the information for his book from an Irish working girl he lived with named Mary Burns, who took him with her into the homes of working-class families. There he watched and listened. What he saw convinced him that England was on the verge of revolution. He was not a trained economist, and the main thesis of his book proved to be wrong, but what he said was true even if it was not the whole truth.

His contributions to the review, which were along the lines of his book, opened the eyes of Marx to conditions across the Channel of which he knew nothing. The conclusions to which Marx was groping were suddenly illuminated by the conclusions at which Engels had arrived. While Marx was making his way toward communism by pondering over the significance of the French Revolution, Engels had been converted by what Mary Burns had shown him in the slums of Manchester. One travelled by the hard road of reason, the other by the easier path of observation and intuition.

The long friendship between Marx and Engels, which developed into one of the greatest partnerships in history and ended only with Marx's death in 1883, has never been satisfactorily explained. It was not as if Engels were a Boswell eager

[8] *The Condition of the Working Class in England in 1844* (London, 1892), p. 15.

to shine in the reflected glory of a greater man. In many ways he was the more competent man of the two, able to earn his own living, which Marx never was, and able to win men to his opinions instead of antagonizing them. Jenny Marx described him as "healthy, fresh, merry and good-humored." Evidently he was what the Middle Ages would have called a "sanguine man." No one would ever have called Karl Marx "sanguine." The thick-set, pugnacious figure, the glittering eyes under beetle brows, the irritability and the intellectual arrogance marked him unmistakably as a dangerously "choleric" man. Upon Carl Schurz, who met him in the early days of the Revolution, he made an abidingly unpleasant impression.

> I have never seen a man [wrote Carl Schurz sixty years later] whose bearing was so provoking and intolerable. To no opinion which differed from his own did he accord the honor of even a condescending consideration. Everyone who contradicted him he treated with abject contempt; every argument that he did not like he answered either with biting scorn at the unfathomable ignorance that had prompted it, or with opprobrious aspersions upon the motives of him who had advanced it. I remember most distinctly the cutting disdain with which he pronunced the word "bourgeois"; and as a "bourgeois," that is as a detestable example of the deepest mental and moral degeneracy, he denounced everyone that dared to oppose his opinion.[9]

Yet this was the man to whom the pleasure-loving Engels was utterly devoted and to whom he lent money "without hope of return and without expectation of gratitude." [10] Engels knew that he did not lack ideas of his own and that on certain aspects of economics he was better informed than Marx, but he never thought of claiming credit for his share in the partnership. Possibly there was something feminine in Engels' nature that made him cling to the stronger nature and at the same time seek to efface himself. If so, the Marx-Engels Institute in Moscow, which has set itself the task of collecting, in original or photographic copies, everything written by or about Marx and Engels, has by its very title redressed the balance in Engels' favor.

[9] *The Reminiscences of Carl Schurz*, 3 vols. (New York, 1907), I, 139.
[10] E. H. Carr, *Karl Marx* (London, 1934), p. 94.

After the collapse of Ruge's *Jahrbücher* Marx contributed a few articles to another short-lived radical paper called *Vorwärts* (1844). An unsuccessful attempt on the life of King Frederick William IV had prompted the editors of *Vorwärts* to express a desire for a more accurate shot. The Prussian Government seized on the occasion to petition Guizot for the suppression of the paper and the expulsion of the editors and contributors from France. The *Vorwärts* had been a thorn in their flesh since the publication of Heine's *Die Weber*, written at the instigation of Marx on the occasion of the revolt of the Silesian weavers. This revolt marked the beginning of the German working-class movement. The story has been made familiar in modern days by Gerhart Hauptmann's drama, *Die Weber*, in which Hauptmann drew on recollections passed down by his family and neighbors. It was only natural that Berlin should wish the incident forgotten. Frederick William had exerted himself to relieve the distress, but the rioting was only ended by the usual Prussian expedient, the firing of soldiers on the crowd.

Guizot was willing enough to comply with the Prussian request, but unfortunately Heine was a difficult man to expel. He had lived in Paris for fourteen years, and the French people considered him one of themselves. Suddenly to order a poet of his reputation out of the country would bring down a storm of criticism from the liberal press. Heine himself therefore was not molested, but a number of other Germans who had contributed to the *Vorwärts*, including Marx, were ordered by the Paris police in January, 1845, to leave France within the month.

Driven out of France, Marx and his family gathered up their few belongings and moved to Brussels. In order to avoid any further difficulties with the Prussian Government he relinquished his Prussian citizenship and at the same time promised the Belgian authorities not to publish anything about current Belgian politics. The promise, as he understood it, did not affect his determination to make Brussels the headquarters of the international communist movement. In Paris he had been so absorbed in his books that he had found little time to attend the meetings of workingmen's associations. Those that he did attend convinced him that the French were on the wrong track. The followers of Saint-Simon and Fourier indulged themselves in fantastic dreams of a new society. They constructed the outlines of an ideal state out of their heads, and then looked about for a capitalist to launch it. Without any philosophy of history they could not understand that socialism was a necessary product of historical development. Marx was determined to establish socialism on a more scientific basis.

Brussels was not a bad headquarters for his purposes. From there he could keep in touch with developments in London, in Cologne and in Paris, the three points upon which his organization was to be based. Engels, who could only stand a few months of business at a time, soon joined him. He proposed a visit to England where the processes of capitalism could be observed at their best or at their worst. In the summer of 1845 Marx crossed the Channel for the first time and, in the company of Engels, spent some six weeks in Manchester and London. The England they set out to explore was the stagecoach England of the young Queen and Sir Robert Peel, of Mr. Pickwick and Becky Sharp, but it was also the England of the Corn Law agitation and of the Chartists, whom Marx believed to be already locked in a life-and-death struggle with the bourgeoisie. Marx met some of the Chartist leaders, and, what interested him even more, he met a group of German workmen who had settled down in London in pursuit of their respective trades and founded there a German Workers Educational Union. These men had previously belonged to a revolutionary organization in Paris called the "League of the Just." Their leading spirit was Wilhelm Weitling, one of the most picturesque figures among European radicals, in whom Marx at once recognized a dangerous rival.[11]

If Marx was to found a German Workers Association in Brussels, as he planned to do, and if it was ever to become the center of communist activity in Europe, he knew that he would have to oust Weitling from the position of leadership in the communist world. Weitling had the unquestionable advantage of being a workingman himself. He was the illegitimate son of a French officer who had been stationed in Magdeburg during the Napoleonic wars. His father had disappeared without making any provision for him, and young Wilhelm was apprenticed to a Magdeburg tailor. During the years of apprenticeship he picked up a smattering of education, enough to give him a sense of the injustice of the world but not enough to

[11] See Carl Wittke, "Marx and Weitling" in *Essays in Political Theory* (Cornell Univ. Press, 1948), pp. 179–93.

make him aware of his own mental deficiencies. When the moment arrived for him to do his military service, he left home with a pack on his back and a hatred of the army, government and all those in authority, in his heart. He drifted to Paris where he joined the League of the Just, and escaped to Switzerland when the League was broken up by the Paris police. In Switzerland he fell foul of the magistrates by publishing a book, *The Gospel of a Poor Sinner*, which depicted Jesus as a rebel and a communist, "the illegitimate child of a poor girl Mary." This thinly veiled piece of autobiography resulted in an indictment for blasphemy, six months' imprisonment and expulsion from the country. Having served his term he set forth on his wanderings again and eventually reached London in 1844, where he was enthusiastically entertained by the German Workers Educational Union.

Among those who met him in Switzerland was Bakunin, who found in him "plenty of undisciplined fanaticism, of honourable pride, and of faith in the future of the enslaved majority." [12] Undisciplined fanaticism was not a quality that appealed to Karl Marx. He had no patience with communism such as Weitling's that was founded on nothing more substantial than a burning personal grievance. Weitling must be shown up. Marx lured him to Brussels on the plea that those who were working for the same cause, namely the emancipation of labor, should sit down together and work out a common program. The details of the meeting are recorded for us by a Russian celebrity hunter, Paul Annenkov, who had come to Brussels to meet Marx, and whom Marx invited to attend the interview with Weitling. It appears that the meeting had hardly come to order before Marx jumped to his feet and challenged Weitling to stand and deliver:

> Tell us, Weitling, you who have made so much stir in Germany with your communist preaching, and have drawn after you so many working men, depriving them of their jobs and their crusts of bread, on what grounds do you justify your revolutionary and socialist activities, and on what basis do you propose to establish them for the future? [13]

Weitling was completely taken aback. The workingmen he had

[12] Quoted from E. H. Carr, *Michael Bakunin*, London, 1937, p. 122.
[13] Quoted from E. H. Carr, *Karl Marx*, p. 44.

addressed so passionately in Germany, in France and in Switzerland were not like Marx. They had not asked him for any theories. They were content to know that he had suffered, and they were grateful to him for talking to them so eloquently about justice, solidarity and fraternity. Weitling felt that his contribution to the cause was no less important than all this talk of theory and analysis conducted in the calm of the study by men who were utterly detached from those they professed to help. What did Marx know about workingmen? He had never had to earn his living, never been in prison, never suffered. Yes, he gloried in his ignorance of economic theory. Stung by this attack, Marx shouted back: "Ignorance has never yet helped anybody."

On that note the meeting broke up. It was the old quarrel between the staff and the line, the college-trained expert and the ignorant man who knew nothing beyond what his experience had taught him. Weitling knew he was beaten. He had no weapons with which to face the chilly scepticism of his learned opponent. Fortunately a German workers organization in New York heard of his controversy with Marx and invited him to become editor of the socialist *Volkstribun*. Weitling accepted and disappeared from Europe. We shall hear of him again in America as the founder of one of those short-lived utopian communities that were so popular during the forties and fifties. With such foolishness Marx had no sympathy. He cared nothing for socialistic experiments that affected only a fragment of society. Meanwhile he and Engels were busily engaged building up an organization and establishing the machinery of collaboration between communists of various countries. The word communist was of no special significance in their minds. They adopted it as a practical matter so as not to be confused with the socialist parties already in existence. Marx used the words "socialism" and "communism" interchangeably, but he made the sharpest possible distinction between his own rigorous doctrine and what seemed to him the cloudy, sentimental socialism of men like Owen and Louis Blanc.

While Marx stayed in Brussels writing, studying, and quarreling with everybody who did not agree with him, Engels was scurrying between London and Paris, interviewing those who might prove sympathetic. His letters to Marx are not those of a fanatic; indeed, he seems to have enjoyed the flesh-pots of Paris as much as any bourgeois. On the whole, the *grisettes* seem to have been more impressionable than the socialists. He sees Cabet, who was friendly enough (*der alte Knabe war recht kordial*), and Louis Blanc, who might go far if he could shake himself free from his ideology, but nothing much seems to have come of these interviews. Apparently French radicals were not yet ready to join any international organization.

Engels fared better in London, where, thanks to the Chartists, the proletariat had reached a stage of development unknown on the Continent. There were plenty of difficulties to be ironed out, but by the summer of 1847 Marx must have felt that they were beginning to see the light at the end of the tunnel. The federated "Leagues of the Just" held an international congress in London, which led to the welding of all existing proletarian forces into one single Communist League. The next step was the drafting of a constitution and what the delegates called a "confession of faith." This task was assigned to Marx and Engels. The original draft of the confession was sketched out by Engels but he was not pleased with it. In a letter to Marx, November 24, 1847, he suggests giving up the question and answer form in favor of an outright statement of principles or manifesto.[14] The change in the name from "League of the Just" to "Communist League" was no less significant than the change in the slogan from the eighteenth century "All men are brothers" to the nineteenth century "Proletarians of all countries, unite!"[15]

There was some delay in the writing of the Manifesto. Citizen Marx had to be prodded by the Central Committee in London, but the manuscript was finally finished and sent over to England early in 1848. It was printed in German—an octavo pamphlet of thirty pages. The copies were still damp from the press and had not yet been placed on sale, when on February 24 Louis Philippe fled from Paris, and the forcible overthrow of the whole existing order, promised by the Manifesto, appeared to have come to pass.

For the moment it looked as if the storm of revolution would engulf all Europe. From Sicily to the Baltic, rulers were

[14] "Ich glaube, wir tun am besten, wir lassen die Katechismusform weg und titulieren das Ding: Kommunistisches Manifest."

[15] As Professor Hans Kohn pointed out at a recent meeting of the American Historical Association, in Washington, December 29, 1948, the emphasis had shifted from the individual to the class.

tumbling over themselves in their hurry to grant the reforms demanded by their peoples. In every state existing ministers were jettisoned and more liberal ministers appointed. Metternich fled from Vienna, and King Frederick William IV bowed to the will of the Berlin mob. Except in Russia and England, the two empires that flanked the Continent, the peoples of Europe had got the bit between their teeth and were running away with their rulers. "Everything is demanded of us," wrote the distracted Duke Ernest of Saxe-Coburg, "even the establishment of perfect health and the gift of long life!" Benjamin Disraeli made a speech in the House of Commons about the "modern, new-fangled, sentimental principle of nationality" that was threatening one nation after another with civil war.

Marx was not satisfied. The great engine of revolution lumbered through Europe knocking over a few governments, but it did not plough up the stiff soil of society in the way he had hoped. In the *Communist Manifesto* he drew up the program of the revolt of the proletariat and its triumph over the bourgeoisie. Communists must everywhere support every revolutionary movement against the existing social and political order of things. A revolution that fell short of this program was no revolution at all. The adoption of universal suffrage and parliamentary government, which seemed the solution to many so-called socialists, was no solution to Karl Marx. While Ledru-Rollin and his friends charged Louis Philippe and the Bourgeois Monarchy with responsibility for the economic depression of 1847, Marx exonerated them and laid the blame squarely on the capitalistic system. Hegel, whom he called "the world philosopher of our time," had argued that true freedom was to be found in working in line with the trend of history. Marx agreed. He was all in favor of surrendering to the trend of history, but whereas Hegel believed that the Prussian state represented the culmination of the historic process Marx was convinced that the forces of history led elsewhere—to the overthrow of all states, including Prussia, and the emancipation of society at large from all exploitation, all national and class distinctions.

The *Communist Manifesto*, like all good propaganda, is full of sweeping generalities couched in a deceptively simple style. "A spectre is haunting Europe—the spectre of communism. . . . The history of all past society is the history of class struggles. . . . Society as a whole is more and more splitting into two great hostile camps, into two great classes directly facing each other—bourgeoisie and proletariat. . . . The bourgeoisie has subjected the country to the rule of the towns. . . . You reproach us with intending to do away with your property. Precisely so; that is just what we intend." So it goes on for thirty trenchant pages, the most arresting declaration of principles since Jefferson's.

In England the more thoughtful Tories were already aware of the ever-widening gulf between the rich and the poor, but no remedy they suggested went to the heart of the problem. The various factory laws passed during the forties, such as the Ten Hours Bill, might mitigate the appalling conditions under which men worked, yet they did not remove the indignity of an unemancipated class. Disraeli's "Young England" movement, inspired by Carlyle, was merely harking back to a romantic and paternalistic feudalism. Engels had already dismissed it in *The Condition of the Working Class in England* as "unattainable and ridiculous." In the *Manifesto* Marx put in more picturesquely: "The aristocracy, in order to rally the people to them, waved the proletarian almsbag in front for a banner. But the people, so often as it joined them, saw on their hindquarters the old feudal coats of arms, and deserted with loud and irreverent laughter." Nor was Marx any more kindly disposed to the utopianism of Cabet, the *petit bourgeois* socialism of Sismondi, or the Christian socialism of Lamennais. Christian socialism "is but the holy water with which the priest consecrates the heartburnings of the aristocrat."

Having thus excoriated the bourgeois civilization evolved by capitalism, and derided the simpletons who would cure the cancer by rose-water methods, the *Manifesto* goes on to cite ten reform measures as "pretty generally applicable in the most advanced countries."

1. Abolition of property in land and application of all rents from land to public purposes.
2. A heavy progressive or graduated income tax.
3. Abolition of all right of inheritance.
4. Confiscation of the property of all emigrants and rebels.
5. Centralization of credit in the hands of the state, by means of a national bank with state capital and an exclusive monopoly.

6. Centralization of the means of communication and transport in the hands of the state.
7. Extension of the number of state factories and instruments of production: the bringing into cultivation of waste lands, and the improvement of the soil generally in accordance with a common plan.
8. Equal obligation of all to work. Establishment of industrial armies, especially for agriculture.
9. Combination of agriculture with manufacturing industries; gradual abolition of the distinction between town and country, by a more equable distribution of the population over the country.
10. Free education for all children in public schools. Abolition of children's factory labor in its present form. Combination of education with industrial production.

In 1848 these proposals must have sounded like the ravings of a lunatic, but they are mild and reasonable—many of them indeed have been adopted by conservative governments —compared to the ringing peroration: "Let the ruling classes tremble at a Communist revolution. In it the proletarians have nothing to lose but their chains. They have a world to win. Workingmen of all countries, unite." [16] Posterity has chosen to remember the exhortation to revolution rather than the demands for a graduated income tax, a national bank, conservation of natural resources, and free education.

The immediate effect of the *Manifesto* was slight. The fact that its publication coincided with the outbreak of revolution prevented its receiving the attention it might otherwise have had. Had it come out a few months earlier or a year later it would at least have attracted the interest of the police, but at the moment that it appeared there were more important things to think about than the supposedly scientific communism of two unknown young Germans. It is only after living through the tornado that one wants to read about the meteorological disturbances that caused it. The explosive power of the *Manifesto* was reserved for future generations. It is like

[16] The translations from the *Manifesto* are taken from the English edition of 1888, which was supervised by Engels himself. The first English translation appeared in George Julian Harney's *Red Republican* (London, 1850). The more popular form of the communist slogan, "Workers of the world, unite," was not used by Marx or Engels.

a diabolic time bomb that gathers fresh force from every explosion. The French socialist who maintained that the *Manifesto* had been more read than any other book in the world except the Bible was drawing a long bow, but its persistent popularity cannot be denied.[17] Lenin was not exaggerating when he declared that "the whole organized and fighting proletariat of the civilized world lives and moves in the spirit of the *Manifesto* to this day."

Less than a week after the declaration of the French Republic Marx received a letter from Flocon, one of the members of the Provisional Republic, inviting him to return to Paris.[18] He had already been arrested in Brussels, treated according to his own account with unheard-of brutality, and ordered to leave the country within twenty-four hours. The Belgian Government, startled by the blaze of revolution across the frontier, decided that it had already tolerated Marx's presence for three years, and that that was enough. Marx wrote a long article for the *Réforme* about the persecution to which he had been subjected by a reactionary government.[19] He arrived in Paris on March 4, took rooms at 10 rue Neuve Ménilmontant, just off the boulevard Beaumarchais, and began to study the processes of revolution in actual operation. The Communist League in London had already transferred executive authority to district representatives in Brussels, who in turn handed it on to Marx in Paris. He was now President of the Communist League. If only there were a few more communists! After the excitement of the first week he wondered whether the revolution was not going to peter out into a mere change of rulers— in France a Proudhon or a Lamartine instead of Louis Philippe, and in Prussia a bourgeois liberal instead of Frederick William IV. If this were to be the result of the revolution, Marx predicted a stampede of the working class to America and a compromise with the well-to-do bourgeoisie from which the proletariat would gain nothing.

Would the Revolution, victorious in France, reach out to

[17] Ernest Labrousse in *La Revue Socialiste*, January, 1948.

[18]
> Paris, le 1er mars 1848
>
> Cher et vaillant Marx,
> Le sol de la République francaise est le refuge de tous les amis de la liberté. La tyrannie vous a banni, la libre France vous ouvre ses portes à vous et à tous ceux qui luttent pour la sainte cause de la fraternité des peuples. Salut et fraternité.
>
> FERDINAND FLOCON
> Membre du Gouvernement provisoire.

[19] *La Réforme*, March 8, 1848.

the other nations of Europe? The outlook was not promising. The Provisional Government, eager to consolidate the advantages it had won, wanted peace at any price. From the very first day Lamartine, as Minister of Foreign Affairs, was assuring all foreign governments of the peaceful intentions of the French Republic. It was this prudent conservatism that determined the attitude of the Provisional Government toward the various foreign legions that were being recruited in Paris and that were to carry the torch of revolution into less enlightened countries. Certain that these ill-equipped volunteers would be easily dealt with by the armies of the countries they were invading, and glad to rid themselves of foreigners who added to the unemployment problem, the members of the Provisional Government outdid themselves in making polite speeches and in cheering the delegations on their way. It cost nothing to assure a few Poles, a few Germans, or a few Irishmen that France was always on the side of liberty, and it cost very little to ease them out of the country, though the funds donated by the Government for this purpose excited angry protests from the foreign ambassadors.

Marx saw through the tactics of the Provisional Government at once. He was particularly indignant at the support given by Lamartine to the German Legion, which was nothing but a device for handing over to their respective governments workmen whom France could not use. Two thousand Germans, headed by the poet Herwegh and his millionaire wife, proposed to invade the Fatherland, brush aside any resistance they might meet, and proclaim a republic. "I do not doubt for a moment," wrote Herwegh on March 15, "that if today we received a signal to rise, we could stand on the frontier thoroughly equipped within eight days." [20] A week later the signal was given, and the first battalion of the Legion marched out of Paris. Meanwhile the Prussian, Baden and Württemberg ministers in Paris were communicating with their governments. As soon as the Legion crossed the Rhine it was intercepted by a small force of Württemberg troops. With the first volley the legionaries, who had no cartridges with which to answer the fire of the enemy, took to their heels. Some thirty of them were killed, a few trickled back into France, and the rest, including the Herweghs, escaped into Switzerland. So ended the invasion

[20] Quoted by J. G. Legge, *Rhyme and Revolution in Germany*, p. 361.

of Germany. The other foreign legions that set out with fanfare of trumpets for Belgium and Savoy fared no better.

From Marx's point of view the whole enterprise was insane. Instead of engaging in this revolutionary foolery, the foreigners in Paris should have been girding themselves for the real struggle that was to come. He and Engels had been building for the future by starting a German workingmen's club in Paris in opposition to Herwegh's Legion. As soon as the workingmen were indoctrinated, they were to make their own way into Germany, settle in the industrial centers or wherever the revolutionary movement showed signs of activity, and there build up communist cells. In the meantime, the Central Committee of the Communist League, including himself, Engels, Wilhelm Wolff (a schoolteacher from Silesia to whom *Das Kapital* was afterwards dedicated), and three German workingmen who had come over from England—Karl Schapper, a typesetter, Heinrich Bauer, a shoemaker, and Joseph Moll, a watchmaker—issued a statement of seventeen specific reforms demanded by the Communist Party in Germany. These were more or less a restatement of the points already made in the *Communist Manifesto,* but they contained also a demand that Germany should be proclaimed a republic, one and indivisible.

The program was more adapted to France than to Germany. In Germany there was no question of overthrowing a bourgeois regime, for such a thing had never existed. The problem in Germany was to create a bourgeoisie powerful enough to cope with the absolute rulers and the feudal nobility. In France "freedom" meant universal suffrage and a republic that would guarantee a living wage to all workers, but in Prussia, or Hanover, or Bavaria, freedom meant nothing more than establishing the sort of government that the French had just upset. In 1848 there was still no such thing as Germany. The great shapeless area stretching across the middle of Europe included five kingdoms and innumerable duchies, grand duchies, and even republics. There was a German language spoken by 25,000,000 Germans; there was a German art and a German culture, but there was no such thing as a German flag or a German state. "You Frenchmen are lucky," remarked Hegel on one occasion to his friend and disciple Victor Cousin, "you are a nation." The same note of frustration recurs throughout

Treitschke's *History*: "In Rio no less than in New York people would disdainfully inquire, 'Where is your Germany? . . . We have never seen a German flag, a German consul to represent its interests, or a German warship to defend it.' " [21]

Napoleon had simplified the political geography of Germany in the interests of efficiency, but the Congress of Vienna reintroduced the confusion by creating the Confederation of Germany. The political problems of the Confederation were further complicated by the peculiar character of the component parts. While the most powerful members of the Confederation were Prussia and Austria, two thirds of the peoples of the Austrian Empire, mainly non-German, were not included. Yet the interests of these Hungarians, Poles, Croats and Czechs might dictate the policy of the Austrian delegates. The Kingdom of Prussia represented another problem. It was built up of provinces that had been shifted about like the pieces in a jig-saw puzzle. Prussian Poland had been taken away and then partially returned. After Waterloo, when the Powers decided to make Prussia the warden of the German gate against France, she was given the Rhineland and Westphalia. The gift was not entirely welcome, for it created a kingdom of widely separated provinces. Between the new Rhineland province and the original Brandenburg nucleus lay the Kingdom of Hanover, always jealous of Prussia, and other smaller states. Furthermore, though eastern Prussia had several windows opening on the Baltic, western Prussia had no outlet to the sea at all. Kiel was Danish, Hamburg and Bremen were free cities, Emden belonged to the duchy of Oldenburg, and the mouths of the Rhine were Dutch.

The haphazard collection of provinces which had been dumped into Prussia's lap, each with its own fiscal and tariff policy, had to be welded into some sort of political and economic unity. As long as Frederick William III lived it was generally accepted that no changes would be made in the political institutions of Prussia, but by 1848 the advent of railroads, together with the *Zollverein* or Customs Union, had already begun to lift Germany from its economic stagnation. The *Zollverein* came first. In 1819 Prussia established a single tariff for all her own lands. The next step was to declare her willingness to accept neighboring states as partners in the new

[21] Treitschke, *History of Germany in the 19th Century*, 7 vols., London, 1915, VII, 203.

system. The advantages of the system were so apparent that all the states in the Confederation except Austria and Hanover soon wanted to be included. By January 1, 1834, when the *Zollverein* first came into effect, throughout three quarters of Germany long trains of wagons stood waiting to cross the frontier lines, with goods now for the first time toll free.[22]

The growth of the railroads stimulated the policy that the Customs Union had begun. One of the chief champions of the railroad in Germany was King Ludwig of Bavaria, who brushed aside the assertions of the Bavarian College of Physicians that railroad travel would give horrible headaches to both travellers and spectators, but it was Friedrich List, the great German economist, who conceived and advocated the idea of a German railway system. List was the Alexander Hamilton of Germany, the man who first realized that the German states must develop their manufactures, and at the same time build an adequate transportation system, if they were ever to aspire to nationhood. He foresaw, though no Prussian, that the railroad network would have to radiate from Berlin, and it was thanks to him that Germany, disunited as she was, forged far ahead of France in the construction of railroads. With the help of the Saxon Government he organized the company that built the first commercial line in Germany, between Leipzig and Dresden. Reports show that in 1839, when the line was opened, it carried 412,000 persons, "including ladies who kept needles between their lips to check familiarity in the single tunnel."[23]

Thus, thanks to the *Zollverein* and the railroads, Prussia had become by 1848 a prosperous state, but owing to the lack of natural frontiers it was a "made" state rather than a natural one like France or England. Surely the next step would be representative government, which in turn would lead to German unification. So at least thought such German liberals as Baron von Bunsen, the Prussian Ambassador in London. The accession of Frederick William IV in 1840 raised high hopes. Nature had endowed the new king with an agreeable personality and a quick, sympathic intelligence. He was a clever artist—he excelled in sketches of romantic castles—an eloquent speaker and a charming letter writer. He was something of a

[22] J. H. Clapham, *Economic Development of France and Germany, 1815–1914* (Camb. Univ. Press, 1945), p. 97.
[23] J. H. Clapham, *op. cit.*, p. 151.

mystic too, if mysticism can be stretched to include a belief
that he had been divinely appointed to promote the welfare
of his people, about which he claimed to know far more than
the people did themselves. The personalities of the court were
invariably attached to him even when they saw his faults. Leopold von Ranke, the historian, described him as a young
man full of intelligence and knowledge "who, excuse the
professor in me, has by some mischance failed in his examina-
tion."

The reign began in the conventional liberal way with an
amnesty to political offenders. Arndt, the author of patriotic
poems against Napoleon, who had subsequently fallen foul of
his own Government by criticizing the reactionary policy of
German princes, was restored to his professorship at Bonn;
Turnvater Jahn, the father of gymnastics in Germany, another
old patriot suspected of liberalism, was relieved of police supervision; and the brothers Grimm, victims of despotism in Hanover, were called to Berlin. In his first speech Frederick
William let it be known that he intended great changes. He
regarded the protection of the lower classes as a sacred Christian duty. The press hailed him as the reformer for whom all
Germany was longing, and Herwegh wrote a poem comparing
the King to the magnetic north, to which the people, like the
needle in a compass, were always turning. But it was not long
before they were disillusioned. There was in the King's character an almost pathological element of vacillation that prevented him from following any one straight line. Unfortunately
this vacillation was not incompatible with an equally objectionable vein of stubbornness. He insisted on having his own
way without ever being quite sure what it was that he wanted.
Marx and Engels were delighted by the stubbornness, which
they knew must ultimately lead to revolution, whereas a constantly vacillating king might always just manage to avoid a
crisis. But they need have had no fears.[24]

Within a few months of his accession the King refused
categorically to redeem the promise of a constitution made by
his father in 1815. Later he went half way by summoning com-
mittees of the various provincial Diets in Prussia to meet as a

---

[24] "Wenn doch der FW IV sich starrköpfig hielt! Dann ist alles gewonnen,
und wir haben in ein paar Monaten die deutsche Revolution . . . Aber der Teufel
weiss, was dieser launige und verrückte Individuum tun wird."—Letter from Engels
to Marx, March 8, 1848.

United Diet in Berlin. At the opening ceremony on April 11, 1847, he delivered his famous "scrap of paper" speech:

> I am impelled to the solemn declaration that no power on earth shall ever move me to transform into a conventional and constitutional relationship that bond between prince and people whose intrinsic truth it is which renders us so mighty, and that neither now nor ever will I allow a scribbled sheet of paper to intervene like a second Providence between our God in Heaven and this land of ours, to rule us by paragraphs and oust our time-honoured and sacred fidelity to each other.[25]

That speech set the tone of the meeting, and it is not surprising that the United Diet separated shortly afterward under a general cloud of dissatisfaction and distrust. The King's attempt to escape from an honorable obligation was not forgotten. For the first time representatives of all Prussia from the Rhine to the Vistula had met in Berlin, and regardless of court traditions they had discussed their common interests. A few months later, early in 1848, he was willing to promise anything and everything, but by then it was too late.[26]

Frederick William had chosen a bad time to fall out with his people. France was overthrowing not only Louis Philippe but the whole principle of monarchy as well. In Bavaria the prestige of monarchy was already suffering from King Ludwig's infatuation with a Scottish dancer who called herself Lola Montez. Royal mistresses do not necessarily make for revolution, but Lola's demand for the removal of the university from Munich was more than even the good-natured Bavarians could stand. Finally the King abdicated and Lola Montez, like so many Continental fugitives in days of trouble, fled to England where she had no difficulty finding adequate substitutes for the King of Bavaria. Baron von Brenner, the Austrian Minister in Munich, reporting to his Government on the King's abdication, remarked that "the people grew twenty years riper in these few days." [27]

In the Rhineland men were maturing even more rapidly.

---

[25] Quoted by J. G. Legge, *op. cit.*, p. 150.

[26] The utterly unpredictable character of Frederick William IV is brought out by D. R. Strauss, the famous German theologian and man of letters, in *Der Romantiker auf dem Thron der Cäsaren* (1847), in which Strauss drew a parallel between Julian the Apostate and Frederick William IV.

[27] Veit Valentin, *1848: Chapters of German History*, London, 1940, p. 88.

On February 27, only four days after Louis Philippe's flight, the citizens of Mannheim convened a public assembly at which they formulated demands for freedom of the press, trial by jury, and a German parliament. In Hanover, the Duke of Cumberland, a cast-iron Tory who had ascended the throne of the newly created kingdom as King Ernest Augustus, forestalled serious trouble by concessions liberal enough to satisfy the least progressive of German states. Everywhere patriotic associations were springing up overnight. On March 5 a group of professional men met together in Heidelberg, proclaimed the fusion of Germany, and named a committee to study ways and means of summoning a preliminary parliament. This was indeed the *Völkerfrühling,* the people's springtime, when it looked as if all the ills of mankind were going to be washed away in a torrent of beautiful words. Never before had people believed so implicitly in the magical power of resolutions and speeches. A captious critic at the Heidelberg meeting might perhaps have discerned a small cloud on the horizon. There seemed to be some disagreement between Heinrich von Gagern, who wanted to proceed cautiously according to parliamentary rules, and the impetuous Friedrich Hecker, who was all for declaring a People's Republic at once. Heinrich von Gagern, an old-fashioned liberal from Hesse-Darmstadt who had been wounded at Waterloo before he was sixteen, warned those present to beware of setting up a new republican Confederation of the Rhine. "I will have no mob rule and no coquetting with the mob," he exclaimed. Hecker retorted that he wanted no freedom if it was to be only for the privileged or for the rich.[28] Marx observed the rift between the moderates and extremists, and saw that it was good. German unity, as the Frankfort Parliament was to show still more clearly, was in itself a question big with disunion, and he was determined to make the most of it. For republican idealists like Hecker he had nothing but contempt.[29]

Like all the other rulers in Germany, Frederick William found himself swept along by the revolutionary current. He was always, as his tutor described him, "the prey of the passing moment," but though he was ready enough to make concessions he never really understood the meaning of constitutional government. The people insisted on a genuine parliament that

[28] J. G. Legge, *Rhyme and Revolution in Germany,* p. 247.
[29] Karl Marx, *Revolution and Counter-Revolution,* chap. 3.

could initiate legislation. The King still clung to the notion of a *Landtag*, a glorified debating society of whose futility they had long since grown tired. That was the issue that the King, forever dreaming of some rigmarole of feudal Estates, could never bring himself to face. No one could fail to see that the revolution in Paris, closely followed as it was by the fall of Metternich in Vienna, was an ominous danger signal. The charged atmosphere was certain to produce riots, but as in Paris the Army was considered strong enough to restore order and maintain absolutism. On the morning of March 18, the Berlin chief of police learned that a great demonstration in front of the castle had been planned for the afternoon. The King issued a conciliatory proclamation, but it was too late. By midnight he was besieged in his castle by an ugly crowd demanding that the troops should be withdrawn from Berlin. He could either submit to the people or he could give the Army a free hand. General von Prittwitz, in whom the Army had complete confidence, was willing and ready to stamp out the insurrection, but the King was a man of feeling and he recoiled from the idea of street fighting. Unable to make a clear-cut decision he ended by forfeiting the respect both of his people and of the Army.

What had happened during those few hours was a curious repetition of the mysterious shot on the boulevard des Capucines, on the night of February 23, that kindled the fires of revolution in Paris. While the people of Berlin surged into the open square in front of the palace, clamoring for the King to appear on the balcony, two shots "accidentally" discharged by soldiers on the edge of the crowd threw everybody into a panic. The effect of those shots, accidental or not, was disastrous. No one was wounded, but a regiment of dragoons seized the opportunity to advance upon the crowd and clear the square. The revolution was now in full swing. The people, believing they had been purposely lured into the palace square to be butchered, began throwing up the inevitable barricades. M. de Circourt, the French Minister, who had seen the Paris risings of 1830 and 1848, wrote Lamartine at the end of the first day's fighting that the frenzied resolution of the Berlin mob made these March days stand out in his mind as more horrible than anything that had happened in Paris.[30] The actual fighting, though fierce, did not last long, but its impor-

[30] A. de Circourt, *Souvenirs d'une Mission à Berlin* (Paris, 1908), p. 188.

tance was heightened by the pitiful collapse of the King. At first he was determined to put down the insurrection at any cost. Then he changed his mind and issued a proclamation to his "dear Berliners" representing the revolution as the work of foreign agents. In the midst of the fighting he displayed a white banner bearing the word "misunderstanding" in great letters, but the people were too embittered to discuss misunderstandings. Nothing would satisfy them but the unconditional evacuation of the city by all the troops, and this at last the King ordered. Officers and men marched out of the city, disgusted and bewildered. The Prince of Prussia, Prince "Grapeshot" as he was called, who was supposed to have given the order to fire, fled to England.

The King was now completely in the hands of the populace, and the scene was set for his own personal humiliation. First, he was made to come down from his palace to inspect the mutilated corpses of those who had fallen in the barricades.

"Hats off!" the multitude shouted, and the King took off his hat to the dead below. Then a deep voice among the crowd intoned the old hymn, 'Jesus, meine Zuversicht'—'Jesus my Refuge,' in which all present joined. The chorus finished, the King silently withdrew, and the procession moved away in grim solemnity." [31] A few days later the King formally capitulated to the revolution by issuing a decree ordering the Prussian Army to wear a cockade with the revolutionary colors—black, red and gold—alongside of the regular black and white Prussian cockade. His army had just been fighting against the black, red and gold flag of the revolution. Now he himself seized the hated enemy colors and flaunted them in the street. At the same time placards were posted "To the German Nation," announcing that for the salvation of Germany Frederick William had placed himself at the head of the whole fatherland. Perhaps he felt that by assuming the pose of constitutional leader of Germany he might extricate himself from the tangle of humiliation in which he had become involved.

To make the degradation still more complete the wretched King was compelled to liberate all political prisoners and to greet them as they left the prison. Among those pardoned was the famous soldier of fortune Mierolawski. Half Polish and half French, Mierolawski was one of those ardent spirits who are always organizing unsuccessful insurrections. In 1848 he

[31] Carl Schurz, *Reminiscences*, I, 121.

organized a rising which was to begin in Posen and Galicia, and thence to extend over Russian Poland. It was easily suppressed, and Mierolawski was arrested by order of Frederick William and imprisoned at the request of the Czar.[32] The speech made by the liberated Poles has a not altogether unfamiliar ring about it: "The people of Berlin are beginning to realize what the exigencies of the time require. For the security of a free Germany an independent Poland must be reconstituted to resist the pressure of the Asiatics." [33] The speech chimed in well with the sentiments of the German people who have always looked upon Poland as a bulwark of civilization whenever war with Russia appears desirable or unavoidable.

In the meantime the Prussian Government had been reconstituted with a view to the task awaiting it. The administration was for the first time entrusted to business men belonging neither to the nobility nor to the official class. Ludolf Camphausen, the prime minister, no soldier and no aristocrat but an ex-President of the Chamber of Commerce of Cologne, undertook the impossible task of reconciling the old order and the new. He was a cautious liberal, not lacking in courage but more interested in the development of railroads and shipbuilding than in the thorny constitutional problems he was called upon to solve. David Hansemann, the Minister of Finance and the next most important figure in the cabinet, was another of those industrial magnates who, in Germany as elsewhere, were just beginning to make themselves felt in the political world. Under the new ministry the Prussian National Assembly came into being, signifying the moral and political victory of the citizens of Berlin over the absolute rule of the King. Constitutional government, trial by jury and freedom of the press had suddenly been conjured out of the air. Revolution was winning all along the line—in Saxony, in Hanover, and in Württemberg, no less than in Prussia. In Vienna the fall of Metternich, far from satisfying the people, had precipitated a demand for far-reaching reforms.

In Cologne, where the ground had been better prepared than elsewhere, men were talking about a national guard, the

---

[32] After spending two years in a Prussian prison, Mierolawski cropped up again in command of rebel forces in Sicily in 1848, and in Baden in 1849. Later on he served in Garibaldi's Legion, and he was with Gambetta in 1870. He is said to have combined "recklessly radical convictions with the personal prejudices of an aristocrat and a dictator."

[33] A. de Circourt, *Souvenirs*, p. 212.

abolition of the regular army, free education, and the right to
guaranteed employment. It was no time for German radicals
to be lingering in Paris. Marx had been expounding the *Communist Manifesto*, just arrived from London, to the followers
of Blanqui and Barbès, but the time had come when his presence was more needed in his own country. The bourgeoisie,
represented by such men as Camphausen and Hansemann,
must not be allowed to divert the spontaneous enthusiasm of
the people for their own benefit. In Paris the revolution had
fizzled out into a squabble between different groups of bourgeois democrats. In Germany it might still be possible to drive
the progressive forces on from the reformist outlook to the
revoluntionary stage where a direct attack is made on private
property.

The directors of the Communist League left Paris in
April. Wolff went to Breslau, Schappen to Wiesbaden, Engels
to Elberfeld, and Marx to Cologne. Camphausen invited Marx
to settle in Berlin, but he preferred to remain in Cologne where
he was already known and where the Code Napoleon, still in
operation, assured him greater liberty of action than he would
have had in Berlin. The Code Napoleon, unlike the law in
force elsewhere in Prussia, provided for the trial of political
offenses by a jury. Marx decided that if he ever should get
into trouble his own townspeople would take a more lenient
view of his case than a government-appointed judge.

The immediate problem that faced him was the eternally
boring question of money. Propaganda was the crying need of
the moment, as always with Marx, and propaganda could not
be conducted without funds. He must have his own newspaper
—it was to be the *Neue Rheinische Zeitung* this time—and the
faithful Engels must see to the financing. It was not an easy
task. Engels' own father was a rich man, and Marx hopefully
suggested that he might do something substantial for them,
but Mr. Engels thought otherwise. He was one of those people
who avoid the discussion of social questions as they would the
plague. Pure incitement, that is what it was, and Caspar
Engels would not give them a penny.[34] His son Friedrich was
equally determined. The newpaper, as he explained to some
of his less suspicious bourgeois friends, was not to be considered

---

[34] "Die Leute scheuen sich alle wie die Pest vor der Diskussion der gesell-
schaftlichen Fragen; das nennen sie Aufwiegelei."—Letter from Engels to Marx,
April 25, 1848. See also, Marx to Engels, April 24, 1848.

as a herald of communism. On the contrary, it was to be a herald of democracy. On this understanding a few shares were subscribed, and on June 1 the *Neue Rheinische Zeitung* made its appearance with, sure enough, the words "Organ of Democracy" on the title page. "We joined the democratic party," said Engels years later, "as the only possible means of getting the ear of the working class." [35] In other words, the noble end justified the rather shabby means. Obviously the sin that the world attributes to the Jesuits, though no political party has ever been free from it, was already beginning to eat its way into communism.

Under the sheep's clothing of democracy Karl Marx soon found himself championing the German bourgeoisie and avoiding any suggestion of a possible rift with the proletariat. This was all the more necessary in view of the fact that by June 1, 1848, German liberals were growing weary of revolution. It was no use preaching communism until the bourgeoisie had cleared the way by winning the battle for German unity. There would be plenty of time then to show that the victory was only an illusion. In Prussia the Camphausen Ministry had run into difficulties already. With the re-establishment of order Frederick William plucked up courage to the extent of thwarting the mildly liberal reforms the Government was trying to carry out. Once again he insisted that the ministers were merely agents of his will. As Bunsen regretfully noted, "the idea that subjects, and those such as he felt to be inferior to himself both in abilities and experience, should direct his policies, was intolerable to him." [36] Under these circumstances Camphausen resigned. It was obviously impossible to found a liberal state if the King refused to abide by the recognized rules of constitutional government. The situation was further complicated by the simultaneous elections to the Prussian National Assembly and the Frankfort Parliament. Several men had been elected to both bodies. Which of the two assemblies held the prior claim? Should one build from the ground up, or from the top down? Should one devote all one's energies to remodelling Prussia, or concentrate at once on the greater Germany to be? Could one be free and united at the same time?

[35] Letter to Florence K. Wischnewetzky, January 27, 1887. Quoted by L. Schwarzschild, *The Red Prussian*, p. 181.

[36] *A Memoir of Baron Bunsen, Drawn Chiefly from Family Papers by His Widow*, 2 vols. (London, 1868–69), II, 211.

Such were the questions that puzzled good German liberals during the springtime of 1848, while those who made no pretense to liberalism, like Engels' father, wondered whether these speculations would not inevitably lead to anarchy and recurrent revolution.

In the speech from the throne with which Frederick William opened the Prussian National Assembly on May 22, he expressed regret that the internal affairs of Prussia had not permitted her to wait for the results of the Frankfort Parliament. He himself was ready to merge Prussia with Germany. The King revelled in generalizations. Vague talk about a greater German *Reich* was much more his affair than the meticulous questions involving his prerogative that the Prussian National Assembly was likely to discuss. But events moved too quickly for him. Only a few days after the outbreaks in Vienna and Berlin the preliminary Parliament, conceived by the assembly of notables at Heidelberg, had met in Frankfort, in the old church of St. Paul's, to settle the question of a constitution for all Germany. The National Assembly, to which in turn the preliminary Parliament gave way, held its first meeting on May 22. This Frankfort Parliament, the one Parliament worthy of the name that Germany has ever had, was a body of extremely able men. Carl Schurz, in summing up the various political bodies he had seen in operation, thought the American Congress the most representative, the House of Commons the most businesslike, the French Assembly the most turbulent, and the Frankfort Parliament the most dignified and orderly. Unfortunately it had at its immediate disposal no administrative machinery, no army, no treasury, only its moral authority and the brains of its members. There was one laboring man among them, a Polish peasant from Silesia. All the rest were well-educated men, most of them products of university education. There were 49 university professors, 57 professors and other teachers from higher schools, 157 judges, 118 civil servants, 66 lawyers, and a liberal sprinkling of Catholic priests, Protestant pastors, mayors, doctors, diplomats and librarians—all in all an imposing gathering, though perhaps too academic for the rough-and-tumble business of making a nation. "Too much of a university and not enough of a political stock exchange" was the terse comment of one German historian.[37] Nevertheless for a moment it looked as if the long-

[37] Veit Valentin, *op. cit.*, p. 271.

standing disputes between the rulers themselves, and between the rulers and their peoples, would be melted away by the eloquence of these learned men.

One of the many difficult questions the Frankfort Parliament had to consider was the meaning of the word "Germany." Did Germany include all of Austria, such parts of Austria as were German-speaking, or no part of Austria at all? The German was the most influential element in the Austrian Empire. Metternich himself was a Rhinelander, the professional classes were overwhelmingly German, and Germans, though only one third of the population, paid two thirds of the taxes. After long discussions the Frankfort Parliament voted to include in the new *Reich* only the German-speaking provinces. The decision was promptly repudiated by Vienna. Complicated as was the situation in Germany, owing to the number of small states and the overlapping of Austria and the German Confederation, the tangle within the Austrian Empire was still more intricate. In view of the current of nationalism that was sweeping through Europe, how was Austria to keep the diverse elements in her Empire—the Germans, Magyars, Czechs, Croats, Poles, etc.— welded together? The same force that was working slowly but surely for German unity, the feeling that Prussians and Bavarians, Saxons and Hessians, possessed a common cultural heritage, spoke the same language and therefore should come together, was working conversely in Austria to drive the different sections of the Empire apart. But the Austrian Empire in spite of its cumbersome administration could still draw on a fund of vitality that kept it alive for another seventy years.

Another and no less prickly problem that the wise men of Frankfort had to resolve was the form of the new government. Should Germany be an empire or a republic? In some states, particularly Baden, the sentiment was strongly republican, whereas Prussia and Bavaria were still devoted to the idea of monarchy, provided the monarchy was not too absolute. But before any of these questions could be settled the Frankfort Parliament felt that it must lay a firm foundation of philosophic principles. Accordingly the debates on the constitution were prefaced by a discussion of the fundamental rights of the German man, a list of which had been drawn up in a hundred paragraphs. Days passed into weeks, and weeks into months while the Parliament was still busy with underlying principles.

It was all very thorough and very German, but in the meantime the ardor of the people was beginning to cool.

The editors of the *Neue Rheinische Zeitung* followed the proceedings at Frankfort with the greatest satisfaction. Everything was going wrong, as Marx had predicted and hoped. The first act of the National Parliament should have been to proclaim the sovereignty of the people, and the second to draft a constitution based on that sovereignty. In the very first issue of the paper Marx pointed out that neither of these obvious steps had been taken.[38]

As to the question of German unity, which split the Parliament into two camps, the advocates of a greater Germany including Austria as the senior partner, and the advocates of a little Germany headed by Prussia, he was completely indifferent. Nor was he interested in the political jockeying between the two groups which ended in the election of the Austrian Archduke John as the provisional head of the nation (*Reichsverweser*). The Archduke's popularity was due to a certain bluff good humor coupled with the fact that he had married the daughter of a postmaster, which was taken as a proof of his democratic leanings. Marx decided that Frankfort was going the way of all bourgeois parliaments. It was headed for conciliation, or what we might call appeasement. Instead of affirming its solidarity with the people it was bent on coming to an understanding with kings and princes. That the German revolution was a travesty of the great revolution of 1789 was only too obvious. Within three weeks of the fall of the Bastille Frenchmen had rid themselves of the last vestige of feudalism; but in Germany, four months after the fighting on the Berlin barricades, the feudal rights of the aristocracy had not yet been seriously challenged.[39] How could one describe the revolution in Germany except as a case of much ado about nothing (*die wenige Wolle von dem vielen Geschrei*)!

The drift toward counter-revolution was hastened by the lurid course of events in Paris. The desperate fighting of the June days had struck a chill through Europe. Paris as usual set the fashion in revolution, and it was all too likely that what had happened in Paris would be re-enacted in Vienna or

---

[38] "Die deutsche Nationalversammlung hat nun schon an ein Dutzend Sitzungen gehalten, und hat von dem Allen Nichts getan."

[39] *Neue Rheinische Zeitung*, July 30, 1848.

Berlin. If all the noble speeches about liberty and the brother-hood of man were to result in the slaughter of thousands of soldiers and workmen on the barricades, then surely revolution was an evil thing, and anyone who talked of perpetuating a revolution instead of putting the brakes on and bringing it to a halt was an enemy of society. The *Neue Rheinische Zeitung* was the only paper in Europe, with the exception of the Chart-ist *Northern Star*, that took the side of the proletariat. Up to the end of June, Marx and Engels, anxious to appear as demo-crats rather than communists, had not touched on social ques-tions at all, but the fighting in the streets of Paris convinced them that the time had come to throw off the mask. The *Mani-festo* was beginning to be known throughout Germany, and there was no hiding the fact, developed so clearly in the *Mani-festo*, that the bourgeoisie and the proletariat were sworn enemies. While Engels wrote a series of articles glorifying the courage and skill of the insurgents, Marx undertook to show the social significance of the struggle. In spite of their defeat, argued Marx, the proletariat had made a great step forward on the road to liberation. Henceforth they would know that they had class interests at stake no less than the bourgeoisie. The idea of fraternity was a farce. Never again could there be any talk of fraternity between the bourgeoisie and the working classes. Terrified by the future they had evoked, the bour-geoisie were tumbling over themselves in their hurry to patch up their differences with the ruling classes.

The defeat of the proletariat in Paris had still another consequence. The peoples who were struggling for national in-dependence, the Poles, the Italians and the Hungarians, all of whom a revolutionary France should have championed, were now abandoned to the mercy of the reactionary powers, Prus-sia, Austria, and Russia. Thus it appeared that the cause of nationalism, which the Provisional Government in Paris pro-fessed to believe in as the natural corollary of democracy, and the cause of social equality, which they shied away from, were really inseparable. Until the proletariat won their battle with the middle class, there would be no Poland, no Hungary, and no Italy. Confronted by the apathy of prosperous liberalism, Marx and Engels clamored for war as the only means of "sav-ing" the revolution—war with Denmark over Schleswig-Holstein, war with Austria to free the Hungarians and Italians from Habsburg domination, but above all for war with Russia. Only amidst the general confusion of war could they hope to attain their ends.

War with Russia was always a popular cry. Russia was the arch oppressor of Poland. In the eyes of nineteenth century democrats the cause of Poland became a symbol of international righteousness, a touchstone for genuine liberalism. Ever since the brutal Russian repression of 1831, and the Austrian annexation of the free republic of Cracow in 1846, with the connivance of Russia and Prussia, Poland had become the most popular oppressed nation. If the eye of a Frenchman or an Englishman did not glisten at the mention of the word Poland, he was no true liberal. It is one of the well-known characteristics of democracies to turn a blind eye to abuses at home and to indulge the liberal sentiments they profess by sympathizing with injustices they cannot remedy. Never was this tendency more prevalent than in 1848. Liberal opinion in England was bitterly critical of Austria's conduct in Italy, while Metternich could hardly bring himself to contemplate British policy in Ireland. France, who ruled over no subject nations in Europe, was particularly affected by the woes of Poland. In one of his more caustic moments Kossuth once remarked that Poland had relied on French sympathy, and that the sympathy still existed but that Poland didn't.

The fact was that it was just as difficult for the French Republic to do anything about Poland as it had been for the Monarchy. There was no solution short of a European war, and that was precisely the solution Marx and Engels wanted. They cared nothing about Poland, but they were perfectly ready to use Poland or any other oppressed nation as a stalking horse. Under cover of Poland they could advance toward world revolution. In a private letter to Marx, Engels made no bones about it. The more he thought about the Poles, the more convinced he was that they would never amount to anything as a nation, and that they were a serviceable instrument only until Russia herself was swept into the agrarian revolution.[40]

[40] "Je mehr ich über die Geschichte nachdenke, desto klarer wird es mir, dass die Polen *une nation foutue* sind, die nur so lange als Mittel zu brauchen sind, bis Russland selbst in die agrarische Revolution hineingerissen ist. Von dem Moment an hat Polen absolut keine *raison d'être* mehr." May 25, 1851.

This letter is included in *Karl Marx and Friedrich Engels: Selected Correspondence*, translated by Dona Torr (London, 1934).

From that moment Poland lost all excuse for existence. There is a breezy ruthlessness about Engels that dictators will always find refreshing. It is not surprising that Lenin should have admired him. Marx was more discreet. In the *Neue Rheinische Zeitung*, August 19, 1848, he claims that the establishment of a democratic Poland is a primary condition for the establishment of a democratic Germany. The situation in Poland was complicated, as Marx well knew, by the existence of two opposing factions. One hoped for a "liberation" which would leave the landed gentry masters of the new Poland. This was the point of view represented by the Polish *émigrés* in Paris. It was they who made Proudhon wonder whether a Polish serf would be any better off under Polish aristocracy than under Russian government. Then there was the other faction that sought freedom not only from the alien Russian yoke, but also from the no less galling tyranny of the Polish landowner. Marx was not affected by these disputes. In his eyes nationalism, however plausibly it might be tricked out, would always be a reactionary phenomenon. The liberation of Poland was important only in so far as it led to war with Russia. It was for this reason that he was so much more sympathetic with the Poles than with the Czechs or the Croats. These subject peoples of the Austrian Empire were victims of a new heresy, Pan-Slavism, a ludicrous movement, according to Marx and Engels, aiming at the subjugation of the civilized West under the barbarous East.

The prophet of this new religion, Michael Bakunin, was one of those strange creatures moved by impulse rather than reason whom Marx found so difficult to understand. As a rule he had found no difficulty in annihilating those who disagreed with him, but the big Russian had a protean quality about him that eluded Marx's grasp. The contrast between the two was too striking to have escaped the notice of biographers:

> The Russian aristocrat and the middle-class German Jew; the man of generous uncontrollable impulses, and the man whose feelings were so perfectly subdued to his intellect that superficial observers disbelieved in their existence; the reckless begetter of incoherent and ill-regulated ideas, and the disciplined thinker; the man of magnetic personal attraction, and the man who repelled

and intimidated by his coldness—every element of contrast is present in the matching of this incongruous pair.[41]

Both wanted a new social order but they differed fundamentally over the methods by which it was to be achieved. Marx staked everything on the development and organization of the political power latent in the working classes, particularly the proletariat of the towns, by which means he hoped to capture the state machine. Bakunin was an anarchist who would have wanted to capture the state only in order to destroy it.

In 1848 these issues were still below the horizon. Marx was systematically spinning his web in Cologne, while Bakunin was charging about Europe from Paris to Berlin, to Prague, to Dresden, wherever there was a chance of finding a fresh seedbed of revolution. "What a man!" exclaimed Caussidière, the newly appointed prefect of police in Paris. "On the first day of a revolution, he is a perfect treasure; on the second, he ought to be shot." Bakunin arrived in Prague at the end of May in time to hear Palacky, a Czech historian, propounding the doctrine of Pan-Slavism. As a professor Palacky had been invited to the preliminary parliament of intellectuals which was preparing for the German constituent assembly at Frankfort, but he had refused on the grounds that Bohemia, being inhabited predominantly by Slavs, could never form part of a German state. Instead of going to Frankfort he formed a Czech committee which issued a general open invitation for a Slav congress to assemble in Prague at the end of May. In this year when every state was convening a parliament to assert its rights it was surely fitting that Slavs should demonstrate to the world that freedom need not necessarily express itself through nationalism. Palacky was convinced that only within a strong Austrian Empire could the Slavs ever be free. Just as St. Paul was proud of being a Roman citizen, so the Slavic peoples should be proud of their membership in the Austrian Empire. If Austria did not exist already it would be necessary to create it.

Bakunin, an outcast from his own country, was delighted to find himself in the heart of a great Slav family. He was not as ready as Palacky to put his faith in the Habsburgs, but his quick enthusiasm was easily kindled by the conception of a Pan-Slavic union. The enthusiasm took shape in a flamboyant

[41] E. H. Carr, *Karl Marx*, p. 224. See also Schwarzschild, *op. cit.*, p. 97.

manifesto to the peoples of Europe which was considerably toned down by Palacky before publication. It expressed hopes for the liberation of the Slavs of Turkey, the transformation of the Austrian Empire into a federation of free peoples, and the termination of the Russian-Polish quarrel on mutually satisfactory terms.

Marx and Engels treated the whole movement with withering contempt. It was sentimental, it was unhistorical, it was everything they despised. The Slav brothers could not even communicate with each other, as they spoke no common language. When Bakunin was twitted with this inconvenient fact he replied that there was one phrase at least which was understood by all Slavs from the Elbe to the Urals, from the Adriatic to the Balkans: *Zahrabte miemce!* ("Down with the Germans!")[42] Marx and Engels were not impressed. Germans might be hated but they were nevertheless indispensable, and nowhere more so than in Bohemia. The fecklessness of the whole Pan-Slavic movement was proved to their entire satisfaction by the outbreak of an insurrection in Prague, which provided General Windischgrätz with an excuse for occupying the town with imperial troops. Incidentally, the insurrection had nothing to do with the Congress—it was organized by students and workmen—but the result of it was to send the members of the Congress scurrying home. Bakunin of course was an exception. He joined the insurgents at once and slipped away only after they had surrendered.

We hear of him a year later in Dresden, where he played an important part in one of the last flare-ups of the revolution. The King of Saxony had refused to recognize the German constitution promulgated at Frankfort. Popular opinion was irritated by the royal explanation that until Prussia had accepted the constitution it was unreasonable to expect Saxony to do so. Why should Saxony wait on the convenience of Prussia? On May 3, barricades began to appear on the streets, and the Civic Guard went over to the rebels. Bakunin was not particularly interested in the cause of German national unity or the Frankfort constitution, but the sight of a barricade was something he could never resist. On the following day he established himself in the Town Hall, the headquarters of the insurgents, and "gave advice and information in every direction with wonderful sangfroid." Among his companions in the

[42] E. H. Carr, *Michael Bakunin*, p. 158.

Town Hall was one of the junior conductors of the Dresden Opera, Richard Wagner. The picture of the great musician, a rather tentative revolutionary, and the utterly reckless Bakunin, has been preserved for us by Wagner himself in the amazingly vivid pages of his autobiography. Just before the outbreak of the revolution Bakunin had attended a rehearsal of Beethoven's Ninth Symphony. "At its close he walked unhesitatingly up to me in the orchestra, and said in a loud voice, that if all the music that had ever been written were lost in the expected world-wide conflagration, we must pledge ourselves to rescue this symphony, even at the peril of our lives." [43] Wagner could not help being drawn to this exuberant giant, and only narrowly escaped being captured with him. Several of the leaders slipped through the hands of the police after the fall of Dresden, but Bakunin was arrested at Chemnitz and handed over to the Russian authorities. After a few years in a Russian prison he was sent to Siberia in 1855. From Siberia he escaped by way of Japan and the United States to England. He arrived in London in 1861 with his appetite for revolution still unsatisfied. His turbulent career did not end until 1876, when he died in Berne.

While Bakunin was floundering in the quicksands of Central Europe, Marx from his vantage point in Cologne watched the tide of revolution receding. The *Neue Rheinische Zeitung*, still calling itself an organ of democracy, had been steadily losing ground. In August Marx visited the industrial centers of Germany and Austria, where the faithful were still active, in the hope of picking up new subscribers. He returned, without having had much success, in time to find the Hansemann ministry being forced to resign over the Schleswig-Holstein issue. The Frankfort Parliament had requested Prussia to go to the support of the two duchies which the new King of Denmark was seeking to incorporate into his kingdom. Glad of a chance to prove itself after the fiasco in Berlin when it had been compelled to evacuate the city, the Prussian Army invaded the northern provinces and was well on its way to ousting the Danes, when Frederick William under threat of Russian intervention accepted an armistice. This armistice, which left the two provinces still under the control of Denmark, was sharply criticized by liberal opinion all over Germany. By no one was it more sharply criticized than Karl Marx. For him it was

[43] Richard Wagner, *My Life*, 2 vols., New York, 1911, I, 466.

merely another Poland, another spark that might ignite a European war. For the Frankfort Parliament, the Malmö Armistice, as it was called, constituted a serious loss of prestige. It accepted it reluctantly, as it had no army of its own with which to enforce its will, and in any case it was in no position to thwart the might of Russia. For Frederick William the Schleswig-Holstein affair was a godsend. One of the reasons he had agreed so readily to the truce with Denmark was that it enabled him to bring the army back to Berlin, and thus to overawe the Prussian Assembly. When a few of the more liberal members plucked up courage enough to protest, the King dismissed Hansemann and replaced him with a general who had more suitable ideas about the relative importance of kings and parliaments.

On September 17, the *Neue Rheinische Zeitung* staged a mammoth open-air demonstration on the banks of the Rhine near Cologne. The object of the meeting, which was attended by all democratic organizations in the neighborhood, was to warn the people that their liberties were threatened. Marx himself did not attend the meeting. Having forfeited his citizenship, he may have felt that as a foreigner he ran a greater risk than his colleagues of being expelled from the country. The Government reacted more severely than he had expected. The *Neue Rheinische Zeitung* was suspended for three weeks, and those members of the editorial staff, including Engels, who had sponsored the demonstration fled across the frontier to avoid arrest. The finances of the paper were now in a desperate state. Marx sacrificed the rest of his personal fortune to keep it alive.

Meanwhile, the cause of liberalism had fallen on evil days in Austria as well as Germany. By the end of October, Vienna, which had been enjoying six months of uneasy liberty, was surrounded by the Imperial forces. The Emperor Ferdinand abdicated, and the eighteen-year-old Francis Joseph, a decent young man but completely ignorant of the modern world, began a long reign dedicated to the maintenance of his dynasty at any price. In Prussia, Frederick William, fortified by the events in Vienna, informed the Assembly that it had been moved from Berlin to Brandenburg, and that until the resumption of its sittings in Brandenburg its debates were to be discontinued. A few of the more radical deputies refused to leave Berlin. They held meetings wherever they could, in cafés and beer cellars, and voted a proclamation to the people urging them to refuse to pay taxes until constitutional government was restored.

Marx took up their cause eagerly. Here was a clear-cut issue on which to fight the Government. By now he must have known that the revolution was doomed, but he was determined to prove that the failure was due to the cursed principle of moderation, which had prevented the people in every country from exploiting the advantages they had won. "Insurrection," wrote Engels, "is an art quite as much as war or any other, and subject to certain rules of proceeding, which, when neglected, will produce the ruin of the party neglecting them." One of the rules is to keep up the moral ascendancy which the first successful rising has given to you. Marx decided that the people of Cologne must recapture that ascendancy. Refuse to pay taxes! Resist the taxpayer by force! That was their first duty as citizens. (*Die Steuereinzahlung ist hochverrat, die Steuerverweigerung erste Pflicht des Bürgers!*) The Prussian authorities countered by bringing the editors to trial on a charge of seditious utterances. The trial, which took place in February, 1849, created intense excitement. Marx made a masterly defense in which he argued that it was mere hypocrisy to invoke the laws which the crown had flouted against those who had upheld them. The refusal to pay taxes did not shake the foundations of society, as the public prosecutor contended. On the contrary, it was an act of self-defense on the part of society against a Government which threatened its foundations. At the end of the speech the jury, consisting exclusively of those bourgeois whom Marx so despised, acquitted all the accused and thanked Marx for his interesting presentation of the issues involved.

The acquittal was a great personal triumph for Marx, but it did not alter the fact that revolution for the moment was a lost cause. In France, another Bonaparte was on his way to the Tuileries; Italy had been "pacified" by Radetzky; Austria had fallen out of the frying pan into the fire by getting rid of the aged Metternich only to find herself being governed by the far tighter hand of Schwarzenberg. In England, the Chartist leaders had been arrested, and in Ireland the potato famine had left the population too miserable and too hungry to think of revolution. In Germany, liberalism and nationalism were pulling in different directions. The difficulty of uniting the fatherland without alienating Prussia or Austria proved insuperable. The Frankfort Parliament, instead of making good its work before the Austrian and Prussian Governments could recover from their revolutions and challenge its supremacy, had become involved in a war with Denmark from which it emerged with seriously diminished prestige. The old conflicts over frontiers—in Poland, in Bohemia, in Schleswig and Holstein—had blinded even the liberals in the Frankfort Parliament to the importance of social reforms. Which comes first, security or domestic legislation? Theoretically they should go hand in hand, but in the richly variegated patchwork of Europe where the strands of interest all run counter to each other they seldom do.

Marx himself did not realize that the wars he was advocating would produce armies, and that unless armies were controlled by some sort of democratic regime they would become the tools of absolutism. Nor would that absolutism bear any relation to the dictatorship of the proletariat he had in mind. By the end of 1848 the Frankfort Parliament knew that the Germany of their dreams must be hitched either to Prussia or to Austria. In view of the fact that so much of Austria was non-German the choice fell on Prussia, and on March 28, 1849, after endless debates Frederick William was elected emperor of a newly constituted empire. It was not so long ago that the King of Prussia had posed as a champion of a united Germany, but he was now in a different mood. If the crown had been offered to him by a council of princes he might have accepted it, but a crown that was voted to him by a Parliament smelled too much of Master Butcher and Master Baker. It had no aroma of magnificence about it. No, he could not accept it. The world must never think that he could be chained up to the revolution by any such paltry manoeuvres. He would rather remain King of Prussia by the grace of God than become Emperor of Germany by the grace of democracy.

Frederick William's refusal to accept the throne offered to him knocked the bottom out of the Frankfort Parliament. The high-minded, moderate liberals, those who had always believed that a nation could be fashioned out of winged words, resigned, and the control of the Assembly drifted into the hands of extremists. This radical minority decreed new elections and called upon all German governments to accept the constitution. By this time Prussia, weary of the farce of popular representa-

tion, rejected the constitution and called upon all its delegates
to withdraw. Bavaria and Saxony followed suit and by the end
of May the pitiful rump of the once-dignified Frankfort Parliament, surrounded as it was by Prussian troops, transferred its
sittings to Stuttgart. The little kingdom of Württemberg, not
being willing to offend Prussia, locked the doors of the meeting
place, and the members were finally dispersed like any mob at
a street corner.

So ended the honest efforts of an exceptionally able body
of men to unite Germany. The German people had acclaimed
their National Assembly of 1848 as a goddess of liberty, only
to let the goddess die a year later "like a street woman in the
gutter." [44] Why did all the splendid dreams never come true?
Partly because the King of Prussia never overcame his terror of
democracy. To him it was always a Jacobin thing born of the
French Revolution. Partly, too, because the German people
were, as indeed they still are, politically inept. They had been
excluded from all participation in government for so long that
political liberty seemed to them a matter for philosophical
speculation in which only the highly educated could indulge.
Germany had its full quota of brilliant men in 1848, but unfortunately they were not statesmen. In Austria, the counter-
revolution produced a statesman in Prince Schwarzenberg, who
resuscitated the Empire with amazing efficiency and stemmed
the tide of democracy which was threatening to undermine it.
In Germany, Bismarck made speeches in the *Landtag* about
the divine right of kings, but the time was not yet ripe for him.
The thirty-three-year-old Pomeranian squire watched the
birth pangs of German democracy with undisguised contempt.
Years later he phrased that contempt in memorable words:
"Not by speeches and resolutions of majorities are the great
questions of the time decided—that was the mistake of 1848
and 1849—but by blood and iron." The popular movement to
unite Germany ended in the conviction that nothing could be
accomplished by persuasion, that the give and take of democracy was a synonym for chattering inefficiency. That was the
real tragedy of the revolution.

The popular risings in Saxony, Baden, and the Bavarian
Palatinate may be regarded as the last rumblings of the storm.
In spite of the ardor that inspired them, these were feeble
affairs badly organized and badly led. Apparently there was an

[44] Veit Valentin, *op. cit.*, p. 263.

unwritten law in 1848 that all revolutionary uprisings should be commanded by gallant but incompetent Polish officers.

> Men who had served as officers in the great Polish revolutionary wars appeared at that time with a sort of halo of revolutionary heroism around their heads. The popular legend attributed to them not only extraordinary bravery, but also all possible military talent, and exceptional familiarity with the secrets of the military art. It was as if at the rallying places of the Polish refugees, especially in Paris and in Switzerland, a stock of generals was kept in store, to be occasionally disposed of for revolutionary enterprises in any part of the world.[45]

So wrote Carl Schurz,[46] who, as a young man, took part in the Baden uprising and barely escaped with his life. Fifteen years later he and Franz Sigel and Alexander Schimmelpfennig and many other German liberals who had joined the insurgents in Baden were to find a broader scope for their talents on the battlefields of the American Civil War.

It was hardly to be expected, now that Prussia was methodically stamping out the embers of revolution, that Karl Marx would be allowed to continue on his way unmolested. The Cologne jurymen might refuse to convict him, but there were other ways of putting a stop to his seditious utterances. Being a foreigner, Marx could be expelled from Prussia by government decree. On May 11, 1849, an order of expulsion was issued depriving Marx of the "privileges of hospitality which he had so disgracefully violated," and requiring him to leave Prussian soil within twenty-four hours. Karl Marx was not easily intimidated, and he accordingly took his own time about leaving. There were many questions to be decided. What was to become of the *Neue Rheinische Zeitung*, and still more important, what was to become of himself and his family? As for the paper, the other editors decided that without Marx it could hardly be kept alive. The final issue, a flaming defiance of the Government printed in red type, appeared on May 19. Marx decided to go down with flags flying. As for himself, his wife and family—there were now three small children and Jenny was expecting a fourth—like all good exiles

---

[45] Of all these Polish soldiers of fortune, General Bem, who commanded the Hungarian armies in Transylvania, was the only man of outstanding ability.

[46] *Reminiscences*, I, 188.

they would go to Paris, where, in spite of Bonaparte's police, revolutions were always hatching. But first Marx must visit Baden, where the last weak flame of insurrection was still flickering and where Engels was serving as adjutant of a volunteer corps. After having been arrested by Hessian troops on suspicion of having taken part in the insurrection, and released the next day, he arrived in Paris early in June. Paris was gloomy, in the throes of cholera, but he was not discouraged. "A tremendous outbreak of the revolutionary volcano had never been nearer." [47]

Paris, in the summer of 1849, was not quite as ripe for revolution as Karl Marx believed. It is strange that any man who prided himself as he did on his coldly dispassionate approach to history should have so invariably ignored the inconvenient facts that did not fit in with his theories. Marx ignored the fact, for instance, that Louis Napoleon, the Prince President, was the choice of the rural masses of France and that he and they had one great interest in common—the prevention of disorder. The dubious Roman expedition, upon which he had embarked in the hope of ingratiating himself with the Church and the Army, was sharply criticized by the republicans in the Chamber, but when Ledru-Rollin attempted a *coup d'état* against the Government it was crushed without difficulty. One of the first victims of the repression that followed this insurrection was Karl Marx. The police had discovered that a certain M. Ramboz, who was living at No. 45 rue de Lille, was no other than the notorious agitator Karl Marx, and they decided that "M. Ramboz" and his family would live more comfortably in the isolated *département* of Morbihan in Britany than in Paris. Marx was outraged. He was convinced that Morbihan was a pestilence-ridden swamp, that the sentence of banishment was a death sentence in disguise. It was like being sent to the Pontine marshes.[48] The prefect of police was sympathetic. It was always possible to leave France altogether. Switzerland and England were the two countries most favored by exiles, but in Switzerland Marx felt that he might be caught like a rat in a trap. It would be better to go to England where,

[47] "Paris ist *morne*. Dazu die Cholera, die ausserordentlich wütet. Trotzdem stand ein kolossaler Ausbruch des Revolutionskraters nie näher bevor als jetzt zu Paris."—Letter of Marx to Engels, June 7, 1849.

[48] "Das Department Morbihan, das man mir angewiesen, ist in dieser Jahreszeit tödlich—die Pontinischen Sümpfe der Bretagne."—Letter to Engels, August 17, 1849.

though the people were deplorably backward in revolutionary theory, at least one was not pestered by the police. London had now supplanted Paris as the great center of revolutionary activity. In any case, it would only be a few months before he was back in Germany riding the whirlwind of revolution.

Little did Marx realize when he arrived in London in September, 1849, that he would never again live in Germany. He visited Germany occasionally, but for the rest of his life, nearly a third of a century, his home was in England. Nor did he realize that with his arrival in England the whole course of his life was to change. Almost from the day he graduated from the University of Jena he had been living in an atmosphere of intense excitement. The police had been continually on his trail. He had been banished twice from his own country, twice from France, and once from Belgium. He had been the editor of a paper that Lenin years later called "an incomparable organ of revolution." From now on it would be different. Life was still going to be hard and, if it had not been for the generosity of the ever-reliable Engels, the Marx family might well have gone under, but the British police paid no attention to him and he could say what he wanted without fear of arrest. The gigantic *Das Kapital* still lay ahead of him, representing long hours of study in the British Museum, but the chapter of adventure was over. For Marx, as for so many other men, the preposterous hopes and fears of 1848 would never be recaptured.

CHAPTER

IV

THE REVOLUTION IN THE
HABSBURG MONARCHY

1

METTERNICH, SZECHENYI, AND
KOSSUTH

MAZZINI'S description of Metternich—"Immobility personified, the Chinese principle in its highest expression, the Status Quo incarnate"—has never been seriously challenged by posterity.[1] Everything the man stood for was wrong, but there was a fascination about his very consistency that even Mazzini could not deny. At least he grasped the nature of the principle he represented, which was more than could be said for anybody else on the monarchical side. What Mazzini grudgingly admitted, others acclaimed with delight. Stendhal, for instance, chose Metternich as the model for Count Mosca in the *Chartreuse de Parme*—Count Mosca, the lover of the beautiful Duchess Sanseverina, the most brilliant diplomat in Italy, the man who was at home in every court in Europe. Whatever his limitations, Metternich was the personification of self-confidence and elegance, two qualities that the world hates and secretly admires. The portraits by Lawrence, the smile with which, according to Balzac, one would deceive God himself, show us the *grand seigneur* in all his glory. In the long struggle against Napoleon it was not the great captain who had triumphed, but the quiet-spoken diplo-

[1] Mazzini, *Scritti*, IV, 351.

mat whose sinuous policy had held the coalition together until the whirlwind had spent its force. Ever since he had been appointed Minister of Foreign Affairs after the defeat of Wagram, Metternich, then thirty-six years old, had devoted himself to the overthrow of Napoleon, the restoration as far as possible of the world that was, and the maintenance of peace. The long years following the Congress of Vienna were an epilogue, almost an anticlimax. He had no illusions about Austria. He knew, better than any of his contemporaries, the weakness of the Government and the peasant obstinacy of Emperor Francis for whom he prepared endless memoranda which nobody ever did anything about. It was not in Metternich's nature to force a decision. Gradually, like many diplomats, he came to mistake a careful diagnosis for a remedy. After the revolution had driven him from office, he explained that though he had sometimes governed Europe he had never governed Austria.

One of Metternich's recent biographers recalls a speech made by Briand to the League of Nations in 1928: "If any act of justice were proposed which would disturb world peace and renew the troubles of yesterday, I should be the first to call upon these promptings to stop, to abandon it in the supreme interests of peace . . ." [2] These words might well have been uttered by Metternich at any time between 1815 and 1848. They are easy to criticize, but to a people who have lived through a long war, a people whose country has been occupied by the enemy, they are terribly convincing.

One afternoon in December, 1825, Metternich and a young Hungarian officer, Count Stephen Széchényi, fell to discussing some of those acts of justice which Metternich thought would inevitably disturb world peace and renew the troubles of yesterday. Széchényi was one of those liberals whom Metternich instinctively distrusted. Liberalism was nothing but a veil behind which lurked the ghastly face of revolution, and the fact that those who professed liberalism were often high-minded made it all the more dangerous. As a young hussar Széchényi had made a celebrated dare-devil ride through the French lines at the Battle of Leipzig, bearing despatches to Blücher's headquarters. Later on during the campaign he had been overheard by one of Metternich's spies to say that Austria was fighting only to prolong its exisence and that within a century it would certainly fall to pieces. From Metternich's

[2] H. du Coudray: *Metternich*, London, 1935, p. 349.

point of view these two incidents were highly significant. They proved that Széchényi was a hot-headed Hungarian radical whose recklessness might some day plunge the Empire into civil war. Actually, Széchényi was anything but a radical. After the Napoleonic wars he had travelled a good deal, particularly in England, where he had become enamored of the English aristocracy. The country gentleman's way of life, the interest he took in his estates, his knowledge of agriculture and horse-breeding—these were things that might well be introduced into Hungary. His friends, most of whom were idling away their time in Vienna living off the revenues of their Hungarian estate, regarded him as an Anglomaniac.

It was true that he brought back from England a taste for horseracing and English clothes, but along with the jockeys and the exquisite breeches he brought back a new faith in his own country. Széchényi felt that Hungary could never hold up its head among the nations of Europe until its aristocracy, like the aristocracy of England, acquired some sense of its responsibilities. Though it had formed an integral part of the Habsburg Empire since it had been liberated from the Turks in 1699, Hungary had never lost its identity. The Emperor of Austria, absolute in his own domains, was simply a constitutional king in Hungary, and the Pragmatic Sanction, which secured the succession of Maria Theresa, confirmed the rights of the Hungarian Diet and, what was even more important, preserved those county assemblies which enshrined the principle of local self-government. Unfortunately, with a population of ten million serfs and 400,000 landowners, many of whom never lived on their estates, Hungary was in no position to resist the Habsburg policy of centralization. Maria Theresa had taught the serf to look to the Court of Vienna rather than to the Diet of Pressburg for help in his troubles. Her successor, Joseph II, an idealist and a doctrinaire, went even further in trying to weld the polyglot races of his dominions into a single people.

Among other so-called reforms he issued a language edict which made German the official language of the common state. How could these evil tendencies of the Habsburgs be arrested? Széchényi set himself to persuade Metternich that national aspirations in the different provinces of the Empire need not necessarily run counter to the imperial system. He wanted to avoid conflict with the dynasty, but at the same time he was determined to create a new Hungary out of the old.

The first step was to get the nobility to surrender their exemption from taxation. Otherwise the peasants would always be found fighting on the side of a foreign government against a supposedly freedom-loving aristocracy. That was the rock upon which the Polish struggle for independence had always struck. The Diet of 1825 gave Széchényi an opportunity of setting an example in patriotism that caught the imagination of the public. One of the deputies had been protesting against the idleness of the Hungarian magnates who dissipated their fortunes at court, regardless of their country, and who did not even speak their native tongue with sufficient accuracy to make use of it in the Diet. Széchényi rose to reply. He spoke Hungarian badly—he would have been more at home in German, the language of society, or in Latin, the language in which the debates were usually held—but his earnestness held the attention of his audience. He offered to give a whole year's income, 60,000 gulden, to found a society for promoting the study of the Magyar language. His example was followed with more or less zeal by other nobles, and a few years later a Hungarian Academy of Science was established by royal decree. One of the more sceptical deputies asked the count what he intended to live on if he gave away all his revenues for one year. "My friends will keep me," replied the count.[3]

Széchényi was sometimes criticized for his lordly manner, but whatever his idiosyncrasies, he was one of the most far-seeing, practical reformers of his age. Granted the feudal conditions of Hungary, it was obvious that nothing could be accomplished unless the reforms started at the top. The aristocracy must lead the way. With England as his model he founded what he called the National Club at Pest, equipped it with all the comforts of the best clubs in London, and developed it into a rallying point for the more progressively minded members of his class. Before long the National Club, fired by Széchényi's energy, had launched forth into a hundred projects. Construction of roads, building of steamboats, dredging the Danube, scientific cattle breeding, importation of stallions from England, founding of a Hungarian insurance company and a Hungarian national theatre—there was no limit to Széchényi's

[3] Otto Zarek, *Kossuth*, London, 1937, p. 34.

activities. In another age or in another country he would have been a great empire builder, but there was nothing of the ruthlessness about him that empire-building sometimes suggests. His energy was inexhaustible, but at the same time he walked delicately and never trampled on other people's rights.

The work by which he will be chiefly remembered was a suspension bridge connecting Buda and Pest. Hitherto traffic between the two cities had been confined to a mediaeval pontoon bridge. Széchényi's enthusiasm for a suspension bridge might have seemed exaggerated but there was more significance in the project than met the eye. He used the bridge as a means of persuading the magnates that they must share the expenses involved in embellishing the city. Once that point has been won they might gradually be led to accept a more just distribution of taxes in general. The problem of financing this undertaking plunged Széchényi into the unfamiliar waters of economics. In England he had studied the doctrines of Adam Smith and Jeremy Bentham. Now he began to study the economic situation of his own country. Suddenly the man who had been laughed at as a dandy and an anglomaniac produced what was to remain for a long time one of the standard books on economics in Hungary.[4]

All this seething activity Metternich watched with disfavor.[5] Theoretically he was not opposed to the economic development of Hungary but he scented revolution in the distance. It was all very well for Széchényi to insist that he wanted to avoid all conflict with the dynasty and with Austria. Could he express to his friends the kindly feeling to the Austrian Government he had just expressed to Metternich? Széchényi admitted that would be difficult in view of the way the laws were being interpreted to the Emperor's advantage and to the disadvantage of Hungary. Metternich brushed him aside. He was acting as a traitor to himself and to his friends.[6] The two men parted company each thinking he must have made some impression on the other. Both of them were destined to be swept away by forces they had foreseen yet could not control.

[4] *Credit (Hitel)* (Budapest, 1830).

[5] "Le Pays, à qui l'on aurait du offrir les moyens de tirer un meilleur parti du sol et d'ouvrir les voies les plus commodes pour exporter l'excédant de ses produits, a eu des courses à chevaux, des casinos, un théâtre hongrois et un pont qui a couté un million et auquel aboutit pas une seule route carrossable."—Metternich, *Mémoires*, 8 vols., Paris, 1880–84, VII, 59.

[6] Metternich, *op. cit.*, IV, 245.

The downfall of Széchényi—he committed suicide in 1861 after spending many years in an asylum—is one of the most poignant tragedies of the revolution. He who was by nature a builder was suddenly obsessed by the fact that he had brought nothing but confusion into the world. As he watched his country plunging into civil war he cursed the day that he had ever embarked upon a policy of reform. It has become a truism that revolutions always devour their young, and Széchényi was no exception to the rule. The moderate, level-headed leaders of the early stages in a revolt are always thrust aside by the pitiless enthusiasts, the "nothing but" men who would rather die than compromise. Széchényi stood midway between the two extremes of reaction and revolution represented by Metternich and Kossuth. If either of them had been willing to listen to him the Austrian Empire might well have been spared the storm that was uprooting governments all over Europe, but one was convinced that Széchényi harbored designs against the Empire, while the other, though he called him the greatest of Hungarians, always suspected him of being more of an aristocrat than a patriot.

By the time we reach 1848 the cracks in the Metternich system were growing more and more visible to the outside world. The old diplomat's prestige had been badly shaken. He had always posed as a champion of legality, but by the annexation of Cracow, the little Polish republic created by the Congress of Vienna, he had forfeited his right to be considered a stickler for the sanctity of treaties. He had antagonized the Italians by trying to browbeat Pius IX, and he had antagonized the Swiss by threatening them with a commercial blockade if they attempted to make any change in their constitution without his consent. In England Lord Palmerston seemed to take a savage delight in thwarting him on every possible occasion. In France, Guizot usually proved more amenable to reason, but Guizot had recently appointed Rossi, a Lombard exile, French Ambassador at Rome, and Rossi was known to be unsympathetic with the Austrian policy of repressing every sign of Italian nationalism. Metternich's experience with Napoleon had implanted in him the conviction that Austria must never act without the support of some, if not all, of the Great Powers of Europe. That support was now lacking. Wherever he looked, the ranks were wavering. The Czar Nicholas, the one reliable despot in Europe, was so busy preventing an insurrection in

Poland that he could not count on his support in western Europe. In Prussia, the unaccountable Frederick William IV had virtually surrendered to the temptation of leading the new national Germany. Metternich considered that he was headed for the abyss and would have nothing to do with him.[7] From the diaries of Princess Mélanie, his adoring third wife whom he married when he was fifty-eight, it is obvious that Metternich knew that the world around him was crumbling. There is a certain dignity as well as pathos in the way he remained at his post sharpening the old weapons of diplomacy for one last battle against the forces of liberalism.

The immediate issue in 1847 was the independence of Switzerland. The Congress of Vienna, bowing to the fact that Switzerland could not be absorbed into any other nation, had seen to it that the Swiss Confederation should remain a loosely tied parcel of separate cantons rather than a compact independent republic. The advantages of such a system to the powerful nations on her borders were obvious. It would always be easier to intervene in the affairs of a canton than in those of a sovereign state. On the other hand, the weaknesses of the Federal Diet made Switzerland a paradise for political refugees. We have already seen how Mazzini used Switzerland as a base of operations from which to spread his revolutionary network all over Europe, and how near Louis Napoleon came to plunging Switzerland into war with France. The Great Powers might assert with perfect truth that the troublesome little republic in their midst was becoming a hotbed of radicalism, but as long as they denied her the privilege of creating a strong federal executive they could hardly complain if the activities of "dangerous" political refugees were not controlled. The right of asylum in Switzerland had become a by-product of the weakness of the central government.

When, in 1841, the Protestant canton of Aargau suppressed the monasteries within its borders, and when, a few years later, the Catholics in Lucerne countered by calling in Jesuits to fill all the important educational posts in the canton, it was obvious that a new element of confusion had been introduced into the picture. The hatred felt for Jesuits by liberals

---

[7] "Il y a plus de quatre à cinq mois que le Roi de Prusse m'a engagé à me rencontrer avec lui dans le courant de l'été. Je m'y suis refusé, par la raison que rien de véritablement utile ne peut résulter pour la Prusse de mon contact avec celui qui conduit le pays vers un abîme . . ." Metternich to Apponyi, July 19, 1847.—Metternich, *op. cit.*, VII, 99–100.

all over Europe during the nineteenth century was perhaps unreasonable, but it was none the less a fact, and the summoning
of Jesuits to Lucerne was intended and accepted as a challenge
to the rest of Switzerland. The country was now splitting into
two camps—Catholics and conservatives who stood for the
retention of the Jesuits and who resented any attack on can-
tonal rights, versus Protestants and radicals who wanted to
separate church and state and to amend the federal pact of
1815 so as to bring it more in line with the necessities of national life. The formation of a separate league (*Sonderbund*)
by the seven Catholic cantons—Lucerne, Uri, Schwyz, Unter-
walden, Zug, Fribourg and the Valais—brought matters to a
head. These seven cantons voted to secede from the Federal
Diet on the ground that their rights under the pact of 1815
were no longer safe. Like the Confederate States in America
they had a tenable legal case, but the spirit of the times was
against them. It was the old question whether the sovereignty
of one part of the nation should take precedence over the
sovereignty of the whole. The majority opinion in Switzerland,
in 1847, like the majority opinion in America in 1861, decided
that it should not.

With the formation of the *Sonderbund* Metternich began
to think that the moment had come to arrest the spread of
democratic decay that was threatening to make Switzerland a
compact, indivisible country.[8] He thought of sending troops to
the frontier, but to make the gesture effective he needed the
collaboration of the other Powers. Would Europe never understand the necessity for common action? Guizot promised that if
Austria would open the breach France would follow. In other
words, Austria was to incur the odium of intervention and
France was to play the grateful role of coming in as the
apparent protector of Swiss independence. Once before, in
1832, that was exactly what had happened in Italy. Austria
had lent her support to the Pope, and France had promptly
occupied Ancona on the ground that Austrian troops had invaded the Papal States. Metternich was disappointed by
Guizot's reply. It did not seem to him helpful,[9] but he lived in
an age when diplomats still kept their tempers. He remained

[8] "Le chancelier autrichien chercha à aider 'la cause de la justice' contre
'la société en fermentation de pourriture démocratique' qui voulait la Suisse une
et indivisible." V. Bibl, *Metternich*, Paris, 1935, p. 274.

[9] "un pareil système est l'opposé de celui que nous regardons comme utile."
Metternich, *op. cit.*, VII, 335.

unruffled. Irony rather than invective was the favored weapon.

The difficulty of a union of the Great Powers was increased by the policy of England. Palmerston always enjoyed playing a lone hand, and while Metternich was trying to produce a united front in favor of the *Sonderbund* Palmerston backed the Protestant cantons. By apparently assenting to the necessity of eventually intervening to keep the peace, and then trumping up one excuse after another for doing nothing, he enabled Switzerland to set her house in order before any of the Powers could intervene. As it turned out, Palmerston's delaying tactics were largely responsible for the final liberation of Switzerland from the foreign yoke that had lain so heavily on her ever since Napoleon established the Helvetian Republic in 1798.

In 1847 Switzerland was faced by a greater danger than Napoleon. Metternich had already lent the partisans of the *Sonderbund* 100,000 gulden, 3000 rifles, and the services of a well-known officer, Prince Schwarzenberg. By the end of the year, impatient at Palmerston's delays, he was ready to intervene still more actively, but by that time it was too late. The Federal Diet declared war against the *Sonderbund* on November 4, and after a campaign lasting only three weeks the Catholic cantons laid down their arms. Thanks to the energy and moderation of General Dufour,[10] commanding the federal troops, peace was soon re-established. The essential reasonableness of the Swiss people was never more clearly demonstrated. The war was so short and the losses were so trifling—only 78 men in the Federal Army were killed—that there was no exultation over victory and no bitterness over defeat. After the rebellious cantons had paid a small indemnity, the troops were withdrawn and everybody in typically Swiss fashion went back to work. There were none of the wholesale executions, imprisonments, and deportations that were to follow on the heels

---

[10] Those who have had some experience of the problems of an occupying army will appreciate the full value of Dufour's instructions to his senior officers. As for instance:

"Si une troupe est repoussée faire soigner ses blessés comme les nôtres mêmes et avoir pour eux tous les égards dûs au malheur. Désarmer les prisonniers, mais le leur faire aucun mal, ni leur addresser aucune injure. Les traiter, au contraire, aussi bien que possible pour les désabuser. Les laisser rentrer chez eux, s'ils s'engagent sur l'honneur à poser leur uniformes et à ne pas reprendre les armes. Empêcher à tout prix la violation des églises et des établissements religieux. Pousser l'attention jusqu'à ne point loger des troupes dans ces établissements et y poser des sauvegardes."—Quoted from *The British Ski Year Book* (1948), p. 193.

of revolution in other parts of Europe. Nevertheless, the significance of the War of the Sonderbund was not lost upon the rest of Europe. It was a victory for individualism as well as for nationalism. By her own efforts Switzerland had consolidated her union and gained admittance into the ranks of the genuinely independent states of Europe. At the same time, the Swiss citizen had won those rights for which the bourgeoisie all over Europe was clamoring—the right of free speech and the right of assembly guaranteed by a written constitution.

For Metternich the War of the Sonderbund represented one more rebuff. He and his allies had insisted that the conflict between the Catholic and Protestant cantons was not just a local squabble but a question of principle, and as such it was generally accepted. The radicals, or what Metternich called radicals (*parti du mouvement*), had won an important victory and the effect of that victory was felt like an electric shock throughout the Austrian dominions. In Rome, in Florence and in Prague, wildly enthusiastic crowds gathered outside the Swiss consulates to do honor to the staunch republic that had withstood the great Austrian Empire. In spite of the imperial censorship, letters of congratulation poured into Switzerland. It was as if men realized that the War of the Sonderbund was, as Treitschke afterwards called it, the forerunner of European revolution.

The situation at home in Vienna was no more promising. In the 1840's Vienna was a somewhat provincial city placidly occupied with her own concerns, but to those who lived for music and the theatre it had never been more delightful, never more conscious of its individuality, never more definitely the capital of the pleasure-seeking world. Fanny Elssler's dancing, a new Strauss waltz, the next appearance of Jenny Lind—these were the things that mattered. How long would it all last, wondered the poet Bauernfeld. "Government! Administration! Vienna's slogan: Conversation!" [11] Many besides Bauernfeld knew that there was a restless Vienna below the glittering surface, a Vienna that should have been, but was not, the clearing house for the political aspirations of all the peoples of the Empire. Deputations of Hungarians, Czechs and Croats, Serbs and Poles were forever passing through the antechambers of Met-

[11] "Was Regierung! Was Verwaltung! Wiener Schlagwort: Unterhaltung!" Quoted from Josephine Goldmark, *Pilgrims of '48*, p. 14.

ternich's palace and going away dissatisfied. University students and professors came to protest against the censorship, but nothing was ever done.

It was a difficult time for patriots. On the throne sat the feeble-minded Emperor Ferdinand, who had succeeded Francis in 1835, and alongside him a disillusioned old man who saw nothing but danger and difficulty in every suggestion that was made to him. Metternich liked to think of himself as the oldest and most experienced doctor in Europe. He knew how to distinguish between curable and incurable diseases. Austria's disease was definitely incurable. The great lumbering governmental machine was grinding to a halt. The council of state, composed of the timid and incompetent Archduke Louis, uncle of the Emperor, the equally incompetent Count Kolowrat, Minister of the Interior, and the clear-sighted but stubbornly negative Metternich, was not even capable of administering, far less of governing, the Empire. Of the members of the imperial family the only one of will and determination was the Archduchess Sophia, mother of the future Emperor Francis Joseph. Sophia had convinced herself that if the feeble Emperor Ferdinand abdicated in favor of her son, and if Metternich resigned, the storm in the Empire would subside. After all, Metternich was responsible for the intolerable bureaucracy in which he and everybody else was slowly strangling. The Government seemed to be employing one half of the nation to govern the other half. Whether or not this were true, Radetzky, who had the soldier's contempt for politicians, seriously maintained that the civil officers of the Empire, not including Hungary and Transylvania, actually outnumbered the Army. Not the least important function of this vast bureaucracy was the regulation of opinion within the Empire by an elaborate system of censorship, espionage and intimidation. Everybody of any importance was watched, and the correspondence of ambassadors, bankers and foreign agents was invariably opened, examined and copied. Believing as he did that every hint of criticism was inspired by revolutionaries, Metternich devised what he considered effective counter-measures. The only sure way for the civilian to avoid the dungeons of Spielburg was to observe a discreet silence on all political and social questions. Modern dictators have so far outdistanced Metternich in the art of silencing the independent thinker that the methods of his police seem to us, accustomed to all the horrors of the

Gestapo, comparatively benign; indeed in all the refinements of torture the nineteenth century was immeasurably inferior to ours.

2

Rumors of the revolution in Paris reached Vienna on the last day of February, just a week after the event had occurred. The news was immediately confirmed by the Russian Ambassador. He had received a telegram from Rothschild announcing the fall of Guizot and the abdication of Louis Philippe. How was it that the Rothschilds always heard the news before anybody else! These amazing bankers, the secret victors of the Battle of Waterloo, were once again able to provide accurate news while statesmen and diplomats were snatching at rumors. Metternich was momentarily stunned when the Russian Ambassador told him that the French had set up a republic. *Eh bien, mon cher, tout est fini.* But after the first shock was over his mind slipped back into the old channels. Once again he would build up a Holy Alliance. The Czar, the King of Prussia, England—even Palmerston must now see how wrong he had been—could still throw up a dyke against the rising tide of revolution if only they would act together. The Czar responded to his appeal with a loan of six million gulden, but events were moving so fast that before the six million gulden could bring the rusty old machinery into operation the revolutionary movement had engulfed all Central Europe. "What remains standing in Europe?" wrote Czar Nicholas to Queen Victoria, on April 3, 1848. "Great Britain and Russia!" [1]

The overthrow of Metternich was brought about by various forces that happened to converge upon the person of the unhappy chancellor at the same time but otherwise had nothing to do with each other. Metternich had to deal with enemies within the council, in particular Kolowrat and the Archduchess Sophia. Kolowrat was the jealous subordinate who hoped to be able to step into Metternich's shoes; the Archduchess, the scheming mother who believed that while other thrones were tottering the Habsburg throne might still be saved for "Franzi" —there were only a few months to wait until he attained his majority—if Metternich were only removed in time. Sophia's

---

[1] *The Letters of Queen Victoria.* Ed. by A. C. Benson, 3 vols. (London, 1907), II, 196.

supposed liberalism in siding with the opposition has been described as the result of "passionate maternal anxiety." [2] She knew exactly what she wanted, and she got it. Within a year "Franzi" became the Emperor Francis Joseph, and he was still ruling over the Habsburg Empire when he died sixty-seven years later, in 1916, just in time to be spared the final break-up of his dominions. Metternich might have been able to cope with his enemies at court if he could have rallied the people of Vienna to his side, but the people of Vienna had come to look upon him as personally responsible for all their sufferings.

Vienna had not escaped the usual aftermath of the Industrial Revolution. With the introduction of manufactures, the growth of cities, and the expansion of commerce, wages had fallen, living conditions had deteriorated, and women and children had been sucked into industry. The lower bourgeoisie, threatened with the competition of the machine, was clamoring for government protection—so far unsuccessfully. In the suburbs of Vienna, just as in the suburbs of London or Paris, independent workmen were fighting their long-drawn-out losing battle against modern industry. Especially was this true in the case of spinners and weavers, who were now experiencing for the first time the horrors of poverty and unemployment. Idle men and women were willing to join any movement which might bring them relief from starvation. Their situation was different and in some ways worse than that of the workingmen in other countries. In England the Chartists, though they failed and made themselves for the moment ridiculous, at least provided a program for the future. In France, the social theories of Louis Blanc, of Proudhon and of Cabet were on everybody's lips, but the Viennese workingman had no one to guide him. He was fighting in the dark against some power he did not understand that was crushing him.

Leadership finally developed in an unexpected quarter. For very different reasons the students of the university were as determined as the workingmen to get rid of Metternich. To them the name of Metternich would always be hateful on account of the notorious Carlsbad Decrees. The Emperor Francis had once made an address to university professors enjoining them to be careful not to teach their students too much; he did not want learned or scientific men but obedient subjects. Metternich seconded his master only too well. He called a confer-

[2] H. du Coudray, *Metternich*, p. 356.

ence at Carlsbad to crush the revolutionary spirit of the universities. A special government official was attached to each university to direct the minds of students and faculty to sound political conclusions. All dangerous teachers were to be removed. No government was ever to accept a teacher so expelled from any other university. It was on account of the Carlsbad Decrees that Arndt, the poet of the War of Liberation and one of the most popular figures in Germany, was dismissed from his professorship at Bonn on a charge of democratic intrigue. It is not surprising then that the lead in the actual outbreak of revolution was taken by the university. Professor Hye of the law faculty, who had already challenged the Government once by denouncing the seizure of Cracow, drew up a petition embodying the students' demands and submitted it to the Emperor. He was supported by three young doctors, Lohner, Fischhof, and Goldmark, each of whom was to play an important part in the coming revolution. What they wanted was the freedom of the university from government supervision, the dismissal of Seldnitzky, head of the secret police, and the resignation of Metternich. No one must ever interfere again with the freedom to teach and the freedom to learn. At the same time they were not antimonarchical or republican.

It is significant that whereas in France there was no affection for the monarchy, in Austria no one dreamed of any other form of government. The Habsburgs, even the feeble-minded Ferdinand, were always popular, particularly with the Viennese. It was Metternich who was responsible for every act of injustice and every breakdown in the administration. It was Metternich, too, who had never understood that liberty was the strongest link in the chain of loyalty binding the people to the throne. He might have been able to hold his own against his his enemies at court, to temporize until they fell to quarrelling among themselves, and he might have made his peace with the students by easing the censorship, but there was an attack from a third quarter against which he had no defense.

On March 3, just a week before the students presented their petition, a Hungarian deputy named Louis Kossuth, already known to Metternich as a troublemaker, mounted the rostrum of the Diet of Pressburg and delivered what has come to be known as the baptismal speech of the revolution. The debate of the day happened to be on the subject of banking conditions, and in his analysis of these conditions Kossuth seized the occasion to discuss the whole question of Hungary's relations with Austria. It was not until he had been talking for some time that the audience realized that they were listening to a great revolutionary speech. Kossuth called their attention to the "stagnant bureaucratic system" that was leading the Empire to destruction and jeopardizing the future existence of the dynasty. He spoke of "the pestilential air blowing from the Vienna charnel house and its deadening effect upon all phases of Hungarian life." [3] Finally he came to the climax of his speech—parliamentary government at once for the whole monarchy and a separate Ministry of Finance for Hungary. The deputies greeted the speech with a long uproar of applause. Széchényi was in despair. This little provincial lawyer with that cursed eloquence of his did not understand what he was saying. Such talk might lead to revolution; it would certainly never lead to reform. Never before in the Hungarian Diet had anyone dared attack the Monarchy so openly. As Széchényi foresaw, Kossuth's speech marked the end of that peaceful evolution of Hungary from a feudal to a modern state that had always been so close to his heart.

Pressburg, the meeting place of the Diet, was only twenty miles from Vienna, and in spite of the censorship, copies of Kossuth's speech were soon circulating all over the city. On March 13 a body of students followed by an enormous crowd marched to the State Chancery. One of the students then read Kossuth's speech under Metternich's windows, and the excitement of students and citizens rose to fever pitch. Contrary to their usual principle of stifling all agitation before it was fully under way, the police did nothing. In the afternoon, when it was too late, the Archduke Albrecht ordered the troops to clear the Ballplatz where the crowd had congregated. The Archduke's order produced the inevitable volley that united students, bourgeois and workmen, just as it had done in Paris and Berlin, and thus transformed the revolt into a revolution.

In the midst of the confusion the Emperor, the archdukes, Metternich and Kolowrat met to deliberate. According to the story of Count Flahault, the French Ambassador, who told Princess de Lieven, who told Greville the diarist, Metternich talked uninterruptedly for an hour and a half. He talked pleasantly with that smooth serenity that was so exasperating to his

[3] O. Zarek, *Kossuth*, p. 138.

hearers. Finally the Archduke Louis pulled out his watch. They had only half an hour left. A civic deputation had delivered an ultimatum demanding Metternich's resignation. What was to be the answer? Kolowrat said that in his twenty-five years' experience he had never known Metternich to give a definite answer to anybody. Metternich, still imperturbable, pointed out that there was a point of order involved that Kolowrat might not understand. He could not resign. The Emperor Francis before his death had made him promise never to abandon his son. His son alone could absolve him from that promise. A message was accordingly sent to the Emperor which produced a thoroughly characteristic reply: "I am the Emperor, and it is for me to decide; and I yield everything. Tell the people I consent to all their demands." [4] "And thus," adds Greville, "the *Crétin* settled it all; and the great Minister, who was in his own person considered as the Empire, and had governed despotically for forty years, slunk away, and to this hour nobody knows where he is concealed." The great Minister was not concealed for very long. He left Vienna secretly the following night. At the last moment one of the Rothschilds lent him a thousand ducats—otherwise he was penniless—with which he made his way partly by coach and partly by railroad, as befitted one who belonged to both the eighteenth and nineteenth centuries, through Germany and Holland and eventually to England. We catch a glimpse of him en route playing the violin all by himself in the chateau of Weinsberg. His host was mystified by his behavior. He insisted that the red flag be hoisted over the tower where he lodged. There he sat playing the *Marseillaise*, always the *Marseillaise*, over and over again, but he played it, his host admitted, very well.

Metternich would have been very glad to stay on in England. However mistaken the English may have been in their foreign policy, there was no mistaking the genuineness of English hospitality. His old friends of Napoleonic days were delighted to see him.[5] The Duke of Wellington and a host of other notabilities called on him at once. The Duke in particular was full of attentions. He brought Metternich a portrait of himself in the uniform of an Austrian field marshal, and, what was perhaps even more welcome, a short jacket to wear over

---

[4] *The Greville Memoirs*, 8 vols., London, 1896, VI, 163.
[5] "J'y retrouve mes vieux amis et cette hospitalité qui est non pas un vain mot, mais une qualité particulière de cette nation." Metternich, *op. cit.*, XIII, 155.

his clothes—the ideal present for anyone not accustomed to the temperature of English houses, as many visitors to England since Metternich have come to know. Disraeli sat at his feet. Metternich, he decided, was the only philosophical statesman he had ever met. Everybody came to see him, even Palmerston, though the two did not talk politics. Yes, London society was extraordinarily agreeable, but in spite of it all his wife, Mélanie, was restless. She hated the interminable streets of London, where you might be jostled at any moment by the revolutionary riff-raff of Europe. No doubt the Brunswick Hotel in Hanover Square was a sorry substitute for the beautiful castle of Johannisberg or the smiling villa outside Vienna. Even the visits to Richmond and Brighton, and to the Duke of Wellington at Strathfieldsaye, began to pall.

Metternich bowed to her wishes, and by the spring of 1851, they were on their way homeward. It was a satisfactory homecoming, almost a triumphal progress. The satirists had made the most of his fall from power and his flight across Europe, but now the laugh was on his side. Once more he was back in Vienna, not in office—he was too old for that at seventy-nine—but sitting comfortably in the stage box watching a new set of actors playing the old familiar parts. How familiar the story was—Act I, Agitation; Act II, Revolution; Act III, Reaction. Metternich did not think much of the new players, Schwarzenberg, Bach and Stadion, but that was natural enough. To the old trouper the new men always seem hopelessly lacking in style.

His last years were very peaceful. Death finally caught up with him in 1859, just after the outbreak of the war with Italy. If he had been consulted there would have been no war. "For God's sake, no ultimatum to Italy," had been his last words of advice to Francis Joseph, but they came too late. The ultimatum had already been sent. If by some miracle Metternich had still been alive in 1914 we can be sure his plea to Francis Joseph would have been exactly the same, "For God's sake, no ultimatum," and it would have been disregarded just as it was in 1859. It was not so much the cry of a pacifist as of a good European. Metternich hated to see the fabric of Europe torn apart, and he never accepted the fact that the spirit of nationalism was bound to tear it apart unless adequate concessions were granted in time. Mazzini had roused Italy, and Széchényi, as we have just seen, had warned Metternich as long ago as

1825 of the newly awakened national consciousness in Hungary, but by 1848 Széchényi himself had been swept aside by a more obviously popular figure.

3

Louis Kossuth, the country lawyer whose amazing eloquence precipitated a revolution, is one of those heroes of the nineteenth century about whom history has reversed its opinion. A hundred years ago he was regarded in England and America and by a large section of his own countrymen as a man of irreproachable integrity, the hero of a lost cause, the undaunted champion of the rights of small nations. We know now that his conception of liberty and patriotism was by no means as ideal as was generally supposed. A modern historian has described him as "the first dictator to rise to power by prostituting idealism to the service of racial passion." [1] The history of the last ten years, the knowledge that nationalism can so easily degenerate into Hitler's *Herrenvolk* rubbish, goes a long way toward explaining the divergence between yesterday's point of view and today's.

Kossuth was born and grew up in the little village of Monok in northern Hungary, near the Galician border. His father, the village lawyer, belonged to the gentry but he owned no land; only a porticoed, high-roomed manor house. He was a man of some cultivation who had read his Rousseau and his Voltaire but still clung to the strict Protestantism of his ancestors. One of Kossuth's earliest recollections was of his father reading to the family every Sunday from the Hungarian Bible. The four children—Louis was the oldest and the only boy—grew up to be as nearly as possible trilingual. The mother, who was of Slovak origin, preferred talking German to the children, but they spoke Hungarian with their father, and Slovak with the people of the village. Later on, Louis learned Latin, which was the language then spoken in the Hungarian Diet. He got his first schooling from a Protestant clergyman, who at once perceived that Louis Kossuth, with his Werther-like sensibility and his ferocious independence, was different from his other pupils. Afterward he was sent to a Catholic school, then to the Calvinist college of Sáraspotak, and finally to the University of Budapest. His father was determined that he should have

[1] A. J. P. Taylor, *The Habsburg Monarchy*, London, 1942, p. 56.

the best education available. It was taken for granted that like most cultivated men of his class in Hungary he would be a lawyer. His career was already mapped out for him. He would return to Monok, enter his father's office, and gradually take over the practice.

The talents and amiability of the young lawyer soon won him great popularity in the neighborhood. Here was a man equally in demand in the houses of country families and in the cottages of the peasants. Being now of age, he took his seat in the *Comitât,* the county meeting, where his knowledge of law and his natural, unpretentious eloquence marked him out for a more distinguished future than the village of Monok or the county of Zemplen could offer. An outbreak of cholera gave him an unexpected opportunity of proving both to the peasants and to the local aristocracy that he was something more than an able young lawyer with a gift of ready speech.

The story of the cholera epidemic in the remote districts of upper Hungary has been aptly described as "a catalogue of horrors." The aftermath was even ghastlier than the plague itself. Medical science was in its infancy. There was no sanitation to speak of, and there was one dreadful, murderous ally of the pestilence—stupidity. In the Middle Ages epidemics were often attributed to the Jews, who were accused of poisoning the wells. Rumors now began to circulate that in this epidemic the wells were being poisoned by the nobles. The fact that the cholera outbreak happened to coincide with the Polish Revolution of 1831 gave this rumor a certain credibility. A number of unfortunate Poles, driven from their country, had sought refuge in Hungary, and they brought cholera with them. Most of them were aristocrats or small landowners; in any case they were not peasants. The Viennese Government, always friendly with Russia, forbade all subjects of the Austrian crown to harbor these rebels, but the sympathy with the Poles was so strong that the order was not enforceable. Among others, Kossuth's mother gave shelter to some of these exiles and strained the resources of the family to the utmost to provide for their needs. At the same time his three sisters had volunteered as nurses to fight the epidemic which had overrun all northern Hungary. The county of Zemplen was known to be harboring a number of Poles, and it was there, too, that the cholera was most virulent. A mob of peasants and beggars armed with guns, scythes and flails started to terrorize the neighborhood and threatened to burn down the houses of the gentry.

This was the crisis that gave Kossuth a chance to prove himself. He spoke to the people from the steps of the church, explained to them the ridiculous delusions they were under in ascribing the scourge of cholera to the upper classes. The disease was no respecter of persons. It descended on the rich as well as the poor. Hospital facilities of all kinds were lacking. He recommended borrowing several large buildings on the outskirts of the town for the use of the sick, and he urged the inhabitants to equip those buildings as best they could with beds and linen. By the time he had finished he had not only pacified the mob but even organized them into a national guard for the preservation of the community from the marauding mobs of other villages.

The danger of anarchy and destruction had been averted, but at the same time Kossuth's eyes had been opened to the existence of a class hatred he had never suspected. What value had the historic constitution and all the liberties which the nobles so proudly defended if the privileged class left the peasants in a state of such ignorance and fanaticism that they readily believed stories about the nobles poisoning their wells? There and then Kossuth decided that the material improvements put forward by Széchényi and other magnates were not enough. Surely it was more important to educate the people, inform them what was going on in the world around them, than to found a National Club for the enjoyment of the more enlightened aristocracy or to open up the Danube to steamboats. Kossuth wanted to plough deeper than Széchényi. He had proved what he could do in the little world of Zemplen; now he began to long for the larger arena of Pressburg where the National Diet held its meetings.

In September, 1832, Kossuth was thirty years old. His youth had slipped away. He was a capable provincial lawyer with no prospect of ever being anything else. Only two years before, another provincial lawyer, Louis-Adolphe Thiers, about the same age as himself, had played an important part in driving Charles X from the throne of France and installing Louis Philippe in his place. In France the bourgeois had come into his own. Might it not be that in Hungary, too, an unknown country lawyer might thrust his way into fame? The opportunity, when it came, did not look particularly golden. Kossuth

was appointed to the Diet of 1832 as the delegate of a certain
Baron Hunyadi who was unable to attend the meetings himself. As a delegate of an absentee member, Kossuth took his
place on the side benches reserved for those who had a seat but
not a voice. For an ambitious young lawyer, eloquent, able and
restless with the desire to serve mankind, it must have been
peculiarly tantalizing to be a member of the Diet but condemned to perpetual silence.

At first, Kossuth was content to watch the proceedings, to
listen to the debates, and to study the idiosyncrasies of his colleagues. These members of the Diet were worth watching, they
were the great men of Hungary. Some day he hoped to pit
himself against them, against Széchényi, exasperatingly elegant in his English clothes but with an aura of greatness about
him that was not to be denied; against Kolcsey, the poet philosopher who seemed out of place in the workaday world of politics; Wesselényi, a giant from Transylvania who thrilled
Kossuth with his thundering denunciation of the Viennese
Government; and Francis Deák, a solid-looking bourgeois in
old-fashioned clothes whom these others unexpectedly deferred
to as the leader of the liberal party. Deák was a year younger
than Kossuth but he had already "arrived." At first glance
there was nothing arresting about him. The stocky figure, the
twinkling eyes peering out of a round face, the ivory-handled
walking-stick with which he came stumping into the chamber,
suggested a comfortably prosperous shopkeeper rather than a
great statesman. No one ever owed less to the graces than
Francis Deák. He was not a finished speaker, he was not a
scholar or a writer, but he had in him two qualities that will
always be welcomed in any political gathering—he was completely without ambition for himself, and he had the faculty
of seizing the main point of an argument and sticking to it.

Kossuth measured himself mentally against all the great
figures in the Diet. Then he began, at first as a kind of game,
to scribble down reports of their speeches, in which he tried to
catch not just the argument but the character of every speaker.
It amused him to fit men into categories—the lukewarm and
the fanatics, the hedgers and the diehards, the hypocrites and
the honest men. These reports, originally intended only for the
absent member he was representing, were soon being read all
over Pressburg. Just as a brook that has been dammed up will
dig another channel for itself, so Kossuth, deprived of a voice

in the Diet, found another outlet in journalism. If a phrase was heightened here and there, if he gave more space to the liberals than to the reactionaries, he was merely exercising the right of selection. Gradually he came to think of himself not just as a reporter, but as an editor and finally as a pamphleteer. The unknown substitute deputy from Zemplen was suddenly discovered to be an extraordinarily competent political journalist. There was no precedent to guide him. Hitherto the work of the Diet had not been known to the main body of the people. Metternich's system of censorship forbade the printing of reports of debates, but there was no law against lithography, and Kossuth's reports, written out in longhand, were secretly lithographed and despatched to every corner of the country, where they found thousands of eager readers. Before long the name of Kossuth was known all over Hungary.

The Viennese Government now saw that Kossuth was forcing an entrance for the public into the sacred mysteries of legislation. Metternich did not dare proceed against him while the Diet was still sitting, but in 1837, when the meetings were over, both Kossuth and Wesselényi, who had been reporting the debates in the Transylvania Diet in much the same way, were indicted for treason, arrested and sent to prison. The Government dispensed with the formalities of a trial.

The Diet of Pressburg had been dissolved but the Government soon found that the discussion of burning questions was being carried on with unabated energy in fifty county assemblies instead of in the Diet of Pressburg. Nor was it possible to stop the distribution of reports of the debates. Kossuth's poison was working in the remotest corners of Hungary. The peasants learned from his *Parliamentary Messenger* that Deák was pressing for the very reforms they wanted—freedom from the mediaeval dues, the right to buy land, and better security for person and property. The Edict of Maria Theresa, called the Urbarium, had granted the peasant the right of leaving the land when he pleased, or of remaining if he liked, while he complied with certain conditions, but the Urbarium had never been enforced. Now, in one county assembly after another the discussion ended in instructions being given to the deputies to keep on driving for the reforms Deák had initiated.

Meanwhile Kossuth's imprisonment was turning to his advantage. Metternich had raised him from obscurity to martyrdom; it was just the kind of publicity he wanted. More than

that, imprisonment gave him the leisure he might not otherwise have had to learn English. He knew French already, but
he must learn English too. English was the language of practical men. Széchényi's knowledge of Adam Smith and Bentham
and Cobden had made him feel that until he had read the
works of these great men he would not be able to discuss questions of economics with any authority. With the help of Shake-
speare and an antiquated grammar he set to work and learned
English so thoroughly that ten years later his amazing mastery
of the language held British and American audiences spell-
bound.

By the time the prison doors swung open in 1840 the clever
journalist Metternich thought to discipline had become a
hardened revolutionary. Hungary had changed too. Kossuth's
journal, like the wand of a magician, had conjured up a new
spirit in the land. When the Viennese Government demanded
four million florins and thirty-eight thousand recruits as Hungary's share of the defense program, the Diet made it clear
that no royal demands would be considered until the political
prisoners were set free. Deák led the opposition in the lower
house, and Count Louis Batthyány came forward as the champion of freedom in the house of magnates. Batthyány was not
as able as Széchényi, but Széchényi was growing restless at
what seemed to him the radical tendencies in the new Diet
and he had yielded his position to the younger and more reckless man. It was a long struggle, for the majority of the great
land-owning magnates sided with the Government, who met
the fierce attacks of the opposition by identifying loyalty to the
King's ministers with loyalty to the King, and denouncing
hostile criticism as high treason. In the end the opposition won,
and the money was granted only after the political prisoners
had been released.

After three years of enforced silence Kossuth came out of
prison bubbling over with ideas, eager to talk, eager to write,
eager to argue with anyone and everyone who would listen to
him. The Diet was not sitting at the moment, otherwise he
would certainly have been elected, but another and even better
forum soon presented itself. A bookseller from Pest had just
received permission from the Government to publish a newspaper. Would Kossuth undertake the editorship? There was no
question about the policy of the paper. If he accepted, his
name would be the program. Nothing could have suited Kos-

suth better. Metternich was approached and strangely enough gave his consent, perhaps on the theory that so unusual a concession would conciliate a dangerous opponent, or at least deprive him of the terrible popularity that those whom the Government was forced to punish somehow always acquired. The first number of the *Pesti Hirlap* (Pest Gazette) appeared in January, 1841. Almost immediately it acquired immense influence. For the Hungarians the *Pesti Hirlap* marked a new departure in journalism. It was not a pamphlet, nor was it a mere chronicle of events. The *Pesti Hirlap* was a modern newspaper, the first modern newspaper in Hungary. Kossuth secured the services of men of real ability who presented a picture of day-to-day life in Hungary as it actually was. Wisely he avoided questions that would obviously embroil him with the authorities, such as the position of Hungary in the Habsburg Monarchy, but every article in the paper, however innocuous it might look, was a signpost pointing toward revolution. It was impossible to write about life in the provinces, the reform of the municipalities, or the assessment of taxes, without hinting at the backwardness of the country and the necessity for change. Széchényi's warning against appealing to the passions of the people was ignored, and the circulation soon rose to seven thousand, more than that of all the other papers in the country put together.

The topic that aroused most controversy and that definitely alienated Kossuth from Széchényi and the more moderate reformers was the apparently harmless one of language. By the middle of the eighteenth century the Magyar language was in very real danger of dying out. Latin had become the language of government, and German of society. It was the mistaken attempt of Maria Theresa and Joseph II to establish German as the universal language of their dominion that roused Hungary from her lethargy. Széchényi, as we have already seen, was one of the first of the magnates to protest against the Germanization of the aristocracy. The founding of the Hungarian Academy of Sciences, the result of his generosity, marked an important stage in the renaissance of the Magyar language. With every year the tide of national feeling ran more strongly. In 1835 the Diet decreed that laws were to be published no longer in Latin only, but in Latin and Magyar. A few years later, in 1839, when Deák was leading the still moderate opposition, the Addresses to the Sovereign were drawn up in the Magyar language only—an innovation which was met with the greatest enthusiasm. Finally, in 1843, after a brilliant campaign of agitation in the *Pesti Hirlap* the Diet passed a new linguistic law making Magyar the exclusive language of the legislature and the only language to be taught in the schools. The three Slovak counties in Hungary were exempted for six years in order that at least the officials, if no one else, might during that period acquire a knowledge of Magyar. As a concession to the Croats it was agreed that in their schools Magyar was to be a compulsory subject but not the language of instruction.[2]

Kossuth ignored, consciously or unconsciously, the fact that the majority of inhabitants in Hungary were not Magyars. Hungary was a polyglot nation of Magyars, Germans, Slovaks, Croats and Rumanians, within the still more polyglot Habsburg Empire. Thus the truculent policy of Magyarization of which Kossuth was the apostle inflicted great injustice on the various minority groups which together outnumbered the Magyars. It was no idle phrase of Széchényi when he accused Kossuth of "goading into madness against the Magyar nation" all other races of the Crown of St. Stephen.[3] The word self-determination had not yet been coined, but the idea was already familiar, and men were beginning to wonder as they have been wondering ever since how far down the scale the principle of self-determination applies. If Magyar was to be acknowledged as the official language in Magyar-speaking communities, surely Kossuth could not grudge the same liberty to the Croats and the Slovaks. But Kossuth did grudge it, with the result that in Hungary the revolution developed into a contest on two fronts—against Vienna on the one side, and against the non-Magyar races on the other.

If Széchényi could have had his way there would have been no revolution. He believed just as ardently as Kossuth in the desirability of assimilating the non-Magyar elements, but unlike Kossuth he was willing to wait. The steady growth of a vigorous national culture and literature along the lines already started would lure the other races into the fold, whereas Kossuth's policy of force would inevitably provide a spirit of separatism. Nor would he have quarrelled with Austria. Pro-

[2] The history of the language question in Hungary is treated extensively in R. W. Seton-Watson, *Racial Problems in Hungary* (London, 1908).
[3] Quoted by R. W. Seton-Watson, *op. cit.*, p. 93.

vided everybody kept his temper the essential reasonableness of his position would ultimately prevail. Unfortunately
those who are blessed with the dangerous gift of galvanizing
their fellow men into action by dramatizing the injustices
under which they labor are not attracted by a long-term policy
of sweetness and light. Kossuth came more and more to look
upon Széchényi as the lost leader, and Széchényi in the loneliness of his moderation courted unpopularity with what the
Hungarian poet Aranyi has called "the snow of equanimity
and the ice of disdain."

The one man who might have saved the country from
heading into revolution was Deák. He was more approachable
than Széchényi, and, being a Magyar born instead of a convert
like Kossuth, he knew the limits of Magyar strength. Utterly
devoid of personal vanity, a landowner, though not one of the
great proprietors, as well as a lawyer, Deák was peculiarly
fitted to lead the conservative party, but at the moment when
his leadership was most needed he was not a member of the
Diet. He had been elected in 1843 but he had flabbergasted
his supporters by refusing to take his seat. After the election
was over and while he was still being congratulated, he found
out that bribery, intimidation and even murder had been
freely resorted to by both parties. Deák felt this electioneering
violence to be a "cancer at the very root of public life in
Hungary." He would always see "bloodstains on his mandate"
if he were to accept an election won by such methods. Whether
or not he was too squeamish, as some of his friends complained,
his retirement from public life at this particular moment was a
great loss to Hungary. Though he returned to politics in 1847
and was appointed Minister of Justice in Batthyányi's cabinet,
it was not until many years later that he resumed the first place
in the Hungarian national movement. The cynics thought he
had sacrificed himself to no purpose, but he lived to become
Hungary's most successful statesman.[4]

In the few years that remained before the storm broke, the
legislature was chiefly occupied with embittered debates on
the introduction of Magyar as the official language throughout
the kingdom, on the whittling down of feudal rights, and the
full emancipation of the peasants. Kossuth, now the unchal-

[4] For Deák's subsequent career and the part he played in the Austro-Hun-
garian compromise in 1867, see Mrs. F. O'Brien, *Francis Deák, Hungarian Statesman* (London, 1880).

lenged leader of the liberal party, had redoubled his activities.
Life had not gone easily with him since his release from prison,
but his energy surmounted every difficulty. The sensitive, frail-
looking substitute deputy, always suffering from ill-health, had
developed into one of the most effective agitators of the nineteenth century. The *Pesti Hirlap* had finally fallen under the
ax of censorship, and an interview with Metternich in which
Kossuth hoped to induce the great man to change his mind
produced an uncompromising "no." Unfortunately no record
of the interview has come down to us. Kossuth was not discouraged. If he could not edit a newspaper he would do something else. At one moment he made an unsuccessful sortie into
the realm of economics. He founded a tariff-protection union
and dreamed of converting Hungary into an industrial state.
The fact that Széchényi was a disciple of Cobden and free
trade was enough to make Kossuth an ardent protectionist. He
would build up manufactures just as Széchényi was building up
agriculture; he would boycott Austrian goods and create a new
self-sufficient Hungary.

After the first wave of enthusiasm these undertakings all
failed, and the Trading Company, the most important of the
companies founded by Kossuth, went bankrupt. Nevertheless
Kossuth's popularity kept on growing. He forgot his own failures, plunged into other activities, and the people followed
him. The world is generally supposed to worship success, but
the popularity of a Mazzini whose life was a long succession of
failures, and of a Kossuth who experienced one rebuff after
another, suggests that in time of revolution success and failure
really are the impostors Kipling believed them to be.

In the election of 1847 Kossuth, already a member of the
county assembly of Pest, was elected to the National Diet and
became the uncontested leader of the radical group in the
reform party. Reform was in the air. Metternich's concessions,
which three years before would have been received with acclaim, were now regarded as inadequate. He had recently
appointed administrators to supersede the Hungarian county
assemblies, and these he now agreed to remove upon certain
conditions. The conditions he imposed were rejected by all
parties. The debates on the administrators were still in progress when news arrived of the February revolution in Paris.
Széchényi entered in his journal the laconic comment: *Tout
est perdu.* The consternation which the fall of the July Mon-

archy produced in Vienna encouraged the Magyars to step up their pace. Kossuth's great speech of March 3, demanding that a system of responsible government should be introduced in Hungary, let loose an avalanche of reforms adopted almost without discussion. Within the space of one month Hungary was transformed from a land of aristocratic privilege and semi-feudal traditions to a constitutional monarchy which recognized the equality of all citizens before the law.

A glance at the twelve points of the Hungarian program shows that the much dreaded republican element had not yet come to the front. What Kossuth, and more particularly Deák, had in mind was a liberal-bourgeois state connected with Austria, just as the self-governing dominions are with England, by sentimental rather than legal ties.

1. Freedom of the press and abolition of censorship.
2. Ministerial responsibility.
3. Annual parliaments elected by universal suffrage.
4. Equality of all in the eyes of the law.
5. Formation of a National Guard.
6. Taxation of the clergy and the aristocracy.
7. Suppression of feudal rights.
8. Elected juries for criminal cases.
9. Creation of a National Bank.
10. A national army.
11. Liberation of political prisoners.
12. Union of Hungary and Transylvania.

Hungarian historians insist that the Revolution of 1848, as far as Hungary was concerned, was an act of self-defense, and that it had little to do with abstract principles or theories of government. The Hungarians were fighting for the ancient independence of their kingdom, not for an experimental republic.

4

Only two days after the delivery of Kossuth's speech the leading supporters of German unity met at Heidelberg. The demand for a wider national life was flooding through the backwaters of every little principality in Germany. Everywhere men were clamoring for written constitutions. Within ten days Metternich had fallen. Immediately afterward Kossuth, accompanied by a host of dignitaries, made a triumphal progress along the Danube from Pressburg to Vienna. The actual head of the deputation was the Archduke Stephen, a Habsburg himself who had espoused the cause of Hungary. The little river steamer bedecked with flags puffed its way past the cheering crowds. In Vienna the arrival of the Hungarian delegation was the signal for the wildest enthusiasm. The horses were taken from the Archduke Stephen's carriage, and it was dragged by students from the waterfront to the imperial palace. But the center of attraction was Kossuth. He had the demagogue's mysterious faculty of exciting a crowd by his mere presence. Széchényi, one of the few members of the deputation who was disturbed by the febrile enthusiasm, made a note of Kossuth's extraordinary popularity: "If Kossuth demands it, the people will pull down the palace itself." [1]

The Emperor Ferdinand, who was still in the mood for yielding, consented on March 17 to everything Kossuth had demanded. A constitution was granted to Austria, and the formation of a responsible ministry under the presidency of Count Batthyány to Hungary. However hateful to the court the administrative revolution might be, it was obvious that it could not be put down with bayonets, at least not at the moment. After all, the situation might have been worse. The most devoted absolutist could hardly maintain that a cabinet which included Batthyány, Esterházy, Széchényi and Deák would be likely to have much in common with the defenders of the barricades in Paris or with the leaders of the revolution in Berlin or Vienna. Kossuth was more dangerous. How much more dangerous nobody knew.

After the first inevitable concessions had been made, the court party headed by the Archduchess Sophia decided that the revolution had gone far enough. They had wanted to get rid of Metternich, and that had now been accomplished. The new cabinet headed by Kolowrat and another bureaucrat named Pillersdorff was too weak to oppose the revolutionary forces openly and too tricky to abide honestly by the concessions they had made. The Government's policy, according to the American *chargé d' affaires*, was characterized only "by indecision and duplicity." [2] Accordingly they fell back on the old policy of "divide and rule." Metternich had always believed that the demand for constitutional government in

---

[1] O. Zarek, *op. cit.*, p. 146.

[2] W. H. Stiles, *Austria in 1848–49*, 2 vols., New York, 1852, II, 118.

Vienna might be used to crush the independent spirit of Hungary by absorbing the Hungarians into a common Austrian parliament. He believed also that Croatia, already antagonized by Kossuth's policy of Magyarization, might become the focus of the anti-Hungarian movement. With this purpose in mind, just before the nomination of the Hungarian cabinet, General Jellachich had been created Ban (Viceroy) of Croatia.

Baron Jellachich was not by any means the extraordinary man that the sycophants around the imperial throne represented him to be. He was a colonel in a frontier regiment of the Austrian Army when he was picked out for royal favor on account of his pronounced Slavic, and therefore anti-Hungarian, sentiments. Something of a scholar and a poet, besides being a good-looking cavalry officer, he was the ideal leader for what at first appeared to be a lost cause. Croatia was one of the several outlying provinces of Hungary that had no intention of being absorbed. The people were determined to maintain their identity together with their virtual independence. No doubt Hungary's linguistic laws, as Széchényi said, were goading the other races within the kingdom into madness, but it is at least equally true that the Austrian Government was delighted to turn these quarrels to her own advantage. As the twentieth century knows only too well, anarchy is the bridge over which expelled absolutism returns to power, and it was on that theory that the Austrian Government encouraged every movement for autonomy that might embarrass Batthyány's cabinet. "There were indeed two governments," says Deák, "the one manifest (with this one we treated), while the doings of the other were kept secret even from Austrian ministers." [3] It was this duplicity quite as much as their own radical tactlessness that drove a naturally loyal people into war.

By the end of the summer Hungary was ringed with hostile nationalities in arms. Along with the Croats, the Serbs and Rumanians were also threatening insurrection. The moderate party among the Magyars were quite willing to grant the just demands of peoples who were their natural allies. Wesselényi, now a blind old man after his long years of imprisonment, urged the Diet to remember that Hungary was isolated in the vast ocean of nations: "I ask you therefore to pass a law that the nationality of the Rumanians shall be respected." [4] Kos-

[3] Quoted from *Letters and Journal of Count Leiningen*, London, 1911, p. 25.
[4] Stiles, *op. cit.*, II, 60.

suth opposed the motion, declaring that he knew nothing of a
Rumanian or a Croatian people, and that he recognized only
Hungarian citizens. The more moderate members of the ministry did what they could to avoid a conflict. They even promised to send 40,000 troops to reinforce Radetzky's hard-pressed
army in Italy. It was an unpopular move in view of the threatening attitude of Jellachich to denude Hungary of its embryo
army, but Batthyány was determined to give Austria a convincing proof of Hungarian loyalty. Kossuth consented un-
willingly. He alone seems to have realized that war was inevitable. Always suspicious of Austria, and haunted by the
spectre of an all-devouring Slavism, he had no illusions about
the future. Hungary would have to fight several enemies at
once, and she would have to fight them alone. King Charles
Albert, whose armies looked as if they might drive Radetzky
out of Lombardy, had announced that Piedmont would seek
no allies from outside of Italy: *Italia farà da sè*. Hungary, too,
would have to fend for herself. She would have the sympathy
of England and France for what it was worth, but the governments of those two countries were not composed of knights
errant. Kossuth should have known that nations do not go to
war unless their own interests are directly involved.

As soon as the new Diet met, elected for the first time by
the whole people, Kossuth asked for 200,000 men and 42,000,-
000 florins "for the defence of the country, the restoration of
order, and the security of the throne." The proposal brought
the deputies to their feet, cheering and shouting with applause.
He had been appointed Minister of Finance in the new cabinet,
not President, but the deputies recognized him as their leader
and voted for his proposal unanimously. It was one of Kossuth's great moments. He waited for the applause to die down,
then he spoke again: "I bow before the greatness of this
nation. If Hungary's energy is equal to her patriotism even the
gates of Hell will not prevail against her!" [5] Fashions in oratory change, and from the distance of a hundred years Kossuth's words begin to look garish and shopworn, but to the
Hungarian patriots of 1848 these same words were inconceiv-
ably fresh and gleaming. It was with such words that new
nations were being conjured into being.

Still there was no open breach between the Governments

---

[5] D. Iranyi, *Histoire Politique de la Révolution de Hongrie, 1847–49*, 2 vols.
Paris, 1859–60, II, 17.

of Vienna and Budapest, but with the unexpected victories of Radetzky in Italy and of Windischgrätz in Prague, the prospects of peace grew fainter. Austria had now so far recovered herself that she would be able to give her entire attention to Hungary. In September, Batthyány and Deák journeyed to Schönbrunn on one last effort at reconciliation. They invited Ferdinand to come to Pest himself, thereby giving his ministers his support and sanction. As the King of Hungary, and as one who had declared Jellachich a rebel, he was still popular. After keeping the Hungarian deputation waiting for two hours in an anteroom Ferdinand gave an equivocal, ungracious reply, and the deputation returned to Pest to find that Jellachich had crossed the river Drave, separating Hungary from Croatia, and that he was actually being encouraged to pursue "his loyal undertaking." [6] In the following months the Batthyány cabinet resigned. In order that the country might not be left without any sort of executive government, a committee of national defense was nominated by the Diet with Kossuth as president. With marvelous energy he organized a national volunteer force (the *Honved*) and girded the country for war.

In a last-minute effort to avoid the conflict the Emperor now appointed Count Lamberg, a Hungarian and a friend of Batthyány's, commander-in-chief in Hungary. Lamberg's mission was to take over command of all troops, Hungarian and Croatian alike, and arrange an armistice. On the very day that he arrived in Budapest, to which the Hungarian Diet had now been transferred, Kossuth carried a resolution through the Diet calling on the Hungarian Army to refuse all recognition of Lamberg's authority. Ignorant of what had happened, the unfortunate man proceeded to Buda, the ancient city on the left bank of the Danube, to present his credentials to the president of the Hungarian ministry, Count Batthyány. Batthyány was away. He went on to the residence of the general commanding the fortress. The news that Lamberg was visiting the fortress seemed to the excited Magyars a sufficient proof of his intentions. A cry was raised that Buda was going to be occupied by Austrian troops and military law established. An armed mob followed him, and as he was driving back in an open fiacre across the bridge into Pest, he was dragged from the carriage and murdered.

Vienna responded to the murder with a proclamation

[6] *Francis Deák, a Memoir*, p. 96.

charging Kossuth and his colleagues with direct responsibility. Hungary was placed under martial law, the Diet was dissolved, and Jellachich was appointed dictator. The extremists in Vienna and Budapest regarded the appointment as a challenge, and when certain Viennese regiments were ordered to Jellachich's support in Hungary, the Vienna mob behaved in exactly the same way as the mob in Budapest by murdering the Minister of War, Count Latour, in broad daylight in the open street.

War between Hungary and Austria was now at last an acknowledged fact. The difficulties of Austria were complicated by the outbreak of the October revolution. Though the Austrian Reichstag had been slow to realize that the defeat of Hungary would inevitably lead to the end of constitutional government in Austria, the appointment of Jellachich disclosed the two divergent paths stretching ahead of them. Either the Reichstag must support the imperial policy of centralization, or they must be prepared to accept the idea of a loose federation of the eleven nations constituting the Empire.[7] By the time they understood the nature of the choice, the revolution had broken out, and the deliberations of the Reichstag—whether they should demand the withdrawal of the declaration of war against Hungary, whether they should transfer the sittings to some point outside of Vienna—had become a matter of importance only to themselves. The day after Latour's murder, the Arsenal was stormed and the city was reduced to a state of anarchy. The Emperor fled to Olmütz after appointing Windischgrätz commander-in-chief of the army charged with the relief of Vienna and the stamping out of revolution. At the same time Jellachich gave up the idea of conquering Hungary, which he was beginning to think too much for him, and hurried to Vienna to join forces with Windischgrätz.

By the end of October, Vienna was besieged by two armies. Now or never was the moment for the revolutionary parties in Austria and Hungary to join forces. Left to their own resources, the radicals in Vienna were doomed unless they could get immediate assistance from national Germany or national Hungary, the two causes for which they were fighting. The Frankfort Parliament sent them a radical delegate, Robert Blum, once a Leipzig bookseller and now one of the great agi-

---

[7] The eleven nations were Germans, Magyars, Czechs, Slovaks, Croats, Serbs, Slovenes, Italians, Rumanians, Poles and Little Russians.

tators of revolution. Blum had grown tired of the endless speeches in Frankfort and had come to believe that the only hope for Germany lay in the triumph of the Vienna radicals.

A man of much greater importance in a siege than Robert Blum arrived in Vienna at about the same time. This was Joseph Bem, a Polish general, one of the most successful of those meteoric soldiers of fortune of whom Poland has always produced such an ample supply. Bem had had a story-book career. He had served in Davoust's corps in Napoleon's expedition to Russia, won the Legion of Honor at Danzig, commanded the Polish artillery in the insurrection of 1830, escaped to Paris where for a time he taught physics, and endeavored to raise a Polish Legion to fight for liberalism in Portugal. Now, in October, 1848, he gravitated naturally to Vienna, and was immediately appointed to the command of the National Guard. Unfortunately the men he had to deal with did not understand the nature of a revolution. When he ordered them to march out of the city against the army of Jellachich they refused to follow him, on the ground that they were only intended for the defense of the city. At the end of the siege Bem slipped through the Austrian lines into Hungary and offered his services to Kossuth. He was given command of the Hungarian Army in Transylvania, where his exploits against the greatly superior Austrian forces made him an almost legendary figure. After the surrender of the Hungarian armies he escaped, seriously wounded, into Turkey. There he turned Moslem and died a year later, in 1850, as Governor of Aleppo.

With the absence of any real support from Germany or Hungary the defeat of the Viennese revolutionaries was inevitable. A Hungarian army advanced gingerly to the plain of Schwechat, within sight of the church towers of Vienna, where it made contact with Jellachich's army, but the ensuing attack was not pressed home. On the Vienna side there seems to have been some bungling in the negotiations with Kossuth. The Viennese had been urged by their Hungarian friends to tear up the railway line, but they neglected this precaution, and thus Windischgrätz was able to bring up more troops to meet the threat of the relieving army. On the morning of October 30 it was clear to the observers on St. Stephen's tower that the Magyars were not coming nearer. "Soon it became unmistakably certain that they were steadily and quickly retreating.

One after another the observers slipped away down the dark steps of the tower." [8] The heavy fog had for a time concealed the truth. Windischgrätz and Jellachich were in fact carrying everything before them. The bombardment of Vienna began on the thirty-first, and by that evening imperial troops were in possession of the city. Robert Blum and a few of the other leaders were shot, and a new ministry took office under Prince Felix Schwarzenberg, a cold, clear-headed, iron-willed aristocrat. The Reichstag left Vienna and reconvened in the little Moravian town of Kremsier. There it embarked on a long series of constitutional debates, which were finally cut short on March 4 by Schwarzenberg's announcement that the Imperial Government had resolved to impose a constitution of its own devising.

The Army had come into its own. Windischgrätz, the Metternich in army boots, Jellachich, the Slav poet-cavalryman, and Radetzky, the eighty-year-old veteran who had been almost driven out of Italy and then fought his way back—these men were the heroes of the hour. It was by their efforts that the Habsburg dynasty had been propped up on the throne and given a new lease on life, a lease that was to run for another seventy years. Wherever democracy or nationalism had raised its head—at Prague (June 12 to 17), at Milan, and now in Vienna—these men had struck it down.

The capture of Vienna was the turning point in the history of 1848. The fall of Milan destroyed the link between Italy and the nations north of the Alps that were fighting to free themselves from Metternich's bureaucracy, but with the fall of Vienna the whole fabric of revolution seemed to collapse. The original insurrection in Vienna and the downfall of Metternich had caught the attention of the whole world. It had suggested that the old order was passing. The victory of the counter-revolution, therefore, was looked upon as correspondingly significant. The old order was reasserting itself. The new policy formulated by Schwarzenberg demanded a new and more aggressive Emperor. Ferdinand, who had long been impossible as a ruler, was persuaded to abdicate in favor of his nephew the Archduke Francis, who now assumed the name of Francis Joseph.

At eight in the morning on December 2, 1848, the imperial family, the field marshals and a few high-ranking digni-

[8] Josephine Goldmark, *Pilgrims of '48*, New Haven, 1930, p. 122.

taries assembled in the archbishop's palace at Olmütz. The abdication ceremony was short. Schwarzenberg was not interested in pageantry. "It has been the motto of our Government to be a protector of the law," so spake the Emperor to his peoples for the last time.[9] But now, apparently, the law needed a more vigorous protector. Ferdinand was accordingly dismissed. He made one last fleeting appearance on the stage of history when the Prussians occupied Prague in 1866. "Even I could have done as well as this," was his comment on the achievements of his successor.

The new monarch came to the throne with fair promises on his lips, but his accession marked the end of reform in Austria for many years to come. Schwarzenberg taught him that he could under his guidance become a great figure in history "if he possessed the force, the self-confidence and the firmness to oppose to the disastrous ideas and aims of European revolution and the folly of western democracy, the will of a true ruler who brings happiness to his people." The first task that lay before him was the subjugation of Hungary. In Vienna, the war against Hungary was officially represented as a struggle against the revolutionary forces that were seeking to overthrow law and order in every country of Europe. In Hungary, the war was also represented as a clear-cut struggle against lawlessness. Hungary had not been consulted about the abdication, the new Emperor had not been crowned King of Hungary, and in the new constitution promulgated at Olmütz Hungary had been reduced to the state of a mere province of Austria. Of the attitude of the Hungarian Diet, Kossuth could say with perfect truth: "We have rebelled against no government, we have not broken our allegiance; we have no desire to separate from the Austrian Empire, we desired no concessions and no innovations; we were satisfied by what was ours by law." [10] But the time had now come when no reference to the Pragmatic Sanction or to the laws of 1848 could avert a crisis. With Schwarzenberg determined to build a highly centralized modern state, Hungary found itself compelled either to submit unconditionally to the form of government designed for subject provinces by imperial wisdom at Vienna, or to embark upon a

[9] Cited by Adolph Schwarzenberg, *Prince Felix zu Schwarzenberg,* New York, 1946, p. 35.
[10] Extract of a letter from Kossuth to Francis Pulzsky, the Hungarian envoy in London, dated February, 1849, quoted in *Francis Deák,* p. 105.

war of self-preservation. Thus, owing to the turn of events in Vienna, Hungary's parliamentary revolution of 1848 developed into the war of independence of 1849.

The battle of Schwechat had brought into prominence the great difficulties against which the Hungarian Government now had to contend. While Kossuth's power was supreme in the newly appointed Committee of Defense, it was anything but supreme among the officers of the Hungarian Army. These men were torn between their love of Hungary and their allegiance to the Emperor. Civil war invariably presents a problem in loyalty. A hundred years ago many conscientious Americans were beginning to wonder whether they owed their allegiance to the state or to the nation. In Hungary, by the end of 1848, officers in the Army found themselves face to face with a very similar dilemma. Theoretically no problem in loyalty was involved. The Emperor of Austria and the King of Hungary were one and the same person, but since the revolution, imperial authority had broken down, and the Habsburg viceroy in Budapest had proceeded from one concession to another without any reference to Vienna. With the accession of Francis Joseph and the appointment of Schwarzenberg as his prime minister, all this was to be changed. The new Emperor had no intention of being crowned King of Hungary as his predecessors had always been. Hungary was to be made to understand that it was in no sense a separate state. The Pragmatic Sanction was a dead letter. Under these conditions about seven hundred officers resigned from the Austrian Army and joined the revolutionary cause. Whether they were "pricked forward by the spur of ambition or galvanized by the new credo of liberty" [11] it was none the less a difficult decision, and they did not make it lightheartedly. As one of them, Count Leiningen, who was afterward hanged for treason, wrote to his wife: "I will not lull myself to sleep with vain illusions; I know that in the light of human law my actions must be condemned . . . my fate is bound up with that of Hungary." [12]

The most famous among the secessionists and the most ambiguous character of the revolution was a young officer, Arthur Görgei, who had already been picked out by Kossuth for his brilliant conduct at the battle of Schwechat. Görgei had grown up in the army, but being a man of intellectual

[11] Adolph Schwarzenberg, *op. cit.*, p. 50.
[12] *Letters of Count Leiningen*, p. 214.

tastes he soon tired of the routine life in a garrison town, and sent in his resignation with the idea of devoting the rest of his life to the study of chemistry. For some years he taught chemistry at Prague University, but by the time the revolution broke out he had retired to a little village in Galicia to study new methods of cloth manufacture. Revolution offered this restless, proud, discontented man the opportunity for advancement and distinction that he might otherwise never have known. On arriving in Budapest he was appointed major in the *Honveds*, the Hungarian National Guard, and he was serving in that capacity when Kossuth discovered him.

The relationship between Kossuth and Görgei was not to prove an easy one, but for the time being Kossuth was so busy rousing the nation to a consciousness of its dangers that he overlooked the insubordination of his generals. Few men have possessed as he did the qualities of the orator and of the organizer. Recruits poured in so quickly in response to his appeal that it was difficult to equip them. At the same time he had to find the right leaders. To Bem, the indefatigable little Pole who had defended Vienna, he gave command of the army in Transsylvania, and to Görgei, who had shown more initiative at the battle of Schwechat than the commander-in-chief, he gave a corps in the main army that was to defend Budapest. There is no question that Kossuth did his utmost to choose the best among those officers who rallied to the national colors. Many of them were men of real ability, and the odds against which they fought fired the imagination of freedom-loving people all over the world. The very word "Hungary" made "the world's dead spirit leap again." [13] But there was a reverse side to the medal. The generals were always quarrelling among themselves. They acted like feudal barons, jealous of their prerogatives, suspicious of each other, and still more suspicious of the central authority. When Dembinski, one of the Polish officers, was appointed commander-in-chief, Görgei called his staff together and told them to accept "this apparent humiliation" with the same indifference as he did himself. This same indifference, really insubordination, characterized all his relations with Kossuth.

The differences between these two men, more than the might of their enemies, was what caused the downfall of Hungarian liberty. That Hungary should have been able to hold out

[13] Matthew Arnold, "Sonnet to the Hungarian Nation," 1849.

for nearly a year, in spite of incessant squabbling among the leaders, was in itself remarkable. In the last weeks of 1848 the military situation looked hopeless. The imperial troops started an invasion from the north and the west. The Croats, ready and eager long before the Court at Vienna gave its sanction, marched against Budapest from the south. Transylvania was in revolt, and in the east the Serbs were advancing under their nationalist leader Stratimirovitch. If only Kossuth had not goaded these other races into madmen by insisting on his policy of Magyar domination!

Windischgrätz occupied Budapest in January, but the Hungarian Army under Görgei's skilful leadership withdrew without being defeated. On January 1, Kossuth ordered the removal of the Government to Debrecen, a hundred-odd miles east of Budapest. The evacuation was carried out with all precautions, and the crown regalia and the banknote printing press, that most important instrument of civil defense, went with the Government. Meanwhile Batthyány and Deák made one last effort at a compromise peace, but Windischgrätz met them coldly. Unconditional surrender (*unbedingte Unterwerfung*) were the only terms he would consider. Those fatal words, which have so often broken the hearts of peacemakers and forced them to fight for a cause in which they did not believe, cleared the way for Kossuth's next move. Obviously it was impossible to come to terms with the Habsburgs. Ferdinand, whom loyal Hungarians still regarded as their Emperor, had been deposed, and his successor, an eighteen-year-old boy dominated by Windischgrätz and Schwarzenberg, was determined to rule by force. The moment had come, so Kossuth thought, to convince the last doubting Thomas that Hungary must stand on her own feet without either the support of the Habsburgs or the co-operation of the other races within her borders. Encouraged by a series of Hungarian victories during the winter and early spring of 1849, the Diet, meeting in the great Protestant church of Debrecen on April 14, proclaimed the independence of Hungary and the deposition of the Habsburg dynasty. Kossuth, who had engineered the whole proceedings, was appointed Governor. Of all the statesmen who had been prominent in the struggle against Metternich, he was the only one who survived. Batthyány had resigned, Széchényi was suffering from a breakdown, Deák had never wanted to lead a revolution. Only the little lawyer of Monok remained. His eloquence, his amazing energies in providing for the needs of the armies, and the intensity of his Magyar patriotism had clothed him with an authority which none of the other leaders of the movement had ever possessed.

Independence had been proclaimed, but no resolution as to the form of government was passed. Hungary was still at war, and the choice between constitutional monarchy and a republic could well be deferred until after the victory. The exploits of the Hungarian armies were applauded by all Europe, but the proclamation of independence did not meet with as much enthusiasm from the Hungarians themselves as might have been expected.[14] Kossuth was accused of personal ambition. Some people suspected him of wanting to seize the crown himself. Even those who trusted him and believed in his high-mindedness thought that the proclamation was badly timed. The successes in the field might have been used as a basis for reopening negotiations with Austria, instead of which Schwarzenberg, now more than ever determined to crush Hungary at any cost, swallowed his pride and appealed to the Czar for help. The Czar Nicholas needed no urging. He had always been convinced that there could be no permanent peace in the world unless the great empires were kept intact. So it was that when, a few years later, the United States was threatened with disunion, Russia was the only one of the Great Powers who would have no truck with the Confederacy. Not that the Russian Government was inspired by any passionate admiration for the American Constitution, but the revolt of a province, secession—call it what you will—was too dangerous a practice for any nation to condone. There was good reason therefore for the Czar's quick response to the appeal of his young fellow Emperor. A free Hungary might easily be tempted to threaten his Polish dominions. Decidedly it was his duty, as God-appointed guardian of conservative institutions, to intervene.

In May, the Russian forces already standing guard near the passes of the Carpathians poured into the fields of Hungary. Despite the victories won by Görgei and Bem the sands in

[14] Even before the declaration of independence Görgei had issued a statement to the Army condemning the policy of the Committee of Defense, and calling upon the officers to declare that the Army was fighting for the maintenance of the Constitution of Hungary as sanctioned by King Ferdinand V. By that time King Ferdinand V, alias the Emperor Ferdinand, had been deposed, and his policy repudiated by his successor. Görgei's position was unrealistic, but his officers agreed with him rather than with Kossuth.

the Hungarian hourglass were now running out. The country was overrun by enemies. The Austrians, Croats, Serbs, and now the Russians with an army of 130,000 men, were all determined to strangle this new country at birth. At the last moment Kossuth offered the Rumanian leaders independent commands in the Hungarian Army, while the Diet discussed a law guaranteeing the free development of all nationalities upon Hungarian soil, but it was too late. A law which, if voted in March, 1848, might have rallied the whole of Hungary in support of Magyar independence, was worse than useless, a mere signal of distress, now that masses of Russian and Austrian troops were closing in upon every side. On August 11, Kossuth issued a proclamation renouncing the office of Governor, and transferring all civil and military power to Görgei. Two days later Görgei, finding himself hopelessly sandwiched in between the Austrian and Russian armies, capitulated to the Russian general Paskievitch at Vilagos.

The decision to surrender to a Russian general rather than an Austrian proved a terrible mistake. Paskievitch's famous despatch, "Hungary lies vanquished at the feet of the Czar," only intensified Austrian bitterness against the Hungarian leaders. Had Austria herself been victorious, an amnesty would have been possible. As it was, General Haynau, who had succeeded Windischgrätz, exacted a terrible penalty. Thirteen Hungarian generals were condemned to death, of whom four by special favor were shot, and nine hanged. Görgei, protected by the Czar, was banished to Klagenfurt, where he spent most of the rest of his long life—he died in 1916—trying to explain how it was that, while he survived, the generals whose only fault was that they had served under him were ruthlessly put to death.

Görgei's character has always been a subject of controversy among Hungarians. For many years Kossuth regarded him as a traitor, but he finally withdrew the charge and stated that Görgei was no traitor, only "a man of ambition." On the other hand, Count Leiningen, one of the generals who was executed, regarded him as a hero and a man of the highest character.[15] From Görgei's own account it would appear that Kossuth had entered into negotiations with Russia before resigning, and that he had even gone so far as to offer the crown of Hungary to the

[15] *Letters and Journals of Count Leiningen*, p. 30.

dynasty of the Romanoffs.[16] The fact was that regardless of who was mostly to blame, the quarrels between Kossuth and Görgei had reached such a point that the efficiency of the Hungarian Army was seriously affected. Under these circumstances Görgei probably felt that the war was lost on the day Russia intervened.

The capitulation of Vilagos marks the end of the great revolutionary upsurge of 1848. Venice held out for another ten days, and the fortress of Komorn in northern Hungary did not surrender until September 26, but there was no hope of any dramatic reversal of fortune. The fires of revolution were methodically extinguished one by one.

Kossuth, Bem, Dembinski and about 5000 fugitives escaped into Turkey. Some entered the service of the Sultan, others eventually found a refuge in England and America. Hungary, entirely defenseless, was left to the mercy of the Austrian Government. Not content with the shooting and hanging of generals, Haynau promptly rounded up some 1700 civilians of whom 114 were put to death, among them Count Batthyány whose crime consisted in having tried to mediate between the Vienna Government and the revolutionary forces. No execution was more deeply resented than his. The London *Times* compared it to the execution of Egmont by the Duke of Alba.[17] The brutalities of Haynau made his name a byword even among the Austrians themselves. In Italy he had been known as "The Beast of Brescia" on account of his mass execution of Italian patriots, and Radetzky, who was not squeamish, had finally had to get rid of him. "Haynau," he said, "is like a razor; after it has been used, it should be placed back in its case." [18] Europe felt that Schwarzenberg had put the razor back too late, but Europe's sympathy did not stop the Austrian firing squads.

Kossuth had already appealed to England, as Mazzini had done, to give up the cherished policy of non-intervention which actually played into the hands of tyrants, and he had appealed no less eloquently to France to live up to the principles of her new constitution and not to abandon Hungary to her fate, as she had already abandoned Poland and Italy. To these despairing cries there was no answer. In France, Louis Napoleon was

---

[16] A. Görgei, *My Life and Acts in Hungary*, 2 vols., London, 1852, II, 390.
[17] October 17, 1849.
[18] A. Schwarzenberg, *op. cit.*, p. 57.

far too occupied in putting his own house in order to interfere in Austria's domestic affairs. In the *Collège de France* Michelet made a fervent speech in support of Hungary, but French foreign policy was not decided in the *Collège de France*. In the same way Cobden described for England the Calvary of Hungary under Habsburg rule, but no one in England or France was ready to die for Hungary.[19] Palmerston indeed believed that the independence of Hungary was quite incompatible with the essential task Austria had to perform—the turning back of the tide of Russian aggrandizement in Europe. To carry out that task it was not necessary for Austria to hold her Italian provinces, but to detach Hungary from Austria would be to cripple the Monarchy in its most vital organ. Palmerston's policy was never based upon sentimental considerations of nationalism but upon the enduring principles of the balance of power. Kossuth jumped to the wrong conclusion when he thought that Palmerston must champion Hungary as long as he had lent his support to Piedmont. In Palmerston's mind the issues involved were very different. It was only when the Austrian Government, as if determined to place itself utterly in the wrong, adopted the most brutal methods of repression that Palmerston began to express strong sympathy with the Hungarian cause. As usual, he carried the British people with him. Whatever inconsistency there may have been in his foreign policy, he always reflected popular opinion.

By the time Kossuth arrived in England, in October, 1851, he had become a romantic hero, the modern Prometheus defeated but unconquered, standing alone amid the wreckage of European liberalism. During the three weeks of his visit people turned out to greet him as they had turned out for no other foreigner. The Lord Mayor of London gave him an official reception, and he was equally feted in Birmingham and Manchester. Wherever he spoke he pleaded the cause of his unhappy country, and he pleaded it with amazing eloquence. Cobden considered him a phenomenon. "Not only is he the first orator of the age, but he combines the attributes of a first class administrator, high moral qualities, and unswerving courage." [20]

[19] Drouin de Lhuys, Louis Napoleon's foreign secretary, stated the Government's case in the Assembly very simply: "Si on veut autre chose, si l'on veut la guerre, que l'on apporte la propagande à la tribune." No one answered the challenge.

[20] J. Morley, *Richard Cobden* (London, 1905), p. 570.

Queen Victoria was made very uneasy by all this enthusiasm over a revolutionary, and particularly by the fact that Lord Palmerston, her foreign secretary, announced his intention of inviting Kossuth to his house. The incident was responsible for one of those delightfully crisp letters that Victorian statesmen were in the habit of writing to each other. Egged on by Queen Victoria, Lord John Russell, the prime minister, "positively requested" Lord Palmerston to decline to receive Kossuth. The reply, written while the messenger waited, read as follows: "There are limits to all things. I do not choose to be dictated to as to who I may or may not receive in my own house. . . . I shall use my own discretion. . . . You will, of course, use yours as to the composition of your Government." [21]

Kossuth sailed for America before the meeting could take place, but Palmerston managed to annoy the Queen still further by allowing a deputation of radicals to present an address to him at the Foreign Office in which the Emperor of Russia and Austria were stigmatized as "odious and detestable assassins" and "merciless tyrants and despots." Palmerston met the deputation most cordially, thanked them for their complimentary references to himself, and ignored the references to the two sovereigns. Once again the Queen protested to the unfortunate Lord John Russell, but the remarks could not be withdrawn. Lord Palmerston was incorrigible.

Kossuth's departure to America was well-timed. He left England while still at the height of his popularity, the most picturesque of innumerable refugees who for the most part were eking out a bare living in London boarding houses, quarrelling among themselves and hoping, working, planning for the better world that was to be. The London that he left behind, the London of Karl Marx and Mazzini, would soon have tired of his eloquence. The British people had cheered him, but he wanted something more than cheers. Ahead of him lay the incalculable New World. What would America do for him? The first wave of Hungarian immigrants, the aftermath of the war of independence, had already reached American shores. Some of these immigrants wanted to build a Hungarian New Jerusalem on the untamed soil of America. Others were practical people, ready to forget the past and eager to throw in their lot with a new civilization and a new way of life. Kossuth was different. He did not want to settle down in New Budapest, Iowa, or

[21] *Letters of Queen Victoria,* II, 393.

anywhere else. He wanted to go back to his own country with funds and diplomatic backing. Frankly, he wanted the United States to divert her energies to the establishment of Hungarian independence. Those who heard him were touched by his eloquence, but at the moment America was too deeply engrossed in her own manifest destiny to give much thought to the sorrows of Hungary. The nation was not yet ready to take on Europe's burdens. Kossuth made his appeal just one hundred years too soon.

CHAPTER

V

REPERCUSSIONS IN AMERICA

1

ONE AFTERNOON in February, 1838, President Van Buren and his cabinet were entertained by a private demonstration of a curious new invention called the telegraph. The inventor, Samuel F. B. Morse, was an artist by profession who had only gradually come to realize that he was more interested in electricity than in the study of old masters. Subsequently Morse offered his invention to the Government for $100,000, but on the recommendation of the Postmaster General, obviously a hardheaded business man—not the kind of man to be bowled over by a mere novelty—the offer was refused. The Postmaster doubted whether the revenue to be derived from the new toy could be made to equal the enormous outlay. Ten years later Morse made a formal application for a patent, which was granted on October 24, 1848, but it was still another ten years before the first cable was laid between the Old World and the New.

The reports of the overthrow of the French Government, therefore, took nearly a month to reach America. The *New York Evening Post* published the news of the abdication of Louis Philippe on March 18, twenty-three days after the event. But if the news travelled slowly there was a burst of enthusiasm when it finally arrived. What could be more gratifying than the knowledge that at long last Europe was following in the footsteps of the United States! Public opinion in America was convinced that Europe, too, was now to enjoy the blessings of liberty and justice. Resolutions were offered in the Senate and in the House tendering the congratulations of Congress to the French people on their new republic. Jefferson Davis in the

Senate, and Lincoln in the House, voted in favor of the resolutions. The French were greatly impressed by what they considered the unprecedented action of Congress.

A monster meeting held in City Hall Park on April 3 to rejoice over the freedom of France was described by Bayard Taylor as "one of the most sublime meetings I ever beheld." Cheers were given for Pope Pius IX, Lamartine, for the Swiss and for Poland. "At seven o'clock the City Hall was illuminated on all sides except the north with 1500 sperm candles— one to each pane of glass—and produced a most magnificent appearance."[1]

American opinion was more interested in the revolutionary events in France than in the movements which were going on at the same time in Italy, Germany and Austria, but the Administration was eager to welcome revolutions in Europe, wherever they might occur. Andrew J. Donelson, the American Minister to Prussia, was ordered to proceed to Frankfort to watch the course of the Frankfort Assembly, and in August he was definitely appointed envoy extraordinary and minister plenipotentiary to the Federal Government of Germany. The fact that there was no federal government of Germany did not matter. There would be one by the time the order reached him, or at least the Administration hoped so.

The official attitude of the Government and the feeling of the people remained friendly to any revolutionary movement that resulted, or looked as if it might result, in the establishment of a republic. The only exception was Mazzini's Roman Republic, which was never recognized. It was obvious to Lewis Cass, hurriedly sent to Rome as diplomatic representative in December, 1848, that the Republic was not likely to last long, and recognition was accordingly withheld. In this case the traditional American sympathy for the underdog clashed with the equally traditional liking for success. With France and Austria determined to bring the Pope back to the Vatican and to reestablish his temporal authority, and with England committed to a policy of non-intervention, Mazzini's gallant venture was bound to fail. Horace Greeley and Bishop Hughes, the truculent Catholic bishop of New York, argued the issue in the pages of the New York *Tribune*, while the State Department, which had grown cautious after its hasty recognition of the French

[1] *New York Evening Post*, April 4, 1848.

Republic, watched and waited. Only two years before, in 1846, James Buchanan had spoken of the Pope as the instrument chosen by Providence to effect the political regeneration of his country.[2] The ways of Europe were difficult to understand, and the State Department was not willing to antagonize Catholic opinion in the United States by backing a forlorn cause in Europe.

Meanwhile, the conservative element in the country, temporarily silenced by the unexpected collapse of the Louis Philippe government, was recovering its voice. Daniel Webster noted that the men who had seized the reins of government in France were poets and editors. Few if any of them had any knowledge of affairs, and none of them had been elected by the people. In a frantic effort to retain popularity they had undertaken to guarantee employment and prosperity. Mr. Webster thought nothing of such foolishness. A government of poets, indeed! No wonder France was in difficulties. Henry Clay was slightly, but only slightly, more sympathetic. In expressing his congratulations he pointed out that the United States was not committed to the sanction of any excesses that might be perpetrated in the name of the republic. John C. Calhoun was the most pessimistic of the three. A government that had started its career by suppressing slavery in its colonies, on the ground that slavery was an affront to human dignity, was not likely to win his approval. Obviously France was not prepared for a republic. Frenchmen were making the same mistake as the abolitionists in confusing the liberty that existed in some mythical state of nature with the liberty painfully evolved by society. The Savannah *Republican* echoed the same thought:

> The greatest danger that now seems to face the young republic is the desire of its directors to do too much. Not content with what they have achieved of national freedom they seem disposed to rush into socialism, and that still more cruel absurdity of immediately emancipating the slaves in all the colonies of France. We sincerely hope that the sober second thought of their statesmen may induce them not to mar their great triumph, and the respect of foreign nations, by the adoption of measures at once so

[2] Howard R. Marraro, *American Opinion on the Unification of Italy* (New York, 1932), p. 7.

visionary and so fatal in their consequences to the well-being of the Republic.[3]

For the most part the men of letters applauded the revolution. Lowell wrote odes to France and Lamartine. Whittier was naturally enthusiastic for anti-slavery reasons. His *Songs of Labor and Reform* include many references to the events of 1848, and incidentally illustrate the dilemma that always confronts the Quaker reformer. As a Quaker, he was convinced that war was invariably an evil, and as a reformer he knew that there were certain evils, such as slavery, that could only be overcome by force. His poem "The Peace Convention at Brussels" is a good example of the infinite optimism of his generation. Emerson was sceptical, but then Emerson was in Paris during the spring of '48 and was therefore better informed than any of his contemporaries at home of the difficulties the Provisional Government had to face. "At the end of the year," he wrote in his journal, "we shall take account." [4] It was a question in his mind whether the revolution was worth the trees that had been cut down to make the barricades. Another sceptic was that determined individualist Henry Thoreau, who thought that "the sudden revolutions of these times have acquired a very exaggerated importance." Thoreau was never impressed by mass movements. The one man who might have been expected to acclaim the sudden surge of democracy in Europe, Walt Whitman, makes no mention of it at all. In 1848 the obscure editor of the Brooklyn *Eagle* had not yet found himself. If he gave any thought to Europe he probably comforted himself with the reflection that across the Atlantic feudalism was fighting its last battle while America was setting an example that the rest of the world was bound to follow. It was only as he grew older that Whitman began to take an interest in the revolutions of '48. The lines to "Europe, the 72nd and 73rd Years of These States" were published in 1855, and "To a Foil'd European Revolutionaire," in 1856. The reaction of 1849–50 seems to have moved him more than the upsurge of 1848.

There is no doubt but that President Polk's farewell mes-

---

[3] Quoted by E. N. Curtis, "American Opinion of French Historical Revolutions," *Am. Hist. Rev.*, XXIX, 258.

[4] Emerson, *Journals*, 11 vols. (Boston, 1912), VII, 452.

sage in 1848 voiced the sentiments of the great majority of his countrymen: "Peace, plenty and contentment reign throughout our borders, and our beloved country presents a sublime moral spectacle to the world. . . . While the enlightened nations of Europe are convulsed and distracted by civil war or intestine strife, we settle all our political controversies by the peaceful exercise of the rights of freemen at the ballot-box."

In the thirties and forties America was still so intoxicated with its own runaway growth that it could not afford more than a passing glance at Europe. The initial excitement soon died down. The traditional enthusiasm for republican institutions interfered with any objective estimate of the struggles of democracy in other lands. It was enough to know that the older nations were sitting at our feet. President Polk had every reason to be satisfied with his administration; he was the only President who had entered office with a definite policy of expansion, and he had carried out his policy with remarkable success. Over a million square miles had been added to the national territory. The Mexican War may not have been popular in certain sections in New England, but it was popular with the nation as a whole. There was no denying that it was our "manifest destiny"—the phrase was coined in 1845—to overspread the continent. At one time or another growing nations invariably succumb to the plea of manifest destiny. It may be an opium war in China, a fascist empire in Africa, or the march of a land-hungry people across America. The argument is always the same—inevitability, that "it had to be that way." So it was that Oregon, California, New Mexico and Arizona became a part of the national domain, and the Mississippi River, so lately the frontier, suddenly found itself in the center of the United States.

If the President had listened to his Secretary of State, James Buchanan, later President Buchanan, we should probably have gobbled up Mexico too, but Polk, realizing that territorial expansion must go hand in hand with the extension of slavery, decided that for the time being a million square miles was enough. The anti-slavery men already regarded the Mexican War as a conspiracy to "get bigger pens to cram with slaves." It would be better to forgo manifest destiny for a while in order not to emphasize the demands of what the southern planters called their "peculiar institution." Slavery was extended down to the Rio Grande, but Oregon was organized as a territorial government without slavery in 1848, while California was admitted to the Union as a free state in 1850. Webster might assert that we wanted no accession of new states, no extension of territory, but President Polk knew the American people better. In nations, as in individuals, growth can only be deflected. It can never be arrested or even entirely controlled.

More than anything else, changes in transportation—the steamboat and the railroad—had contributed to the gangling growth of America. In 1850 the Republic boasted nearly 9000 miles of track. Work on the Baltimore & Ohio Railroad, the first to be built in America for the general transportation of passengers and freight, was begun in 1828. Boston and Albany were connected by railroad in 1842, Boston and New York in 1849. When Dickens travelled from Boston to New York in 1842, he went by train to Springfield, and from there by steamboat down the Connecticut River to Hartford, "thus saving a land-journey of only twenty-five miles, but on such roads at this time of year that it takes nearly twelve hours to accomplish." From Hartford he went on by train to New Haven, and then on again by boat to New York.[5]

Transportation was still to a large extent based on water. Steamboats were plying on the Mississippi long before railroads or even turnpikes had stretched out that far. In 1844 the famous steamboat *J. M. White* did the twelve-hundred-mile run between New Orleans and St. Louis in under four days. There was no comparable record for railroads, for nowhere in the country was there yet a continuous stretch of track for anything like the same distance. It was the golden age of steamboat travel. Mark Twain has immortalized the Mississippi, but the cleancut Hudson River liners were equally regarded as among the finest products of American material civilization.[6] Not until the generation after the Civil War did the railroads catch up with the steamboats, and trade seek an outlet by rail to the Atlantic seaboard instead of flowing south to New Orleans along the Mississippi. In 1848 cotton was king. Nearly three quarters of a million bales were being handled annually through New Orleans.

Charleston and New Orleans reminded travellers of Paris.

[5] John Forster, *The Life of Charles Dickens*, 2 vols. (London, 1874), I, 220.
[6] C. R. Fish, *The Rise of the Common Man* (New York, 1927), p. 74.

Cincinnati was a thriving city of 50,000 inhabitants. "I have not often seen a place," says Dickens in his *American Notes*, "that commends itself so favourably and pleasantly to a stranger at the first glance." Dickens was charmed by its clean houses of red and white, its well-paved roads, and "footways of bright tile." Dickens visited Cincinnati in 1842. Anyone visiting there fifty years earlier would have found nothing but a few scattered log huts. Boston was another city that delighted the traveller with its spick and span wooden houses and its general air of politeness and good humor, but these places were exceptions. The average American city was not impressive. In 1845 Chicago was a muddy frontier station, not nearly as important as Nauvoo, the Mormon settlement on the other side of the state. Washington was a big sprawling village with an unfinished Capitol. Cows and pigs, not to mention chickens and geese, roamed the streets at will. Carl Schurz, fresh from Germany after the revolution and eager to like everything in the United States, thought it a slouchy and unenterprising city. To the sightseer New York was almost as much of a disappointment as Washington. No remarkable public or private buildings, no picture galleries, no museums except Barnum's museum of curiosities on the corner of Broadway and Ann Street, opposite St. Paul's Church, which was pointed out to strangers as a sight really worth seeing.

Judged by Old World standards the American scene was not on the whole an inviting one. Nature had been generous enough, but wherever man had interfered with nature he had usually spoiled it. And yet, though Americans were carelessly skimming off the surface treasures of the land, slashing the forests and building untidy cities, they were also bringing to bear upon the problems of everyday life the most extraordinary ingenuity the world had ever seen.[7] It was during the forties

[7] American "handiness," or, more particularly, the handiness of the Connecticut Yankee, finds apt expression in a poem by the Rev. John Pierpont written for the Litchfield County celebration in 1851:

Thus by his genius and his jack-knife driven,
Ere long he'll solve you any problem given;
Make any gimcrack, musical or mute—
A plough, or coach, or organ or a flute;
Make you a locomotive or a clock,
Cut a canal or build a floating dock,
Or lead forth Beauty from the marble block;
Make anything in short for sea or shore,
From a child's rattle to a seventy-four.

that Cyrus McCormick began manufacturing reapers in Chicago, thus pointing the way to farming on a big scale. In 1846 Richard Hoe perfected the rotary printing press, and Elias Howe patented the sewing machine which was to make possible that peculiarly American product, the mail-order dress. In 1847, as a result of the Mexican War, Samuel Colt was given a government order for a thousand revolving pistols. Following the lead of Eli Whitney, Colt developed the manufacture of interchangeable parts, and thus begot the assembly line of the twentieth century. In this same decade telegraphy became one of the accepted facts of life, Dr. Morton administered ether at the Massachusetts General Hospital, and Matthew Maury initiated a system of recording observation of winds and currents that was to prove of untold benefit to navigation and to win him recognition in all parts of the civilized world.

Yankee ingenuity became proverbial, but it was not the only distinguishing American characteristic. The American people were spiritually, as well as mentally and physically, restless. Freedom and all that it connoted was fermenting in men's minds. In the election of 1848 a new party presented itself at the polls—the Free Soil Party, advocating free soil, free speech, free labor and free men. In 1848, after years of discussion, the New York Legislature passed a Married Women's Property Law that gave to women certain limited rights in the control of their own property. Women's rights were very much in the air. Feminists like Margaret Fuller and Susan B. Anthony were beginning to make themselves heard. Lucretia Mott organized the Women's Rights Convention in 1848, which among other things called upon "the women of this country to secure to themselves their sacred right to the elective franchise."

It was a quiet-spoken but militant schoolmistress, Dorothea

Make it, said I? Ay, when he undertakes it,
He'll make the thing, and the machine that makes it;
And, when the thing is made—whether it be
To move on earth, in air, or on the sea,
Whether on water, o'er the waves to glide,
Or upon land, to roll, revolve or slide,
Whether to whirl or jar, to strike or ring,
Whether it be a piston or a spring,
Wheel, pulley, tube sonorous, wood or brass,—
The thing designed shall surely come to pass;
For, when his hand's upon it, you may know
That there's "go" in it, and he'll make it go.

Litchfield Co. Centennial Celebration (Hartford, 1851).

Dix, who forced upon every state in the Union a recognition of its responsibility to the insane. After pestering the Massachusetts state legislature to do something for the insane persons confined within the Commonwealth in "cages, closets, cellars, stalls . . . chained, naked, beaten with rods and lashed into obedience," which finally shamed them into action, she went on to petition Congress to provide for national hospitals. Introduced in 1848, her bill was finally passed in 1854, only to receive the veto of President Pierce on the grounds that it was unwise for the national government to assume the support of the nation's paupers.

The year 1848 was the heyday of reform. Every kind of injustice, not merely Negro slavery, was to be eradicated. Many of the reformers reached across the ocean. It was in 1848 that Elihu Burritt, the learned blacksmith of New Britain, stirred by the revolutions in Europe, organized the Brussels Congress of Friends of Peace, which was followed by a still more impressive congress held in Paris in 1849. Victor Hugo took the chair, and among the 2000 delegates who attended were such men as Charles Sumner from Massachusetts, and England's great advocate of arbitration, Richard Cobden. A series of resolutions were passed, asserting the necessity of a simultaneous reduction of armaments and the arbitration of all international disputes. Every step in the practical application of American democracy was eagerly watched by liberals across the seas.

Society could and must be perfected. It was merely a question of pulling the right lever. Political conventions, mass meetings, lectures, debates, pamphlets, torchlight processions, prayer meetings—by one method or another the goal could always be reached. In Maine temperance crusaders were gathering their forces for the first major victory of prohibition. This, too, was advocated on the score of freedom. It was only the sinner who regarded prohibition as an unjustifiable assault upon the liberty of the individual. Actually the cardinal aim of prohibition was to relieve the individual, to secure a real freedom from the domination of drink. If Harriet Martineau thought that the people of New England "did good by mania," that, too, was an American characteristic.

One of the curious paradoxes of the period was the coupling of intense individualism and extreme gregariousness. For the American, individualism meant freedom from government restriction. It did not mean then, or at any time since, independence of other individuals. In 1848 we were already a nation of joiners.[8] Just as in the Middle Ages men entered monasteries, sometimes to practise their chosen craft and sometimes to stake a claim on paradise by good works in this world, so in America men joined societies, communities and religious sects for economic as well as religious reasons. Logging was one of the main industries of the Oneida community; the Shakers were competent farmers, and many of the Latter-Day Saints became notoriously shrewd business men. All through 1846 and 1847 the Saints were creeping westward over the Iowa prairies. Wherever they made a protracted halt log houses were put up, wells were dug, land was ploughed, and seed was planted for the benefit of those still to come. The Mormons had made enemies in Illinois, and the hostility had culminated in the murder of their prophet, Joseph Smith. Nauvoo, one year so prosperous, was deserted the next. It fell to Brigham Young to lead his followers, 16,000 of them, on the long march to the promised land in the valley of the Great Salt Lake. By the end of 1848 five thousand had arrived. They knew—better even than Longfellow—the meaning of "the bivouac of life."

Late that summer there spread through the country east of the Mississippi a strange tale from beyond the mountains. Daniel Webster had said that California was not worth a dollar, but even before the words were spoken John Wilson Brown had found yellow grains of gold at Sutter's Mill on the American River. In a few weeks the news spread along the Pacific coast and then, gradually, very gradually, it found its way east. Indifferent or frankly sceptical at first, as soon as the news was confirmed a great restless horde started trekking across the plains, struggling through the jungles of Panama or sailing around the Horn, bound for California on the quest of the golden gravel that made men mad. By the end of 1849 some 80,000 people had found their way to the gold diggings, 30,000 by sea and 50,000 overland. These westbound emigrants, farmers, workmen, mechanics, even clergymen, moved as in a trance. To them the difficulties of the pilgrimage were mere fantasies. Nothing was real but the El Dorado that lay at the end of their wandering. On February 25, 1849, William H. Seward wrote to his wife from New York:

[8] A. M. Schlesinger, *Paths to the Present*, New York, 1949, p. 23.

Thus far on my way to Washington, I find myself floating on a strongly-increasing tide of people, who hinder,
annoy, and embarrass each other. The world seems almost
divided into two classes, both of which are moving in the
same direction: those who are going to California in
search of gold, and those going to Washington in quest of
office. How many adventurers are preparing themselves
for disappointment, revenge and misanthropy.[9]

Such was the America that greeted Europe's refugees in 1849
—a great sprawling giant of a country where everything was
changing overnight, a country where there was room for everybody and where nobody need be poor.

2

During the years of revolution, 1848 and 1849, over half
a million immigrants arrived from Europe. The numbers had
been stepping up since 1845, the first year in which the figures
had topped 100,000. These newcomers were not political refugees but Irishmen driven from their country by hunger, and
Germans, Englishmen and Scots drawn to America by the hope
of improving their position in the world. For the Germans it
was largely a question of acquiring land free from any encum-
brances. In England it was not so much the farmer who wanted
to emigrate as the artisan. Ever since 1823, when the American
Chamber of Commerce opened an office in Liverpool, the
United States had been enticing skilled workmen to emigrate.
During the first decade of Victoria's reign exports from Great
Britain in manufactured articles declined, and many an artisan
short of work heard from an older relative, now prospering in
the States, of land where there was a growing market for whatever he could do. For the British workman the States were the
place for the urban pioneer, the man with a trade.[1] But the
emigrants from England and Scotland were a mere drop in the
bucket compared to the Germans, and still more to the Irish.
In a country where over half the population lived on potatoes
the failure of the potato crop was a catastrophe to which emigration or death seemed to be the only answers. Disraeli was

[9] Cited in C. R. Fish, *op. cit.*, p. 310.
[1] *Early Victorian England*, 2 vols. (London, 1934), II, 364.

hardly exaggerating when he said that "the mysterious but universal sickness of a single root changed the history of the world." The blight appeared in America in 1844; it reached Europe the following year, attacking Holland and Belgium, Hungary, Germany, and Ireland, where its worst effects were felt. The British Government carried out extensive food distribution, but the famine took a terrific toll of Irish life. Over 500,000 died, many of them on board ship on their way to America. If Ireland had been alone in her misery other countries might have come to the rescue, but the failure of the grain harvests in France and Germany in 1846 and 1847 unfortunately coincided with the potato disease.

The famine was a turning point in Irish history, marking the beginning of mass emigration. The time and circumstances of this emigration were never forgotten. The large numbers of emigrants prevented any effective competition to provide good conditions. The ships were crowded and filthy, and they carried no doctors. What food was given was uncooked, and to get near the fires it was necessary to bribe the sailors. The Chief Secretary for Ireland informed the House of Commons that of a hundred thousand Irishmen who fled to Canada in one year 6100 perished on the voyage, 4100 on their arrival, 5200 in the hospitals, and 1900 in the towns to which they repaired. "This was the fate," says Sir Charles Duffy, "which was befalling our race at home and abroad as the year '47 closed. There were not many of us who would not have given his life cheerfully to arrest this ruin, if only he could see a possible way." [2] The people fled before the famine, carrying with them not only disease and death but the seeds of an anti-English tradition, based on absentee landlords and a foreign established religion, which was cherished and handed on from one generation to another.

The Irish potato famine, coinciding as it did with the revolutionary movements of '48, helped to swell the unprecedented flood of immigrants that swept over America in the late forties and early fifties. The Irish element provided what the new life in America was demanding and did not yet possess—a laboring class willing to accept any kind of work that was offered. Unlike the Germans or the Scots and the English, the great majority of Irish immigrants brought with them no capi-

[2] Sir Charles Gavan Duffy, *Four Years of Irish History, 1845–49* (London, 1883), pp. 527–32.

tal and no skills. They were peasants in the Old World, and in the New they became, for the first generation at least, hewers of wood and drawers of water. The Irishman was employed in the building of canals and railroads, in excavating ditches for gas and water mains. His willingness to live in squalor frightened those who were already beginning to talk about the American way of life, but it was only the Irish who were willing to do the pick and shovel work required by America's new material civilization. Why was it, we may ask, that the Irishman whose principal grievance at home was that he could not own land should not have wanted to occupy the almost free lands in the West? Some of them of course did, but far more preferred to remain on the crowded eastern seaboard. The Irishman was not a frontiersman by instinct. If he loved land he loved people too, and the great emptiness of the frontier where there was no companionship and no church of his faith did not attract him.

The coming of the Irish marks the beginning of the native American's dislike of immigrants. Provided the immigrant adopts American ways he is readily accepted, but those who do not comply with American habits and standards of living meet with no mercy. The native workman sure of employment at good wages has never been prepared to face the competition of immigrant labor. Nor was he always tolerant of a religion rooted in Europe that seemed to him alien to republican institutions. So strong was the anti-Catholic prejudice that a new political party, the Know Nothings, was founded in the early fifties with the object of depriving the Irish of their civil rights, and if possible making it a penal offense to profess the Catholic faith openly. The Know Nothings appealed, just as the Ku Klux Klan was to do seventy-five years later, to all the familiar prejudices of jealousy and bigotry. Only native-born Protestants were allowed to join. Members when questioned by outsiders answered, "I know nothing." In the state elections of 1854 they almost carried New York, and did carry Massachusetts, but the triumph, signalized by an elaborate investigation of Catholic schools, was short-lived. The party disappeared after the elections of 1856, when the Southern members obtained control and passed pro-slavery resolutions.

The chief result of Know Nothing agitation was to intensify nationalistic feeling among the foreign stocks, particularly the Irish. As their numbers increased they were shrewd enough to realize that if they consolidated their hitherto scattered forces they might swing closely contested elections to the party of their choice. As between the Democrats and the Whigs they chose the Democrats as being less rigidly American and therefore more hospitable to the foreigner. This was the period when Tammany Hall won the hearts of the immigrants by offering all kinds of relief and facilitating their naturalization. When the Republican Party was founded, astute politicians like Seward tried to woo the Irish vote by fulminating against England, but the bid for popularity was too obvious. While the Irish would cheer anybody who gave a passing twist to the British lion's tail, they could never be weaned from the party that had first befriended them.

The Know Nothing movement was not directed only at the Irish. The Germans who were streaming across the Atlantic in almost as great numbers were subject to the same criticism of clannishness and failure to conform to American habits. Out of the 30,000 Protestant Germans living in Philadelphia in 1849 only 3000 went to church regularly. The taverns were full enough, but the churches were empty. In Cincinnati, also full of Germans, Sunday seemed to be a day for concerts and play-going. Americans did not smile upon such practices. Pessimists in Germany warned prospective emigrants of the unbelievable arrogance of the native-born American. The German intent on emigrating to America must be prepared to rid himself as soon as possible of all the earmarks of his descent, and by translating himself into a complete Yankee put an end to the insults from which he suffers.[3] Another German author speaks of the deeply ingrained American hatred for everything German.[4]

And yet America was a lodestone the Germans could not resist. They came not single spies but in battalions—34,000 in 1845, 58,000 in 1846, 74,000 in 1847. When it looked as if Germany might be a place worth living in after all, in '48 and '49, the numbers dwindled, but after the failure of the Frankfort Parliament to make a nation, emigration soared again, reaching the record figure, in 1854, of 215,000. In some villages the population left in a body. Learning that it was impossible

---

[3] Karl Büchele, *Land und Volk der Vereinigten Staaten von Nord Amerika,* Stuttgart, 1855, cited by Edith Abbott, *Historical Aspects of the Immigrant Problem,* p. 145.

[4] "der tief eingewurzelte Hass der Anglo-Amerikaner gegen alles Deutschtum."

to get passages from Bremen or Hamburg, emigrants flocked down the Rhine to Dutch and Belgian ports. Treitschke wrote that Germany was without resource in the face of this concerted movement.[5] In Baden and Württemberg the authorities positively recommended emigration to avert the danger of overpopulation. The yearning to emigrate, stimulated by the transportation companies and by glowing letters from those already settled in America, spread like a fever. Our own generation is familiar enough with the problem of a Europe unable to feed its people or to offer any hope of a good life to those unable to emigrate. Conditions in Germany were not as desperate a hundred years ago, but the lure of America was, if anything, even stronger than it is today.

America was indeed the promised land, a land where the taxes did not amount to anything, where the public official had no advantage not shared by the farmer, the merchant, or the teamster, a wonderfully fertile land where the cost of living was less than in Europe and where the prices paid for labor were higher. There were certain disadvantages, of course. A press that pandered to national prejudices, an educational system that was defective as well as expensive, and a galling contempt for strangers—this was the price one paid for republican institutions.

Actually it was not so much the republican institutions that attracted immigrants as the desire for immediate well-being. Europe in 1846 and 1847 was restless and hungry. It was also in financial difficulties. The potato famine and the unprecedented failure of the harvests necessitated enormous imports from long distances—south Russia and America. These had to be paid for, and the payment drained away gold. Meanwhile the inexorable increase of population was making the German peasant more than ever land-hungry. Americans might choose to believe that republican government was the bait that drew immigrants to their shores, but free land was a more powerful attraction than any institution made by man. Not only free land, but along with it freedom from laws and customs that curbed individual enterprise. "What I like about this country," wrote one immigrant, "is that the farmer can dismiss his hired hand any day he wants to, and the hired hand can leave when the impulse strikes him. As a result, each is more careful with respect to the other than in countries where

[5] Treitschke, *op. cit.*, VII, 274.

the terms and conditions of service are drawn up in a legal contract." [6]

In other words, what men sought in America was the freedom to come and go, to sell and bargain, to work and to enjoy the fruits of their labor, or, as Whitman put it, to "lean and loaf at their ease observing a spear of summer grass." It was this, rather than any theory of government, that brought men to America. The forty-eighters would have agreed with Thomas Paine that government even at its best was a necessary evil. They had had enough of government at home. The peculiar utopian charm of America, the characteristic that distinguished it more than anything else from Europe, was that in America the government lêft men alone.

The German states were not prepared to leave men alone even in emigration. Those who gave any thought to the question, and the newspapers of the period prove that there were a great many who did,[7] could not help regretting that German emigrants, whether they went to Canada or to the United States, to Australia or to Algiers, were as a rule forever lost to the fatherland. German emigration was compared to the annual sending out of an army of more than 100,000 fully equipped, which, as soon as it steps over the frontier, disappears forever. Could not something be done to protect emigrants and retain them for the old national stock? The suggestion was made that Germans should form massed settlements in the new homelands for the preservation of the German language and civilization.

The idea of establishing German states within the United States, which might or might not become members of the Union, had haunted German imaginations at least as early as 1841. In that year the Teutonia Order was founded in Texas "for the preservation of German national individuality, the furtherance of German immigration and the facilitation of correspondence between Texas and Germany." The attractions of Texas were obvious. Here was an enormous tract of country, easily accessible from Europe, which might quite conceivably become an extension of Germany in the New World. Germans were already settled there in great numbers. One of the most

---

[6] Cited in Marcus L. Hansen, *The Immigrant in American History,* Cambridge, Mass., 1942, p. 81.

[7] Cf. the bibliography in M. L. Hansen, *The Atlantic Migration,* Cambridge, Mass., 1945.

popular books of the frontier, *Nathan the Squatter; or the First American in Texas,* was written by a German.[8] Earlier in the century Texas had belonged first to Spain and then to Mexico. In 1837 Andrew Jackson recognized it as an independent state—the Lone Star Republic. This infant republic was the pioneer in the land-grant boom business, willing to make generous concessions to any foreigner making application. All a promoter had to do was to promise to settle a certain number of families on the land, pay for the survey and record the deeds.

The greatest of the Texas colonizers was Stephen A. Austin, son of a roving Connecticut Yankee who established the first permanent American settlement at San Felipe de Austin on the Brazos River. Austin was the ideal colonizer, honest and resourceful, but there were many others, Americans, French, and German, who possessed neither of his qualities. The Teutonia Order soon petered out, but it was followed in 1842 by a more ambitious undertaking. In that year a group of German princes and noblemen, including Prince Leiningen, a half-brother of Queen Victoria, and Count Solms-Braunfels, a student friend of Prince Albert, founded a society called the *Adelsverein* for the protection of German immigration in Texas. The society was the outgrowth of a typically German philanthropic imperialism—philanthropic in that the leaders hoped to alleviate social conditions in Germany, and imperialistic in that they envisaged a feudal German state overseas. Texas was to be peopled by Germans and they were to remain German. Treitschke dismissed it as one of those well-meant undertakings inaugurated with the superficiality of distinguished persons knowing nothing of their business.

The *Adelsverein* launched its experiment on a wave of optimism.[9] Each settler was to receive a tract of land far more extensive than anything he could hope for at home—160 acres for singlemen and 320 for the father of a family. Even if the property were divided, the grant would still take care of several generations. Everything was in favor of the settler. The soil was unbelievably fertile, animals cost nothing to raise, good

---

[8] Charles Sealsfield, *Nathan der Squatter oder der erste Amerikaner in Texas* (Zürich, 1837). Sealsfield's real name was Carl Postl.

[9] The official publication of the *Verein—Ein Handbuch für deutsche Auswanderer* (Bremen, 1846)—makes it perfectly clear that the colony was to be an extension of Germany overseas.

markets were always available. The Bremen shippers, who had agreed to transport the colonists, waxed enthusiastic, and a regular campaign of publicity was begun. The association promised to provide good ships for the passage, wholesome fare on board ship, agents to receive the immigrants on landing, and vehicles to transport them free of expense to their place of destination. Prince Charles of Solms-Braunfels had gone ahead to make all the necessary arrangements. Possibly he was not the ideal leader for a colonizing enterprise, but the account he wrote of his stewardship is good reading. Prince Charles was the typical noble of a small German state, a survival from the Middle Ages, full of courage and eager to face the hazards of the New World, but curiously unconscious of the fact that his rank would not carry as much weight in Texas as it did in Solms-Braunfels.[10]

The first shipload of immigrants arrived at Galveston in November, 1844. No sooner had they landed than the disappointments began. Apparently the rights purchased in 1842 had lapsed in 1843, and the President of the Republic refused to renew them. Prince Solms managed to buy the rights of two other promoters. The new land was described as a second paradise. In reality it lay in the heart of a wilderness, hundreds of miles beyond the remotest settlement. This wretched mistake was to prove the ruin of the whole enterprise. Unaware of the situation that awaited them, more than 2000 families joined the association, sailed from Germany, and were landed on the flat coast of the Gulf of Mexico without finding any of the wonderful facilities promised them in the prospectus. In the meantime Prince Solms had gone home. He had borne himself, he tells us in his report, "as a German and a man." It was not his fault if the dreams of a German state in Texas had vanished with the incorporation of Texas in the United States, nor was it his fault that the war with Mexico had stripped the country of provisions, supplies and transport. He had at least succeeded in laying out the town of New Braunfels on the Guadalupe River to which about 2500 immigrants eventually found their way. Of the remainder, some returned to Germany, five hundred enlisted in the Army for the Mexican War, and another five hundred died.

[10] Carl, Prince of Solms-Braunfels, *Texas, 1844–45*, translated from the German (Houston, 1936).

The story of these immigrants dragging their way through the wilderness to New Braunfels, beset by fever and starvation, was later turned to account by the German radicals of 1848, who were fond of alluding to the sturdy peasants who had fallen victims to princely stupidity on the fever-stricken shores of Texas.[11] The survivors learned to fend for themselves, but they melted into the American scene instead of remaining outposts of Germany. When Frederick Law Olmsted visited New Braunfels in 1855 he was struck by its air of contented prosperity. Olmsted was not only the father of American landscape architecture, but also a shrewd observer of social conditions. He noted that these indefatigable Germans had already founded an Agricultural Society, a Mechanics Institute, a Society for Political Debates, a Harmonic Society, and, what must have pleased him more than anything else, a Horticultural Club which had expended $1200 in one year on trees and plants.[12] With the Revolution of 1848 a new and more radical element was introduced into the German population in Texas. Olmsted deplored "the free thinking and devotion to reason, carried in their turn to the verge of bigotry." At the same time the German churches in Texas, Lutheran and Catholic, were both prospering. The *Verein* had promised that churches would be established under its auspices, and when New Braunfels was founded a pastor was imported from Illinois to minister to the settlers' needs.

While the *Adelsverein* had collapsed and gone into bankruptcy, the pioneers who lived through the first terrible year had become prosperous American citizens. By 1849 there were said to be thirty thousand Germans in Texas, half of whom had come directly from Germany and the other half from other states in the Union. Not all of those who came from Germany belonged to the *Adelsverein*. Henri Castro, a former soldier in the Napoleonic armies, founded a French settlement which contained many Germans, and there were a certain number of Germans who found their way into Texas before the great exodus of the forties. Today the population of western Texas is largely German by extraction. The annexation removed all possibility of those special privileges to foreigners which an independent Texas might have offered. Eager for

[11] Treitschke, *op. cit.*, VII, 274.
[12] F. L. Olmsted, *A Journey through Texas*, New York, 1857, p. 179.

immigrants though it was, the United States never wanted to see a German commonwealth, or indeed any other commonwealth, established within its borders.

The history of attempts to form foreign colonies within the borders of the United States is almost monotonous in its record of failure. It was not only the United States that resisted it. The immigrants themselves soon tired of the restrictions imposed upon them by the colonizing society at home. While they were determined to keep up their choral societies, their gymnastic societies, their German language and their German customs the uneasy stirrings of liberty were not to be denied. Sometimes that liberty might assume forms of which they did not approve. Viktor Bracht, one of the original settlers at New Braunfels who later became an American citizen, was shocked by the behavior of American girls:

> Until he has become acquainted with the peculiar conditions under which women of American are born and reared, their demeanor may sometimes appear a little informal to a stranger. For example, many have been shocked to hear girls thirteen to seventeen years of age converse by the hour, without reserve or embarrassment, with young men about marriage and matrimonial relations. This subject appears, on the whole, to be their favorite topic. . . .[13]

Bracht also complained, like so many travellers, of "the disgusting American habit of chewing tobacco and the incessant expectoration that goes with it," but he was not overwhelmed by these shortcomings. Almost in the same breath he maintained that it was to "social independence" as well as to political freedom that America owed "the rapid development of her present power and greatness." Every nationality becomes mongrelized when it cuts loose from the parent stock, but the mongrel enriched the pattern of life in the New World by weaving into it the heritage of the Old.

3

The Germans were not the only people in Europe to feel the call of Texas. While the aristocratic society for the protec-

---

[13] Viktor Bracht, *Texas in 1848*, translated from the German by Charles Frank Schmidt (San Antonio, Texas, 1931).

tion of German immigrants was struggling to maintain its authority at New Braunfels, a group of Frenchmen had embarked for Texas with very different ideas. Instead of wanting to establish a French colony they dreamed of founding a utopia. These Frenchmen, Icarians as they called themselves, were the advance guard of a community founded by Etienne Cabet, one of those rarely sincere communists of the nineteenth century who conceived of the perfect state, and then came to the New World to put it into effect.

In the 1840's, when the evils of the Industrial Revolution were beginning to make themselves felt, the discontented, the restless, and the idealistic elements in society, of which there were an ever-increasing number, sought refuge from the drabness of life around them in glorious visions of the ideal community. A new world had come into existence, a world of coal, steam and machinery, which in turn had created problems not to be solved by the old familiar methods of political revolution. Wherever industry had made most strides, men were beginning to think less of the tyranny of princes and more of the tyranny of capital. The idea gathered strength that the good things of this world, particularly land, should be more evenly distributed. In France the materialism of the Bourgeois Monarchy and the callous indifference of Guizot to everything except politics gave great incentive to utopian thinking. The ideas of Saint-Simon, Fourier, and Proudhon were germinating in men's minds. Saint-Simon, the first of the technocrats, had predicted that before the end of the century the business man would have replaced the aristocrat, just as the scientist was replacing the priest. Fourier had dreamed of regenerating society by making men live in phalansteries, independent and self-sufficient communities which combined the functions of an up-to-date modern factory and an enormous summer hotel. Proudhon, the most individualistic of revolutionaries, "the Robinson Crusoe of socialists," a man without a party, a class or a creed, was already protesting against the evils of mass civilization.

Etienne Cabet, the founder of the Icarian communities, may not have been as profound a thinker as these men, but he was more determined to put his ideas into effect. He was the author of a utopian romance, *Le Voyage en Icarie*, which became so popular that it ultimately drove him to Texas, to Illinois, to St. Louis, there to demonstrate the truth of his theories. Cabet was born in Dijon in 1788, the son of a well-to-do cooper. The boy grew up in the midst of shavings and barrels, destined to ply his father's trade, but a delicate constitution which unfitted him for work in the shop induced his father to allow him to study law. He must have shown extraordinary aptitude, for at the age of fifteen we hear of his being appointed professor of the class in which he was a student. At that time the manpower of France was being drained into the Napoleonic armies, so perhaps the honor was not as exceptional as it sounds. As soon as the Bourbons came back he settled in Paris, where he affiliated himself with the secret revolutionary societies with which the capital was honeycombed. Although a republican at heart he acquiesced in the supposedly constitutional monarchy of Louis Philippe, who appointed him Attorney General for Corsica. Cabet, as a reluctantly converted republican, was the kind of adherent kings prefer to keep at a distance. Back in Paris before the end of 1831, he was elected to the Chamber of Deputies where his persistent criticism of the Government finally caused his arrest on a charge of *lèse-majesté*. He was given the choice of two years of prison or five years of exile. His friends persuaded him that he would be safer in exile than in prison—political prisoners were sometimes never heard of again—and accordingly he crossed the Channel and settled in London. In the great desert of London, where so many other republicans were eating the bitter bread of exile, he would at least be able to say and write what he thought.

The chief result of the years in exile was the utopian *Voyage en Icarie*. As a novel it is neither better nor worse than dozens of other novels about the world as it might be. In all such tales, from More's *Utopia* to Aldous Huxley's *Brave New World,* the author adopts the framework of a novel upon which to hang a scathing criticism of the present social structure. Cabet, who had no mean opinion of himself, warns the reader in the preface not to pay too much attention to the unfortunate love affairs of his hero, Lord William Carisdall. Under the guise of a novel he maintains that the *Voyage en Icarie* is really a treatise on morality, philosophy, social and political economy. Furthermore, it is the fruit of endless labor and immense researches. The story, such as it is, relates the experiences of Lord William Carisdall, a young English nobleman who has learned by chance of the existence of a remote country known as Icaria. His curiosity is piqued, and he decides to

visit this strange country which is apparently so free from the
evils that afflict his own land. *Voyage en Icarie* purports to
be a journal in which he records his observations and his
experiences.

Throughout all these utopian romances there runs a fearful symmetry. Icaria is peopled by such uniformly flawless
characters that the reader yearns for an occasional scoundrel.
Liberty implies the right to go wrong, and in Icaria no one
ever goes wrong. Why should they? Everything is run by the
state with unbelievable efficiency. Everybody's hours of work,
hours of sleep, recreation, even diet, is decided for him, and
no one seems to object. Among the measures advocated by
Cabet in order to achieve this state of perfection are the abolition of the rights of inheritance, state regulation of wages,
national workshops—very different, presumably, from those
instituted by the Second Republic—eugenics and, above all, a
comprehensive system of state education. Children were to be
taken from their homes and entrusted to the state at the age
of five. There is nothing new in these proposals; they are the
common stock of all utopias. Only occasionally, as in his ad-
vocacy of mass production, which he applied particularly to
the making of hats, did Cabet stumble on a really original idea.[1]

Voyage en Icarie was one of those books that catch the tide
of public taste. It told the public just what they wanted to
know—that material well-being for all its citizens was within
the reach of every government, and that it could be realized
without violence. Published in 1840, it ran through five editions
before the end of 1848. The attack on the existing social order
and the glowing account of the happy brotherhood of man
made it immensely popular with the working classes. This new
Koran was read not only in Paris but throughout France. Encouraged by its reception, Cabet, back in France after his
years of exile, plunged into Icarian propaganda. At first he
believed that time and the ardor of his disciples would inevitably bring about the acceptance of his ideas, but the endless controversy arising out of the book, the enthusiastic friends
and taunting enemies, finally constrained him into vindicating
the truth of his theories by a practical demonstration. No one
should say that he was a mere theorist, that he lacked the
courage of his convictions. In a new country, on virgin soil, he
would build a model of his communist ideal.

[1] E. Cabet, *Voyage en Icarie*, 2nd ed., p. 137.

In May, 1847, he published in his weekly paper, the *Populaire*, under the heading *Allons en Icarie!* a long manifesto written in his usual grandiloquent manner. There was no longer any hope of realizing his dream in France. Emigration was the only solution. "We can count on ten or twenty thousand Icarians . . . our plans will be carefully worked out in advance, and out there, in Icaria, with our Icarian principles, what marvels we shall achieve." [2] But where was Icaria? Asia, Africa or America? That was still a secret. Exhaustive inquiries were under way to secure the selection of the perfect site. Finally, in November, after six months of waiting, the secret was revealed. They were going to Texas. The "exhaustive inquiries" consisted of a conversation with Robert Owen, who, on the strength of his experience at New Harmony, was regarded as an authority on America. Owen had at one time received a promise from the Mexican Government of an immense tract of country, but at the last moment the Mexican Government had stalled, and Owen had never taken up the concession. That land now belonged to Texas, which was busily seeking to populate its vast unoccupied territory. Large grants were being made by the new state to private concerns on condition of their securing settlers. The representative of one of these concerns, the Peters Company of Cincinnati, happened to be in London just at the moment when Cabet was casting around for the ideal location for his Icarians. Owen put the two men in touch with each other, and on January 3, 1848, they signed a contract whereby the Icarians were to receive 320 acres per family, provided the land was occupied before July 1, 1848. The exact limits of the colony were not specified. The agreement merely stated that Cabet would start colonizing at the ninety-seventh degree longitude and that he would continue to the western limit of the Peters concession, which extended along the Red River and the Trinity River.

Cabet naturally knew nothing about Texas, but his sanguine temperament convinced him that everything was all right. Even before the contract was signed he announced in the columns of the *Populaire* that "after examining all available countries" he had chosen a beautiful, healthy, and fertile tract of land in Texas for the proposed colony. The land bordered the Red River, which was easily navigable along its

---

[2] Cited by J. Prudhommeaux, *Icarie et son Fondateur, Etienne Cabet*, Paris, 1907, p. 206.

whole extent. Steam, by diminishing distance, had made the whole matter of emigration a simple affair. Cabet certainly knew how to generate optimism. The office of the *Populaire* was swamped with applications and gifts from would-be members. Every day brought its quota of shotguns, fishing tackle, pictures, books, eiderdowns, clocks, even silver dishes. A tailor contributed his best pair of scissors, and a furniture dealer sent in fifty folding chairs. Cabet would have preferred more of the ten thousand franc subscriptions he had been promised, but no doubt the scissors and the folding chairs would be useful too.

The advance guard, sixty-nine pioneers, the cream of the party, according to one of the survivors, sailed from Havre on February 3, 1848. What a moment it was! Sixty-nine soldiers of humanity bound for a new paradise across the seas, not like other emigrants to make their fortunes but to fashion a new society and prove to the world that the communism propounded by Étienne Cabet was something more than an idle dream. Cabet himself did not go with them. His duties kept him in Paris organizing the departure of the main body.

On March 27, after fifty-three days at sea—distance had not been so terribly diminished after all—this advance guard arrived at New Orleans. The town was in holiday mood, not at all to greet them but to celebrate the overthrow of Louis Philippe and the establishment of the Republic, news of which had been brought by a faster ship. These shattering events had happened while they were at sea. Some of them could not help regretting that they had left France. It might be that under a really popular government their Icarian ideals would be realized at home, but it was too late to think of going back now. That way madness lay. After all their splendid speeches and high promises it was impossible to go back to the lovable, humdrum world they had left behind. But there were more serious problems ahead of them than the pangs of nostalgia. A closer inspection of the map revealed that Icaria was not on the Red River, nor was there any national route connecting it with Shreveport, as Cabet had led them to suppose. It appeared that, like so many others, he had been the victim of the smart business methods of American land agents, and that he had taken the statement of the Peters Company too literally. Instead of reaching their new home by boat from New Orleans they had to strike 250 miles inland from Shreveport across a trackless wilderness of swamps and forests. To get to Icaria at all was a formidable business requiring guides, ox carts and provisions for several weeks, all of which cost money, and money was precisely what they lacked. They were warned to hurry on account of the heat and the rains, but how could they hurry when they did not speak the language, and when everything they needed had to be bought at the lowest possible price? Fortunately they were a stout-hearted band not easily discouraged even by the swarms of mosquitoes, which compelled them to walk single file, each man waving a branch over the head of the one in front. The mosquitoes, the heat, the tangled wilderness and the unfordable rivers had not been mentioned in any prospectus, but they staggered on, eventually reaching Icaria on June 2.

Even then they could not afford to rest, for the extent of land they acquired depended on the number of log cabins they were able to put up before July 1. Working with desperate energy they managed to build thirty-two, which entitled them to some ten thousand acres. The million acres Cabet talked so glibly about presupposed the construction of three thousand cabins. The ten thousand acres secured by the advance guard would have satisfied the needs of the Icarians for some time to come, but there was another yet more fatal misunderstanding with the Peters Company, or with the State of Texas, which proved insurmountable. Texas had divided its unoccupied territory into square sections of 640 acres. Whenever a large tract of land was sold, as to the Peters Company, the state reserved alternate sections of land for itself. In other words, the black squares on this enormous checkerboard belonged to the state. The Peters Company in turn divided their white squares into halves, of which they retained one and leased the other to the Icarians. By insisting that the sections they sold should be occupied and built on, the Peters Company automatically raised the value of their own unimproved lands. Eventually these lots would be sold too, and the fact that they were surrounded by land that was occupied and worked would make them more valuable.

The Icarians probably never dreamed that their ten thousand acres were not contiguous. To establish a communistic colony with a central administration and a co-operative system of agriculture on many scattered and disjointed parcels of land must have struck them as a hopeless undertaking.

Nevertheless they built their log cabins and started ploughing as if they were going to live there forever. They knew nothing about western farming. The ploughs broke and they exhausted themselves and their oxen without achieving any results. Such was the condition of affairs when they were joined by the second wave of emigrant Icarians. Only nineteen arrived of the 1500 Cabet had promised, and of these ten were already stricken with fever. The newcomers had been buoyed up on their journey by the belief that they would be welcomed by a prosperous community, not entirely settled perhaps but at least tolerably comfortable, instead of which they were greeted by a gaunt, despondent group of settlers who, hating to admit failure, knew they must either perish or return to civilization.

Under these circumstances there was nothing to do but to start the weary trek back to New Orleans, where they arrived shivering with fever and broken in spirit. There they were joined by new deteachments including finally Cabet himself. He too had had his difficulties. With the establishment of the Republic and the promulgation of the famous guarantee of employment, French workmen were thinking more about the new order that was blossoming before their eyes and less about the advantages of emigration. The great army of prospective Icarians had dwindled to less than five hundred and even these as soon as they arrived at New Orleans began to quarrel among themselves. There were ugly stories afloat about misappropriation of funds. Two hundred broke away from the community to go back home, others to strike out for themselves in New Orleans. The American virus was already at work. In a country where wages were so high and land was so cheap, co-operative action hardly seemed necessary.

Cabet was not discouraged; two hundred and eighty faithful adherents still remained with him. If the first settlement had proved a failure it had given them a much needed experience, and in a less relentless climate and in less remote surroundings his irrepressible optimism told him they were bound to succeed. Early in 1849 they settled in Nauvoo, Illinois, a town that had been built up by the Mormons and subsequently abandoned when Brigham Young started the great migration across the plains to Utah. With its large stretches of cultivated land and well-built houses Nauvoo must have seemed to the Icarians the paradise of their dreams. For the next six or seven years fortune smiled on them. They began cautiously this time, renting only 450 acres but along with it cattle, tools, forage, a flour mill, sawmill, and distillery. To be sure, they did not realize the dream city Cabet had conjured up in his romance, but they did make a living and they did establish a miniature communist state. Each man worked for the whole community, never just for himself. Families were allowed separate houses, but men, women and children all took their meals together, and the manual labor was scrupulously divided. Nor did they forget that, in the communist state particularly, man does not live by bread alone. Cabet's report on the varied activities of the colony, a little rose-colored, like the prospectus of a progressive school, speaks of the writing and printing of the two newspapers, one in French and the other in German, the laboratory experiments, the plays, concerts and debates that filled the waking hours of the happy Icarians.[3]

But beneath the surface trouble was brewing. At first Cabet had exercised his almost unlimited powers very discreetly, but as time went on the Icarians began to chafe under his arbitrary rule, and when he returned to Paris to answer a charge of embezzlement brought by some of the disgruntled colonists who had gone back home, the supposedly happy family developed an ugly attack of individualism. Communal work ceased, and each man carved out for himself a piece of private property. Cabet hurried back to Nauvoo only to find that the majority of Icarians, having once tasted liberty, refused to obey his orders any longer. In 1856 the association split into two parties, the smaller of which, comprising one hundred and eighty faithful members, headed by Cabet, abandoned Nauvoo and started off again to found a new colony. They settled at Cheltenham, on an estate of twenty-eight acres lying six miles west of St. Louis, but to their great sorrow without Cabet. On the eighth day of November, 1856, he had succumbed in St. Louis to a sudden attack of apoplexy. Active and optimistic to the end, he was struck down while making extensive plans for the new settlement.

The subsequent history of the Icarian settlements falls outside the range of this book. Altogether there were seven settlements—the original Texas colony, Nauvoo, Cheltenham, three settlements in Iowa, and one in California. The first

[3] Etienne Cabet, *Colonie Icarienne aux Etats Unis d'Amérique* (Paris, 1856), pp. 15–17.

split in the ranks affected every new colony. Whenever there was a disagreement, and the administration of a model community offers exceptionally favorable opportunities for disagreement, one group always felt that they could expel another, or failing that, that they could secede. So the process of fission went on until finally, in 1898, at Corning, Iowa, the few surviving Icarians agreed to disband. This time there was no squabble about money, no dispute about administration; it was simply that the flame of communism had burnt itself out. Icaria had survived for fifty years, during which time it had evoked a very real spirit of devotion, but it finally succumbed to that passion for independence which lays hold of every immigrant as soon as he sets foot in America. Utopias flourish in America as nowhere else in the world. It is the one country which inspires every kind of social experiment and at the same time breeds a distrust of the regimentation that those experiments necessitate.

Another Frenchmen driven by the revolution of '48 to found a colony in Texas was Victor Prosper Considérant, a graduate of the École Polytechnique in Paris, who had fallen under the spell of Fourier and resigned from the Army to spread the Fourier gospel. Considérant was the real founder of the French co-operative movement. Fourier was a theorist, Considérant a practical man who pruned the Fourierist doctrine of its absurdities and directed it into the path of modern socialism. Elected to the Assembly in 1848, he helped to draw up the constitution which was later torn up by Louis Napoleon. In the following year he protested against the Roman expedition, and along with Ledru-Rollin and many others was driven into hiding. From Brussels, where he took refuge, he conceived the idea of following Cabet's example, but his first visit to America was more in the nature of a sight-seeing trip than anything else. He was welcomed by Albert Brisbane, one of those earnest puzzled men—Whitman described him as looking "as if he were attempting to think out some problems a little too hard for him" [4]—who felt that human misery could be alleviated only by a fundamental reconstruction of society. Like many others before him Brisbane was impressed with the necessity of dignifying and somehow embellishing the manual labor of mankind. The doctrines of Fourier, whom he had met in Paris,

[4] Cited from Arthur M. Schlesinger, Jr., *The Age of Jackson*, Boston, 1946, p. 363.

seemed to offer the only hopeful solution. Associationism, as Brisbane christened Fourierism for American consumption, provided an escape from the evils of a rapidly expanding society in which everybody was seeking his own advancement rather than the welfare of his fellows. By living in rural surroundings with a few carefully selected spirits, and engaging in a little light manual labor, associationists would enjoy a more wholesome and more simple existence than was possible amid the pressure of competitive institutions. Such was the theory underlying Brook Farm as well as the more strictly Fourierist phalanxes founded by Brisbane.

After a few months in New York and a visit to the North American phalanx in New Jersey, Brisbane and Considérant set forth to explore the possibilities of founding another socialist community in Texas. Considérant was wildly enthusiastic. The climate, the fertility, the availability and cheapness of the land, everything convinced him that they were certain of success. Foreign travellers in America usually manage to see only what they want, and Considérant found just what he wanted in Texas: "The prodigality of nature provides nine-tenths of what man in Europe has to create by the sweat of his brow. . . . One can find in Texas a combination of favorable conditions which enable the settler to achieve the most wonderful results with a minimum of effort." [5] Considérant's account of Texas is one long paean of praise. No Fourth of July orator could have been more eloquent on the glorious opportunities offered by the unfolding civilization in America. He knew all about Cabet's difficulties, but he felt he was more practical than Cabet and that he would profit by his mistakes. Few of the original Icarians knew anything about agriculture, hence their sufferings.

Upon his return to Belgium after the tour in Texas, Considérant announced his intention of founding a colony, and appealed for funds and for settlers, stipulating particularly farmers. The response was a tribute to his personality, but the people who besieged his office, far from being farmers, were artisans, scholars and musicians, cultured men weary of the Napoleonic regime, and determined to emigrate to a land where they could experiment with their ideas of social reform. Considérant's colony ran into the same difficulties with which we are already familiar. Founded at La Réunion on a lime-

[5] Victor Considérant, *Au Texas*, 2nd edition (Paris, 1855), pp. 63, 80.

stone bluff near Dallas, the site was more suitable for vines than for farming. Perhaps it reminded the colonists of the chalk country in Champagne. The co-operative principle was put into effect at once, but the colony did not prosper. Apparently the scholars, musicians and artists did not take kindly to pioneer life. After two years of drought the four hundred colonists gave up the attempt at farming, co-operative or otherwise, and went their separate ways. Within three years the settlement melted away, and today only two houses are left to mark Considérant's colonizing venture. There were no outbreaks, no town meetings, no official winding up of affairs; the people just quit. Considérant himself was among the first to leave. He settled in San Antonio and remained there through the Civil War, writing letters to Renan about his *Vie de Jésus*, and to Bazaine about the folly of Napoleon's Mexican venture. The Confederate Army, remembering that he had been an officer in the engineers, offered him a commission but he refused it. After 1871 he went back to France, when the doors were opened to political offenders, and lived on in Paris until 1893, the last of the voluble, talented, impractical figures of '48.

Though the story of La Réunion is a chronicle of failure, many of the individual colonists stayed on in Texas and contributed much to the cultural and scientific life of the communities where they settled. One of them, who had been conductor of the orchestra at the Odéon, brought the first piano into Dallas County. Another of the subsequently well-known emigrants was Julien Reverchon, the naturalist, whose name survives in the red-thorn *crataegus reverchonii*, and in a campanula named after him by Asa Gray. Reverchon's career is symbolic. All through the forties and fifties Texas, first as an independent republic and later as a state, was a vortex into which flowed currents from every part of Europe. Often the current spent itself without result, as men became exhausted in the struggle to maintain themselves in a new and strange environment. It was only toward the end of his life that Reverchon was able to spare time from farming to devote himself to botany.[6]

The failure of the Icarian communities, and of Considérant's colony at La Réunion, must be attributed primarily

[6] For further details on the life of Reverchon see Samuel Wood Grier, "Naturalists of the Frontier" in the *Southwest Review*, XIV, 321–30.

to the character of the members. At a period of great stress in Europe it was not only the idealists who came to America but, in even greater numbers, the adventurers and the crotchety who jump at any new movement that seems to offer a short cut to success. The earlier religious communities, the Rappites and the Zoarites, composed of German peasants skilled in the tillage of the soil, were more successful than the later groups of communists and socialists. At the same time it may be argued that America owes more to the cranks, the adventurers, and the discontented who came over for social or economic reasons, than to the more seemingly reliable religious communities. The German colonizers at New Braunfels, the Icarians, and the co-operative farmers at La Réunion, as soon as they struck out for themselves were very apt to become leaders of the communities where they settled, whereas the mute inglorious among the sects of Rappites, Zoarites and Amanites, whatever height of spiritual perfection they reached, contributed little to the growth of the country.

One of the most interesting of the "failures" was William Weitling, founder of a short-lived communist colony in Iowa and precursor of American socialism. We had left him in Brussels being worsted in an argument with Karl Marx, whose fierce logic had paralyzed him. Since then he had emigrated to America on the invitation of a group of German-American Free Soilers to take charge of their weekly magazine, the *Volkstribun*. Upon his arrival he found that the *Volkstribun* had suspended publication, but he immediately plunged into other activities. He organized the League for Liberation among German-American workers, which generated a wave of enthusiasm for revolution. Rumors of the great events in Europe sent him hurrying back to Germany, but the ray of light caused by the uprising in Baden was quickly extinguished, and by the end of 1849 Weitling had returned to America to devote himself for the rest of his life to the welfare of the German-American workingman.

Early in 1850, he founded a monthly magazine, *Die Republik der Arbeiter* (The Republic of the Workingmen), in which he preached co-operative handicraft enterprises and exchange banks as the method by which the workers could free themselves from state and capitalist domination. Eventually Weitling became a German-American version of Horace Greeley, not an original thinker but a warm-hearted champion of the under dog, an "emotional socialist," as Karl Marx put it, bubbling over with a love of all humanity. At the same time he had real gifts as an agitator and reformer. German immigrants had already formed a number of labor unions, but there was no connecting link between them, and no unity of purpose, until Weitling organized a "Central Committee of United Trades." This was a delegated body of labor organizations, representing some 2500 members. A meeting was held in New York, and before long similar bodies were organized in other cities in the Union to combat the anti-foreign propaganda of the Know Nothing Party. So successful were Weitling's efforts that the movement enlisted the sympathy and co-operation of workingmen of other nationalities, including native Americans. The next step was a nation-wide convention of workingmen, which was held in Philadelphia in October, 1850. Weitling seized the opportunity to put forward his pet scheme of an Exchange Bank. Morris Hillquit describes it as "an institution where every producer of a useful commodity could deposit his product and receive in exchange a paper certificate of an equivalent value, with which in turn he could purchase any article contained in the bank store at cost." Through the operation of the Exchange Bank Weitling hoped gradually to undermine the whole system of capitalism.

At the Philadelphia convention Weitling reached the high-water mark of his career, but though the convention adopted his proposals without modification his Exchange Bank never materialized. While the workingmen voted for him, not enough money was subscribed even for an experiment on a modest scale. Meanwhile his Communia settlement in Iowa had gone the way of all such ventures owing to quarrels among the colonists. Try as they would, no communistic utopias in America could compete with the absurdly high wages of the forties—two dollars a day and roast beef. Some of those whose faith in communism survived the disaster at Communia threw in their lot with the Icarians at Nauvoo. Weitling's prestige never recovered from the setback at Communia. His failure seems to have provoked his natural self-assertiveness and to have irritated his colleagues in the Workingmen's League. After a sharp quarrel he withdrew from public life, a bitterly disappointed man, and passed the remaining years of his life as a clerk in the Bureau of Immigration. His Workingmen's League will be remembered as the first convention of German workingmen on American soil, but it never attained the significance that its bright beginnings had promised.

Weitling himself, if not a great man, is certainly a figure to be reckoned with in the history of American socialism. He was the first man in America to organize foreign labor and to dream of an independent political party. His followers espoused many reforms, such as homestead legislation, public libraries, adult education, and "a program of public works that sounds strikingly modern." [7] Against a dark background of economic distress he might have played a more important role on the political stage, but in the forties and fifties America was still too full of enticing perspectives for any widespread acceptance of the gray future offered by communism. In an army where every soldier really believes he has a *bâton* in his knapsack there is no use talking about the abolition of rank.

A very different type from Weitling but equally important in the history of the labor movement in America was Joseph Weydemeyer, a former Prussian artillery officer who had been converted to Marxism by the articles in the *Rheinische Zeitung*. Weydemeyer emigrated in 1851 with the deliberate intention of laying the foundations of scientific socialism in the United States. On the outbreak of the Civil War he joined the Union Army and served with distinction in the armies of Frémont and Sigel, but throughout it all he remained a convinced Marxist. When he had first thought of emigrating, Engels had warned him of "the necessarily increasing tempo of the country's prosperity which makes people consider bourgeois conditions as a *beau idéal*." [8] Weydemeyer heeded the warning. While he participated actively in American life, he never became Americanized in the way that Engels had feared. He was an abler man than Weitling, who disliked him on account of his admiration for Marx and Engels, and persistently belittled his efforts as a builder of labor organizations, but in the long run he was no more successful. The country was not ripe for socialism. The fluidity of life, the ease with which successive waves of immigrants settled on the land, made socialism of any kind, Weitling's utopianism or the orthodox Marxism of Weydemeyer, seem curiously irrelevant. In the booming circus of American life in the nineteenth century socialism could never be anything but a sideshow.

[7] Carl Wittke, *We Who Built America*, New York, 1939, p. 240.
[8] Cited by Karl Obermann, *Joseph Weydemeyer* (New York, 1927), p. 28.

In addition to the hungry and the restless, the Marxists, and the utopian dreamers, there was still another group that fled from Europe during these years, attracted to America by the enticing prospect of political freedom. They did not want to eliminate competition or to isolate themselves from the surrounding world and its corrupting influences, but they did want rights that were denied them in Europe. They were the genuine forty-eighters, men like Carl Schurz and Franz Sigel, who could have had a rich life in Germany if they had not preferred the freer air of the United States. The descendants of every German who came over in '48 would have it that it was despotism that sent their ancestors to America, and a longing to enjoy the blessings of the American Constitution. Actually, the strictly political refugees who emigrated, as opposed to those who came here to make their fortune, numbered only a few thousand, but the influence of these few thousand refugees was out of all proportion to their numbers.

Carl Schurz, the son of a schoolmaster and grandson of a peasant farmer from the Cologne district, had fallen in love with America long before he ever left Germany. As a child he had watched peasants from a neighboring village load their wagons with all their worldly possessions and disappear over the horizon on their way to the New World. He had heard his father and his uncles talking of that immeasurable country on the other side of the ocean, "where the people were free, without kings, without counts, without military service, and, as it was believed in Liblar, without taxes." [9] One morning while he was still a student at the University of Bonn, a friend burst into his room with the news of the fall of Louis Philippe. The flames of revolution were soon licking the frontiers of every petty state in Germany. Universities were particularly inflammable, and within a month of the great events in Paris the professors as well as the students of Bonn had laid aside their books and were touring the countryside preaching democracy and German unity. No one enjoyed it with more gusto than young Carl Schurz. A ready speaker, full of infectious enthusiasm, he was in demand at every democratic rally. For a moment it looked as if democracy in Germany were winning a bloodless battle, but the political horizon soon began to darken. Nowhere was there any concerted action. Most of the liberals in Germany did not demand anything beyond the

[9] *The Reminiscences of Carl Schurz*, I, 29.

establishment of national unity and a constitutional monarchy on a broadly democratic basis, but the republican extremists were not willing to halt at any halfway house. In south Germany they insisted on forcing the issue before it was ripe.

While the Germans in America were sending messages of congratulation to the Frankfort Parliament, fighting had broken out in the little duchy of Baden. The Grand Duke fled, and a provisional government composed of popular leaders assumed the place of his ministry. For a moment King Frederick William IV of Prussia looked on uneasily. Could he afford to see a popular state so near to his own borders? His generals decided the question for him by marching the Prussian Army into Baden and crushing the republic before it had had time to establish itself. One of the rebels who decided not to surrender was Carl Schurz. He escaped from the town of Rastatt through a sewer at the time of its surrender, and made his way into Switzerland. The next year he returned to Germany at the risk of his life to rescue Gottfried Kinkel, one of the prominent democrats of the day, from prison. Not only did he get him out of prison, he even managed to spirit him out of the country. One day the famous pair appeared in London where they were greeted as heroes. Kossuth congratulated him on his exploits, and Mazzini took him into his confidence, hoping no doubt to enlist his interest in the conspiracy of the moment. It would have been easy enough for Schurz to lose himself in revolutionary intrigues, but America was beckoning to him.

Other men could stay in Europe hatching plots and dreaming of revolutions, Schurz wanted to face the challenge of life in a new country. In the summer of 1852, he and his young wife, the daughter of another German exile, landed in New York, determined to make the United States their permanent home. They were the ideal immigrants—young, adaptable, not too sensitive, well-balanced, and as honest with other people as they were with themselves. Like all immigrants, they had their black moments, but Schurz knew that if he could once identify himself with the busy life surging around him the black moments would soon be forgotten. Politics was in his blood. It was not long before he sensed the impending struggle over slavery and the dangerous alliance with slavery of the timid conservatism and the far-reaching material interests of the Northern states. He must know more about

America and the strange processes of democracy, more than he could glean from his conversation with Mr. Jefferson Davis, the Secretary of War, or Mr. Stephen Douglas, Senator from Illinois. How could men profess to love liberty, and at the same time practice slavery? He must soak himself in the political history of the Republic, but above all he must go west where the new states were growing up and where he could see for himself new political communities working themselves out of the raw.

Wherever he went—Illinois, Missouri, Wisconsin—friends and relatives seemed to spring up out of the ground to greet him. In Chicago, people were too busy to pay much attention to him, but in Milwaukee he found an atmosphere that was thoroughly congenial. Milwaukee had received rather more than its proportional share of the German immigration of 1848. It was already to a large extent a German city, one of the few in America where the homesick forty-eighter could have heard a Beethoven symphony rendered in acceptable style. Fredrika Bremer, the Swedish novelist who travelled through the west in 1849, noted that "the Germans in the Western States seem to band together in a clanlike manner, to live together, and amuse themselves as in their fatherland. Their music and dances, and other popular pleasures, distinguish them from the Anglo-American people, who, particularly in the West, have no other pleasure than 'business.' " [10] From Milwaukee Schurz found his way to another German colony in Watertown, Wisconsin, where one of his uncles had already settled. In this pleasant community, surrounded by Mecklenburgers and Pomeranians, hard-working and thrifty people, and a few Irish and native Americans from New England, he decided to make his home.

The only thing that grieved him about his German neighbors was that they were almost all Democrats. As a rule, foreign immigrants drifted naturally into the Democratic Party, which presented itself to them as the protector of the political rights of the foreign-born population, whereas the Whigs were suspected of nativist tendencies, hostile to the foreign born. Schurz set himself to wean his compatriots from their allegiance to the Democratic Party. Any party that approved the opening of the Territories to slavery under the guise of popular

[10] Fredrika Bremer, *Homes of the New World*, 2 vols. (New York, 1853), I, 616.

sovereignty was anathema to Carl Schurz. It was the forty-eighters, and particularly Carl Schurz, who swung the German vote in the west to the newly formed Republican Party. In 1856 they supported Frémont, and in 1860, in even greater numbers, they voted for Lincoln. The Illinois Central proved an unexpected ally. The immense tract of land it received from the federal government had been sold off rapidly to German immigrants, and it was the votes of these foreigners that helped Lincoln to carry Illinois in 1860.[11]

Astute western politicians—and no politician was more astute than Lincoln—did not forget the importance of the German vote. It was characteristic of Lincoln that he should have tried to master the complexities of German grammar, and that prior to his first nomination he bought a German-language newspaper.[12] At the meeting of German Americans held at the Deutsches Haus in Chicago in May, 1860, the assembled Germans put themselves squarely on record as adhering to the Republican principles of 1856, "in a sense most hostile to slavery." [13] The men at this convention made up a notable roster. Carl Schurz was the most distinguished member but there were many others of importance: Reinhard Solger of Massachusetts, who was as influential in bringing Germans in the east into the Republican fold as Carl Schurz had been in the west, George Schneider the editor of the Illinois *Staats Zeitung,* Joseph Weydemeyer, and Friedrich Hecker, formerly a member of the Baden Assembly and one of the first men to proclaim the German Republic.

These and many others at the Deutsches Haus convention were genuine forty-eighters, men who had emigrated from Germany or Austria for political rather than economic reasons. Hecker had sacrificed a promising career as a lawyer to lead a motley army of unemployed workmen against trained Prussian soldiers. He had announced that he would march through Germany, through Poland into Russia, bearing the torch of revolution wherever he went, but his poorly equipped force was easily routed, and he followed the usual route of political refugees to Switzerland and ultimately to America. After being

---

[11] "The election of Lincoln and, as it turned out, the fate of the Union was thus determined not by native Americans but by voters who knew least of American history and institutions." W. E. Dodd, *Am. Hist. Rev.,* XVI, 787.

[12] Carl Sandburg, *The Prairie Years,* 2 vols. (1926), I, 449. M. L. Hansen, *The Immigrant in American History,* p. 148.

[13] J. G. Randall, *Lincoln the President,* 2 vols. (1945), I, 163.

welcomed as a conquering hero by the Germans in New York and Philadelphia, he moved on out west and became a successful farmer, viticulturist and cattle raiser in Illinois. He never accepted public office, but he threw himself into the fight against slavery and stumped the country first of all for Frémont, and later for Lincoln. When the war came he enlisted in the Union Army, rose to be colonel of the 24th Illinois, and was severely wounded at Chancellorsville.

The forty-eighters were all Union men, as were most of the recent immigrants. Even the Germans in Texas, many of whom had emigrated from Germany just before the revolution, had to be coerced into accepting secession. The belief in an easy victory for the North prevented many of these Texas Germans from taking decisive action, though one of them is said to have offered Sam Houston 2000 "Dutchmen" to break up the Secession Convention.[14] Some of the forty-eighters who had served in the Baden revolution, among them Schurz, Franz Sigel and Schimmelpfennig, rose to be generals in the Union Army. For the German immigrants in general the war hastened the melting-pot process. It broke down the clannish tendency which was beginning to arouse bitterness on both sides. The *North American Review* complained that the New York *Staats Zeitung* had been started expressly for the purpose of re-Germanizing Americanized Germans, and went on to warn the immigrant that "he who has not the good sense to adapt himself to our social habits and our modes of thought is bound to fail." [15] This was hardly the way to win the affection of the homesick immigrant who looked back with longing to the comfortable beer gardens, the theatre, the music and the free commerce in ideas that were so terribly lacking in the raw society of the New World. The highest praise some of these newcomers could give to anything in America was to describe it as *gerade wie in Deutschland*. The compliment was not always appreciated.

But among the forty-eighters the disgruntled were the exception. Far more typical were those who came to America determined to make a success in spite of the difficulties. Many who had been professional men at home took up farming in America, and became known as Latin farmers because of their university education. Olmsted gives an unforgettable pic-

[14] G. G. Benjamin, *The Germans in Texas*, New York, 1910, p. 109.
[15] *N. A. Review*, LXXXII, 264.

ture of these Latin farmers in his *Journey Through Texas*: "You are welcomed by a figure in a blue flannel shirt and pendant beard, quoting Tacitus, having in one hand a long pipe, in the other a butcher's knife; Madonnas upon log walls; coffee in tin cups upon Dresden saucers; . . . a Beethoven's symphony . . . a book-case half filled with classics, half with sweet potatoes." [16] The German university man turned farmer became a figure of tradition in many other states besides Texas. Next to farming, journalism seems to have been the most popular profession. Between 1848 and 1852 the number of German newspapers in the United States jumped from 70 to 133.[17] Among the forty-eighters there was also a group of medical men who had been trained for their profession in European universities. They found medical education and medical practice in the United States in a deplorable state— "not a single eminent physiologist . . . and few biologists." [18]

There was hardly a field of activity in which these exiles did not distinguish themselves. Even those whose names are not known to the general public often contributed something significant to American culture. The colored postcard and the Christmas card owe their origin to Louis Prang, a refugee forty-eighter from Breslau. He was the first man in America to make cheap reproductions of famous works of art. The word *chromo,* which he invented, is now almost a term of reproach, but seventy-five years ago Prang's colored lithographs were enormously popular. Another refugee lithographer, Julius Bien, who had been trained in the art institute of Cassel, supplied Sherman with a field-map printing outfit for his march to the sea.

One of the most striking stories of a successful readjustment to a new way of life is the saga of the Wehle and Brandeis families. The twenty-six persons in this party sailed from Hamburg in 1849 with two grand pianos, all their cooking utensils, china and glass, featherbeds, dowry chests of the two engaged daughters, and "to civilize the wilderness" paintings and sketches they had made in Italy.[19] The whole troupe settled at Madison in the Ohio Valley, but a few years later the two

[16] F. L. Olmsted, *op. cit.,* p. 430.

[17] New York *Tribune,* March 5, 1852.

[18] Josephine Goldmark, *op. cit.,* p. 248. See also Carl Wittke, "The German Forty-Eighters in America," *Am. Hist.* Rev., LIII, p. 720.

[19] Josephine Goldmark, *op. cit.,* p. 211.

Brandeis brothers moved to Louisville, one to build up a large medical practice, the other to develop a wholesale grain and produce business. Adolph Brandeis, founder of the pioneer grain firm of Kentucky, was one of the immigrants who fell in love with his new-found country at first sight. That love was transmitted in full measure to his son Louis, later Justice Brandeis, who never forgot how much he owed to the tradition of 1848.

The only other racial group who, like the authentic German forty-eighters, emigrated for political reasons were the Hungarians. Compared to the Germans and Irish, who were pouring into every port on the Atlantic seaboard from Passamaquoddy to Galveston, the Hungarian invasion was small, homogeneous, and select. They were the only refugees from Europe who had inherited a knowledge of self-government from their ancestors. They had already fought for their freedom under Kossuth. That in itself guaranteed them a warm welcome in the United States.

In December, 1851, when he landed on Staten Island, Kossuth was already a popular hero in America. There was no exaggeration in Emerson's words of welcome at Concord: "You have got your story told in every palace and log-hut and prairie camp, throughout this continent." Of all the confused struggles for liberty in the years 1848–49 none had excited more sympathy in American than that of the Hungarians.

Wherever Kossuth spoke, and he spoke to enormous audiences in New York, Washington, throughout New England, in Pennsylvania, Ohio, and Kentucky, he was acclaimed as no other foreigner had been since Lafayette. In New York he was greeted with an enthusiasm that may well have deceived him. Governors Island fired a salute in his honor, and Hungarian flags broke out on every public building. The opening reception at Castle Garden was the signal for a series of dinners and deputations, balls, benefits and torchlight processions. This round-shouldered little man with a heavy beard and a wrinkled forehead, who pleaded his country's case so eloquently, swept New York off its feet. "He is here," said Horace Greeley, "to arouse us to a consciousness of our national position and the responsibilities it involves." Sitting in his office in the Department of State, Daniel Webster read of the excitement and found it all rather embarrassing. Provided Kossuth would be satisfied with expressions of sympathy, a few receptions, and an introduction to the White House, no harm would be done. "I am a good deal at loss what to do," wrote Webster to one of his cronies, "and what to say. I hope I may be able to steer clear out of trouble on both sides." [20] In accordance with his plans, Webster escorted Kossuth to meet President Fillmore, who received him "with great cordiality" and invited him to dinner at the White House.

Congress played up too by giving him an elaborate subscription dinner, at which Webster so far forgot himself as to offer as a toast, "Hungarian Independence." In the course of his impromptu remarks he went on to say, "We shall rejoice to see our American model upon the lower Danube and on the mountains of Hungary." Unfortunately the notes of these "impromptu" remarks were picked up under the table after the dinner and transmitted to Chevalier Hülsemann, the Austrian *chargé d'affaires*. The relations between Webster and Hülsemann were already strained owing to the fact that the State Department was known to have promised recognition to the Hungarians as soon as the revolution attained sufficient success to warrant it. Hülsemann protested to President Fillmore and ultimately withdrew from the country. In the meantime, Kossuth and his suite were being entertained at Congressional expense at Brown's Hotel, where they were said to have enjoyed themselves thoroughly, consuming vast quantities of food and wine, and wrecking a good deal of the furniture. [21] Gradually people began to weary of Kossuth and his Hungarians. "He has injured his dignity," said George Ticknor, "by making speeches for money, and he has injured his respectability by issuing 'Hungarian bonds,' as they were called, down to a dollar, to serve as tickets of admission." [22]

In the end, Kossuth was the victim of the enthusiasm he had aroused. In spite of his triumphal progress and his tremendous personal success he returned to Europe after six months in America a disappointed man. Like so many distinguished foreigners who are nearly killed by American hospitality, Kossuth did not understand the rules of the game.

[20] Daniel Webster, *Writings and Speeches*, 18 vols. (Boston, 1903), XVIII, 280.

[21] Ben Perley Poore, *Perley's Reminiscences of Sixty Years in the National Metropolis*, 2 vols., Philadelphia (1886), II, 405.

[22] Ticknor, *Life, Letters, and Journals of George Ticknor*, 2 vols., Boston (1876), II, 276.

Americans welcomed him, cheered him, and fêted him, but they did not want to become involved in his troubles. He was demanding something that could not be granted. The idea that American freedom and American interests were jeopardized by the reactionary triumph abroad, or that America had a moral obligation to aid the defeated revolutionists in Hungary, was never seriously considered. A New York Whig, Senator Seward, and a Louisiana Democrat, Senator Soulé, pointed to the favorable trade agreements that European republics would extend to their American sister, but most people were convinced that the United States could make its best contribution to the freedom of the Old World by keeping its "lamp burning brightly on this western shore as a light to all nations," as Henry Clay put it, rather than by hazarding its "utter extinction among the ruins of fallen and falling republics of Europe." [23]

While Kossuth wended his way back to Europe, there to consort with Mazzini or with Napoleon III—he would clutch at any ally who promised support for Hungarian independence—his fellow Hungarians stayed on in America. When the war came, twenty per cent of the Hungarian population, a ratio not approached by any other foreign nation, and to be accounted for only by the picked character of the Hungarian immigrants, joined the Union Army. Very few joined the Confederates, and among them only one officer, a certain Colonel Estran who had served under Radetzky in Italy. Even he appears to have been a rather lukewarm Confederate, as he resigned his commission in 1863 and dedicated the account he wrote of his experiences to General McClellan. [24]

In the Union Army the outstanding Hungarians were General Stahel, who won the Medal of Honor, General Asboth and Colonel Zagonyi, both of whom served on Frémont's staff. Zagonyi, who had been a captain of hussars in General Bem's Hungarian Army and had spent two years in an Austrian prison before escaping to America, was one of those picturesque characters whom Frémont delighted to gather around him. Schurz describes Frémont as being surrounded by a "bodyguard consisting mostly of Hungarians, brave soldiers who on

[23] Calvin Colton, *The Last Seven Years of Henry Clay* (New York, 1856), p. 224.
[24] *War Pictures from the South* (New York, 1863). The dedication to McClellan appears only in the German edition.

occasion did excellent service, but who also contributed much to the somewhat unusual 'style' which was kept up at Frémont's headquarters." [25]

The contribution of the immigrants of '48 to the winning of the war is impossible to calculate with any accuracy. Professional southerners have cultivated the idea that the South was defeated by hordes of European-born mercenaries. If we accept the figure of half a million foreign-born volunteers in the Union Army,[26] and a total Confederate Army of only 600,000 which, though it may be low, is the figure inscribed on southern monuments,[27] it is obvious that the foreign-born soldier must have played a substantial part in the winning of the war. Remove those 500,000 men from the Union Army, and the result might well have been different. How many of them were genuine forty-eighters is another problem. During the six years 1847–52 nearly two million immigrants poured into the United States, whereas during the six previous years 1840–46 the figures amounted to 611,000. Prior to 1842 there was no year when the figures topped 100,000. Thus it would seem fair to conclude that at least half the foreign-born soldiers in the Union Army must have been men who for one reason or another had emigrated from Europe during the years of revolution and reaction.[28]

One of the greatest causes of prosperity in a new country is the capital, living and dead, which it acquires from older civilizations. The events of Europe in 1848–49 provided America with a vast influx of living capital. Today no one denies the importance of the immigrant in driving the native stock further and further west. The physical results of immigration are easier to chart than the cultural, but if life in America is richer and more civilized in 1949 than it was a hundred years ago we must be grateful for the revolutions and counter-revolutions, the famines and the economic crises, that sent not only farmers and agricultural laborers but also musicians, doctors and skilled craftsmen of all kinds, streaming across the ocean in search of a freer and a more abundant life.

---

[25] Carl Schurz, *Reminiscences*, II, 344.

[26] M. L. Hansen, *The Immigrant in American History*, p. 142.

[27] S. E. Morrison, *Oxford History of the United States*, 2 vols., London, 1927, II, 168.

[28] The immigration figures for every year from 1820 to 1855 will be found in William J. Bromwell's *History of Immigration to the United States* (New York, 1856).

CHAPTER
VI

CONCLUSION

WHY DID the revolutions of 1848 fail? Why, as G. M. Trevelyan puts it, did history, having reached the turning point of 1848, fail to turn? The political inexperience of the revolutionary leaders, and the fact that they did not agree among themselves, accounts for much of the failure. Nowhere were the leaders united, and nowhere were the revolutionary movements co-ordinated. From the moment he established himself at the Hotel de Ville on the night of February 24, Lamartine must have known that the ill-assorted members of the Provisional Government would never learn to work together as a team. They were agreed on the abolition of the death penalty for political offenses, on the emancipation of slaves, on the benefits that must accrue to France from a republican government founded on universal suffrage, but beyond that they had little in common. While they expressed the greatest contempt for the government they had overthrown, they were in no way equipped to grapple with the economic problems that Guizot had ignored, and that they were now called upon to solve.

In Hungary, the Batthyány cabinet, comprising as it did men of such different temperaments as Széchényi and Kossuth, was just as incapable as the Provisional Government in Paris of presenting a united front and following a consistent policy. At one moment Hungarian troops were fighting side by side with Austrians to suppress Italian nationalist uprisings in Lombardy and Venetia, and at the next they were fighting at home against Austrians in defense of their own rights as an independent nation. In Italy the general apathy of the peasants and the divergent aims of King Charles Albert, Pius IX, and Mazzini precluded any effective action against the Austrians.

In Germany, the fundamental disagreements among those who would build the New Jerusalem were no less startling. The Frankfort Parliament that was to have made a great, united, freedom-loving Germany spent itself in an endless discussion of first principles. It was so intent on laying a firm legal foundation for its deliberations that by the time it was ready to act, it had forgotten that it had no army with which to enforce its decisions. By the late summer the economic crisis was over, the princes had recovered from the panic caused by the overthrow of the Louis Philippe government, supposedly the strongest government in Europe, and the Frankfort Parliament had degenerated into a debating society. The impotence of the wise men of Frankfort was an unfailing source of amusement to Marx and Engels. Their failure proved to the world, though from the communist point of view the proof was hardly necessary, that parliamentary government, so beloved by the bourgeoisie, was bankrupt. It could no longer deal with the increasingly complicated problems of the nineteenth century.

If the revolutionary leaders suffered from inexperience, and from the inability to decide just what it was that they wanted, the people they should have guided were no less bewildered. The working classes wanted a new world, but no one knew just what sort of new world except a handful of communists, and even the communists or socialists—the words were still interchangeable—were divided between the philosophic anarchists like Proudhon and Bakunin, the utopians like Cabet, and the faithful followers of Karl Marx. The middle classes, including the liberal aristocracy, had always been determined to put an end to revolution as soon as they had won certain limited political reforms. As the most recent eminent historian of 1848 has pointed out. "they wanted the revolution to enter like the ghost in Dickens's *Christmas Carol* with a flaming halo round its head and a big extinguisher under its arm."[1] The June days in Paris marked the moment for the extinguisher to be applied. The French fear of communism spread through Europe, infected the German bourgeoisie, and proved the most effective ally to the forces of counter-revolution.

While communism was making its way underground, the

[1] L. B. Namier, *1848: the Revolution of the Intellectuals*, London, 1944, p. 9.

optimists of 1848 who were dreaming of a better world to be were suddenly confronted with another equally serious threat to liberty in the growth of insurgent nationalism. It was in 1848 that nationalism, hitherto the hallmark of the liberal, began to assume some of the ominous characteristics that we associate with the Nazi state. The nineteenth century liberal sincerely believed that once the peoples of Europe were grouped together into strong, self-sufficient nations, a great victory for mankind would have been won. The evils of absolutism that were held to be inseparable from the agglomeration of small states into empires would automatically vanish as soon as Poland, Italy, Hungary and Germany appeared on the map as separate nations. Inspired by Mazzini, poets like the Brownings cast an aura of magic around the words "a free Italy."

The notion that nationalism and democracy were necessarily allied forces making for political righteousness was one of the myths of the nineteenth century. It survived down to our own times, but the dangers inherent in the doctrine were already discernible in 1848. The emotional appeal for a "sound patriotism" led all too easily to the election of a dictator in France and to the demand for *Lebensraum* in Germany. It was not the great landowners, the conservatives and the Junkers who first sounded the clarion call of German nationalism, but the democrats and the intellectuals. The real expansionists in the Frankfort Parliament were to be found on the benches of the Left.

It was Wilhelm Jordan, a democrat from Berlin, who, speaking at Frankfort on July 24, 1848, defended the breaking of the pledges given to the Poles and the consequent crushing of Silesian Poland. He concluded his speech with the cry: "Freedom for all, but the power of the Fatherland and its weal above all!" So began the long list of German claims to Danzig and Königsberg, to the source and mouth of the Rhine, to Alsace-Lorraine and, within our own times, to the rest of Poland, to Austria and to Czechoslovakia.

Kossuth was another eloquent apostle of nationalism who saw nothing inconsistent in expanding the limits of his own country to include unwilling peoples from outlying provinces. Marx supported him on the theory that any movement that broke up the Habsburg Monarchy was worth supporting. Marx was not interested, any more than Kossuth, in the rights of

Serbs, Croats and Czechs. Nor was he at all impressed by Bakunin's mystical faith in Pan-Slavism. The interests of the small Slavic nations were contrary to the interests of the proletariat and would therefore have to be suppressed.

The confusion between the claims of nationalism and democracy, the political inexperience of the revolutionary leaders, the apathy of the great mass of the peasant population in all countries, and the fears of the bourgeoisie that the revolution might go too far, these are some of the reasons why history, having reached the turning point of 1848, failed to turn. But though reactionary governments weathered the crisis, many of the ideals for which men had given their lives on the barricades achieved ultimately a twisted fulfilment. Italy and Germany both fought their way into the family of nations, though the unification of Italy under the House of Savoy seemed to Mazzini a sorry mockery of his dreams, and Bismarck's Germany bore little resemblance to the kindly freedom-loving Germany of the people's springtime in '48. France, guided by a new Caesar, set to work in accordance with the formula of Saint-Simon to improve the moral and material condition of the most numerous and poorest class. There was much that was shoddy about the Second Empire, but the working classes prospered under Napoleon III as they had never prospered before. In England, the programme of the Chartists was gradually carried into effect and, though it did not work the miracles the first Chartists had prophesied, once the workers were given a chance to improve their position within the capitalist system they gave up trying to overthrow the system itself. By the end of December, 1849, when people were reading *David Copperfield*, just available in book form, business was recovering from the shock of revolutions abroad and the railway panic at home. The potato disease had spent itself, factory laws had eased some of the worst pressures of the new industrialism, and the beginnings of an intelligent sanitary policy, of urban parks and free libraries, were making town life more tolerable. Even so, Matthew Arnold's vision of "the armies of the homeless and unfed" was not as easily dispelled as Victorian liberals liked to believe.

In 1848, communism was "a spectre haunting Europe." In 1948, the spectre is an all-too-solid reality, though here again communism has run a very different course from what was laid down in the *Communist Manifesto*. Marx never dreamed that the backward Slav races whom he so despised would be the first to receive his gospel, nor could he have foreseen that the principles he laid down so confidently would be freely adapted to suit the exigencies of Russian foreign policy. It would puzzle him too to see how much modern capitalism had raised the standard of living of the working class. And yet many of his predictions were fulfilled, such as the emergence of giant monopolies, the recurrence of economic crises of increasing intensity, and the gradual shift of emphasis from the individual to the class.

Engels was not far wrong when he maintained a quarter of a century later that the things men fought for in 1848 had mostly come to pass. As William Morris put it in *The Dream of John Ball*, "men fight and lose the battle, and the thing they fought for comes about in spite of their defeat, and when it comes turns out to be not what they meant, and other men have to fight for what they meant under another name."

What remains of the dreams and visions of a better world that seemed almost within man's reach in the spring of '48? It may at least be said that the revolutions crystallized men's ideas and projected the pattern of things to come. They proved that reforms in modern Europe, economic as well as political, can no longer be undertaken piecemeal. The planners of the future must learn to disregard national frontiers. Mazzini seized on this obvious truth long before it had been grasped by his more worldly wise contemporaries. *Italia farà da sè* was an anachronism even when it was uttered. Neither Italy nor any other country on the Continent would be able to put its house in order without consulting with its neighbors.

Economic planning, the charter of the United Nations, the desire to co-operate rather than to compete—these things were all foreshadowed by the revolutions of 1848. On September 20, a Popular International Peace Congress opened its sessions in Brussels at which resolutions were adopted favoring a general and simultaneous reduction of armaments. Other congresses to promote peace were held in Paris (1849), in Frankfort (1850) and in London (1851). These congresses, or conferences as we should now call them, were attended by delegates from the United States, England, Holland, Belgium, France and Germany. Russia was not represented. At the congress held in Paris in 1849 Victor Hugo was elected chairman, and Richard Cobden, always an advocate of disarmament, vice-chairman. The delegates were received by M. de Tocqueville at the Ministry of Foreign Affairs, and the fountains of Versailles were turned on in their honor. Obviously it was regarded as an important occasion. Victor Hugo's opening address was greeted by the 1600 delegates with tremendous applause.

> Do you know [said Victor Hugo] what you will put in the place of armed men, of infantry, cavalry and cannon? . . . You will put in the place of all these a little wooden box which you will call a balloting box, and from that box will proceed an assembly, an assembly which will act as a soul to all of you, a sovereign and popular council which will decide, will judge, will settle all disputes.[2]

On that hot August afternoon just a hundred years ago the 1600 delegates, packed together in the stuffy rooms of the Salle Ste. Cécile in the rue Chaussée d'Antin, listened with rapt attention as Victor Hugo unfolded before their eyes the vision of a peaceful world, from which war had been banished, that lay just ahead of them. Mankind is still waiting for that peculiar blend of nationalism and brotherly love that was to have emerged from Victor Hugo's little wooden box.

[2] The *Examiner* (London), August 25, 1849.

CHRONOLOGICAL TABLE

1847

MARCH 17:   First installment of *The History of the Girondins*, by Lamartine.

JUNE 26:   Teste and Cubières brought to trial.

JULY 18:   Lamartine's address at Mâcon.

SEPTEMBER 19: Guizot replaces Soult as President of the Council.

DECEMBER 27: Opening of parliamentary session; the King's speech on "hostile or blind passions."

1848

JANUARY 2:   Disturbances at Milan; the Tobacco Riots.

JANUARY 12:   Insurrection at Palermo, which spreads throughout the whole of Sicily.

FEBRUARY 10:   Ferdinand, King of the Two Sicilys, grants a constitution.

FEBRUARY 17:   Grand Duke of Tuscany grants a constitution.

FEBRUARY 21:   In Paris, the banquet of the XII*ième arrondissement* is prohibited.

FEBRUARY 22:   The Ministry is heckled in the Chamber of Deputies; street disturbances on the increase.

FEBRUARY 23:   Guizot resigns. Shooting in the boulevard des Capucines. During the night barricades appear all over Paris.

FEBRUARY 24:   Louis Philippe abdicates; the insurgents seize the Tuileries, the Hotel de Ville, invade the Chamber of Deputies and prevent the formation of a regency. A provisional government is formed and the people insist on the proclamation of a republic.

FEBRUARY 25:   Lamartine defends the tricolor. Proclamation of the right to work. The provinces accept the new regime.

FEBRUARY 26:   Abolition of the death penalty for political offenses. Creation of the National Workshops.

FEBRUARY 27:   First news of the Revolution reaches Germany; disturbances at Mannheim.

FEBRUARY 28:   Formation of the Government's Commission for the Workers at the Luxembourg, with Louis Blanc as President.
Publication in London of the *Communist Manifesto*.

MARCH 2:   Universal suffrage proclaimed.

MARCH 4:   Lamartine's manifesto proclaiming doctrine of non-intervention.
Announcement of abolition of slavery in the colonies.
Freedom of the press and freedom of assembly established.

333

MARCH 5:	Charles Albert, King of Sardinia, grants a constitution. Meeting of German liberals at Heidelberg.
MARCH 11–15:	Pope Pius IX grants a series of constitutional reforms.
MARCH 13:	Revolution in Vienna.
MARCH 14:	Metternich resigns. Emperor of Austria promises immediate reforms.
MARCH 15:	Acute financial crisis in France. Peaceful revolutions in Budapest and establishment of Program of Twelve Points.
MARCH 16:	Reactionary demonstration in Paris, the *Bonnets à Poil.*
MARCH 18:	Uprising against Austrian troops in Milan. Revolution in Berlin.
MARCH 19:	Abdication of King Ludwig of Bavaria.
MARCH 22:	Liberation of Milan and Venice.
MARCH 23:	Frederick William IV promises constitutional regime to the Prussian people.
MARCH 24:	Charles Albert appeals to the Italian people to fight the Austrians.
MARCH 25:	Croatian National Committee formed at Zagreb.
APRIL 3:	Republicans in Savoy make an ineffectual attack on Chambéry.
APRIL 10:	In London, fiasco of Chartist petition. Liberal Ministry in Berlin under Camphausen. Charles Albert defeats the Austrians at Goito.
APRIL 20:	*Fête de la Fraternité* in Paris.
APRIL 23:	Elections for Constitutional Assembly under universal suffrage in France.
APRIL 25:	Emperor of Austria grants a constitution, badly received by public opinion. Insurrection at Cracow, suppressed the next day.
APRIL 29:	Encyclical of Pius IX in which he disowns the Italian cause.
MAY 4:	Opening of the Constitutional Assembly in Paris.
MAY 10:	Assembly elects the Executive Commission (Arago, Marie, Garnier-Pagès, Lamartine, Ledru-Rollin).
MAY 11:	At Prague, formation of St. Wenceslas committee, which reasserts the historic rights of Bohemia.
MAY 13:	At Vienna, a central political committee assumes power.
MAY 15:	Demonstration in Paris in favor of Poland; eruption into the Assembly. Counter-revolution in Naples; liberals crushed. In Vienna the central committee stages an insurrection.
MAY 17:	Formation of a commission to prepare the constitution. The Emperor of Austria leaves Vienna and re-establishes the court at Innsbruck.
MAY 18:	The Frankfort Parliament meets in St. Paul's Church. General Cavaignac appointed Minister of War.
MAY 22:	Opening of Prussian Assembly.

MAY 30:	Peschiara surrenders to Charles Albert.
JUNE 2:	Opening of Pan-Slavic Congress at Prague.
JUNE 4:	Supplementary elections: Louis Napoleon (in four *départements*) and Victor Hugo.
JUNE 12:	Fighting between Austrians and Czechs at Prague.
JUNE 15:	Goudchaux demands dissolution of the National Workshops.
JUNE 17:	Prague capitulates.
JUNE 22:	Marie starts measures against the National Workshops.
JUNE 23:	Insurrection in Paris; the workers seize strategic points.
JUNE 24:	The Executive Commission resigns. Cavaignac granted full powers. Intense fighting continues in Paris. Archduke John of Austria is chosen Regent of the Empire.
JUNE 26:	End of the proletarian insurrection in Paris.
JULY 5:	Opening of new Hungarian Assembly in Budapest.
JULY 10:	Opening of Austrian Constitutional Assembly at Kremsier.
JULY 25:	The Italians decisively defeated at Custozza.
JULY 28:	Law enacted limiting the activities of the clubs.
AUGUST 9:	Armistice at Salasco: Charles Albert evacuates Lombardy.
AUGUST 22:	The Emperor of Austria refuses to sanction the measures of the Hungarian Diet.
AUGUST 31:	The Austrian Constituent Assembly abolishes feudal rights.
SEPTEMBER 28:	Lamberg is assassinated upon his arrival at Budapest.
OCTOBER 6:	Uprising in Vienna.
OCTOBER 26:	The troops of Windischgrätz open the attack on Vienna.
OCTOBER 31:	Fall of Vienna: severe repression.
NOVEMBER 9:	*Coup d'état* in Prussia: the Assembly transferred from Berlin to Brandenburg.
NOVEMBER 12:	Fête of the Constitution in Paris.
NOVEMBER 15:	Assassination of Count Rossi in Rome, followed by insurrection.
NOVEMBER 21:	Formation in Vienna of Schwarzenberg ministry.
NOVEMBER 24:	The Pope escapes from Rome and takes refuge in Gaeta.
NOVEMBER 29:	Election Manifesto of Louis Napoleon.
DECEMBER 2:	Ferdinand I, Emperor of Austria, abdicates and is succeeded by his nephew, Francis Joseph.
DECEMBER 10:	Louis Napoleon elected President of the French Republic.
DECEMBER 20:	In Rome, establishment of Triumvirate as the governing body. In Paris, formation of Odilon Barrot ministry.

1849

JANUARY 25:	The German constitution submitted to the various states for ratification.
FEBRUARY 9:	Republic proclaimed in Rome.
FEBRUARY 18:	Republic of Tuscany proclaimed.

MARCH 7:	The Austrian Constituent Assembly dissolved.
MARCH 12:	Charles Albert renounces armistice.
MARCH 23:	Italian disaster at Novara; Charles Albert abdicates.
MARCH 26:	Piedmont agrees to armistice.
MARCH 28:	Frederick William IV elected Emperor of Germany.
MARCH 29:	The Neapolitan troops begin reconquest of Sicily.
APRIL 5:	Austria recalls its deputies from Frankfort Parliament.
APRIL 25:	French troops land at Civita-Vecchia.
APRIL 27:	Frederick William IV refuses the imperial crown.
MAY 5:	Austrians occupy Florence.
MAY 9:	Republican uprisings in Dresden and in the Grand Duchy of Baden.
MAY 15:	Prussia recalls deputies from Frankfort.
MAY 21:	Hungarians re-occupy Budapest.
JUNE 2:	Beginning of siege of Rome.
JUNE 13:	Demonstration of liberals organized by Ledru-Rollin easily crushed.
JUNE 19:	Law against the clubs.
	The débris of the German parliament, having taken refuge in Stuttgart, is dispersed.
JULY 1:	Capture of Rome by French.
JULY 20:	Republican insurrection in Baden suppressed.
AUGUST 13:	Principal Hungarian army capitulates at Vilagos.
AUGUST 22:	Venice surrenders after heroic defense.
	Opening of the Congress of Universal Peace in Paris.
SEPTEMBER 25:	End of Hungarian resistance after the surrender of Komorn.

BIBLIOGRAPHICAL NOTES

THE REVOLUTION IN FRANCE

The student of the French Revolution of 1848 must be prepared to rely very largely on French authorities. In English there are only a few books of any value. Lord Normanby's *A Year of Revolution* will be found useful, 2 vols. (London, 1857). As British Ambassador in Paris, Lord Normanby's point of view is naturally that of a monarchist, but at the same time he got on well with Lamartine, to whose courage and ability during the early days of the Revolution he does full justice. Along with Lord Normanby should be read Louis Blanc's *Historical Revelations* (London, 1858). Louis Blanc was a radical, as bitterly opposed to Lamartine as he was to the Orléans Monarchy, and his *Revelations* are consequently highly critical of Lord Normanby. John Stuart Mill was one of the earliest champions of the revolution. His vindication of the Provisional Government against the strictures of Lord Brougham is still worth reading. See J. S. Mill: Vol. III in *Dissertations and Discussions*, 5 vols. (New York, 1874).

A translation of Lamartine's *Histoire de la Révolution de 1848* was published in London in 1849. Lamartine wrote too soon after the events described to show any perspective, but his history is important as the record of an honest though naïvely conceited man who for three months played a decisive part in the history of France. H. Remsen Whitehouse's two-volume *Life of Lamartine* (Boston and New York, 1918) contains a detailed account of the political events of this period.

For the economic history of the Revolution, Donald Hope McKay's *The National Workshops* (Harvard Univ. Press, 1933), including a comprehensive bibliography, is invaluable. A more philosophic approach will be found in E. L. Woodward's short but compact *French Revolutions* (Oxford, 1939). See also his chapters on Guizot in *Three Studies in European Conservatism* (London, 1929). "Ik Marvel" (Donald G. Mitchell) wrote a lively foreign correspondent's account of the Revolution in *Battle Summer* (New York, 1850). No other writer, certainly no foreigner, paints a more vivid picture of the scenes in the Chamber and in the Hotel de Ville.

Finally, for the reader who is satisfied with a naked and unadorned statement of the facts, accurate and, as far as humanly possible, impartial, there is the Cambridge Modern History. The two chapters by Emile Bourgeois dealing with events in France in 1848 (vol. XI, chaps. 5 and 7) are a good foundation for further study.

No attempt can be made here to list all the French authorities on 1848. The birth of the Fourth French Republic has aroused a new interest in the constitutional experiments of the short-lived Second Republic, and the tide of histories, memoirs and reviews devoted to this period is still mounting. In this connection an important book is Paul Bastid's *Doctrines et Institutions Politiques de la Seconde République*, 2 vols. (Paris, 1942). Bibliographies will be found in

Georges Renard: *La République de 1848* (Paris, 1904), where the emphasis is on social and economic questions, and in Charles Seignobos: *La Révolution de 1848. Le second Empire* (Paris, 1921).

For a general history of the period I have relied on Seignobos. Originally written for the monumental *Histoire de France Contemporaine* edited by E. Lavisse, it represents, like most of the volumes in that series, the middle-of-the-road point of view. It has been criticized by the extreme left and the extreme right as pedestrian, a charge to which historians who keep their sympathies in cold storage are always open.

My right flank has been guarded by Thureau-Dangin and Pierre de la Gorce. P. Thureau-Dangin's *Histoire de la Monarchie de Juillet*, 7 vols. (Paris, 1897–1904), includes a detailed account of the circumstances leading up to Louis Philippe's abdication. A confirmed Orléanist, he regards it as one of the tragedies of the century. Pierre de la Gorce, a conservative magistrate turned historian, is respected by all students of French history regardless of their politics. He himself was a royalist and a Catholic. His *Histoire de la Seconde République Française*, 2 vols. (Paris, 1887), remains one of the essential books on the period.

To guard my left flank I have relied chiefly on Louis Blanc and Daniel Stern. Louis Blanc's *Histoire de la Révolution de 1848*, 2 vols. (Paris, 1880), is a combination of earlier works, notably *L'Appel aux honnêtes gens. Quelques pages d'histoire contemporaine*, and the already mentioned *Historical Revelations; inscribed to Lord Normanby*. Louis Blanc's *Organisation du Travail*, written some years before 1848, has been reprinted together with Emile Thomas' *Histoire des Ateliers Nationaux* in J. A. R. Marriott's *The French Revolution in Its Economic Aspect*, 2 vols. (Oxford, 1913).

Daniel Stern (a pseudonym for the Countess d'Agoult) was a bluestocking with pronounced liberal sympathies. She was interested in the social and economic rather than in the political aspects of the Revolution and, unlike most of her world, she managed to remain friendly with both Lamartine and Louis Blanc. Her *Histoire de la Révolution de 1848*, 3 vols., Third ed. (Paris, 1868), is probably the best of the contemporary histories. Another contemporary history that should be consulted is the *Histoire de la Révolution de 1848*, 11 vols. (Paris, 1861–72), by Garnier-Pagès, a member of the Provisional Government, who was inclined to over-emphasize the importance of his own role.

A more succinct defense of the Provisional Government will be found in Lamartine's *Trois Mois au Pouvoir* (Paris, 1848). This should be supplemented by the three excellent studies on this period written by Pierre Quentin-Bauchart, *La Crise Sociale de 1848* (Paris, 1920), *Lamartine, homme politique; la politique intérieure* (Paris, 1903), and *Lamartine et la politique étrangère de la Révolution de février* (Paris, 1908). The death of Pierre Quentin-Bauchart in World War I was a serious loss to French historiography.

Among the many reminiscences of the period A. de Tocqueville's *Souvenirs* (New ed., Paris, 1942) is in a class by itself. Tocqueville's *Souvenirs* are written with the same honesty, the same common sense, and the same insight into human nature that distinguish his more famous *Democracy in America*.

For Louis Napoleon's rise to power the standard authority is André Lebey,

Louis Napoleon Bonaparte et la Révolution de 1848, 2 vols. (Paris, 1907). F. L. Simpson, *The Rise of Louis Napoleon* (New ed., London, 1925), and Albert Guérard's *Napoleon III* (Harvard University Press, 1943) should also be consulted.

For those who want to get the "feel" of the period there is no substitute for the contemporary press. Apart from the official *Moniteur Universel*, the *National* (organ of the moderate republicans), and the *Réforme* (organ of the left republicans), the weekly *Charivari*, with its inimitable Daumier cartoons, is particularly recommended.

THE REVOLUTION IN ITALY

For an understanding of the background of the Revolution, and of the Revolution itself down to the end of November, 1848, students will do well to begin with the three volumes of G. F. H. and J. Berkeley, *Italy in the Making, 1815 to 1846* (Cambridge University Press, 1932), *Italy in the Making, June, 1846 to January, 1848* (Cambridge University Press, 1936), and *Italy in the Making, 1848* (Cambridge University Press, 1940). Each of these volumes contains a very complete bibliography, but it should be noted that the authors carry the story only down to November, 1848, and that the history of the Roman Republic is not included. Their work largely supersedes Bolton King's two-volume *History of Italian Unity, 1814–1871* (London, 1889), though Bolton King carries the story down to the end.

The conclusions of these volumes on Italy in the making are based on the most recent Italian scholarship. Those who have been brought up on William Roscoe Thayer's *The Dawn of Italian Independence* (1893), and his *Cavour* (1911), will find G. F. H. and J. Berkeley more sympathetic to Pius IX, and to the Catholic position in general, than were the English or American historians of an earlier generation.

No one can read very far in the period of the *Risorgimento* without being aware of his debt to Mr. G. M. Trevelyan. Comprehensive scholarship and a fine sense of poetry combine to make Mr. Trevelyan unique among modern historians. On all matters concerning Garibaldi he is still the final authority. I have leaned heavily on his *Manin and the Venetian Revolution of 1848* (London, 1923), and still more heavily on *Garibaldi's Defence of the Roman Republic* (London, 1907). Garibaldi's *Autobiography*, translated by A. Werner (London, 1889), will be found useful. Of this book Mr. Trevelyan says very truly: "Without knowing that he is making 'confessions,' he gives himself away as much as Augustine or Rousseau, but the gift is pleasant." Jesse White Mario's one-volume supplement to the English translation of the *Autobiography* contains stray pieces of information not found elsewhere. David Larg's *Giuseppe Garibaldi* (London, 1934) is the best one-volume biography of Garibaldi in English. The standard "life" in Italian is by G. Guerzoni, 2 vols. (Firenze, 1882).

No one has yet done for Mazzini what G. M. Trevelyan has done for Garibaldi, but there are several good one-volume biographies in English. Bolton King's *Mazzini* (London, 1912) is an excellent springboard into the subject. The biographies by Gwilym O. Griffith (London, 1932) and Stringfellow Barr (New York, 1935) include the results of more recent scholarship. Along with these should be read Mazzini's *Letters to An English Family*, edited by E. F. Richards, 3 vols. (London, 1920). *The Life and Writings of Mazzini*, a five-volume selection, was published in London in 1891. For a discussion of Mazzini's political ideas see C. E. Vaughan, *Studies in the History of Political Philosophy*, 2 vols. (Manchester University Press, 1925).

For further study, the National Italian edition of Mazzini's writings (Imola, 1906 *et seq.*) is essential. A concise summary of Mazzini's life and thought will be found in Gaetano Salvemini, *Mazzini* (Firenze, 1925). Among the innumerable Italian histories of the period I have relied chiefly on Ernesto Masi, *Il Risorgimento italiano*, 2 vols. (Firenze, 1917). Masi is also the author of the two chapters on Italy in the Cambridge Modern History, vol. XI. The extreme clerical point of view will be found in G. Spada, *Storia della rivoluzione di Roma*, 3 vols. (Roma, 1868–69).

The middle-of-the-road point of view is presented by L. C. Farini, *The Roman State from 1815 to 1850*, 4 vols., translated from the Italian by W. E. Gladstone (London, 1852). Farini was a staunch moderate, if anything a little to the right of center. Gladstone's famous *Letters to the Earl of Aberdeen* on the state of the Neapolitan prisons, in which he described the Neapolitan government as "the negation of God," falls just outside the scope of this book.

For the republican point of view the reader cannot do better than consult Mazzini's own writings, particularly the *English Letters* edited by Mrs. Richards and vol. V of the *Life and Writings*, which contains the articles Mazzini wrote for the London *Spectator* on the causes of the failure of the Revolution. G. Gentile's *Mazzini* (Caserta, 1919) contains a useful analysis of Mazzini's political and social philosophy.

Guizot's *Mémoires pour servir à l'histoire de mon temps*, 8 vols. (Paris, 1850) is an indispensable source book for the diplomatic background of the period. Hübner's *Une année de ma vie, 1848–49* (Paris, 1891) tells the story of the war in Lombardy-Venetia from the Austrian point of view.

THE REVOLUTION IN GERMANY

Karl Marx has been the subject of many biographies. The standard "life" is by Franz Mehring, first published in Germany in 1918. A translation by Edward Fitzgerald, including a useful bibliography, was published by Covici, Friede (New York, 1935). More popular than Mehring is E. H. Carr's *Karl Marx, a Study in Fanaticism* (London, 1934) and Leopold Schwarzschild's *The Red Prussian* (New York, 1947).

E. H. Carr is more detached than either Mehring, the faithful disciple in whose eyes Marx can do no wrong, or Schwarzschild, who goes to the other extreme and writes with all the zeal of an iconoclast. E. H. Carr has also written a "life" of Bakunin (London, 1937) which contains a great deal of information about the relations of Marx and Bakunin not easily available elsewhere.

Of the innumerable critical studies devoted to Marx, Luc Somerhausen's *L'Humanisme Agissant de Karl Marx* (Paris, 1937) deserves special mention as dealing particularly with the development of Marx's ideas during the years 1845–49.

The source from which all writing about Marx stems is the *Marx-Engels Gesamt-Ausgabe*. This is an abbreviation for the title of the monumental collected edition of all the works, letters, etc., of both authors, which has been begun, though not finished, by the Marx-Engels Institute in Moscow. As Mr. Schwarzschild has pointed out, the delay is due to the fact that the two directors of the Moscow Institute were liquidated, one after the other. The quotations from Marx's letters in this book are taken from this *Gesamt-Ausgabe* ("dritte Abteilung, Band 1"). The complete text of the articles written by Marx and Engels for the *Neue Rheinische Zeitung* will be found in the same edition ("erste Abteilung, Band 7").

Among the English and American editions of those works of Marx that deal with the period under discussion, the following are the most important:

(1) The *Communist Manifesto*, originally published under the title *Manifest der Kommunistischen Partei* (London, 1848). There have, of course, been innumerable editions and translations. One of the most interesting is Harold J. Laski's edition (London, 1948), containing not only the *Manifesto* itself, together with the various prefaces written by Marx or Engels during their lifetimes, but also a new appreciation written for the Labour Party, in which Mr. Laski undertakes to prove that the British Labour Party is more truly than Bolshevism the heir of the *Manifesto*.

(2) *Revolution and Counter-Revolution in Germany*, edited by E. M. Aveling (Eleanor Marx), (Charles H. Kerr and Co.: Chicago, no date). This book, consisting of articles written in 1851–52 for the New York *Tribune*, is still excellent reading, though it assumes a more detailed knowledge of the period than the average reader is likely to possess. Charles A. Dana, the managing editor of the *Tribune*, is believed to have visited Cologne in November, 1848, during his tour of Europe, and to have made the acquaintance of Marx at that time. While the articles were attributed to Marx, they were probably written by Engels.

(3) *The Eighteenth Brumaire of Louis Bonaparte*, translated by E. and C. Paul (Allen and Unwin: London, 1926), deals with events that fall just outside the scope of this book, but the vicious attack on Louis Napoleon, a masterpiece of invective, throws light on the revolutionary processes that brought him into power.

For general background of the period the two great German historians, Treitschke and Sybel, are indispensable. Treitschke's *History of Germany in the 19th Century*, translated by E. and C. Paul, 7 vols. (London, 1915), carries the history only as far as 1848. From there on the story is taken up by Sybel's *Founding of the German Empire by William I,* also in seven volumes. The English translation is by L. M. Perrin and Gamaliel Bradford (New York, 1890–98).

Two other more recent histories deserving special mention are A. J. P. Taylor's *The Course of German History* (Hamish Hamilton: London, 1845), a miracle of compression, and Veit Valentin's *1848: Chapters of German History,* translated by Ethel Talbot Scheffauer (London, 1940). A. W. Ward's *Germany, 1815–90,* 3 vols. (Cambridge University Press, 1916), is useful as a work of reference. A. W. Ward is also the author of the chapters on Germany in the Cambridge Modern History, vol. XI.

For the relations between Germany, Poland and Russia in 1848, readers should consult L. B. Namier: *1848, The Revolution of the Intellectuals,* from the *Proceedings* of the British Academy, vol. XXX (Oxford University Press: London, 1944).

One other book, invaluable to students of this period, remains to be mentioned: J. G. Legge, *Rhyme and Revolution in Germany* (New York, 1919). Mr. Legge has translated a number of documents in prose and verse belonging to the revolutionary period. His own comments are invariably illuminating.

REVOLUTIONS IN THE HABSBURG MONARCHY

The student of this period is confronted at the outset by the absence of authoritative works in English. A glance at the extensive bibliography in the Cambridge Modern History, vol. XI, will show how small a contribution has been made to our knowledge of these revolutions by English or American scholars.

The best introduction to the period is C. E. Maurice, *The Revolutionary Movement of 1848–49 in Italy, Austria-Hungary, and Germany* (London, 1887). In spite of the fact that it was published over sixty years ago, it has not yet been superseded. Among contemporary accounts, W. H. Stiles, *Austria in 1848–49,* 2 vols. (New York, 1852), should certainly be consulted. Stiles was the *chargé d'affaires* of the United States at the court of Vienna, and his honest if uninspired narrative is interesting as being the work of a man who was in close touch with the events and personalities he describes. At one point he was the mediator between Kossuth and Windischgrätz, but his efforts to arrange a truce were not successful.

Many of the reminiscences of Hungarian officers have been translated, and among others Arthur Görgei's *My Life and Acts in Hungary,* 2 vols. (London, 1852), deserves special mention. Görgei's book is in the nature of an apologia. The other side of the story is told by General Klapka, *Memoirs of the War of Independence in Hungary,* 2 vols. (London, 1850), and by Johann Pragay, *Outline of the Present Circumstances Attending the Hungarian Struggle for Freedom* (New York, 1850).

Among the many books dealing with the war *The Letters and Journals of Count Leiningen* (London, 1911) stands in a class by itself. Count Leiningen's letters deal not merely with the incidents of the campaigns, but with the political issues involved and with the ethical problem that confronted every Hungarian officer in the Imperial Army.

A vivid account of the Revolution in Vienna is given by Berthold Auerbach, one of the better-known German writers of the day, in his *Narrative of Events in Vienna (September-November 1848)* (London, 1849). Another vivid account of these events will be found in Count Hübner's *Une Année de ma Vie* (no English translation) (Paris, 1891). Count Hübner was an Austrian diplomat, a great admirer of both Metternich and Schwarzenberg. In the spring of 1848 he was sent to Milan, and after witnessing the revolution there he returned in time to take part in the Viennese Revolution of October. Hübner was a shrewd observer, but his sympathies were all with the aristocracy. A very different point of view will be found in Josephine Goldmark's *Pilgrims of '48* (Yale University Press, 1930). Miss Goldmark's father, Joseph Goldmark, was one of the Austrian forty-eighters who, after playing a leading part in the liberal Reichstag of Vienna, emigrated to America in 1850. The account of the Revolution and the subsequent adventures of the family in America, which Miss Goldmark has pieced together from letters and papers of her father and other members of the family, is invaluable to all those who are interested in the various ramifications of the revolutions of 1848. Miss Goldmark's bibliography will also be found useful.

Much of the history of the period will be found only in biographies and memoirs. I have used Metternich's memoirs extensively: *Mémoires, documents, et écrits divers*, edited by R. Metternich, 8 vols. (Paris, 1880–84). The English translation of the *Mémoires* does not include the later years of Metternich's life. The most sympathetic biography of Metternich in English is by H. du Coudray, *Metternich* (London, 1935). The standard German biography is by H. Ritter von Srbik, *Metternich, Der Staatsman und der Mensch*, 2 vols. (not translated) (Munich, 1925). Some new material is included in Viktor Bibl, *Metternich in neuer Beleuchtung* (Vienna, 1928), which is available in a French translation (Paris, 1935).

Kossuth has not been as well served by biographers as Metternich. Unfortunately, most of his own writings have never been translated from Hungarian. *The Memoirs of My Exile* (London, 1880) deals only incidentally with the events of 1848. The best modern biography is by Otto Zarek, translated from the German by Lynton Hudson and published in London in 1937. Zarek is an enthusiastic champion of Kossuth and of all things Magyar. As a corrective to Zarek, or at least as an expression of a point of view that he ignores, the reader should consult R. W. Seton-Watson, *Racial Problems in Hungary* (London, 1908). Seton-Watson states the case for the non-Magyar races in Hungary. Two contemporary biographies of Kossuth, both entirely uncritical, are interesting as showing the immense impression he made on English and American audiences: *Hungary and Its Revolutions with a Memoir of Kossuth*, by E. O. S. (London, 1854), and P. C. Headley's *The Life of Louis Kossuth, Governor of Hungary, Including Notices of the Men and Scenes of the Hungarian Revolution* (New York, 1852).

No biography of Széchényi has been translated into English, but a good deal of information about him will be found in the *Anglo-Hungarian Review* (1922), the *Hungarian Quarterly* (1940), and in any good history of Hungary. Among the best of these is Armin Vambéry, *Hungary in Ancient and Modern Times* (London, 1897). Those who read French should consult Daniel Iranyi, *Histoire Politique de la Révolution en Hongrie*, 2 vols. (Paris, 1859), and those who read German, Heinrich Friedjung, *Österreich von 1848 bis 1860*, 2 vols. (Berlin, 1908). Iranyi was a Hungarian revolutionary, and Friedjung an ardent Pan-German who believed in a unified Germany in which should be incorporated all the hereditary lands of the Austrian Monarchy.

There is a good English biography of Francis Deák by Mrs. Vere O'Brien (London, 1880), and an excellent short study of Schwarzenberg by his great-grand-nephew Adolph Schwarzenberg, published by the Columbia University Press, 1946.

A. J. P. Taylor, *The Habsburg Monarchy, 1815–1918* (London, 1942), is the best short history of the period. A good exposition of Palmerston's foreign policy will be found in Charles Sproxton, *Palmerston and the Hungarian Revolution* (Cambridge University Press, 1919).

While it is impossible to enumerate the articles on the Vienna Revolution and the war in Hungary that appeared in British periodicals of the day, those who are interested in the war of the *Sonderbund* in Switzerland as being the forerunner of the revolutions of '48 should read the seven letters on Swiss politics published in the *Spectator*, 1847, and reprinted in book form (London, 1876). These letters, written by George Grote, the historian, who happened to be staying in Switzerland at the time, had an undoubted influence on stiffening British determination to prevent Metternich's intervening on behalf of the Catholic cantons. While the *Times* took a conservative stand on every issue, weekly papers such as the *Examiner* and the *Spectator* were generally liberal in their sympathies. In America, Horace Greeley lent the support of the *Tribune* to every revolutionary movement.

REPERCUSSIONS IN AMERICA

American reaction to the revolutions of 1848 is reflected in many newspapers of the period, but it has never been made the subject of a comprehensive study. American correspondents in Europe were naturally sympathetic to the cause of revolution. The despatches of Charles A. Dana in the New York *Tribune* and "Ik Marvel" (Donald G. Mitchell) in the *Courier and Enquirer* are particularly useful. *American Opinion on the Unification of Italy*, by Howard F. Marraro (New York, 1932), summarizes their reports together with those of many others, though of course it does not deal with events in any country except Italy.

"American Opinion of French Historical Revolutions," by E. N. Curtis, an article in the *American Historical Review*, vol. XXIX, covers the ground for France, and "American Opinion of German Unification," by J. G. Gozley (Columbia University Studies, vol. CXXI), does the same for Germany.

For the impression made by America on an unusually well-educated immigrant nothing can take the place of *The Reminiscences of Carl Schurz*, 3 vols. (New York, 1907). It is the best of the many accounts written by forty-eighters. The immigrant has only recently come into his own as a constantly important factor in American history. Two books by Marcus L. Hansen, *The Immigrant in American History* (Cambridge, Mass., 1942) and *The Atlantic Migration* (Cambridge, Mass., 1945), give him the place he has so long deserved. Chapters 11 and 12 of *The Atlantic Migration* deal particularly with the great wave of migration that followed the European revolutions. Edith Abbott's *Historical Aspects of the Immigrant Problem* (Chicago, 1926), actually an immigration anthology consisting of selections from books, newspaper articles, political speeches, etc., includes an excellent bibliography. J. G. Randall's *Lincoln the President*, 2 vols. (New York, 1945), discusses the part played by the forty-eighters in the nomination of Lincoln. (See vol. I, chap. 7.) The influence of German immigration on American political and cultural life is dealt with in Carl Wittke's *We Who Built America* (New York, 1929). See also his very informative article "The German '48-ers in America" in the *American Historical Review,* July, 1948.

The early histories of Texas, which will be found listed in C. W. Raines, *Bibliography of Texas* (Austin, 1896), deals extensively with the German and French immigration of the forties. F. L. Olmsted's *A Journey through Texas* (New York, 1857) contains a good deal of interesting information on the attitude of the early German settlers to slavery.

For the history of the Icarian settlements I have relied chiefly on Albert Shaw's *Icaria: A Chapter in the History of Communism* (New York, 1884) and on the standard biography of Etienne Cabet by Jules Prudhommeaux: *Icarie et son Fondateur, Etienne Cabet* (Paris, 1907). The best source for Victor Considérant's socialist venture in Texas is an article by Eusibia Lutz, "Almost Utopia," in the *Southwest Reviews*, vol. XIV, 321–30. Maurice Dommanget's *Victor Considérant*, the best of several biographies, is disappointingly silent, as are all the French authorities, on this period of Considérant's career. As a friend of Albert Brisbane, the most persistent of American Fourierists, some information about his experiences in America can be gleaned from Brisbane's autobiography. This autobiography was incorporated by Redelia Brisbane in her *Albert Brisbane, A Mental Biography* (Boston, 1893).

Kossuth's visit to America, including the speeches he made and the receptions he attended, was copiously reported in the press of the period. The *Select Speeches of Kossuth, Condensed and Abridged, with Kossuth's Express Sanction*, by F. W. Newman (London, 1853), will be found useful. "Kossuth in New England," by George S. Boutwell, *New England Magazine*, July, 1894, is the most discriminating of the many eulogies Kossuth received during his tour. His own *Memoires of My Exile*, translated by Ferenc Jansz (New York, 1880), deal only incidentally with the visit to America. A complete collection of documents relating to Kossuth's visit in the United States has been published by Denes A. Janossy, *The Kossuth Emigration in America* (Hungarian Historical Society: Budapest, 1940).

Weitling is not included in the *Dictionary of American Biography*—an unfortunate omission—but a sketch of his career is included in Morris Hillquit's *History of Socialism in the United States* (New York, 1906). Professor Carl Wittke has promised a full-length biography, and in the meantime his paper "Marx and Weitling" in *Essays in Political Theory*, edited by M. R. Konvitz (Cornell University Press, 1948), will be found useful.

Joseph Weydemeyer is the subject of a biography by Karl Obermann (New York, 1947).

INDEX

Adams, Henry, quoted, 178

Aberdeen, Lord, Mazzini and, 133

Adams, Samuel, American patriot, 37

Adelaide, sister of Louis Philippe, 16, 20; death of, 28

Adelsverein, society, 299, 301

Affre, Monsignor, Archbishop of Paris, 79; murder of, 101

Agoult, Mme. d', Louis Napoleon judged by, 94–95; National Workshops and, 98

Albert, workman, member of government, 50

Albertists, moderates, 138, 162, 163

Albrecht, Archduke, revolution started by, 252

Alembert, d', *Encyclopedia* by, 6

Algerian conquest, consolidation of, 23

Alsace-Lorraine, claims to, 329

Amanites, sect, 314

America (*See also* United States), immigrants disliked in, 295; advantages of, 297, 298; passion for independence in, 311

American girls, description of, by German, 302

Anita, Garibaldi and, 165, 166; flight and death of, 190–191

Annenkov, Paul, quoted, 203

Anthony, Susan B., American reformer, 290

Antonelli, Cardinal, power of, 179; appeals made by, against Mazzini, 184

Anzani, Garibaldi's chief lieutenant, 165; illness of, and death, 166, 168

Arago, François, astronomer, 23; election of, 45; as Minister of the Navy and of War, 46–47, 54, 59, 69; votes for, 75; revolt against government questioned by, 100

Aranyi, poet, 263

Arenenberg, Switzerland, Louis Napoleon at, 83, 86, 87

Armellini, yielding of, to Mazzini, 183

Army, forming of, from unemployed, 58; eventually rebels against the state, 60; National Workshops and, 97

Arndt, Ernst Moritz, poet, author, political offender, 214, 251

Arnold, Matthew, vision of, 330

Artois, Comte d'. *See* Charles X

Asboth, General, Hungarian, 325

Ashurst, Emilie, quoted, 135

Ashurst, William, Mazzini and, 134–135

Ashursts, Mazzini writes to, about Pius IX, 142

Aspre, General d', Garibaldi and, 172, 173

Assembly. *See* National Assembly

Associationism, Fourierism called, 312

Augsbürger Zeitung, 195

Aumale, Duc d', arrival of, 5; opposition of, to Guizot, 31

Austin, Stephen A., colonizer in Texas, 299

Austria, influence of, in Italian peninsula, 115, 116; information sent to, concerning Mazzini, 133; Milan and, 135, 149–151, 154, 155; moderates views concerning, 136, 137; Charles Albert declares war on, 138; feeling that Pius IX was against, 140; strength of, 159; Pope's attitude in regard to war with, 160; victory of over Charles Albert, 170; Garibaldi and, 170–174; Rossi does not approve of war with, 177; victories of, 185; question of whether Germany included, 223, 224; Empire resuscitated in, 234; Metternich and, 239; balance of power and, 243; Switzerland and, 245, 247; constitution granted to, 266; Hungary at war with, 270; end of reform in, 273; task of, in regard to Russia, 280; claims to, 329

Austrian Empire, elements of, 223; Palacky and, 228, 229; might have been spared the storm, 243

Azeglio, Marquis Massimo d', moderate, 136, 137, 138; Austrian brutality condemned by, 150; advice of, 151–152; Garibaldi described by, 166